D1309261

A NEUROPSYCHOLOGIST'S JOURNAL:
INTERVENTIONS AND "JUDI-ISMS"

A NEUROPSYCHOLOGIST'S JOURNAL

Interventions
and
"Judi-isms"

Dr. Judith Bendheim Guedalia

URIM PUBLICATIONS
Jerusalem · New York

A Neuropsychologist's Journal: Interventions and "Judi-isms"
by Judith Bendheim Guedalia

Typeset by Ariel Walden

Printed in Israel

First Edition
ISBN 978-965-524-123-5

Urim Publications   Lambda Publishers, Inc.
P.O.Box 52287   527 Empire Blvd.
Jerusalem 91521 Israel   Brooklyn, NY 11225 U.S.A.
                                 Tel: 718-972-5449
                                 Fax: 718-972-6307

www.UrimPublications.com

Contents

Editorial note

All the names of patients and family members have been changed to protect their privacy. Some identifying details have been changed.

Most of the names of physicians have been changed.

Chaim K. is a nom de plume of the author's co-writer in the essays in the section titled "Life-Wizened Chaim K."

Acknowledgements

THE COMPILATION OF most of the articles I have written combines a labor of love with a sense of ordering loose ends. I am hopeful that this book will be the first of many compilations and not stand as an "only child." As with the birth of a child, the first and most grateful Thank You goes to Hashem (God).

I wish to acknowledge many who were so important to me in my very fortunate life. My friends, colleagues, students and, of course, my patients who have trusted my "Judi-isms," taught me so much and have been there for me in so many ways.

Naomi Klass Mauer is not only the co-editor of *The Jewish Press* who published my bi-monthly and later monthly pieces, but my friend of many years who is and was an important enabler of this endeavor.

Thank you, Shaare Zedek Medical Center, for being MY home-away-from-home for over twenty years.

During the many Mass Casualty Events (MCE) (generally terrorist actions but also traffic accidents) in the Emergency Room, as Chief Psychologist I worked shoulder-to-shoulder with Amalia Oren, the Director of Social Work. I learned much about traumatology from her, from the patients and their families, that continues to enrich my psychological and neuropsychological skills.

Shaare Zedek's Director General, Professor Jonathan (Yonatan) Halevy, has been a leadership role model for me and a keen supporter of the Pediatric and Adult Neuropsychology Unit I head. To him I owe major accolades.

The peer review journals gave my Neuropsychological voice an opportunity to express itself along with those Ethics, Science and Religion journals that permitted me to research and write about the "intersect" of my Psychological and Judaic selves.

To Tzvi Mauer, the publisher of Urim Publications, and the very able Batsheva Hashkes Pomerantz, my editor, who made this book happen. Of course, any errors are mine alone, and for those I apologize.

My parents, Els Salomon-Prins Bendheim and my late father, Charles Henry Bendheim, were The Source. I owe my siblings, in birth order, Jack Bendheim,

Debby Eisenberg, Aviva Sussman, Philip Bendheim, Edna Zussman and Karen Levine, so much for being with and behind me through thick and thin.

My wonderfully loving children who have given me my "raison d'etre" and who have defined my identity as a mother, grandmother and great-grandmother, (in birth order) Allison Siffre Guedalia Kupietzky, Jacob Leon Guedalia, Isaac David Guedalia and Joshua Siegfried Guedalia, and their spouses.

My grandchildren who are wonderfully independent human beings – be they one year to over a quarter of a century old – are an eternal source of wonder and joy. The "icing on the cake" are my four great-grandsons. May all the children find their blessed lives under the watchful eye of Hashem and follow in His path and be guided by His ways.

No one has been more important to me than my wonderful husband, Rabbi Dr. Harris Guedalia. Since I was fifteen and a half years old, he has enveloped me with his whole being. He has been my best friend, and has nurtured, honored, educated, supported and, above all, loved me. To him and Hashem I am eternally grateful.

Judi
Jerusalem, Israel
Adar 5772, March 2012

IN THE BEGINNING

September/Elul and
New Beginnings

Sᴇᴘᴛᴇᴍʙᴇʀ/ᴇʟᴜʟ ʙʀɪɴɢs ᴡɪᴛʜ ɪᴛ the sense of new beginnings, the beginning of the Jewish New Year and the beginning of the School New Year. During the more than two decades as director of the Neuropsychology Unit at the Shaare Zedek Medical Center in Jerusalem, I have trained over eighty interns in the field of psychology, specifically Neuropsychology, Medical, Developmental, and Rehabilitation Psychology. Each year I await the new graduate students who are doing either their first year of fieldwork, senior fieldwork, and interns. I am never sure who is more nervous, them or me.

In recent years, I've had a group of six to eight students. Imagine, if you can, having octopulets, earnest young students anxious to please and eagerly waiting to learn. They are older than their American co-graduate school students. They have finished the army; many have been officers, having added extra years and responsibility, to the mandatory three years for men (five years if they served within the Hesder Yeshiva), and two years for the women. Most then went on the year trip – an almost mandatory cultural norm of getting "ooout" of Israel and the constrictors of life here, and army life in particular (to the outback of Australia, India, South America or wherever). Then they take entrance exams for university, study for a three-year BA in psychology, attain a 94 percent average, are accepted to graduate school in neuro, or medical, or rehabilitation, or developmental psychology, maintaining the 94 percent average, and only then begin the requirements for clinical fieldwork and internships. For the great majority, all this takes place as they are working part-time to support themselves, as their parents are not able to do this.

These students are very smart, competitive and capable, but many have never seen a child or people culturally different than their immediate circle, nor any of the disorders they have learned about. They know this year (or three years) will include learning about interviewing, assessment and therapy and seeing the real world of developmental, neuropsychological disorders and psychopathology under a fair but tough taskmaster (me!?!). At the beginning of the year, they are observers, as the year progresses they begin to see their own patients under my supervision. I feel the pressure of fulfilling their expectations as well as being the first step in their professional career. The case vignettes below are just a small example of what awaits them:

– A referral from pediatrics with a request to speak to a young couple in their twenties: their nine-month old son was just diagnosed as having Cystic Fibrosis (CF). The father was born in Europe; the mother, in the States. The father's family is Ashkenazi (of Central European origin); the mother's Sephardic, descendants from the Spanish Inquisition. They never would have joined their genetic history had they not met at Hebrew University during their junior year abroad, both have the recessive gene for CF, which sadly plagues their son. With the advent of the Internet they are not only drowning in the sorrow of the diagnosis, loneliness without family in Israel, but also information – too much and too soon.

– They flew up from Eilat. The child is seven years old with his mother, a single parent. The child was diagnosed as psychotic and retarded in Eilat. The mother reported that a child-psychiatrist comes to the health clinic every two weeks. She feels her son cannot be retarded, as he is so clever in so many ways. She collected money so that they could fly up to Jerusalem for an assessment by a neurologist. The mother seems to be correct. The neurologist diagnoses Tourette Syndrome but feels that this diagnosis does not tell the whole story. The child is then referred for a neuropsychological evaluation, which means another flight up to Jerusalem. After six hours of assessment, the data seems to point up to a child of average intelligence with a Non-verbal Learning Disorder and Tourette Syndrome.

– The distraught mother brings in a beautiful 7-year old girl. The principal will not let her back into school as she has had her fourth incident. The little girl describes the incident. A child bullied her friend. She threw rocks at the child, causing bruising. As I am wont to do, I ask about the stones, were they round? Were they grey or another color? And other such questions. In the conversation that ensues, she mentions that she had looked for glass shards but couldn't find them. They are better, she says, because they draw blood, and the bully deserved more than just a bruise. The intelligence scores are low, belying what clinically presents as a highly intelligent child. Her projective tests give us direction. She may have an incipient form of schizophrenia. From where does this aggression stem? I refer her for psychiatric evaluation.

– "The school wants to place my child in a school for the retarded, he was never retarded, he's just ill." The mother had convinced my secretary to bypass the four-month waiting list. When I see the child, I understand why my usually determined secretary caved in. The 13-year old has ALD, Adrenoleukodystrophy, better known as the disease described in the movie "Lorenzo's Oil." It is an autosomal (through the mother) degenerative disease, presenting at about 6–9 years of age with a not so slowly degenerating neurological and muscular functions until death. In the assessment of this young teen, he was strapped to his wheelchair and could barely be understood through his slurred speech. His cognitive function was "generously" plotted at about four years of age. His school did not know how to handle and "teach" him. I explain the disorder to the school and end the conversation agreeing that trying to "teach" him may not be the most rewarding of activities, neither for him nor for the teacher. It was decided to let him keep attending his regular school, with an aide, as well as with his classmates with whom he entered first grade, until medically it would be impossible for him to continue. The teaching would be of *chesed* (kindness) to his classmates, and by letting him stay in class with an aide, we might help address mother's plea to be heard that "my child was not born retarded," not to speak of his feelings of joy at being allowed to "remain in regular school like all his other childhood friends."

– Her brother is Autistic. In further intake sessions it seems he has Fragile X. She, an attractive 12-year old, is having extreme difficulty in mathematics. She has almost no friends, doesn't "get it," her classmates say; can't organize her materials for school and has difficulty attending to task. ADD, said her teachers; she needs to be on medication. The mother wanted to do an assessment before going to the family doctor to get the meds. The assessment profile is consistent with Fragile X-F (the female presentation of the mostly male Fragile-X, a genetic disorder that in its mildest form causes ADD). We will not know for sure, because the parents don't want her genetically tested, they have "enough on their plate right now." I agree and present the school with a detailed remediation and realistic expectation plan, as well as recommendations for easing testing requirements and "release" from the requirement to take *bagruyot* – statewide matriculation tests – in math.

– She was referred for consultation by the Genetics Department; they don't want to test her. They referred her to me. Her parents were divorced when she was five years of age, and her father lives abroad. She is an only child. Her grandmother, mother, and only aunt, have all died of ovarian cancer. She wants to do the genetic testing for the genetic marker for BRCA-1 and BRCA-2, the Jewish gene for breast and ovarian cancer. She is twenty years old. If she has the gene she has almost a 70 percent chance of getting the disease. The only therapy at this point in time is prophylactic oophorectomy and mastectomy (ovary and breast removal). This is generally not done until the patient has had children and is over the age of forty. In the course of our meeting, she tells me that she really knows already that she has the gene. She knows she is going to die and leave her daughter with the same pain and loneliness, and then die young as well. Why should she go out on a date? Why should she get married, even if someone would have her? She feels compelled to tell all on the first date. I ask her if she would rather be dead now and save years of uncertainty. "What are you talking about?" she yells at me. "What kind of a psychologist are you anyway, aren't you supposed to help people! No one knows when he or she is going to die. A terrorist might even kill me when I step out of the hospital." We make an appointment for the following week to discuss dating.

– At the beginning, she came in weekly for therapy. Now this burn survivor, a victim of a booby-trapped car bomb, comes once a month when she has follow-up occupational therapy appointments. One week she came twice. The "anniversary" of the bombing was coming up, as was the final healing of her "exposed" scars. I'm not sure which is more traumatic for her at this point in time.

– She was three months old in her mother's arms when a car hit them. This three and a half year old Arab girl is just beginning to speak. The developmental neuropsychological assessment shows a delay in abilities that are thought to be localized in the left hemisphere of her brain. I advise her lawyer not to settle the case, rather get speech and language therapy for the moment and re-evaluate her in two years.

– I am asked to see a woman in the cardio-thoracic surgery ward. "We put in a new valve and she'll do fine," said the nurse. "What's the problem," I ask. "If we could, we would want to take it back. She's a nightmare of a patient." I visit her and hear her complaints of all and sundry. I tell her that she seems more afraid and anxious than my regular post-surgery patients. I tell her about EMDR, which she agrees to try.[1] We started and she began to laugh hard and loud, I started to really get worried. In the course of EMDR, she talks about a picture she sees of herself in Russia, separated from her mother at a train station. Then she told me that when that happened she was around four years old and now she's fifty-four. "I guess I feel the same now, and you are my mother who just found me." The nurses told me the next day that they couldn't believe she was the same patient.

Some of my friends, who are not in the field, ask how it is that I enjoy my work so much. I answer, that I see my job as finding the healthy part of the child, adult, and situation in each individual case. I hope I am able to communicate and teach this to my students.

---

1. EMDR, Eye Movement Desensitization and Reprocessing integrates elements of many effective psychotherapies in structured protocols, which are designed to maximize treatment effects. These include psychodynamic, cognitive behavioral, interpersonal, experiential, and body-centered therapies. See www.emdr.com.

So Much to Be Grateful For

As ROSH HASHANAH approaches we have to be grateful for many things. The Second Intifada began Erev Rosh Hashanah in October 2000. There were many families mourning day after day for those killed and maimed during those years. It is hard to remember that we should be thankful, too!

From a total of 135 successful attacks, the Israel Defense Forces thwarted 406. At the beginning of the March 2002 Operation Defensive Shield, there were 135 casualties from 17 successful attacks. Eight were thwarted. In June 2004, the IDF managed to stop 22 (twenty-two!) murderous terrorist attacks from happening. In July, six attacks were prevented. In August, they caught five but unfortunately one terrorist team got by and shot and killed a father of eight.

When visiting in the States and in Europe, I told people where I have been living for over thirty years. They asked in puzzlement *why*?

Ironically, with everything that has gone on here since time immemorial, we feel safe to walk in the streets, a feeling that I did not have "outside." Even as we experience the Westernization – read: Americanization – of our world, we are thrilled that our children are growing up with Jewish values. It sounds hackneyed, but when we pray daily about so many things that relate to the Land of Israel, not the least the return of all Jews, we feel pride that we are here already. So much so, that I am usually embarrassed by my good fortune at being granted the ability to live here.

At the end of the summer, everyone walks around wishing the *Shana Tova* greeting for the New Year to all and sundry, and it is September, not December! By the end of Yom Kippur, there will be the constant din of hammering, as yet another *sukkah* or tabernacle gets put together. There seem to be a million types of honey on the market, and we know why. Of course the ever present *apple and honey*, joins the *head and tail* of a fish, but do you know that depending on your ethnic background, the menu for the Rosh Hashanah *Seder Berachot* (blessings) may include quince, leek, black-eyed peas, the head of a lamb, and beets, to name just a few.

In our family we add: lettuce, raisins and celery. Many years ago we hosted a group of yeshiva students, one of whom, unbeknownst to us and him, would become my brother-in-law. He watched in awe, befitting the Days of Awe, as food item after food item was passed around, and then *berachot* were recited using homophones and rhymes beseeching that our "enemies beat/*beet* for cover"; we mark this *date* with sweetness for the coming year; we hope that may "we be as replete in *mitzvot* as the *pomegranate*"; the coming year be sweet as the *apple dipped in honey*, etc.

My husband always asks guests to come up with their own suggestions for blessings. This guest said, you should add lettuce, raisin and celery to your repertoire so that the Almighty may "*let us* have a *raise in* our salary/*celery*." We have done so ever since.

So my recommendation to you all is that when you look at the fish, its head and tail, you should place it on the left side of the table and add: "May we merit to be 'at the front' and not 'left behind' (in the Diaspora) this coming year."

Days of Awe and Fear

A FEW YEARS AGO, immediately after Rosh Hashanah, I received a call from an *askan* (literally, an "activist," but colloquially, the "can-do-man" of a community or Rebbe's court) who worked for a well-known Rebbe, the leader of a Chassidic group. He asked if I would be able to see a grandchild of this leader, adding it was an emergency.

There are neither neuropsychological nor psychological emergencies. In an emergency, go to the nearest ER; there they have the ability to triage and get you the specific medical help required. Emergencies require medical intervention, neurologists for the brain and psychiatrists for the psyche. Serious, though not urgent, neuropsychological and psychological issues can be handled during normal office hours.

So I said that if it is an emergency, it is important to go to the closest ER. "The child has already been there," he said, "and medically he is cleared, but he still has fears."

Living in Israel is frequently awe-inspiring and awesome. In Hebrew, the words for the High Holy Days of Rosh Hashanah and Yom Kippur are called *Yamim Noraim*, the Days of Awe. This connotes both the grandeur of the holiday, the solemnity, and at the same time, the fear pertaining to God's decisions of who in the coming year, will be written in the Book of Life and who will not. With years of *pigu'im* (terror attacks) and war, many people have been left with terrifying fears, so I assumed this was the case of this young boy.

"Never assume," my late uncle (a federal judge) used to say. And once I met the 10-year old boy and his family and heard his story, I again understood the sagaciously succinct: "Never assume."

They started by telling me that the event that caused their son's fears occurred just before the holidays. They explained that before every holiday members of certain Chassidic groups come up to Jerusalem to get their Rebbe's blessings ("up" connotes the holiness of Jerusalem, not the geographic direction). On this occasion over 15,000 gathered, mostly men. In overall orderly fashion, they passed the Rebbe's table (*tisch*).

The Rebbe's table was on a platform, and many disciples – it seems close to five hundred – were standing on this platform built for a maximum of a hundred. This youngster was standing among them, when all of a sudden there was a loud crash, and the whole platform caved in and caused many to topple and fall on one another. He was buried under eight people. Miraculously, no one was killed, and he was pulled free without serious injury.

Up until now the father was speaking. At this point, the mother said: "But now he is so fearful, he won't go out of the house and pulls his mattress into our room at night out of fear and cries out in his sleep from terrible nightmares."

I looked at the parents and the child and said that I'm not sure I can do this alone. They looked at me and said that they would not mind if I consulted with other specialists. "No, that is probably not going to be enough," I said. "I need your help, and especially your son's. Would you be willing to sign a contract that you will help me help him?"

Now, you have to understand that for a Chassidic family, especially father and son, to come to a psychologist is a departure from the norm. To go to a woman is even more unique. On top of that, I am not from a Chassidic following and though I have lived in Israel for over thirty years, my American accent is quite noticeable. Suffice it to say, this was a strange and unusual experience for them. Then this person (I) asked them to sign a contract that all three of them would help me help them – this was even odder. The parents looked at each other over their son's head, the father nodded, and they agreed to sign.

With great flourish, I went ahead and wrote out the contract and all three signed and affixed the date. I signed it too, and said it was now official.

I still wasn't quite sure what I was doing, but went by my instincts, in that I felt the success of the therapy depended on their trusting my expertise. Also they could not just hand over their child for therapy to one so different than themselves. By creating this contractual relationship, I reinforced the fact that I considered them my partners, and we as a unit, would work on the problem.

Then I said to the boy, "I would like to call you Moshe, and we'll use that name when we meet." More looks between the parents, and now "Moshe" was also looking perplexed. "Well then," I said, "didn't Pharaoh's daughter give Moshe Rabbeinu (Moses, our Rabbi) that name when she pulled him out of the water? You were pulled out, saved from drowning in a sea of people." (Again subtly, re-affirming that I knew I was of a different culture, but would try to save their son so that he could retake his position as the Rebbe's grandson and possible future leader of the group.)

"The next thing I need from you," I said to the father, "is the video, DVD, CD or movie of the event."

"We don't watch televisions and we don't have video machines," was their reply. I nodded, but stuck to my guns and, pointing at the freshly signed contract, said, "Please bring it to our next meeting."

Before they left, I asked "Moshe" to draw a picture of how the line of people filing in front of the Rebbe looked, and also where he was standing in relation to the Rebbe. I felt it was important to have him give his perspective of the events, all the while recognizing that he had a special position being close to the Rebbe. Knowing that he was not comfortable speaking to me yet, I requested this sketch. His father looked on, and as the drawing came to life, he often said how good and accurate he thought it was. I asked many questions about the rituals of a *tisch*, and how so many people could line up for hours without pushing or getting into arguments, when waiting for a bus here is a nightmare.

I thanked him for the picture, and pointing again to the contract said, "I'm looking forward to seeing the event." I gave Moshe homework: could he please draw in color what he saw when he was pulled out of "the sea of people." Two days later, we met again. The father brought in a CD disk. He asked how I knew there was one. I said it would not be natural that so many men should be at such an auspicious occasion and there wouldn't be at least one video camera. He smiled and handed it over to me. I had my computer available and loaded it and the four of us saw it together. I felt it was important that Moshe see what happened from the distance of the video images, and that he watch this event in the safety of my office with his parents present.

As it turned out, Moshe and I were the ones who had not seen it before. Both his parents had viewed it a few times.

I replayed the part of the stage falling, the quiet immediately after and the pandemonium that followed as Moshe and others were pulled out of the abyss. We went over his homework and replayed the video again. Show me again, how you got out. Please point out the person who pulled you out. Do you know who he is? Have you spoken with him to thank him? Can you show me again where you were standing before it happened? There were many questions, and there were earnest answers on the part of "Moshe," helping me understand and teaching me about things I didn't know and would never have the opportunity to see for myself.

With each retelling, "Moshe's" body language became more relaxed as did that of his mother. At the end of the session, I returned the disk and said, "We won't need this anymore. Next time, 'Moshe,' could you bring along the *Birkhat HaGomel* you said, and oh, I have a book to lend you." I gave him a children's book on first aid with clear explanations of how to deal with immediate medical problems, how to care for burns, bandage different sorts of cuts and bruises and other skills in helping the wounded.

The next appointment was scheduled for before Sukkot; they called and said that they needed to postpone it until after the holiday. I took this cancellation as a positive sign. The emergency seemed to have abated, I thought, or it might also mean that they found a "real" psychologist. The next appointment was also cancelled; I smiled to myself as I heard the message on my answering machine.

About two months later, I received a package. It was the first aid book and a letter from the mother. She said she had to admit that she and her husband were both very skeptical about the therapy I did with their son. Draw pictures at home, see a video, asking silly questions and then, giving a child of ten a first aid book! All this seemed at odds with what they had envisioned therapy to be.

Moshe had read the book inside and out, she wrote. He had practiced bandaging his siblings' arms and legs. And Moshe went out during Sukkot – on his own. Not only that, he had slept in the *sukkah* which was outside and not attached to the house.

She wasn't sure how, but the unusual therapy had cured him. Young "Moshe" was pulled from the sea of doubt and fear, with a renewed sense of competence and strength, to fulfill his future role.

The Woman with the Scarf
Knotted under Her Chin

During sukkot, the Feast of Tabernacles, we live in temporary dwellings just for a week. The woman in the following story, as so many others, was living in temporary dwellings – under difficult conditions – for years.

She came in, sat down at the table, and in faltering English said, "I just wanted to say goodbye." *Odd*, I thought, *since she had just arrived*! I looked perplexed and a woman to my right said knowingly, in European-accented Hebrew, "She probably just got her visa."

We had found a great deal on a flight that stopped in Europe on the way home from the United States. We would stay in this European country over Shabbat, since with the summer's long days, we would have time on Friday to get our lay of the land and all of Shabbat to walk around. We would then fly out on Sunday.

Besides seeing the sites and visiting museums, we had located three synagogues and decided to pray at all of them, ending with the one that was known for its Shabbat Kiddush, including *cholent* and *kugel* even in the summer. This menu was a great improvement over the vacuum-packed tuna fish that awaited us in our room.

The first synagogue we visited was housed in an old building, where there was no women's section. So I sat out in the hallway. I heard singing from above, and walked up two flights and found a second *minyan* (prayer quorum) in progress. I looked around and though all the eyes seemed to turn and look at me – the outsider – I felt the people were vaguely familiar.

Living in the center of Jerusalem for over thirty years, we often visit different synagogues on Shabbat. Within a 15-minute walk from our home, there are literally hundreds of *minyanim* where people from myriad countries of origin, representing all shades of customs, pray. And so, when I saw the women, they looked somewhat familiar to me – not European at all. I, on the other hand, looked and felt very much out of place. Most of the older women wore scarves over their hennaed hair. One woman beckoned me to sit next to her. She was slim, wearing a pantsuit and a scarf knotted under her chin.

At the appointed time, I pointed to my watch and said, "Shabbat Shalom" and left. I met my husband and we walked through town to the third *minyan*. When the prayer service was over, we were invited to join the rest of the congregation for their advertised Kiddush. There were about sixty men. Eight women were seated behind a curtain/screen (*mechitzah*).

All of a sudden, a woman entered the area. She wore a pantsuit and had a scarf knotted under her chin. I knew her, as she was the one who had greeted me and offered me a seat earlier in the morning. I began to talk with her, and discovered that she had lived in this country for over two years, waiting for a visa to join her children. "Join your children, where are they?" I asked. In halting English she explained that after her husband's death, she worked to pay for her two sons to make the circuitous trip to the U.S. Once they were there, she saved money for her own exit. During the past two years, she was housed in temporary dwellings, learning English and being cared for by organizations that help wayfarers. Now, finally, she had received her coveted visa. She had a ticket for Tuesday and would be reunited with her sons, whom she hadn't seen in over five years. "I came to say goodbye," she said again.

I sat in awe of this woman and the sacrifices she had made to gain her children a new permanent home. By *Hashgachah Pratit* (the Grace of God), I was born at a time and in a place which allows me to move seamlessly between almost any country in the world, and be able to set up home anywhere I choose.

I stood up and went around the table to her. "As an American, let me shake your hand and be the first to welcome you." The woman, with the scarf knotted under her chin, hugged me and kissed me on both cheeks. I continued and said: "As an Israeli, let me say, *L'shana ha'baah b'Yerushalayim* – Next Year in Jerusalem."

SYNTHESIZING THE BIBLE AND LIFE IN THE 21ST CENTURY

"Accidental" Death: Biblical Intervention to Tragic Consequences

T HERE ARE MANY topics that are not usually spoken about, death is one of them. I imagine this discomfort with the topic stems from the fact that for each of us, someone's dying brings to our awareness our own mortality. Frequently, we read about accidents at work, in the armed forces, on the roads, and in the home that result in another's death. I always wonder about what is generally not mentioned: what happens to the person who causes the accident?

A heartbreaking incident was reported on the Israeli news: A young man, a soldier, was home sleeping. He had returned for a break in his hectic and scary schedule as an officer in a special unit of the army. He was safely at home sleeping. It was 3 a.m. when he heard noise outside his window. He lives with his parents and brother on a small *yishuv*, a settlement. He knew his brother was in another unit in the army and his folks were sleeping. He called out to find out if anyone was outside. No one answered. He saw the shadowy figure moving up to his window. He grabbed his gun and shot. The intruder turned out to be his older brother, who wanted to surprise his family with his presence. Tragically, he was killed instantly.

That year, a paper I wrote with Dr. Yocheved Debow, a clinical psychologist, on the topic of accidental killing was published in *Bekhol Derakhekha Daehu, BDD: a Journal of Torah and Scholarship*. In the article, we try to address the issue of what happens to those who are responsible for the accident. Clearly this follows the investigation and designation of the incident as "accidental." Researching the phenomenon in secular literature, we found very little information on methods of dealing/helping the causers of accidents. There is a lot about Post Traumatic Stress Disorder (PTSD), but most of it relates to people who have experienced trauma, not caused it.

In light of the incident mentioned above, I was again reminded of the fact that there is no model for helping the perpetrators of accidental killing accept the consequences of their actions.

In my work as a director of the Neuropsychology Unit at Shaare Zedek Medical Center in Jerusalem, I try to synthesize the many parts of my education, both secular and Jewish. When presented with unique situations, I work under the assumption that Judaism has over five thousand years experience with humanity, which beats any science in use today. So when I was referred a patient with PTSD who was involved in an accidental killing, I turned to the model described in the Bible of the *ir miklat* (city of refuge), a place defined as a sanctuary to protect the "accidental killer." Based on an understanding of the psychic trauma experienced by accidental killers, and using the Torah model, I was sure I would get a deeper understanding of both the problem and the solution.

WHO IS CONSIDERED AN ACCIDENTAL KILLER, A *ROTZEACH BISHGAGA*?

An accidental death becomes a double-edged tragedy for both the bereaved family and the accidental perpetrator, whose experience often sentences him/her to a lifetime of turmoil. In the Bible, the concept of accidental killing is discussed along with both a legal and (we think) therapeutic solution to this difficult experience with the creation of a "city of refuge." The *ir miklat*, a sanctuary to protect the accidental killer, was one of these forty-eight cities established before the Jews entered the Land of Israel. The *rotzeach bishgaga* was sentenced to live there for an indeterminate period of time (Exodus 21:12–14; Numbers 35:9–29; Deuteronomy 4:42; 19:1–13).

According to professional psychological literature the *rotzeach bishgaga* goes through a defined process as a result of this horrifying experience. Shock comes first. Then a brief period of numbness – the mind hides from the full realization that one has caused the death of another human being. This is followed by preoccupation with the event/accident. In the struggle to make sense of the event, many accidental killers replay it over and over in their minds. Anger often engulfs the accidental killer, directed at every aspect and player in the accident, including the victim. Guilt is nearly universal, causing accidental killers to torture themselves for unfounded reasons as well as for error and oversight. Depression, also common, may occur in various forms. Their internal turmoil may cause them to withdraw from family and friends. They usually experience some form of social tension/avoidance of social contact, often resulting from the failure of their friends and associates to respond or act supportively due to their unfamiliarity with the situation. Family stress occurs as well. At some point, virtually all accidental killers begin some process of healing/acceptance. Nevertheless, the aftermath of the event extends throughout their lives. Thus most accidental killers themselves become victims of the event. Remarkably, all the described symptoms experienced by accidental killers are included in the accepted definition of PTSD.

It is interesting to note the similarities of the process which accidental killers experience with the classic model of the stages of mourning described in Elisabeth Kubler-Ross's seminal work, *On Death and Dying*. When we see patients with PTSD following accidents in which they feel culpable, it is striking to note that almost all of them do not experience the final stage: acceptance. They actually remain in the state of mourning. Could they be mourning not only for the victim who actually died but also for themselves, who are still alive, but no longer in their former state of innocence – the person they were before the fatal moment?

Accidental killers are frequently acquitted in court of the crime of manslaughter. Legal exoneration, however, cannot reverse the accident and return the dead person to life, nor can it render the *rotzeach bishgaga* a person who has not killed anyone, albeit accidentally. Often, a *rotzeach bishgaga*'s reaction after being acquitted is to say that the person is still dead, and "it was still my finger on the trigger." Although the law has judged them to be not guilty, their own acute awareness of loss prevents them from accepting that judgment.

HOW THE *IR MIKLAT* MODEL ADDRESSES THE SYMPTOMS OF PTSD

What was the process of getting into the *ir miklat*?

(1) The accident occurs. It should be noted that around ancient Israel signposts directed one to the cities of refuge, making the road to them more knowable by the *rotzeach bishgaga* who is in a numb and shocked state.

(2) The person flees to the *ir miklat* where the family of the victim could not kill them. Outside the *ir miklat* a family member (*goel ha'dam*, the blood avenger) would not be guilty of murder for killing the *rotzeach bishgaga*.

(3) After immediate entry, the court examines the evidence and decides it was indeed an accident. The *rotzeach bishgaga* can remain in the *ir miklat*.

(4) A man was accompanied to the *ir miklat* by his family. His rabbinic mentor was also an option and changed the nature of the exile. (The husband of a woman *rotzeach bishgaga* could opt to join her, or not do so.) Perhaps the purpose of the *ir miklat* was to demonstrate that one's lifestyle should not be altered.

(5) Finally, there is the arbitrary release time. With the death of the High Priest, the *rotzeach bishgaga* was released from "exile." Possibly, we posit, this reinforces the peripatetic nature of the accident itself.

WHO ELSE LIVES IN THE *IR MIKLAT*?

The *ir miklat* was primarily inhabited by Levites – an important sector of the community, mentors of the population. Thus the *rotzeach bishgaga*'s knowledge that they were not being sent to spend their sentence with a socially undesirable community, but were worthy of the company of Levites, may also have served to help them re-acquire a favorable sense of identity. The Levite community, who did not have land or animals to cultivate and care for, also served a primary role in preparing the sacrifices for the Temple. They were known to be people characterized by great precision. It might also have been important for accidental killers to be exposed to this trait as part of their battle against the randomness of the event that had so dramatically changed them.

HOW CAN WE HELP A *ROTZEACH BISHGAGA* TODAY?

The treatment of PTSD remains a challenge not only for friends and family, but also, not the least, for health professionals. The complexity of the disorder underscores the difficulty in establishing a clear treatment of choice, or perhaps a constellation of treatments of choice, for patients suffering from PTSD. There may even be existing facilities that could be redefined in line with the *ir miklat* model. The Israel Defense Forces presently has a facility that seems to have a similar aim. It could certainly serve as a basis from which to launch a more encompassing model that would take into consideration the various symptoms experienced in PTSD. Although the Levite tribe no longer serves the functions it had in ancient times, the psychologists and social workers of today could serve similar functions, at least as a therapeutic staff, if not as a community in which a *rotzeach bishgaga* could live. The fact that biblical practice foreshadows many of the same techniques currently understood and used in modern-day psychotherapies for the treatment of PTSD seems to invite the use of ancient wisdom for those who still suffer today as accidental killers.

Until then, if the community at large is familiar with the concepts in our wealth of biblical literature for all-encompassing approaches to difficult problems, and the treatment of the specific trauma of accidental killers is just one of them, the world will be a more therapeutic and understanding place for us all.

On the Service of the Priests – the Kohanim

My GRANDSON COMMENTED one Shabbat on how quickly I walked "considering . . ." For the sake of his future birthday gifts from me, I felt sure he was referring to my height-challenged state – he being close to six-feet tall and my standing at a mere 5 feet 2 inches (in shoes).

Our quick walk gave me an opportunity to fill him in on how I became so skilled in fast walking. On the holidays of Rosh Hashanah, Yom Kippur, Sukkot, Pesach, and Shavuot I would accompany my father, z"l (OBM), as he almost ran between the two synagogues which my two grandfathers attended. As the oldest in my family, I can recall being about eight years old and joining my father, a Kohen (a priest), first at the S & P (Spanish and Portuguese Synagogue in Manhattan) where my mother's father prayed (they began *davening* very early), and then running to the WSIS (West Side Institutional Synagogue) where he joined his father in *duchaning* (giving the Priestly blessing) on the holidays. If you have never been to the S & P on a Shabbat or even gone to the annual Tisha B'Av service (in the dark!), let me describe what attending to a Kohen before he was "on" entails.

In the S & P, the Kohanim – at that time my father was one of two – had a special place in the anteroom of the synagogue to sit and change into their plain black sneakers, and their silk top hats! My job was to use a special velvet-napped small pillow to smooth the nap on the hat. As the Kohanim walked down the long path reaching the *Heichal* (Ark) to the accompaniment of the full male choir, they were wearing their top hats and sneakers. At the bottom of the grand marble steps, stood the Levite (or firstborn if a Levite was not present) with a huge silver pitcher and bowl to wash the Kohen's hands prior to his giving the benediction. Then the Kohanim walked up approximately ten steps and facing the *Heichal,* placed their *tallit* (prayer shawl) over their heads, and said the blessing to begin the prayer. After that, they turned toward the congregants and began to repeat the *Hazan*'s (cantor) word for word rendition of the Priestly Benediction. I recall how neat and uniform (flat-headed due to the top hats) the Kohanim looked from the women's balcony (girls, no matter how young, *never* sat in the men's section).

Once the morning prayer, *Shacharit*, was over, we reversed the getting attired bit, and began our fast walk along the six long blocks to the WSIS where there were more Kohanim, Levites and my grandfather, with whom to *duchan*. "Neither snow nor rain nor heat nor gloom" kept us from our job.

It wasn't until my husband became the rabbi of the Syrian community in Los Angeles that I discovered that in some communities Kohanim were in the majority, or so it seemed. Our first Shabbat in our new community was an eye opener: when the *Hazan* called up the Kohanim, it seemed as though 90 percent of the men took off their shoes and went up to the *Heichal*. Outside of Israel, only the Sephardic communities *duchan* on Shabbat; in Israel, both Ashkenazim and Sephardim do so.

Kohanim who *duchan* together form a bond, a club of sorts. However, little did my grandfather and one of his *duchaning* buddy's imagine that over fifty years later their great-grandchildren would meet and marry in Israel!

The Gift of the Crowning Glory

I LOOKED AT HER thinking of my grandmother, who used to refer to one's hair (especially girls) as "your crowning glory." There she stood before me, all of fourteen years old, hair shorn in a kind of choppy, very short ponytail ("*kuku*" in modern Hebrew; "fringe" in UK).

"I didn't want to tell anybody until I did *it*," she said. Other girls have done *it*, too. *It* was first growing her hair the longest it has ever been and then cutting it so that it can be used to make a wig for a young cancer patient.

I thought of the oft-told story of two brothers who loved each other so much that each night they crept over to the other's property and added wheat to the beloved brother's daily harvest so as to help him be more successful. The story goes on to say how one night they met, and on that site the Beit HaMikdash – Holy Temple was built; a story emphasizing unadulterated selfless brotherly love, as the foundation of the earthly presence of Hashem (God).

L'havdil (to differentiate between the sublime and mundane), there is a famous O. Henry short story, "The Gift of the Magi," which comes to mind. Recounted is the story of a financially strapped young couple who want to give each other a special gift. He has a precious watch he inherited; she has beautiful long hair. As O. Henry puts it, they sacrificed for each other the greatest treasures of their house. In order to afford the gift, she cuts and sells her hair and buys him a watch fob, and he "hocks" his watch to buy her beautiful combs for her long hair. Their love for one another is the true gift.

I return to thinking about hair. Hair can be such a bone of contention between teens and parents. Too long, too short, not long enough. For males perhaps, it is cut too near the *pe'ot* (specific areas of the face); for teens and young adults it's shampoo "laced" with H_2O_2, hydrogen peroxide (instead of H_2O – water)! In young marrieds, it's the different opinions regarding *pe'ot* as in *sheitel* or wig hair vs. cloth, *tichel*s or hats used for hair coverings.

Here these few young teen girls, at the height of their opportunity to show off their *own* crowning glory, choose to coddle it, grow it, and then cut it off for a *chesed* – altruistic, meaningful selfless purpose for another.

Wait a minute, I said to myself, *this process sounds a lot like parenting*. We are given the gift of taking and coddling the young, effecting children's growth (home, schools, and communities). This younger generation *forms* our Crowning Glory and finally, we are charged with letting them go off into Life to do the Greater Good for others.

I saw my granddaughter's shorn hair along with the sparkle in her eyes and glow on her face as she showed me the certificate she received from Zichron Menachem – the organization for children with cancer. But more than that, her soft words touched my heart. When she saw the surprised look on my face she said: "Don't worry, Oma Judi, it will grow again."

I relearned life's truth: *growing leads to cutting which leads to selflessness and re-growth.*

May our children's learning and doing the way of *chesed* enhance love for others and speed the rebuilding of the Holy Temple.

A Rite of Responsibility

Israel's supreme court ruled on a case where a mother had "punished" her child by hitting him with a vacuum cleaner. The Court also mandated that all corporeal punishment meted out by a parent to a child be considered abuse, and dealt with by the police and courts accordingly.

Our views and experience at the Clinic would certainly argue for parents and teachers to be made aware that abuse is not condoned. But can a court of law, even the highest in the country, have an influence in this area?

The first step we feel is that society be made aware of the problem. How might we gain a direction on this topic from the Torah? The *egla arufa* (beheaded heifer) seemed to be the Torah's way teaching us the importance of community action and the dire consequences when we just take care of our own.

*

The child sitting in front of me had arrived with a bruised eye. He was accompanied by his mother. When I saw him the preceding week, his eye was not swollen. I ask: "What happened?" My question causes him to be agitated and uncomfortable. I wait.

The mother speaks, and says: "This is what happens to a child who moves while he is being punished."

"With what do you punish him, usually?"

"With a belt." Her tone of voice is as if everyone uses a belt to punish a child. "But this time, he moved, and thus he was hit in the face instead of in the arm."

*

A child was brought to the Clinic because of serious deterioration of his abilities at *heder* (pre-school in the Haredi school system), especially in reading. During the previous school year he had been among the better students, and all of a sudden he cries a lot when home, does not prepare homework and is failing in his studies. The neuropsychological examination did not indicate any learning disabilities.

In a conversation with the parents, they revealed that the first signs of

37

disturbance coincided with the visits a neighbor had begun paying at their home. This neighbor, they said, enjoyed the children. They trusted his judgment implicitly, and sometimes he also helped them out by babysitting.

Based on previous experience with children who show a sudden and drastic change in behavior without any neurological or other medical signs, we recommended that the child be examined both by a social worker and a physician who have experience with "special cases" such as this one. He was found to have been molested.

The young child, seeing that his parents have "entrusted" him to a man such as this, who hurt him, did not have the capacity to doubt that they felt this behavior was acceptable, and felt he could not go to them to complain.

The neighbor was interrogated by the police and was found to have committed this form of aggression on other children in the neighborhood, whose parents were not as attuned to changes in their behavior or distress.

*

The mother arrived with her arm in a cast with a child, who was referred for behavioral problems, especially toward his younger siblings. When the child left the room, I asked her how she broke her arm. She started to cry, but said she had fallen.

In the course of the visit, the child's drawings made me suspicious of verbal or possible physical abuse in the family. The little boy's drawings were full of people with large mouths and especially noses with huge nostrils. The words "charon af" (literally, "nose," but translated as "wrath") kept coming back to me. These drawings gave the words new meaning. Generally the parent is not in the room during the assessment. However, on this occasion, I somehow intuitively felt that she should remain and see him at play in this therapeutic environment. Through play, the child acted out the problems in his family. As the hour progressed, the mother was drawn out by his actions. She understood his games to be what they were – a cry for help. She told of her husband's abuse, which in this case culminated with him pushing her down so that she broke her arm. "He is a good man, and always is so sorry after it happens."

King Solomon in Kohelet (Ecclesiastes) wrote: "Nothing is new under the sun." Motives and behavior have remained unchanged in time. The modern world might be a more sophisticated one (with microwaves, cell phones and the like), but humans have remained the same ever since God created Man.

I perceive the skills I have learned as being instruments of changing behavior, not a tool for judging people. By pointing out certain behavior patterns that are ineffective at best, and damaging to the child or family at worst, we try to effect change.

The people described above are members of their communities. Their children go to school and may be sitting next to yours, or your cousin's. The mother with the broken arm, is someone's daughter, sister, and neighbor. Maybe you saw her at the market crying as she shopped, and ignored her – for her sake of course. At any time, we may be witnesses to situations that we know are not healthy and are damaging. It is our duty as members of the community – parents, educators and professionals – to pay attention to any sign of pain and distress coming from those around us. The importance of social responsibility is reiterated with many examples in the Torah.

In Parshat D'varim, it is told about the *egla arufa*. In an open field, between houses, a dead body was found. As long as the perpetrator of the murder remained unknown the dead person's body was seen as "corrupting the earth." The elders of community closest to the scene of the crime were approached and told they were held responsible for the death.

Two concepts may be inferred from this story. The first pointing at the community's responsibly towards an individual – especially one that is alone, unprotected by the fact of being a stranger.

The second point might be that individuals, even a stranger, have an enormous capacity to influence the community – in this case to effect change. The dead man's blood has the ability to influence the earth, which is common property, and corrupt it, even though only an individual was responsible for his death.

The Talmud explains that the community's elders are *not held responsible* for murdering the man, rather for not helping him. They had not given him food when he had needed it, nor had they provided him with an escort to make sure that he reached his destination in safety.

We read an exhortation to be willing to know instead of pretending to be blind. Not to behave as an ostrich which buries its head so as not to see. It is interesting that the law of *egla arufa* requires that the heifer's blood be absorbed in the earth. Possibly, just as the body's blood impairs the field, so too the exchange of blood, this time under the control of the community, expunges the responsibility. One might say that the community that did not serve the needs of this unprotected individual, God's creation, was prohibited from having God's earth, on which the dead body lies, provide for it – the land becomes barren until the rite of *egla arufa* is practiced. *Middah k'negged middah* (a deed for a deed), the community was not generous with its food for the wayfarer, so the land becomes uninhabitable because food is unable to grow in its environs.

The subject of the *egla arufa* is treated lengthily in the Tractate *Sotah*, a Gemara that is mainly concerned with *shalom bayit*, domestic harmony. The neighbors of the families mentioned above must have undoubtedly heard the sounds of discord, cries of pain; teachers and rabbis must have seen the bruises, the inflammations. Should they not have remarked and been attentive to the deterioration in class work and participation? Should they not have been more available for those parents and children in distress, those who suffered in silence and those whose behavior screamed for help?

In the Book of Judges, we read about the town of Luz. It is said one asked to be shown the way to the town of Luz and promised that the person showing the way would be repaid by God with an act of graciousness. An inhabitant of the place indicated to the person "with a sign" how to reach the destination. For this seemingly inconsequential, tangential behavior, he was repaid by God for generations to come, and the town of Luz was blessed.

The *techelet* (the blue dye for the fringes of the *tzizit*) comes from Luz. The people of Luz were immortal. When Nebuchadnezzar descended upon Israel, he was unable to capture Luz. All thanks to the act of having had shown the way.

Interestingly, the story of Luz is also referred to in Tractate *Sotah* in connection with *egla arufa*. Possibly, another example of how important it is to give help, important even when the help only consists of a sign.

When Pesach annually approaches with its frenzy to clean house, can we not be involved in purging our larger "house," our community of abuse? We clean so well that we have to hide pieces of *hametz* so that we can find it the night before Erev Pesach. Can we be less observant of the signs our friends and neighbors show us that might point to their "*hametz*," their problems? Are we not responsible to help, even if our ability lies only in pointing them in the direction of professionals? *Egla arufa* tells us that God holds us responsible for our communities' very existence. May we merit His blessings.

Me, We, and Them – States and Traits in Our Family: An Experiential Workshop

My husband and I were invited to be scholars-in-residence for a weekend sponsored by Maimonides, the Los Angeles day school (formerly The Sephardic Hebrew Academy). The topics of the weekend were designed to commemorate 800 years since the Rambam's death. Thinking about what to present from my perspective, as a neuropsychologist, I thought about the Rambam's Thirteen Principles (*Yud Gimmel Ikarim* – found in his commentary to the Mishnah in *Sanhedrin*). How do we learn or internalize principles? How do we acquire principles? And more importantly, how can we transmit them to our children? The neuro/psychological concepts of Traits and States came to mind.

Trait concepts permit people to predict the present from the past – how often have we described a people by a stereotype – people from this country are known as stingy/intellectual/spiritual/emotionally labile. More directly we may classify a family based on previous experience with them as a family of sensitive people; people with short fuses, easily angered.

State concepts, on the other hand, identify those behaviors that can be controlled by manipulating the situation – for example shivering when cold. More subtly, Trauma is an experience which can transform a child's world into a terror-filled, confusing state. Research has shown this dramatically alters the child's ability to cope with life's experiences until one-hundred and twenty.

These two complementary schemas are part of the extensive theory of psychological causality that is implicit in language. Traits that we are born with may change depending on the states we are in. Trauma is a case in point. Children who are exposed to fear and traumatic experiences take on different behaviors in life-traits, based upon the physiological states in which their brains have been developed. Positive experience states, too, clearly have their impact on our brains. For example, laughter changes the chemicals in which our brain exists – for it is the human brain that develops, processes and internalizes all traumatic and therapeutic experiences. It is the brain that mediates all emotional, cognitive, behavioral, social and physiological functioning.

What traits do you, as an individual and as a couple, think you have and have evolved based on your experiences? Which have you passed on to your children? What states in the home and school environment will physiologically change the traits your children pass on to their children?

I devised an experiential workshop for that Shabbaton that I am presenting here (we will be experimenting) for you to try with your children.

The first step is understanding your own States and Traits (and your spouse's). The way you might go about this is by taking a list of states and traits. Below is an example (by no way exhaustive). Make a copy or two (or three) of this list.

Trusting	Well-dressed	Confident	Resourceful
Fair	Gracious	Content	Loving
Has convictions	Appropriate	Integrated	Clever
Courageous	Passionate	Self-motivated	Incisive
Truthful	Consistent	Compassionate	Tolerant
Moral	Resilient	Mature	Firm
Loyal	Respectful	Capable	Loving
Accountable	Concerned	Accepting	Understanding
Responsible	Tolerant	Intuitive	Curious
Committed	Sharing	Aware	Quick
Diligent	Kind	Willing	Generous
Honest	Patient	Adventurous	Diplomatic
Prudent	Generous	Spiritual	Wise
Thrifty	Hospitable	Visual	Articulate
Simple	Vision	Present-oriented	Clear
Orderly	Mastery	Future-oriented	Encouraging
Detail-oriented	Productive	Creative	Appreciative
Punctual	Accomplishing	Flexible	Constructive
Balanced	Causal/Initiating	Proactive	Expressive
Trusting	Investing	Adaptive	Friendly
Polished	Effective	Innovative	Analytical
Clean	Practical	Direct	

1. Each of you, separately, choose thirteen (an arbitrary number) words, which you feel represent your strengths. Write them down.
2. Then put them in a serial order what you think is most important.
3. NO PEEKING AT THE OTHER PERSON'S LIST!
4. Take a break.
5. Come back to the list and see if you agree with your choices, change them.
6. Now, sit together and share and discuss your lists.
7. Now together, choose seven attributes. In doing this you will have to convince each other (and yourselves) which are the seven you agree upon.

How to do it at home with the kids?

Do the same thing with the children. Start with a larger number and let them refine the list down, so that the entire family will have seven (or thirteen) priorities in all that will represent your family's prioritized *middot*, attributes. You will be communicating with your children, these conversations need not end with the final choice but can continue for days!

On/Off the Path: An Unusual Travelogue

T HERE IS A LOT OF TALK about "off the *derech*" (leaving the "path" of Jewish observance) and the pain it causes to the identified patients – the children, their families, and the Jewish People. Without minimizing this issue, I often feel we have let our children down by the "narrowness" of the *derech*.

My grandfather was a businessman in Germany in the 1800s, and would travel all over Europe selling his wares (tobacco leaves – don't sue me; I'm not related to Philip Morris!). He learned *shechitat ofot* (ritual slaughter of chickens) so that he could eat wherever he went. How many of us have taught our children subsistence farming or *shechita*?

I remembered my grandfather's realistic skill following our visit to Puerto Plata, the northeast city of the Dominican Republic. The reason we were there was as convoluted as one could imagine. Our granddaughter and her teammates represented Israel in the Women's World Cup of American Flag Football; we felt we should be there. We are generally not sports-groupies, but a seventeen-year old yeshiva high school student . . .

The story begins on a Friday, when the days were longer. Friday afternoon is like an American Sunday. Hours off from school that is not a Shabbat or a holiday. Her brother was in a pick-up game of American football, at Gan Sacher in Jerusalem. She and her friends were also throwing a football around. Eight months later the first (and only) Israel Women's Flag Football team (no tackling, no physical contact, instead pulling one of two flags hanging from a belt) was off to the Dominican Republic for the World Cup.

This team was different, both the men's and women's teams were different. Many of the men sported *kippot* and some played with *tzizit* out, flying in the tropical breeze. The women's uniform was skirts (originally sport-shorts, cut and re-sewn into skirts) on top of pants and long sleeved shirts with players numbers on the back. This special team, representing Israel, flew with *glatt* kosher food for the six-day trip. We brought a small, one-foot high Sefer Torah, and there were three *minyanim* a day (*Shacharit, Mincha, and Maariv*). We had our own *"shul,"* a synagogue that doubled as a dining area and was in reality the veranda of one of the rooms. Shabbat was special. The hotel gave us a room to use as a proper *shul* and dining room. We sang *zemirot*, and had a bunch of *divrei Torah* for each of the three *Seudot*, meals.

Sunday we went on our own tour of the city of Sosua, a haven given by the Dominican Republic to Jews fleeing the Holocaust who were not admitted under the quota to the U.S. in the 1930s. Today 250 of the 1,000 who came remain. The Dominican Republic offered a hundred thousand (100,000) visas; only 1,000, mostly German Jews, took them up on the offer. They survived the Holocaust. One family was the Strauss family who built a dairy that is not only in function today, but supplies the dairy products for the area. There is a one-room *shul* and a larger room that is the museum of the Jewish community.

This special team, made it into the finals, with Cayman Islands, Canada, the U.S., Venezuela and other teams cheering for Israel in their languages, though we came in fourth place (both Israeli teams). This special team proved that keeping Shabbat and observing Kashrut and sportsmanship are in First Place![1]

My premise is that maybe we haven't given our children sufficient tools to know how to stay on the *derech* when they don't have the full L.L.Bean regalia. Based in Maine, the L.L.Bean company's catalogue for outdoor gear and apparel is synonymous with outfitting for the outdoors, and can be a metaphor for how we prepare our children. Maybe we – the parents and educational system – haven't given our youth all the equipment for physical and spiritual subsistence on life's *derech*.

---

1. An enormous amount of credit goes to Toni Sachs, Danny Taragin, Jason Gardner and Coach Yonah Mishan who made this "off the beaten *derech*" trip the unbelievable experience it was.

The Chofetz Chaim's
Observations Guide Us Today

THE ABDUCTION AND MURDER of Leiby Kletzky, *z"l*, in July 2011 should put all *naarishkeit*, frivolity, in its place.

The unspeakable awfulness and its juxtaposition to the Fast of the 17th of Tammuz, the beginning of the Roman siege of Jerusalem which preceded the Great Temple's destruction, should be a lesson to us. The *ahavat achim* (brotherly love) demonstrated by the community of thousands who searched for him, and by the prayers of the Jewish People was unique. How sad that poor Leiby's case was the catalyst which brought the unity to light. May the *sinat achim* (hatred) that was the cause of the destruction of the Temple be banished, and may we all (men, women and children) be of one mind to root out evil.

I am reminded of a story I heard from the late Rav Koppel Kalman Kahana, *zk"l*, of London's Jews' College. As a newly married couple, my husband and I lived and studied in England. My husband had the honor of being in Rav Kahana's *smicha* (rabbinical training) class as well as being the Rav's sometimes driver. As frequently as I could, I would join them in the car. Rav Kahana was an unbelievable scholar of both Talmud and anything else he put his mind to. He arrived in Cambridge, England a penniless refugee. The Rav of the city was fast to recognize his prodigious knowledge. Rav Kahana spent time learning Talmud and learning English – in the legal library of Cambridge. Rav Kahana even wrote a comparative legal paper on Talmudic, Roman and English Law. He received a Masters in Law for his work.

His memory skills where legendary. He once showed me the "pin trick." He asked me to put a pin on one word in a Gemara and then to choose a *daf* (page) which was scores of pages from the pin. After slowly going through each word of the page, he would then be able to tell which word was directly under the pin tens of pages away.

Rav Kahana was the *ilui* (brilliant young scholar) of his day, and was frequently requested by the Chofetz Chaim to accompany him on his journeys. (Rav Yisrael Meir Kagan, 1838–1933, known as the Chofetz Chaim, was a leading Eastern European rabbi whose works continue to be influential today.)

The Chofetz Chaim was asked to spend some time in a distant city and Rav

Kahana was at his side waiting for the train to take him there. When the train arrived, the Chofetz Chaim put his hand on Rav Kahana's leg and signaled him not to board the train. "But Rebbe," he beseeched, "the whole community is out waiting for us." The Chofetz Chaim just shook his head. They waited for the next train.

When they finally arrived at their destination instead of being greeted by their hosts, they saw crowds of people crying, some of whom had *reist kriyah*, torn their clothing in a sign of mourning.

"What happened?" asked Rav Kahana of those around them.

"Haven't you heard? The Chofetz Chaim was in the train that crashed and most of the passengers were killed."

Aghast and traumatized by what he had just heard, he informed those around him that indeed the Chofetz Chaim had survived as he had waited for the second train.

Later, privately, Rav Kahana quietly asked his Rebbe: "Was it a prophecy?"

The Chofetz Chaim shook his head in the negative.

"But, Rebbe, how could you know?"

The Chofetz Chaim answered: "The train was early. It is not in the nature of trains to be early. Something was not right either with the train or the conductor or both."

The whole story, and especially the answer, is one that should guide us today. We need to be more aware of our surroundings; we need to trust ourselves and ask questions if what we see in front of us fits with what our gut tells us.

It doesn't always matter what the answer is. If your gut causes you to pause and ask questions, that is enough.

May the memory of Leiby ben/son of Nachman and Esther be a beacon to us all, to light up darkness and fill nooks-and-crannies of aberrant behavior in our midst with the sound of reporting it, and the light of hope that no child or adult will ever have to suffer.

"Hollyvood" for the Orthodox?

For THE FIRST TIME in Israel, the Haredi community has produced a movie for, by, and with real Haredi actors. Well, really two movies.
The first one, "*Ushpizin*" was a popular movie very professionally done and
available to the public in the standard movie theaters around the country.
The second one "*V'heshiv Lev Avot*" (Turning Back the Fathers' Heart), a more
modest production, is selling like hotcakes in Meah Shearim, Bnei Brak and
other Haredi enclaves, where it's watched on computers. The stories are totally
different, but the impact of this bold move is groundbreaking.

"*Ushpizin*," whose name connotes the spiritual guests who visit the *sukkah*,
opened up a sensitive view of the usually closed (to the public) Haredi *shtetel*
within the larger city of Jerusalem. You are introduced to a middle-aged *baalei
teshuvah* (those returning to observant Judaism) childless couple who are preparing for Sukkot, building their *sukkah* and buying the *Arba Minim* (the Four
Species), including the *lulav* and *etrog*. The story goes on to show a clash of
cultures – the one left behind and the newly religious and spiritual one. How
the well-meaning, intense, and sensitively acted interactions play out is the
heart and soul of the movie. There have been many movies that have attempted
to portray aspects of Haredi life, but this is the first one that is written, acted and
produced mainly by Haredim (with some help from non-Haredi seed money).

The secular people I spoke to found the movie an eye opener. They felt it was
sensitive and a window into a world that they may never see and experience. In
particular, one told me that the movie gave a sense for the pathos of buying the
"right" *etrog* – they may see in the markets or on television (Haredim looking
at *etrogim* with magnifying glasses or a jeweler's loupe) – as an expression of
Hiddur Mitzvah (glorifying the mitzvah).

The second movie was a more modest production. Though not shown in the
movie houses, it was not meant to be. It was meant to be shown in homes, not
houses. The cover recommends that parents watch the film with their children
and talk about it. It was to be shown in schools with the Rebbe or teacher in
attendance. "*V'heshiv Lev Avot*" is the story of an almost Bar Mitzvah aged boy.
He learns in a Talmud Torah and has had a drastic drop in school achievement

and attendance. We watch as he is leaving sign after sign of his pain, his drawings, his chutzpadik answers to his Rebbe, and of course the welt on his brow. All these signs of domestic abuse go unnoticed, until he runs away from home. The story of how his friends, his Rebbe and the community's rabbi go about dealing with the issue demonstrates the power of this groundbreaking movie.

It was the creative idea and produced by Rabbi Noach Korman (a rabbinical pleader at the Beit Din, rabbinical court) and executive director of Miklat Israel, with the untiring help of Mrs. Esti Pallant, the Shelter director. Miklat Israel is a non-profit organization that runs shelters for Haredi married women and their children who suffer from domestic abuse. The organization also runs two hostels for Haredi children and adolescents, one for boys and one for girls in different parts of Jerusalem.

It is impossible to talk about these institutions without mentioning Mrs. Estanne Abraham Fawer. Mrs. Fawer donated the seed money for Nefesh Israel's first four conferences. (Nefesh Israel is a branch of Nefesh International, a networking organization of Orthodox Mental Health Professionals.) I have never met anyone with the vision and "putting her resources where her ideas are" as Mrs. Estanne Abraham Fawer. Not only does she have ideas, but she proposes these ideas with a vision of the finished product. She saw the need ten years earlier to help those speechless in pain – Haredi families, women and children that were suffering in the cruel silence of domestic violence. What was needed was a shelter, a hostel for girls and adolescents and one for boys. In less than a year, those first apartments and then buildings were up and running, with the moral support of the Welfare Department! They are run with class and warmth that is unlike any other institution of its kind. This is an amazing achievement!

As Estanne Abraham Fower says: "Don't miss the opportunity to change the world."

Taking Home the Lessons of
Eden: The Ultimate Kindergarten

Commencing the weekly reading of the Torah after Simchat Torah, and starting the whole cycle of life again, I wondered what I might learn about the "Garden of Eden thing" to help me be a better *shaliach* (agent) of Hashem in my professional life – psychology and neuropsychology. The word *"gan"* (of Gan Eden) translates into "kindergarten," which led me to think that there is a lot to be learned from *that* place! In fact, the importance of what is learned in *gan* (kindergarten) has been stated very well in a popular secular book, the perennial bestseller, *All I Really Need to Know I Learned in Kindergarten*, by Robert Fulghum.

I was mulling over the readings of Eve and Adam in Gan Eden, which speaks of the lost opportunity to live in a world where all is divinely taken care of; where black is black and white is white and never the twain (of alternative grey fuzziness of "truth") shall meet. Simple, is it not? You obey God's injunctions and things work out. You have what Abraham Maslow (1954) attempted to synthesize using a large body of research related to human motivation. His distilled research postulates that our primary needs – food, a cover for your head and a chance to move ahead and enjoy the Glory of God – were found there. If you don't use this gift appropriately, you are "OUT."

Here you have the first woman getting her house in order and chatting with one of the very knowledgeable creatures – the long, many-legged snake. He was created before us humans and has more experience and knowledge of this Gan. Okay, I've been told by "my man, Adam" that we people are a cut above and we know stuff and get our information from *The Source: God*.

So, here I am, Eve says to herself, having a chat about what we can and can't do, and I embellish a bit about the big "No-No" tree. The Tree of Knowledge in the Garden of Eden was to be respected and honored for its presence. No eating from it. Well, I'll just make a *s'yag* (fence), and when talking about it I'll add that you're also not allowed to touch it. What can be wrong with making this beautiful life a little more detailed, a little safer from error? Don't eat, He said. Well, don't touch and don't eat, *I* say. How could I go wrong if I make a fence to protect and respect?

And then, the wily snake picked up on the use of the truth's embellishment. Touch it, he said, touch the fruit of the Tree of Knowledge, for nothing will happen. Of course not, because even fences have logic, and need to be established to protect, define or delineate, not just for the heck of it. Just as with the *Arba Minim* (Four Species) on Sukkot, we don't have five types, or three. This is a lesson of *bal tosif* and *bal tigra* (don't add and don't diminish).

This brings me to the segue of the end of the Festival of Sukkot, a week spent holding and admiring the *Arba Minim*. We are told to hold them in one hand and, as such, achieve oneness from four separate entities. We might have thought: how much better to bask in the glory of Hashem's creations if we just add another, a fifth "type?" After all, four is good, but maybe five will be better.

No, we are told by our Sages, don't add and don't subtract from Hashem's pronouncements. Eve, in her earnestness, just adds a bit, an extra fence and, poof, the rest of us are forever out of the Garden of Eden, and into a world of grey, working for our bread that was once just there; going through difficult labor and childbirth, when they were previously a gift, given without pain.

We were blessed as a nation to have the opportunity to be in Gan Eden, but if not for our overzealousness, we would still be there. Even in the secular world, the period of kindergarten can be understood as the time when we learn the "whole Torah of life." *Gan* is the time for so much learning.

All these associations came flooding into my head when I received a phone message during the Intermediate Days of Sukkot. It was a *barrage* of phone messages. I try to return calls in a timely fashion, but it is reasonable to think that over a holiday, it might take a day or two to return a call. When there are six calls and text messages, my psyche goes into *bal tosif*; don't increase/overload mode. Yes, I appreciate the urgency of the caller, and yes, I will try to return the call, but I *did* leave messages on top of the messages when I called back. And if there is an emergency, they should call or go to their local emergency room. And for a more drastic problem, call the police.

I finally made telephone contact with the urgent caller. *"Baruch Hashem,* thank God," she said. Well, she really said, *"Baruch Hashem; Baruch Hashem; Baruch Hashem; Baruch Hashem; Baruch Hashem; Baruch Hashem."*

Uh-oh, I said to myself, *too much overkill on B"H for just returning a phone call.*

"How do you think I can help you?" I ask.

"Baruch Hashem, He directed me to you. *Baruch Hashem,* you will be the *shaliach* of success. *Baruch Hashem."*

"Excuse me, could you please back up here a bit? I don't really understand why you called me in the first place. In what way do you think I can help you? I may not be the right 'agent'?"

"Baruch Hashem, He guides me and He got me your number."

"*Baruch Hashem*," I say now, for loss of another mantra. "In what way do you think I can help you?"

"*Baruch Hashem*, I am looking for a school for my daughter. I was told that you know many things."

"Your daughter?"

"*Baruch Hashem*, she is out of jail right now; *Baruch Hashem*, the drugs she was taking did not harm her, and now we are, *Baruch Hashem*, looking for a school for her. Yes, even though she is not content living with us and has run away many times.

"*Baruch Hashem*, we have many children who have survived."

"Survived?" I ask.

"Yes, we have had a lot of *tzorot* (trouble) with our children: some have run away; some have gone 'off the *derech*'; some have chosen lives very different than our own. *Baruch Hashem*, He knows what He is doing."

"Besides the drugs, and specifically regarding the daughter you are speaking of, are there any other things you can tell me that might help in my directing you to a school for her?"

"*Baruch Hashem*, she is raising her son well; *Baruch Hashem*, hopefully she will marry the boy's father."

I am a little, or a lot, out of my league here. "You have really had a rough time," I say to her.

"Yes, but *Baruch Hashem*, things are improving for my other children. Right now, they are not being abused by their father. Also, you know, drugs, promiscuity and those other horrible 'off the *derech*' behaviors are improving. *Baruch Hashem*, even though some don't want to live home with me they are, *Baruch Hashem*, beginning to find their ways."

Baruch Hashem, they got out, I say to myself. This is not what Hashem wanted for us in Gan Eden – to be going with the flow! We were given gifts of life, children, a place to live and be protected, but we had responsibilities and obligations to not just praise the Almighty, but put the new world in order – give it definitions, criteria for differentiating. We are obligated to use the earth to produce God's blessings, not just sit there and laud Him.

What I was hearing seemed like a horribly out of whack example of "learned helplessness."

How could these children, or any children for that matter, find their way, when no way was shown? No directives or directions were given. Just go with the flow, and blessed be Hashem.

Cognitive intervention with this family would be *very* challenging. After being taught how to see, hear and listen – not talk (maybe even by teaching them another language like Sign Language) to break the vicious cycle of words with no meaning/understanding behind them, the team of therapists would have to include Maslowian instruction and the unlearning of "learned helplessness."

Prior to Maslow, researchers generally focused separately on such factors as biology, achievement, or power to explain what energizes, directs, and sustains human behavior. Maslow posited a hierarchy of human needs based on two groupings: deficiency needs and growth needs.

Within the deficiency needs, each lower need must be met before moving to the next higher level. Once each of these needs has been satisfied, if at some future time a deficiency is detected, the individual will act to remove the deficiency.

The first four levels are:

- Physiological: hunger, thirst, bodily comforts, etc.
- Safety/security: out of danger
- Sense of belonging and of being loved: affiliate with others, be accepted
- Self-esteem: to achieve, be competent, gain approval and recognition

From hearing this mother's comments, I felt that her children sorely lacked these basic needs; these needs would never be met unless they got out of the rut of "learned helplessness."

While studying the relationship between fear and learning in early 1965, by doing experiments on dogs using Pavlovian classical conditioning, Martin E. P. Seligman and his colleagues accidentally discovered an unexpected phenomenon. In Seligman's experiment, instead of pairing the bell with food (and getting the dogs to salivate when they heard the tone even when no food was present) he paired it with a harmless shock, restraining the dog in a hammock during the learning phase. The idea then, was that after the dog learned this, the dog would feel fear on the presentation of a tone, and would then run away or do some other behavior.

Next, they put the conditioned dog into a "shuttlebox," which consists of a low fence dividing the box into two compartments. The dog could easily see over the fence and jump over it if it wished.

They rang the bell. Surprisingly, nothing happened! (They were expecting the dog to jump over the fence.) Then, they decided to shock the conditioned dog, and again nothing happened! The dog just pathetically lay there! When they put a normal dog into the shuttlebox, one that had never experienced inescapable shock, the dog, as expected, immediately jumped over the fence to the other side. Apparently, what the conditioned dog learned in the hammock was that trying to escape from the shocks is futile. This dog learned to be helpless!

The children in this family never felt the security of having someone care for their psychological needs: hunger, thirst, bodily comforts, etc. They never sensed safety/security and being out of danger at home. They never fit in, and never felt a sense of belonging and being loved, or a common affiliate with others, as they were always being "hit" with new abuse as well as lassitude and absence of direction. How could they fit in when "in" was so ephemeral? How could they achieve self esteem, be competent, gain approval and recognition, when their actions were reactions and the *derech* was so fuzzy?

Again, I reiterated that she had a very tough year, and I would be pleased to direct her to a therapeutic team, who would help her get some direction, and then talk about her children after that.

"Children," she said. "I didn't even mention that I might have had double the number of children I have today, had Hashem not intervened, *Baruch Hashem*, to give me the many miscarriages I have endured."

Baruch Hashem, I said to myself, feeling His control over all of us again.

Partnering with God to Heal the Sick

THE *MADRICH HACHAREDI*, a veritable goldmine, is the Yellow Pages of goods and services of the ultra-religious community here in Israel. One gets just a taste of the *chesed* that abounds in this community from this unique Yellow Pages. One small example is an unusual *gemach* (acronym of *gemilut chasadim* – acts of benevolence, usually used in reference to associations giving interest-free loans). This unusual *gemach* listing can be found under the letter *aleph* and is the *arbes gemach*.

Well, we defined *gemach*, but what is the meaning of *arbes*? *Arbes* are traditionally served at a *shalom zachar* – a Friday night gathering after the birth of a boy. There are many commentaries on this topic; suffice it to say that a proof of the ritual quality of *shalom zachar* is the fact that there is a traditional food served: "*arbes*" = "*niyid*" = "garbanzo beans" = "chickpeas."

And now for the act of kindness: If a baby boy is born just before Shabbat, there is probably not enough time to soak, boil, salt and pepper the *arbes*. So, listed in the *Madrich HaCharedi* is a *gemach* for *arbes*, where someone makes this dish weekly and has it available to give out "just in case."

I bring this as an example of the wonderful thoughtfulness of the community. More times than not, one is unaware – until you require them yourself – of the tremendous acts of kindness and generosity that take place every second of the day. Now, I want to highlight a more serious example, which is the wonderful work of the *Bikur Cholim* volunteers.

What is *bikur cholim*? It is the Hebrew term for visiting the sick. In his book *The Chesed Boomerang; A Bikur Cholim Primer*, by Jack Doueck, the author quotes Rabbi Eliezer ben Isaac (11th century Germany) who wrote in his *Orot Chayim* (Paths of Life): "Visit the sick and lighten their suffering. Pray for them and leave. Do not stay too long, for you may inflict upon them additional discomfort. When you visit the sick, enter the room cheerfully." The rabbis teach that a person, who visits someone who is ill takes away one-sixtieth of their pain.

For example, people from all over the world come to the Cleveland Clinic Cole Eye Institute, a world-famous eye clinic, to be treated. The waiting rooms (and staff too, for that matter) look like a veritable United Nations. People arrive daily for emergencies or scheduled clinic visits.

Amazingly, if you are a Jew, and an Orthodox one at that, without family, friends or even contact persons in Cleveland, the *Bikur Cholim* comes to your rescue. Almost as important as the medical care, is the support and loving kindness shown to the ill and their families. Not only is there a *Bikur Cholim* House, decked out with the patient's every possible medical accoutrement, library of holy and secular books, but also three (if not more) meals a day, freshly cooked, packaged and delivered. As if this isn't sufficient, there are volunteers to drive you to and from doctor appointments, translate for non-English speakers, and, of course, visit the sick.

A community's *Bikur Cholim* is a partner with Hashem in healing the ill!

THE JOYS, TRIALS AND TRIBULATIONS OF LIVING IN ISRAEL

And Don't Forget
Your Germushka!

After tirelessly working "the system" for over three years, a resident of HaGidem St., perpendicular to my street in Jerusalem, was ecstatic. The Municipality, specifically the department in charge of street names, approved his proposal and HaGidem St. has a new name: Trumpledor St. Well, not exactly a *new* name, but rather a more politically correct new name, because "*HaGidem*," as I learned from my grandson, means "The Amputee."

I must sheepishly admit that for the past forty years I have been walking up HaGidem St. and never knew what the meaning of the word was until it was changed. I should have figured out something was off, as streets in Jerusalem neighborhoods are named by topics. The Old Katamon area sports names of 1948 events and battles, Rechov HaMatzor, for example; the neighborhood of Ramat Eshkol, has Rechov Sheshet HaYamim, for the Six-Day War, etc.

My neighborhood of Rechavia and its environs have street names that boast the names of poets and Zionist leaders. Samuel HaNagid (the ruling prince) was the son of Joseph ibn Nagdela, who was born in Cordova, Spain in the Jewish year 4742 (before the close of the 10th century of the CE). He became a vizier and was good to poets – among them, the famous Rabbi Solomon ibn Gabirol, whose name is memorialized by a street a few blocks down. I should have guessed that HaNagid and Menachem Ussishkin (1863–1941), the notable Russian-born Zionist leader, who worked for the revival of the Hebrew language and Jewish settlement in Eretz Yisrael, wouldn't be near just any amputee. So once the street name was changed, I understood to whom it had previously alluded.

Joseph Trumpledor, 1880–1920, was a Zionist leader. He studied dentistry but volunteered for the Russian army, losing an arm during the fighting around Port Arthur in 1905 (hence the *nom de guerre* or wartime nickname, The Amputee). He settled in Palestine in 1912 and worked with Zionist leader Ze'ev Jabotinsky (a street in neighboring Talbiah) to establish a Jewish unit to fight with the British against the Turks. Trumpledor went to Russia and organized pioneer groups to come and settle Palestine. He was killed with others in the defense of Tel Chai (a street not far away in Old Katamon commemorating the pioneer settlement in the Galilee Panhandle).

All this curiosity of etymology was important when the electrician came to fix our problem with the kitchen electrical system.

"It may be the *Birner* (light-bulb) or *Pesulung* (light-bulb housing); could be the *Kabel* (wire) or *Feuse* (got that on the first bounce – fuse). I'll have to check your *trans-for-mator* (transformer from 110 U.S. and Canadian voltage to 220/240 European and Israeli)." He threw these terms at me as he looked around scratching his balding head. All of a sudden a smile of hope lit up his face.

"Have you figured out what's wrong?" I asked expectantly.

"Only if you still happen to have your *germushka*."

Okay, that got me. I called my sister who is an interior architect and designer and works with electricians all the time. "Oh, of course, your *germushka*, the original plans of your apartment remodeling, the wiring, etc."

"*Germushka*," I repeated, awe-struck that she understood this word in Hebrew(?).

"After being here so many years, you've just now heard the word '*germushka*?' It is supposed to mean 'accordion' in some language, as that is what architectural and electrical plans look like – they are folded many times over and open up as an accordion."

Of course, everyone knows that!

Oh, by the way, my kitchen has re-lit up, as the electrician discovered and then repaired the *Erdung*-Earth connection or grounding joint (many of the early German *olim*, immigrants, became electricians).

Orange Is Hot and
Blue Is Calming?

It is 2005. I am in a conundrum. Torn between parts of myself. In Jerusalem, as in many areas of the country, cars are festooned in blue or orange strips of cloth. Orange is for those who don't want the inevitable pull-out from the Gaza settlements, set to take place August 15, 2005. Immediately after the Ninth of Av, the lunar calendar date of the destruction of the two Temples – by the Babylonians and five hundred years later by the Romans. In 1492, this was the date of the Spanish Inquisition's expulsion of Jews. Blue strips are on cars whose owners are in favor of the same inevitable pull-out.

A friend of mine had bought an orange dress and has not taken it out of her closet for fear that wearing it will give the *wrong* message.

The color Orange is associated with warmth, contentment, fruitfulness and wholesomeness. It looks strong and generous.

Blue, a cool color, can slow down your perception of time. Cool colors can also have passive, calming qualities that aid concentration and can create a mood of peacefulness and tranquility and also can produce an environment that seems cold and distant.

There are whole blocks that have orange cloth-stripped cars parked on them and other blocks with blue. When I say "inevitable" am I stating a political remark? A woman was interviewed from her home in a settlement which is in the area scheduled to be evacuated. She was wearing an orange bandana and was packing her house up. She said she is staying. This thing won't happen, how could she be leaving after over thirty years? She is dealing with the unenviable task of packing up and staying at the same time. The cemetery in the settlement is also to be uprooted and the bodies of her family members, some killed in terrorist actions, are to be moved to "central Israel" – the whole country is less than two hours by car wide! The orange part of me aches for her, and the sight of unearthing the remains of her loved ones haunts me.

While orange has a declassifying, broad appeal, it can be used to indicate that a product is suitable for everyone, and can make an expensive product seem more affordable. Blue, on the other hand, represents solitude, sadness, depression, wisdom, trust and loyalty. Wearing blue to job interviews indicates dedication and loyalty.

The Blue part of me senses the total logic and sense in leaving areas where a small number of people are protected by our youngsters in an area that has historically (since before the time of Samson and his Delilah) been a difficult place for Israelites. Beyond that, the pull-out is quite clever, brilliant even. How an elected leader could plan and accomplish a separation without negotiation – because the other side would not sit and talk, and another side who are also the electorate who gave him a landslide, for saying he won't do what he is doing. This feat will be studied by soldiers and politicians and just about everyone else much smarter than me, for years and years to come! Some soothsayers are gearing up for a violent fight, of brother against brother. Others, from within are saying as heart-wrenching as Jew uprooting Jew is, there will be no real violence.

Orange is the color most associated with appetite. If you want to lose weight, cook blue foods. During experiments, when participants were served food dyed blue, they lost their appetite.

This color-war is far different that the one played at the close of the summer camp season, when nothing much is at stake.

So what is the color of peace?

Let's pray that it is prismatic.

We Don't Want to Be on the "Menu" as the "October Surprise"!

On a news program about the American Presidential elections in 2008, the expression "The October Surprise" referred to events occurring in October which have an affect on the November elections. Al-Qaeda's actions in Taba and Ras al-Satan (Head of the Satan!) had shaken its ugly head and may very well have provided such an election's deciding event.

Over the festival of Simchat Torah (Shemini Atzeret outside of Israel), we learned of the mega bombings (three separate incidents that were scheduled to go off at the same time) in which at least thirteen Israelis, six Egyptians and six tourists from Russia and Italy were among the thirty-two people killed. A bomb-laden vehicle crashed into the foyer of the Taba Hilton and twin blasts took place almost simultaneously at the resort of Ras al-Satan, some fifty kilometers away. The two attacks occurred twenty-five minutes apart. The first, close to 9:50 p.m., took place at the Taba Hilton.

As if the idea of killing people by remote control and car bombing is not horrific enough, it is thought that there was also a female suicide bomber involved in the Taba blast. According to eyewitness reports, the woman carried an explosive device, and blew herself up near the hotel's kiddy section of the pool where she chose her victims!

This heartbreaking event reminded me of my first week on a new job. On September 1, 1985, I began working as the school psychologist for a school in the then new neighborhood of Ramot, Jerusalem. I received a phone call on Chol Hamoed Sukkot telling me that some of the students of this elementary school were at Ras Burka in the Sinai and were among those of the seven Israelis killed by a "deranged" Egyptian soldier. What we all later found out, was that one of the dead was the mother of a school child who shielded her daughter with her own body, another was a 10-year old who tried to get his wounded younger brother out of harm's way.

Following the Sukkot attacks, murmurings were going around: Why did people go to Sinai when we read about the difficulties our forefathers and mothers had getting through it? Why Sukkot? Why didn't they listen to the warnings of the army and Secret Service not to go to Sinai at all this holiday?

There are some considerations: Chol Hamoed days are among the few dates in Israel that the country has off, when it is neither Shabbat nor Yom Tov. Israelis of all shapes, ethnicities and religious leanings flock to Jerusalem as well as every park and national recreation area. Yes, the army warned about having inside information regarding heightened danger in the area of Sinai, but haven't we all been living "under the gun" for years! One of the people interviewed, safely back from Sinai, said that she hadn't felt that Jerusalem and Tel Aviv were too safe either. In trying times, I have noticed over the decades in Israel that people become believing (or fatalistic) and develop what I call "the bullet has my name on it" syndrome. They have experienced so many near misses that they "test" *Hashgacha Pratit* (Divine Providence) and might "challenge" God by being careless or thrill seeking, but this is my attempt to explain human behavior and not point a finger in rebuke.

I sincerely think we should be very wary of blaming the victims. How many times do people try to explain away abuse or worse by saying he/she deserved it because _____ (fill in the blank yourselves). No-one "deserves" being abused or killed! Our heart goes out to all the families of the murdered and injured. May God grant us to live in peace and quiet, and with no surprises!

When the Deer Hunter Lost

"The deer hunter" is an anti-war movie about the loss of innocence as seen in three American friends – steel workers – who are soon off to fight in the Vietnam War of the 1960s. One of the most frightening and horrifically memorable scenes is when drunken enemy guards, holding the three, play Russian Roulette with one of the friends. This is regarded as the ultimate gambling "game" (NOT TO BE ATTEMPTED!), played by putting a single bullet in one of the chambers of a gun and spinning it, then pulling the trigger – not knowing if the chamber being fired contains the bullet or if the chamber will be one of the empty ones.

The movie came abruptly into my consciousness on the first day of the new month of Adar 5768 (2008). It is about preparedness for life and the base primitiveness and cruelty that mankind is capable of exhibiting. It goes against so much of Jewish belief and behavior, and yet I recall it because of the events of the same day.

In the yeshiva world and in Israel particularly, we take the joyfulness of the month of Adar seriously. After all, it is the countdown to Purim, the holiday we celebrate when evil Haman's dastardly plot against the Jews of Shushan was overturned and Haman and his sons were hanged for treason against the King of Persia.

The heinous plot in 5768 was devised to occur on a date which was, on the face of it, happenstance, a gamble, as if his planned killing was not planned, but just a matter of luck, the casting of lots. It was with this knowledge that on March 6, 2008, eve of the new month of Adar, a former Arab driver of the students of the Mercaz HaRav Kook Yeshiva high school struck.

He knew, when decked with guns and bandoliers, barging into the *Beit Medrash* (study hall-library) on a clear evening, that the boys would be there, unsuspecting and waiting for the joyful Purim program to begin. He became a killing machine murdering eight and maiming a number of other boys, ages 14 to 17 whose sin was being in yeshiva and, of course, for being Jewish.

We – the psychiatrists, psychologists and social workers of Shaare Zedek Medical Center's ARAN Trauma Team (acronym for Hebrew "mass injured events") – were waiting in the ER, having been informed that a mass terrorist event was going on. We waited for much of the night, only to tearfully discover that very few wounded would come – the majority of the wounded were dead.

Some of the physically and emotionally wounded told horrific stories of how the shooter aimed at his friends and found the gun was empty, reloaded and then proceeded to kill his fellow students. The boy was crouched near another student when the terrorist pointed his gun at him, pulled the trigger and the bullet didn't come out of the chamber. The terrorist moved to the spot where he had more guns and left the boy alone with this Russian Roulette memory seared into his psyche.

A year later, almost to the day, eight-day old Elkana ben Yitzchak Dadon joined the covenant with Hashem and Bnei Yisrael – the Jewish People. This new Jew, named after the holy head of Mercaz HaRav Yeshiva, Rabbi Avraham Elkana Shapira, is the son of the man who located and killed the terrorist.

Ronen Medzini of YNet quoted the heroic dad as saying: "*We hope to gain strength from the terrible event we experienced here and sanctify life with the blood of the victims.*" More poignant was that the *mohel* (circumciser) was none other than Tzemach Hirschfeld, the father of slain Yehonadav Haim Hirschfeld, HY"D, (May God Avenge His Blood) who is quoted as saying: "*This is a very special occasion for me – to circumcise the son of the man who shot the terrorist who murdered my son, and all this just a week before the first anniversary of the attack.*"

During the month of Adar, please co-mingle your thoughts and feelings of joy – "*Mi'shenichnas Adar marbin b'simcha*" (when Adar begins, we increase in joy) with those of the families of the martyrs, the walking wounded, as well as the heroes such as Dadon. May Hashem make Adar truly joyful and hasten the Redemption of all souls in Gan Eden.

On Winter, Smudge Pots, Dirges and S.A.D.

W INTER, HERE IN ISRAEL, connotes rain time. Though I'm not complaining, everyone is concerned. Getting very little or no significant amounts of rain is a real threat to agriculture which all of us in Israel take very personally. Even if hi-tech is on the way of supplanting (sorry for the pun) agriculture, the latter is our financially successful export industry.

We say the prayer for rain with the rest of the Jewish world on Shemini Atzeret/Simchat Torah (here those two holidays are on the same day); then "sealed the deal" with God, with the institution of the added prayer in the Eighteen Prayers, the *Shemona Esrei*. This takes place at the beginning of December, which is the ETA "Home" for those who made the *Aliyat HaRegel* (the pilgrimage to the Holy Land) and returned home. Estimated Time of Arrival, accepted as being sixty days after the holiday period of the month of Tishrei. So in recent years, when we await "serious" rainfall since December, and sometimes approach the end of January with scant rain – all eyes are on the disastrously low levels of the Sea of Galilee!

Winter has changed here as well as in other parts of the globe. I heard a *Global-Warming* report for this area of the Middle East as being "colder winters and warmer summers"! As I sit in layers upon layers of clothes, I can attest to the cold part!

In the late 1960s, when we first moved to Jerusalem, we had to use kerosene heaters, as city-provided steam-fueled central heating was from the "old country," i.e., New York City. I recall that most locals didn't have winter coats, only many layers of handmade sweaters. The ubiquitous army khaki *dubonim* (literally, "teddy bears," refers to quilted storm jackets) filtered down to the populace after the Six Day War, as the Golan Heights and its snow-capped mountains "rejoined" the rest of Israel. Even into the late 1970s, the radio announcer would pass on the army's requests for the knitting of more balaclavas, also known as a balaclava helmet or ski mask, which is a form of headgear covering the whole head, exposing only a small part of the face or sometimes, only the eyes (Wikipedia).

Getting back to agriculture, I recall being up in the middle of the night, turning on the radio, and hearing news bulletins on where help was required to put up and tend to smudge-pots in an effort to save the citrus crop. A smudge pot, also known as a "*choofa*" in Australia, or orchard heater, is an oil-burning device used to prevent frost forming on fruit trees. Usually a smudge pot has a large round base with a chimney coming out of the middle of the base. The smudge pot is placed between trees in an orchard, allowing the heat and smoke from the burning oil to prevent the accumulation of frost on the fruit of the grove (Wikipedia).

In less sunny climes a real problem is S.A.D. – Seasonal Affective Disorder. To quote the Mayo Clinic: "With seasonal affective disorder, [the] fall's short days and long nights may trigger feelings of depression, lethargy, fatigue and other problems. Seasonal affective disorder is a type of depression, and it can severely impair daily life. That said, treatment – which may include light box therapy – can help successfully manage seasonal affective disorder."[1]

One case in particular still echoes in my mind. The person who came for assistance was blind. She was hearing cacophonic music all the time and it affected her ability to function, to such an extent that she stayed in bed all day long.

I told her that, though she may be blind, I am well-neigh "music disabled." I enjoy music but really cannot hum a tune on key. As she began to help me understand the sounds she described, I found myself running down a mental list of diagnoses such as: auditory hallucinations – usually a sign of psychiatric (psychosis?), neurological (e.g., epilepsy?) or middle ear (tinnitus?) problems.

"Before you ask, I was already at a neurologist and ENT (ear, nose and throat) specialist," she explained. "I know what I am hearing," she said determinately.

"Great," I said, figuring that those MDs ruled out more medical diagnoses and sent her on to me, a neuropsychologist, because she didn't exactly fit the profile/diagnosis of a person with a psychiatric disorder. "Please continue to describe it the best you can, because – as I said – I am 'music impaired'."

I asked questions about the music and interspersed questions about her history. It became obvious that every year around January and February she was more ill than the rest of the year.

"I got it," she said, "the music sounds like dirges." Dirges, according to Merriam Webster are: (1) a song or hymn of grief or lamentation; *especially,* one intended to accompany funeral or memorial rites; (2) a slow, solemn, and mournful piece of music. So I gave her homework.

Before our next appointment, would she write (Braille) words to the music she heard – as then, I might be better able to understand the sounds. I didn't share this with her at the time, but I have clinically seen (and research into PTSD

---

1. See: http://www.mayoclinic.com/health/seasonal-affective-disorder/DS00195.

has proven) that once one gives words to "sensed" feelings, their effect on the emotional/visceral self can be better mediated in therapy or by the individual themselves.

She returned and said: "a funny thing happened as I wrote the words to the 'dirge' I heard. I started writing about sunny days, mountain tops, the smell of grass on the hills and the music in my head took on a more melodious sound."

"This sounds like S.A.D. to me," I said.

"No," she objected, "I'm feeling a lot better!"

I explained that I had meant Seasonal Affective Disorder. Once I explained it to her, she said: "That's funny, well not funny Ha, Ha, but you understand," and I did.

Coming to Israel for the Year

Chezi goldberg, hy"d, would focus in *The Jewish Press* column, "Chezi's Corner," on coming on Aliya with children and teens. I am sure, had he lived out his 120 years with us, he would have written about coming on Aliya (the "ascent" to live in Israel) with children, teens, and adults with special-needs.

As a mental health professional in Israel for many years, many parents and adults have asked me about coming to Israel for the year or Aliya with a special-needs family member.

My answer is always a resounding: "Yes."

Then we start figuring out how to make this year in Israel and/or Aliya work. *Ein chadash tachat ha'shemesh* – nothing is new under the sun. In Israel, we have all the challenges that exist elsewhere and then some. The difference here is that our rehabilitation services, special education curriculum, medical and para-medical programs may not be as defined as in Canada or the States, or other countries for that matter. *Baruch Hashem*, we have many schools and organizations that work with special-needs populations, the trick is finding out where they are and the "vocabulary" needed to access this help.

To name a few there is Mercaz Harmony, Sulam, Shalva, Aleh, P'tach, Yad Sarah, to mention just a few in the more Haredi or Hardal (National Haredi) network – though they don't turn anyone not Haredi away! Within the governmental school system, there are special education schools, classes and teachers in both the state-religious general system. These services reflect the religious and cultural shades of the communities they serve. Today, in the more Haredi areas of the country – in Jerusalem, Kiryat Sefer, Bnei Brak as well as many others – these units may have more Haredi professionals working in them, and if not, they are still very aware of the needs of the community.

There is a countrywide network and tremendous source of information for services and professionals around the country. On the medical front, Tipat Halav provides child medical services from after birth till five years of age; the Mercaz LeHitpatchut HaYeled offers child guidance clinics for children with developmental issues, and each municipality has an Educational Psychology

Service. Psychiatric services are also available for all ages, and include special educational and residential facilities, as well as out-patient clinics. As mentioned above, these are countrywide services of assessment and therapy and special-needs placement available to all children from birth through high school. Today there are many Talmud Torahs and yeshivas that have programs for children with special-needs. The universities offer special consideration for students, seeing and hearing impaired, physically disabled and those with dyslexia or other forms of learning disabilities, as does the army and Sherut Leumi – National Volunteer Service.

I recommend doing some homework before, by email or even a visit, but don't cheat yourselves or your special-needs family member out of the *chavaya* – experience – of living/being in Israel.

We are here for you, just come!

"Hypervigilant"
Jerusalem Inhabitants

I HAD A VISITOR. I didn't recognize my visitor immediately because it had been over two years since we had last met. He was in Jerusalem for a wedding and just came by to say hello.

We have had many terror attacks in Jerusalem alone since 2000 until his visit a few years later. Many were left dead, thousands physically injured, so very many of us traumatized. All these events remain etched in my mind; some are still more sharply remembered than others. I try to commit to memory one person, one family constellation from each experience. I guess it is my way of not letting these horrible occasions, their horror, life and death for so many, become diminished and vanish in my memory. Over the years of working as part of the first response staff in times of MCEs (Multiple Community Events/ Injuries), I have developed a means of coping with my own sorrow, exhaustion and *weltsmertz* – I put pen to paper (or fingers to computer) and in so doing find that these thoughts are out of me and on the paper.

I may not have recognized my visitor immediately because his third degree burns had healed wonderfully, but I did remember Saturday Night, Motzei Shabbat, December 1, 2001.

11:30 p.m.
I heard a loud bang. As is the habit of most "hypervigilant" Jerusalem inhabitants, I waited a few seconds to hear the after sounds of a jet signifying a sonic boom, and dreading the eventuality of the sirens, connoting a bomb.

11:45 p.m.
I heard the wailing sirens, checked that all my ducks where in place (all my kids and grandchildren were at home or otherwise accounted for), started to get dressed for the hospital, when my beeper went off with the dreaded "99999" code, a call to the ER trauma support team.

12:00 a.m.
The ER was popping, with ambulances coming and going back to the scene of the two terrorist bombing attacks. The city center on a Saturday night is full

of kids. As so it was that gurney after gurney wheeled in young teens. Our hospital received close to ninety. Some seriously wounded with the nails and screws that were embedded in the bombs, and some with minor wounds of shrapnel (and nails) with gouged out 10 *agurot* and 5 *shekel* (dime and nickel) wounds in all parts of their bodies. One young man was "fortunate" to have the pointy part of the nail just pointing out of his head, others, were less lucky.

Many were not physically hurt, but saw images that are not readily erased from ones mind. Limbs, blood and much more.

Unfortunately, the ER team is very experienced and went into automatic pilot. Doctors and nurses of all specialties doing whatever was immediately needed. The people who normally work as carpenters and the like, doing the "ER jobs" as gurney pushers – to x-ray, to surgery and the like.

The social workers set up for the families an emergency briefing room which is hooked up with the other three Jerusalem hospitals identifying each arrival with an emergency number. This number is matched with their identifying signs and their names if they can speak to entry personnel. As information on the patient's condition and whereabouts (surgery, x-ray, etc.) is known, it is added to the computer station hookup. This enables each hospital to have the information that helps family members get to the right place without undo delay.

The psychiatric and psychological ER staff, talk to those who have been triaged and are waiting for the next stage in their care. Helping, in this case, kids contact their parents. It always amazes me how someone barely in control of their fears, tears and panic will pull themselves together when a cell phone is put to their ear and their parent is on the other end. "I'm okay, but come quickly," was heard again and again, the extent of the speaker's wounds not impinging on the clarity of the voice.

All the inhabitants of Israel have been in a constant state of alert when this type of horror occurs. It is, in fact, a form of "re-traumatization," not just trauma in itself. So with each succeeding event, we see more and more traumatized patients, those wounded and in shock, and those with no external signs, but unable to speak, flat out on their back.

And then each person, each gurney, brings a family constellation to the ER. Some more helpful, some less, some in need of help for themselves.

5:10 a.m.

The last of the ambulatory go through the final "check out" arrangements, one last check up by a physician, and after that final talk with a psychiatrist or psychologist and a social worker. This last part is to prepare them for medical follow-up care. The psych/social "check out" drill includes educating for acute stress and trauma symptoms, and checking that there is a home and someone there to go home to, as well as giving them information and recommendations for therapy, at least for the first month. This therapy is covered in cases of terror attacks by the National Insurance (governmental) Agency.

9:00 a.m.
I just heard the news. A bomb went off in a bus in Haifa. More dead more wounded. The horror continues, and the hypervigilance that we all live with does not abate. Selfishly, I was happy that it was not in Jerusalem.

This is what I remembered two and a half years later.

Si Vis Pacem, Para Bellum –
When You Want Peace,
Prepare for War!

WHAT DO WE DO in times of *pigu'im* and what to expect in order to prepare for Mass Casualty Events given the warnings – a question some of my NYC colleagues asked as they prepared for the Nefesh Israel Convention in Jerusalem.

To paraphrase Monty Python's group: One never expects the Spanish Inquisition. However, since November 2000, we have experienced twenty-six terror attacks in Jerusalem alone. Of the four hospitals in the city, the one where I work received 38 percent of the injured, many psychological trauma victims as well.

Below I will list some of the hints to make the unbearable a bit more user friendly for the medical/psychological/social staff in the ER.

When the beeper or hospital code goes off signifying the call for first response staff:

– First take a deep breath
– Then go to the ladies/mens room
– Have comfortable shoes stashed in your desk. Change immediately. You won't have time later.
– Call home and check "where your ducks" are and tell them you're okay and don't know when you'll speak to them again. They should watch a video and not News Re-Hash!
– ER Kit – I keep a canvas carpenter's belt in my ER file, so that I have extra pockets.
– Mints or the like and tissues go in pockets, too.
– Keep five extra pens (cheapest available because they get lost) in "Kit."
– Some cash for buying coffee or something. We get a lot of volunteers as the night goes on who bring water, cake, sandwiches, etc. (We won't die of starvation!) This stuff usually spans 5–8 hours from influx to when the patients are either released or dispatched to wards, Operating Room, etc. Even "just trauma" patients usually need ENT for collateral bombing sequelae, and then we have release procedure that includes being seen one

last time by an internist (to check that all the blood work, x-ray, etc. were addressed as well as re-check for wounds that might have been missed). A psychologist and social worker sit with them (and their families) to educate about trauma, and give them follow-up info. We try not to give medications to "just trauma" (but that depends on the case) so as not to mask anything else. The next day they can come back and/or see their own doctor.

– I use a small "7 Flag" loose leaf about 4–6 inches tall, to fit in lab coat pocket, with paper so that after I stick on their sticker, I can take notes of the different patients' state and comments on their experience, so that I can refer to it later on when I come back to see them. Also family names, pets, etc. to facilitate conversation as the night/day goes on.

– I don't know about the States, but we need to use our rubber stamp with license number on anything we put in their file, so it also goes in pocket.

– Cell phone, to help them call or call for them. Our hospital (and in the whole country) gave up on limiting cell phone use in the hospital except for CCU and ICU). Nothing goes further to relieve angst than, as ET said, "call home."

– Keep an eye on helping staff (MDs, nurses other psychologists/social workers). If you see tears or burn-out notice them, too – same goes for YOU. Ask for a break if you feel overcome by what you see, or what you have to do/say to a patient or family member!

Si vis pacem, para bellum – When you want peace, prepare for war!

Terrorism Has Many Forms

With the advent of the Internet, we have made "boundriless" contacts. We may be sitting in the office, at home or on the road, but we can connect with faceless friends and foes alike. There is an intimacy that this ahistorical (without history) contact permits us, even encourages. It has many benefits, a closeness of information: "just Google it," the physical contact of touching the computer and "speaking" to someone out there. Immense amounts of information are right at our fingertips. We at Nefesh have created a wonderful ListServ, a forum for communication between like-minded individuals. We are networking day and night (depending where on the globe you reside), asking for referrals to other professionals, consulting on issues and just passing on information that may be of interest to members. The world has indeed become smaller and closer through the Internet.

But clearly there are dangers with horror stories that we read about in the news. One such story took place in Israel. A teenager who was perceived by others and considered himself an outsider and a loner was a computer junkie. He found a contact, a like-minded individual over cyberspace, or so he thought. What seems to have occurred is that the mail, so innocent, so needy, and so desperate for contact, connected with someone with nefarious motives. A date to meet was arranged and the poor young man went unbeknownst to himself and his family, to this first and for him final meeting, his death at the hand of a new form of terrorist.

Just imagine though how easy it is to let someone into your house. You just open the "portal-door," and there they are. I don't want to frighten everyone, but we must be cognizant of this new threat to our families. Clearly this is an isolated case, but worldwide more than a few have been reported.

More common is another form of Terrorism, for Terrorism takes on many forms. One of them, we live through daily in Israel, and those of you in the States experienced fully on 9/11. The namelessness and facelessness of the enemy not only affects the directly injured victim, but in a ripple effect, creates an environment of fear and suspicion. This too is the terrorists' goal.

I am on another List, one of professionals in my specific specialty in psychology. Once, after eight hours in ER on a Sunday, treating, along with our Trauma team, over forty people with acute stress disorder, who were either wounded by shrapnel or had the blood and innards of others on their person (that does not include family members who were no less traumatized by the proximity of their loved ones' escape), I was tired. It was less than a week since the shooter opened up on the same street, killing a few, and wounding and traumatizing scores. My burn patient (second and third degree burns on face, hands and legs) from the attack in December, had just returned to his home in the States. In the wards lay (among others) from the previous week an 18-year old American girl who was on a student program, with chest and internal injuries. She arrived at the hospital with no blood pressure or heartbeat, and possible brain damage.

So when I saw a message from the public relations department about "happy" pictures, I was only too glad to try and open them. Of course, the English wasn't good, since many Israelis' English isn't grammatical, but nonetheless, happy was happy.

Wrong again.

"Happy" was another terrorist ploy. One that definitely achieved its goal. Creating havoc on innocent people in their safe places, reinforcing suspicion, distrust and downright nastiness.

As do most of the people I treat in the ER, I took responsibility for the "illness" I caused those around me by the fact that the virus worm invaded computers of people on the List, and spewed out their saved or sent messages. I apologized for something that was almost totally out of my realm of control. The trauma victims, we see, frequently apologize: "It was my fault, I shouldn't have gone on that bus" or some such other comment. Family members of an abusing spouse or children do this, too. "I'm sorry he wouldn't have hit me had I cooked his favorite soup" or "had I been quieter, Dad wouldn't have pushed me so hard." NO YOU ARE NOT TO BLAME, I tell them, we need to get a handle on things, so even when it is irrational, we try to take responsibility even for abuse!

The case of the virus that caused sickness to other computers on the ListServ is banal and silly by comparison. But the response is one we should all be aware of, because it impacts on how we view other people and their errors, or should we say, other innocent people who were unwittingly taken hostage by deceit and a destructive personality. Soothing comments to my apology were sent back-channel (sent to me privately and not listed on the ListServ for all to see), and the "nothing personal, but you are responsible for what is done to you," ones were sent front channel, out to Everyone on the ListServ, only proves my point. Terrorism succeeds in turning good, understanding, helping professionals into hypervigilant, insensitive ones.

Do continue to use the email, and learn a *musar heskail* (lesson). Don't blame the victim, offer a kind word, a helping hand, because they blame themselves already.

Homeless (for the Year) in Israel

July 2004

– "Mrs. Guedalia, you might not remember me, but I ate at your house on Yom Tov. Right now I am at a pay phone, and have a large piece of glass in my hand."

– The phone rings. It's 6 a.m. "How are you?" I ask the male voice at the other end of the line.

"Not too good," he says, "or I wouldn't call you at six in the morning. I played basketball late last night, after a *shiur*, and I think I broke something. I went to the emergency room here, but they said it's nothing and I don't believe them . . . ." He took a cab, and met me at Shaare Zedek's emergency room two hours later.

– "Hello, I'm so sorry to bother you, I am xxx's cousin who is related to you, right. Well, anyway, I am with a friend of mine in xxx emergency room; she's cut her foot badly and we didn't bring a checkbook, a credit card or enough money. They won't release her until we pay, and it's midnight already . . ." My trusty checkbook and I "sprung" them, and was refunded later by God, for sure, and the two girls.

– It's Erev Rosh Hashanah. The girls we are expecting have not arrived as yet. It is ten minutes until the siren, forty minutes until *shekia*, as the sun sets heralding the holiday. I am somewhat concerned (they called three times previously to ask where we lived, what time to come to help. And, yes, I must admit that I was a bit annoyed that they hadn't arrived yet).

The phone finally rings with a crying and somewhat hysterical young woman at the other end. She and her friend had been on a *tiyul* (trip) for two days, and over-slept. It was after 3 p.m., Erev Rosh Hashanah! And now they could not get a bus and even a cab. So, my very less than thrilled and long-suffering husband went to pick them up by car. How could we leave them for Rosh Hashanah with no one and no food!?

Be we Chasidic or Litvak, Ashkenazi or Sephardic or any hue in-between, for us in Israel, the second day of Yom Tov is either the first day of Chol Hamoed or

Isru Chag. Whichever end of the holiday it falls on, it is the closest we come to Sunday, i.e., not Shabbat or Chag and no school or work. What happens to all those "two-dayers" who are stuck with us Israelis? In our home, I always buy or make extra *challot* for Motzei Sukkot, and by the last day of Pesach all the food in my refrigerator is on paper plates. The night following Pesach, *Rumplenacht* (my Yekkish roots are showing), is a day late. The *sukkah* gets a pot in it, and comes down a day late, too.

My neighbor asks me which of my children has (finally) learned to play such beautiful, though mournful, music on our piano. I don't tell her of the young yeshiva student who came for a Shabbat meal and asked if he could come during the week to practice piano. I said sure, and gave him the combination of our door lock so that he could come when I was at work and the kids were at school. He came for quite a few months. After a while, he left me a note that he had to go back home. His mother had terminal cancer and died not long after.

Not once, but many times, have I had variants of the following conversation: Would you be able to see a friend of mine and convince her/him to see a doctor/ psychologist. S/he won't tell me exactly what is wrong, and will not tell their parents either.

Another time, a yeshiva/seminary may call me at the office (or at home). Could I possibly see someone who has been there for a few weeks/months and is having a great deal of difficulty? "Difficulty," I have learned, can mean anything from psychosis to homesickness; a "great deal of difficulty" is undefineable, but I must say it piques my curiosity. (The Rabbi or Rebbetzin know they have gotten to me). Okay, I say, and much to the chagrin of my staff, as I take yet another person "out of the line" (of people who are waiting for an appointment).

Once it was about a young (19-year old) woman who had been expelled from the seminary she was in, for having been seen "talking to undesirables." That is code, for possibly anyone of the male persuasion, but most assuredly not with a kippa. In this case, the latter was correct; they were young Arabs teens at the Central Bus Station.

Apparently, this young woman had a rare genetic disorder that her parents certainly knew about, and didn't bother to inform the seminary. Similarly, her school in the States could not possibly have not known that she had a serious cognitive and emotional disorder, even if no one bothered to give them the real diagnosis. Yet, no one told any of the individuals or organizations here, who were responsible for this 19-year old, what to expect. After the neuropsychological assessment which I conducted, I had a tentative hypothesis as to her condition. The diagnosis was confirmed when I met a distant relative of hers whose son had a diagnosed version of the genetic disorder. Though, even she did not know this American cousin had it too. The condition causes cognitive defects that affect learning, and cause difficulty in interpreting interpersonal communication. Two conditions that if the seminary, or I as a neuropsychologist, had known at the outset, might have prevented this girl from the hurt and embarrassment of being expelled from her school. She had also unwittingly been in personal danger, as she could not understand the effects of her communication with strangers in general and characters who spoke to her at the Central Bus Station in particular.

I called the States and asked the parents to come here to bring their child home and was told that they didn't want to spoil their daughter's year in Israel. Even though she was past eighteen years of age, I felt like calling the police and reporting child abuse. But my feelings were truly of sadness for this child, let alone my anger and frustration at this glaring case of negligence on the part of the American *chinuch* (education) system. In the end, we prevailed on the parents, and she did go home accompanied by a parent.

In recent years, I have noted a small change. With the advent of email, I am getting contacted, with the parents' permission, by professionals, psychologists and psychiatrists asking me to either take on, or refer their patients who are going to be spending the year in Israel. This is indeed a positive step. These kids will have an easier time navigating the system with an informed professional on their side. The yeshivot and seminaries do not turn away students with problems if they feel they have a professional in Israel with whom they can consult. But these parents are an enlightened few!

The majority of the well-functioning and some of the less so well-functioning are the Homeless Children of Israel. They are the ones whom are sent to "learn" in Israel, without their parents realizing that there is a veritable army of Moms, like me, around the country. This army of Moms is taking care, not only of the feeding of young adult children during the Chagim and Shabbatot, but also their emotional and physical care and sometimes laundry. Throughout the years in Israel, I have heard from three parents, and a few of the kids did come over to say goodbye before they went back home.

My husband read this and said it sounds a lot like I am complaining. I/we are not complaining. We truly are not. We tell each other "can you top this" stories when we meet at weddings and other *smachot*. I have met some of the most charming, smart, *baalei middot* (sterling character), and heard wonderful *Divrei Torah* from the young men and women of the world, many of whom, a generation later, send their kids to Israel.

I, we, just keep wondering if you could possibly know.

P.S. The one thing that I would like to know (in my name and in the name of the hundreds of other Israeli mothers) is that if one of my kids or I were ever stuck in Itchkepoo, Minnesota or Brooklyn, New York for that matter, and it is 2 a.m., what is your phone number?

Collateral Damage

The term COLLATERAL DAMAGE is the military parlance for the damage and destruction of targets or personnel not considered as lawful. When it is used as a euphemism, it is defined as the inadvertent casualties and destruction inflicted on civilians in the course of military operations. In a terrorist war the collateral damage may not be obvious to the eye.

In 2006, on Chol Hamoed Pesach, there was another *pigu'a* (terror attack) in Tel Aviv. Many were killed and more injured.

Erev Pesach, actually two days before Pesach, I was asked to see a family that was in the vicinity of a *pigu'a*. I recalled hearing about the event. I learned since then that they were "just" observers. The family member who called said that they could not get "back on with their lives." I wondered why they had not gone to any of the agencies/hospitals in their locale.

"Well, we felt that since we were not injured (physically) there was no need to complain, and the hospital ER was not for us. Nor, we were told, could we be suffering from PTSD which is only diagnosed after thirty days." Also they could not get insurance coverage as yet for consultation as they hadn't filled out the paperwork.

I told them to come in, and that I was sure that they would work on getting payment after "the holidays." What I understood is that *no one* would go to all that effort two days before Pesach unless they were really in *need* of help! And so I left the cleaning and cooking behind and went back to my office.

What they, four members of the family, first as a group, and then individually, went on to describe was a horrific "viewing" of death and destruction less than five feet from them.

They walked into the office in a slow belabored fashion – heavy with the weight of what they had experienced.

A family session is usually ninety minutes. I had asked the head of the Social Work Department at Shaare Zedek, Amalia Oren, to join me. When dealing with a family, working with a co-therapist helps in modeling couple behavior. We can agree, disagree, interrupt, accept input and reinforce each other in ways that the family system can adopt. We have worked together (and separately) in the ER for years, I know her style and she knows mine. We didn't have any time to prepare ourselves, as we didn't really understand the full extent of what "we were observers to a *pigu'a*" meant, but I know that she works well "on her feet," and I don't do too badly myself.

So we used a combined and distilled version of many years of combined study and experience. We applied the work of Milton H. Erickson, M.D., and his often unconventional approach to psychotherapy, such as described in the book *Uncommon Therapy* by Jay Haley.

Milton H. Erickson's work has always spoken to me, especially his extensive use of therapeutic metaphor and story. He coined the term Brief Therapy for his approach of addressing therapeutic changes in relatively few sessions and influenced the development of Strategic Therapy and Family Systems Therapy beginning in the 1950s. For Erickson, the unconscious mind was creative, solution-generating, and often positive. But more than anything else, his ability to "utilize" anything about a patient to help them change, including their beliefs, favorite words, cultural background, personal history, or even their neurotic habits, fit with my ideas of the goals of therapy: to help my patients solve problems, achieve goals, and change their behavior.

We met with the family for twice the average session-interventions, both because of the extent of their need, and the fact that we all wanted to start Pesach with as little *hametz* (literally, "leavened bread," but metaphorically, "unacceptable material") as was in our control. When we finished the marathon session, we made another appointment for after the holiday.

Maybe I imagined it, but as they thanked us with Chag Sameach wishes for the holiday, they left with a jauntier walk, a sort of lightness that bespoke of relief. Amalia and I looked at each other. We felt metaphorically stooped by what we had heard and absorbed. I guess we were experiencing Collateral Damage ourselves.

He Was Nineteen Years Old

Excitement and joy are meted out here like single M&M's. On a Saturday night in May 2004, the country was thrown into ecstasy by the Maccabi Tel Aviv basketball team's win over Bologna in the European Cup finals. The coach thanking God for His help; the country thrown into a frenzy of parties – one in a Tel Aviv park lasting until the early morning hours and consisting of tens of thousands dressed in the team colors of yellow and black.

Then came Sunday.

Sunday morning was balmy; it hearkened the day the Likud party members were going to the ballot to vote for or against the Sharon Disengagement Plan. Disengagement from the Palestinian area of Gaza first, leaving settlements, towns and farms that previous governments supported and financed as a security ring around Gaza, now deemed a security risk.

Then came Sunday early afternoon.

He was nineteen years old. He is an Israeli soldier in the outskirts near Gaza. He was on duty watching. His post is in a building and the watching he does is of TV monitors placed at various crossing points in the area of Gaza.

She, a social worker who helped people who had lost relatives in terror attacks, was on her way to pick up her husband, a school principal, to take him to a rally opposing the Sharon Plan that meant the dismantling of their hometown of Katif in the area around Gaza. She was thirty-four years old and eight months pregnant. Her children – Hila, 11; Hadar, 9; Roni, 7; and Merav, 2, were in the car with her. They didn't make it to pick him up, nor would they make it to anything else in this world.

As the young soldier was watching the screens, he saw horror unfold before his eyes. On the Kissufim road, terrorists began shooting at a passing car. Their bullets stopped the car in its tracks. The terrorists then approached and rained bullets at the car's passengers from less than a foot away, a pregnant woman and her four young daughters. He sat there helpless watching the massacre, too far away to do anything but gape in anguish.

The number of the victims of terror, those alive and those dead, increase yet again.

Pulling Trees Down the Street

Shortly after pesach, I saw a 10-year old pulling a tree down the street. I saw a group of kids with strollers, thinking how nice it was that they were helping with babysitting. I bent down and looked into the carriages, no babies, but twigs and branches. I said to myself, *Lag BaOmer cannot be far away.* Here Lag BaOmer is a *serious* affair. The bonfires are citywide and, if you come from the States (or anywhere else on the globe), somewhat frightening. When else (except Erev Pesach) do police turn a blind eye to fires on every available space!

I smile at my naïveté when we first came on Aliya. I noticed my kids and their friends eying a wooden chair that I had put on our porch. "Ma, this chair doesn't look safe," said my son to the fervent agreement of his pals. "It is a bit rickety," I noted. No sooner had the words come out of my mouth, when the gang took the chair out of the house and down the steps. They were not this helpful with garbage, what was up? I followed and found that this "dangerous" chair was added to the stash – wood being collected for the *medura*, the bonfire.

Erev Lag BaOmer the city is filled with patches of light. Kids stay up until the wee hours waiting for their potatoes and onions to cook in the fires – I never tasted one that was edible! They sing, but mostly they just watch as these huge fires burn themselves out. The next day the city smells like Atlanta, Georgia might have after General Grant was "done" with it. The air is hazy and full of ashes for days.

I remember barbeques in the States. Charcoal briquettes, smelly chemical liquid and burnt hot dogs, on someone's fire escape or cement porch, or if you were lucky in the backyard (not available in my hometown, Manhattan). Not here. Go to any public green (or sandy) space and you will see a tableau of a *real* picnic unfold. Tents, carpets, *mangal* – local BBQ – and don't forget the *naf-naf*. The *naf-naf* can be a cardboard, large leaf or anything in between, and is *the* fan for the *mangal*'s fire. Hot dogs, no way! Think meat hanging on a nearby tree, *shishlick* – chopped meat, and meat and turkey cubes marinating on *shipudim* – skewers on a card-table (I once even saw a couch being unloaded from a small flatbed truck!). Home was never as airy or friendly.

All over, you see brides and grooms in decorated cars going to scenic sites, especially the Western Wall, to be photographed on the way to and from their weddings.

And finally, of course Lag BaOmer would not be complete without the events at Meron and Safed. They are expecting a hundred thousand people, camping, and doing *halaka* (*upsherin*, or the first haircut for 3-year old boys). I always enjoy hearing (on the radio, I stay away!) the police politely requesting *not* to "borrow" neighboring sheep, nor even bring your own to *shecht* (ritually slaughter) and *mangal* there!

Don't let Lag BaOmer go by quietly, and don't forget your *naf-naf*.

A Miracle of Co-Existence

In JUNE 2004, the Separation Plan – separating Israeli and Arab settlements and villages – was passed in the Israeli Cabinet by a narrow margin.

We live in a strange place, this Israel. It's hard to explain to just about anyone how we (Arabs, Christians and Jews) co-exist even in times of peace, let alone times of war (hot, lukewarm, or cold). You can tell where even the smallest cul-de-sac bistro is located by the armed guard sitting outside. Everyone undergoes bag checks and is electronically wanded before being permitted entrance to supermarkets, museums, libraries, malls and every other public place. Sure we (and you) see the images of war and of Arabs waiting at check-points for access to "greater" Israel, but do you know that in Shaare Zedek Medical Center, of the 687 babies born that June, and the 4,606 babies born in the first half of 2004, 15 percent were born to Arab families.

Coming from the United States, visitors to the hospital are impressed that there are no private rooms – we still consider ourselves a socialistic state. With the exception of patients who need to be isolated because of the contagion of their diseases/conditions or their susceptibility to disease, everyone is in a ward (four or five persons) or at the very least on slow days with one or two other patients. Secondly, it becomes obvious that Jewish patients may be roommates with Arab ones. In no department is this co-existence more obvious than on the pediatric floor, where at any time of the day or night, a mother may be helping out another mother by holding or calming a sick child, the garb and headdress identifying ethnicity, the attention and care identifying motherhood.

As a neuropsychologist and medical psychologist, I see patients with psychological trauma, developmental disabilities and other difficulties related to medical conditions and/or the brain/behavior relationship. My patients come in all sizes, races, creeds, and ages. A car accident or terrorist attack can happen to anyone, so can developmental disorders. There are some "Jewish diseases" that Arabs have, and vice versa (Gaucher disease is one case in point). Language is no barrier – one can always readily find an in-house interpreter for more languages than you can imagine. The easy ones to find are Amharic, Russian, Arabic, French, German, Yiddish and Farsi. But without much ado, I usually call the switchboard – they know *everything* about *everybody*, and have found help in Serbo/Croatian, Dutch, Ladino, Armenian and Georgian.

Doctors and nurses of all denominations work together. A cousin had a baby on a Shabbat. The husband had brought his wife to the hospital before sunset, and after a long and, thank God, successful night in the delivery room, he just wanted to go home to check on his other three young children and get some sleep. Under normal circumstances he would have had to wait until after Shabbat (later that day). Instead, one of the nurses recommended that he take a lift from the mini-bus (driven by a non-Jew) which picks up and drops off the Arab and Jewish doctors and nurses, at set points. He gratefully did.

I'm reminded of a most emblematic story, that of the Bnei Sakhnin winning soccer team. About 30,000 Arabs from Sakhnin (practically the entire town), and other Arab and Jewish fans from the Galilee descended (from northern Israel) on Ramat Gan (in Israel's center). The State Cup game was to decide who would represent Israel in the European Cup. At this game, Bnei Sakhnin played against the Hapoel Haifa team. The Bnei Sakhnin Arab-Israeli team also included two Africans: Guinea goal-keeper Komiko Kamara (a Moslem) and Etche from Cameroon, as well as a Brazilian immigrant. Ayal Lachman was their Jewish coach, and captain of the team was Abass Suwan (Arab). They won, which means that Bnei Sakhnin represented Israel in the European Cup.

Clearly, these are miraculous times, and yes, this is a strange and wonderful place to live!

On the Shoulders of Heroes: Alexander Rubowitz, Aged 16 Forever

T HERE IS A SONG in the musical "My Fair Lady," that goes something like this: "I have often walked down this street before . . ."

Well, I have often walked down Ussishkin Street close to the corner of Keren Kayemet Street. I have also often noticed the blue plaque emblazoned with the Municipality of Jerusalem emblem, designating it a site of note. I am usually rushing to get somewhere and give it a perfunctory glance. This time the date, May 6th, held my attention, because it was soon coming up.

That date is also near the date of my father's *yahrzeit*. At his death, I thought of my grandparents' *yahrzeit*s and how with my Dad's passing, there would be no one to say *Kaddish* for them. On the other hand, I thought, maybe that was Hashem's way of defining mourning and the sadness of losing a loved one. Two generations mourn for each other. A child has to say *Kaddish* for a parent, and *Has ve' Shalom*, Heaven Forefend, if a parent looses a child – the parent is obligated to commemorate that "out of sequence of life" death, by saying *Kaddish* for the child. But grandchildren do not (have to) say *Kaddish* for grandparents. In a sense that is a blessing, for wouldn't the world be a sadder place if we were all mourning generations of family members daily!

But the above sheds some light on the somewhat emotionally weakened state I am in when I read the plaque, which is in both Hebrew and English:

ABDUCTION OF ALEXANDER RUBOWITZ
On Monday the 16th of Iyar 5707, May 6th 1947 at this spot, members of the "special forces" of the British Police abducted 16-year old Lehi [Jewish "underground" fighters] Fighter Alexander Rubowitz while he was carrying Lehi handbills. Alexander was tortured to death and his body has never been found.

Then I started to research this horrible event, using the Internet and I found an official record from July 13, 1947 of the United Nations General Assembly, which I quote:

... the murder of 16-year old Alexander Rubowitz who was kidnapped by a British terror squad under Major Farran is known to you from the press. During the disturbances of 1936–39 a British constable was injured. Thereupon a British patrol picked three youngsters at random in the nearest village, Gilat el Harithiya, and murdered them in the village yard.

JUNE 1947, PALESTINE. The terrorist Stern gang opened fire on British soldiers waiting in line outside a Tel Aviv theater, killing three and wounding two. Another Briton is killed and several wounded in a Haifa hotel. This action was claimed by Jewish terrorists to be in retaliation for British brutality and the alleged slaying of a missing 16-year old Jew, Alexander Rubowitz while he was being held in an Army barracks on May 6.

JUNE 19, 1947, JERUSALEM. Major Roy Farran, held in connection with the disappearance of a 16-year old Jew, escaped from custody in the army barracks in Jerusalem.

JUNE 29, 1947, NEW YORK. The UN Committee votes 9–0 to condemn the acts of terrorism as "flagrant disregard" of the UN appeal for an interim truce as Stern terrorists wounded four more British soldiers on a beach at Herzlia. Major Roy Alexander Farran surrendered voluntarily after his escape from custody in Jerusalem on June 19. He had been arrested in connection with the Rubowitz case.

It seems a long time ago, and we have so many newer tragedies to absorb, that it hardly seems possible to look back to those horribly difficult times before the official establishment of Israel's Statehood, but as I said it captured my attention.

What was Lehi?

Lehi, an acronym for Lohamei Herut Yisrael (Fighters for the Freedom of Israel) was an underground organization that operated from 1940 to 1948. Lehi rejected the authority of the Jewish community's (the Yishuv) elected institutions and the worldwide Zionist movement, and sometimes clashed bitterly with the Haganah. Lehi's goals were maximalist: conquest and liberation of Eretz Yisrael; war against the British Empire; complete withdrawal of Britain from Palestine; and establishment of a "Hebrew kingdom from the Euphrates to the Nile."

In contrast to the scope of these goals, Lehi's strength was limited; it never had more than a few hundred fighters and its arms stores were meager. The disparity between its aspirations and its real power dictated Lehi's method of fighting: bold, extremist actions, intended both to obtain funding and weapons and to demonstrate that it was possible to strike at the enemy successfully.

- February 12, 1942, Avraham ("Yair") Stern, the leader of Lehi, was captured in a Tel Aviv apartment and murdered by British detectives.

- November 6, 1944, two Lehi members assassinated Lord Moyne, the British Minister for Middle East Affairs in Cairo. The perpetrators, Eliyahu Beit-Tzuri and Eliyahu Hakim, were caught, tried by a military tribunal, and hanged on March 23, 1945.

- May 31, 1948, the IDF was established, Lehi was disbanded and most of its members enlisted in the IDF.

- September 17, 1948, Swedish Count Folke Bernadotte, a UN mediator, was assassinated in Jerusalem, and Lehi members were suspected. The government outlawed the organization's branch in Jerusalem and shut down its publication. The leaders of Lehi, Natan Yellin-Mor and Mattityahu Shmuelevitz, were sentenced to long jail terms by a military court, but were released in a general amnesty.[1]

However, how could I just walk by this plaque of the kidnapped, tortured and killed 16-year old Alexander Rubowitz? I wanted to understand more and possibly find out about his family.

So I continued my search on the Internet of the events. And then I saw an article by a British site describing the following:

> In 1948 Rex Farran was killed by a parcel bomb which was delivered to his family home in Codsall. He was the brother of Captain Roy Farran, one of the action heroes of the Second World War. He was involved in the fighting in Crete, where he was captured by the Germans. He escaped and drifted in a small boat for days before being picked up. He was soon back in service in North Africa where he was a founding member of the Long Range Desert Group, the forerunners of the SAS. (He later wrote a very popular book about it – *Winged Dagger* – which is still in print). After the war he was with the British Forces in Palestine where he was involved in the fight against the Jewish Stern Gang, by then renamed the Lehi Group. In 1947 one of that gang's members, Alexander Rubowitz, disappeared. He was never found but Roy Farran was accused of his murder and acquitted. The Lehi group were out to get him.

I was shocked by the violence on every side. But who am I, living here in Jerusalem, as Israel's Independence Day approaches, walking on the shoulders of heroes, teenaged ones at that, who were kidnapped, tortured and murdered,

---

1. Source on Lehi: Israeli Foreign Ministry

to judge anything! I decided on the eve of his *yarhzeit* (16th of Iyar) to light a *ner zikaron* (memorial candle) for Alexander Rubovitz, *HY"D*.

We can only look at the Haggadah service for direction, *V'hi she'amda . . .* When our enemies come up against us, in every generation, Hashem has stood by us and vanquished them. May He continue to do so.

Call Me Crazy . . .

THERE ARE SOME times when, even after thirty years of being in the mental health field, I am left scratching my head and muttering to myself – *Call me crazy, but this is the nutsiest experience I have had.* Each time it happens, and I must say that it doesn't happen often, I feel in awe of the Almighty and all He has to put up with when dealing with us humanoids.

Here are a few such experiences which have left me speechless, a situation which is clearly out of the ordinary for me!

CASE NO. 1

A couple in their late thirties came in with two pre-teens, one boy and one girl. The boy was about twelve years of age and the girl eleven, both looked darkly beautiful, a lot like the mother. I usually do an intake session with a student/ resident psychologist as an opportunity to give them an in situ experience. They usually sit on my left and behind me, while the parents and children sit opposite.

When the family comes in, I let nature take its course, and allow the family to choose who sits where. The mom sat down first with her shoulder to the wall, the girl and boy sat between her. The dad, who sat down last, sat in a chair he had reserved for himself – on entering the room he had placed his briefcase on it.

I looked at them and settled on the kids. After a bit of small talk, I asked them why their parents had brought them to see me. I had already spent time with them, tested their ability to express themselves in language and overall gross motor skills, stability in the chair, fluidity of motor movement, and general signs of a developmental delay. All seemed within normal limits.

They stared at one another and then at their parents. The father looked at me, sharply with his piercing blue eyes and said: "We have a secret in our family, we can't tell you what it is."

"Okay," I say, "you children can leave. You have accomplished what your parents have set out for you to do."

They looked from one to another, their mom nodded in approval and they walked out together. All this time the father is staring at me as if communicating silently, if not somewhat flirtatiously.

What is this all about?

"Well," he says, "the secret is that I am a *ger*, a convert, and my wife isn't – she is Jewish through and through."

"Well, now that you got that out of the way, what is really the secret, because surely you did not come all this way to my office to tell me this shatteringly common occurrence?"

I wasn't sure what made him flinch more, that the information wasn't shatteringly interesting, that it was common or that I didn't fall off my chair in "oos and aahs."

"But, but, but that is the secret," he seemed surprised by his being so not in charge of the conversation.

"No, I don't think so. If that was so much the issue you might have sent a picture postcard."

He looked at my student who by now was close to fainting, as this is not the way I usually deal with patients.

At this point the mom whispers, "May I speak?"

I sit looking at her quietly.

"This past Shabbat my sister came to stay with us. At some point during the day, she came running to me in a panic. She had just seen the two children behaving in a frighteningly non-*tzniusdik*, immodest way. They were both naked and both lying down on a bed together."

"Mmmm," was my sage comment.

At this point, I was sure I did hear the chair which held my student, creak and teeter and almost fall, but now we were finally getting down to the real business at hand. And as far as I was concerned, the real business at hand was what behavior in the household created an atmosphere that allowed a major cultural taboo to be violated.

Ovadia the Prophet was a *ger*.

Call me crazy but we are proud of our converts and don't consider them something to hide.

CASE NO. 2

I receive any number of phone calls regarding young adults in a yeshiva in Israel for the year. Calls come from the yeshiva or from the parents themselves. The following is an amalgam of the cases I see in the course of a year.

For the purpose of clarity, let's call the parents Mr. and Mrs. Gudday. A series of questions is posed to me via email and on the phone: "Are you religious?

Do you cover your hair? What does your husband wear on Shabbat?" None of these questions relate to my professional credentials, but for some reason, many consider the answers even more important.

Okay, I pass the tests (though my answer to what my husband wears on Shabbat continues to be "clothes," which leaves some unamused).

The parents are told my fee, both by phone and via email – it is about a third of what the same neuropsychological evaluation would cost in the States. I tell them that once I take the case, as their child is no longer a minor, he or she will have to sign a release giving me permission to relay the results to them, the parents, the people who have agreed to pay my fee for services. "No problem, we understand completely and agree." I complete the evaluation and sit with my client, their over 18-year old child, who decides not to give consent. S/he will relate the results to them when s/he returns home.

The Guddays call, incensed. How dare I not relay the details to them? Please see the emails that went back and forth regarding this issue: you agreed that your child would decide. Mr. Gudday sends me half the fee by mail – sort of a "that was then, this is now" statement. I advise them to speak with their child, whose main issue has to do with trust – trust, trusting, being trustworthy, keeping to accepted boundaries of behavior both vis-à-vis cultural and religious norms. S/he has pushed the envelope beyond approved personal and yeshiva etiquette which is a sign of social inappropriateness at best and, more sadly and most difficult to remediate, a personality disorder. The yeshiva has felt this strongly and this lies at the base of the referral.

"Okay," says Mr. Gudday. "Can you meet with us and our child, you are on your way to the States anyway." Here I must admit that I erred. Being in this business for over thirty years, I should trust my instincts and rules I pass down to my students – when you cross your own boundaries it is a sign of pathology and not a good deed. No one will benefit in the end.

And so it happened. Unfortunately, I took ill, had to cancel the appointment with Mr. and Mrs. Gudday and their child. However, I had already done my neuropsychological evaluation and gave a feedback session and written report to my client.

So, Mr. Gudday decided not to pay the remainder of what he owed me. Repeated letters explaining the unexpected medical emergency that made me unable to meet with him fell on deaf ears.

No doubt *he* was wearing the "proper" clothes on Shabbat, Rosh Hashanah and Yom Kippur. But clothes don't make a trustworthy man.

Call me crazy.

CASE NO. 3

Again, what type of religion do I practice? What does my husband wear on Shabbat? You'd think that something else is important! At any rate, not withstanding that I was of the female persuasion and did not answer the Shabbat outfit question, the parents agreed to consult with me about their teenage son. Here I will shorten a very long conversation that went round and round before the facts emerged. Their son was in trouble with the police. At sixteen years of age, he was not a really a child in the eyes of the law and though he was not considered an adult, his crime was indeed adult-like. He was arrested with some other boys who had more than a user's amount of drugs on them, making them suspected drug dealers. He was the youngest, though not the only religious one. The State's social service department was giving him a little leeway and placing him in a teen rehabilitation center prior to sentencing.

I asked my standard question: How do you think I can help you?

"Anything you can do, we'll pay anything, just help us and him out," was the answer I received.

"Well this isn't in my bailiwick usually," I said, "so, let me speak to social service and see if they think I can be of assistance."

To make a long story shorter, I did help the social service department see that the parents would be willing to do whatever they could to help rehabilitate their son.

About three months later, I called to find out how things were going. "Oh, he's out of rehab and looking for a job. The job was a condition of his early release."

I suggested that he work on an Orthodox kibbutz where I knew they were in dire need of help and might even be able to pay him, besides giving him room and board.

"You don't understand," I was told, "you are not as religious as we are. Working on even an Orthodox kibbutz would be definitely not allowed by our rabbis."

In this case, the kibbutz I had in mind was Kibbutz Chofetz Chaim which was established on April 25, 1944. The founders were religious pioneers from Germany, members of the Ezra youth movement and members of Agudat Israel who had been living near Kfar Saba. It was the first village founded by Agudat Israel and was named after HaRav Yisrael Meir Kagan, who was also known as the Chofetz Chaim. Not only that, but in 1955, there was only one hectare of hydroponics in the entire world. The project started in Israel, at Kibbutz Chofetz Chaim, as a way of producing fruits and vegetables in water during the Sabbatical year – the Shmita.

Call me crazy, but maybe a little research into the who and what of this ultra-Orthodox kibbutz, which I might add houses a world-renowned *yeshiva gedolah* and *kollel*, might have preceded a "you are not as religious as we are" comment.

Bukra Fil Mish-Mish: Tomorrow when the Apricots Bloom

Od tireh, od tireh
Kamah tov yihiyeh
Ba'shanah, ba'shanah ha'baah.
In the year that will be, we'll sit on our porches
Counting migrating birds as they fly
And the children will run between the houses and the field
Playing catch under the cloudless blue skies.
Come with me, you will see
Just how sweet life will be
In the year, in the year that will be
Come with me, you will see
Just how sweet life will be
In the year, in the year that I see.

(Lyrics: Ehud Manor, Music: Nurit Hirsh)

LATE SPRING AND EARLY SUMMER find me serving only apricots to all and sundry and then ritually drying the *mish-mish* (apricot) pits on my *mirpesset* (porch). Jerusalem boys (generally) can be seen whiling away hot summer days playing *adju'eem* (in the rest of Israel, they are called *go'go'eem*). First with their forefinger and thumb held like a compass, they draw a virtual circle, then take turns shooting the pits to knock other players' *adju'eem*. Whoever has the most, or quits last, wins. The game is similar to marbles played on the streets of my hometown, New York, years ago.

It's a short period of apricot eating, pit drying, collecting and storing the *adju'eem* for the summer season. The saying *"bukra fil mish-mish,"* has the same connotation in the Middle East as *"manyana"* does in Latin America or Spain. All are expressions of: "Tomorrow is another day and then we'll see."

Summertime, and this lackadaisical attitude kind of goes with the warm weather, unless you have been living in the cramped quarters allotted to the former Gush Katif (Gaza area) uprooted, who as of 2006 still haven't been given their roots.

About 1,400 formally Zionistic productive families are squished into *cara-villot*, the large trailers in makeshift trailer-parks. The derisive term is a new two-word combination, from *"caravan"* and *"villa,"* as if the largess of the government's loan of habitation can make up for uprooted and destroyed homes and gardens. A visit to these unsettled settler communities was reported in the Hebrew language daily, *Yediot Ahronot*. The dire statistics say it all: in 2006, 12 young people tried to commit suicide; 20 couples filed for divorce; with the mean age of 29 years, the high percentage of chronically ill is statistically significant; depression is in epidemic proportions.

In 2006, the majority of these previously able contributors to all areas of Israeli society, especially agriculture, were unemployed, and those over 50 had all but given up hope of ever finding gainful employment again. The bureaucracy was paralytic, building the promised housing was delayed and delayed.

The soldiers Eldad Regev, Ehud Goldwasser and Gilad Shalit were kidnapped just one year after the Gaza pull-out. All of us, in Israel and the rest of the world, held our breaths and hearts, when we heard the tremulous voice of Gilad on the cruelly-released tape recording. But who can bear to understand the pain of parents and loved ones trying to sleep, knowing that their children are being held by ruthless captors?

The coffins of Ehud and Eldad were returned in 2008. Gilad Shalit was returned in 2011. The families of the three soldiers had endured endless tomorrows, summertime or not.

Thanksgiving Jerusalem Style 2006: The Triple's Fifth Anniversary

AMALIA OREN, DIRECTOR of social work at the Shaare Zedek Medical Center, came down to show me a well-worn edition of *LaIsha*. On the cover of this women's magazine was a beautiful model. There was something familiar about the eyes. I looked again and again. But it wasn't until I opened to an inside page and saw her as she looked when we first met, that I said: "Leah."

I never give my patients' real names, even though she gave mine while the TV cameras whirred. One evening, there I was standing next to her on the 8:00 news broadcast, when she said, "This is Dr. Guedalia and she did EMDR with me!"

It was December 1, 2001, right after Thanksgiving. In Jerusalem's downtown Midrahov (pedestrian mall), Leah had been there with friends celebrating her 18th birthday. At a table nearby a group of 16-year old boys who were there enjoying the birthday of the twins, A. and L. They didn't know each other – yet.

Not far away, sitting on the *mirpesset* of his dorm room in a Chassidic yeshiva sat M. Within seconds their lives would change.

The first bomb went off; there was silence as if everything in the world had stopped. Within seconds the air and area were punctuated with the sounds of screams and sirens.

Sitting on his *mirpesset*, M. knew it was a bomb. While others in his yeshiva immediately ran to see what was going on, he held back. Shortly before he had become engaged to be married and so was a bit more cautious.

Also, we seasoned Jerusalemites knew or thought we knew, the diabolic plan to set up two bombs and time them so that the second one would get the people who came to help. After he heard the second bomb go off, M. went to see if he could help out.

The first bomb wounded the boys who were celebrating the birthdays. A. had been hit with so many nails and bolts to his body that it was decided not to operate. Miraculously, these additions to the bombs did not puncture any vital organs; they were "just" lodged in his bones, but he was nevertheless a very injured boy.

Leah was more fortunate, or so she thought. She was thrown from her chair by the blast, but after counting all her limbs, she was intact. She wanted to go help others, but the police motioned them to go up an alley.

M. was also sent in that direction. Within minutes a booby-trapped car blew up. It had been filled with flammable material, as if the mere bomb was not sufficient. It was there that Leah and M. were burned.

The group of 16-year olds, Leah, and M. were among those taken to Shaare Zedek. The scores of injured were triaged at the spot and divided by their injuries to be sent to the main Jerusalem hospitals.

The ARAN Trauma Team was beeped immediately, and as the chief medical psychologist of the team, I took up my position in the emergency room.

A sight that remains with me is the long line of gurneys carrying young teens waiting for x-rays of their punctured limbs and bodies. In the entire tally that night were 180 injured. Nearly half of them, mostly teens, were brought to Shaare Zedek.

We worked through the night until morning, went home for some shut-eye and then came back. The wards were full. Many of the injured teens had lost friends and were worried about others in different hospitals. They were in relatively good shape. A. was in ICU (intensive care unit) and was unconscious. His twin was more lightly injured.

M. and Leah did not know each other. They were in rooms on opposite sides of the burn unit, both having suffered second- and third-degree burns on their faces and bodies. M.'s injuries were mostly on his legs and hands, because he had tried to put out the fire on his pants. Leah's burns were more extensive. Most of the injuries were on her face, hands and arms.

I worked with M. using EMDR when he was in the ward, and for weeks afterwards, as an outpatient. It was amazing to see him improve both physically and emotionally. M. returned to his home in the States, and *B"H* was married. (He even came to visit me once.)

Leah's therapy visits were longer and more intense. More than a year later, she was finally able to remove the pressure bandages on her body, and later yet, her arms and hands. Leah became the poster child survivor of the *"meshulash,"* as that triple terrorist night has become known.

Pictures of her were all over, as the beautiful girl she was before the bombings, and now the burnt girl lying in hospital and fighting for her life. As her body healed, I wondered how she would re-identify herself from being a victim/survivor in order to move on.

So it was with great joy that I looked at the model on the cover of *LaIsha* magazine. Her eyes and face were gleaming as she modeled this winter's clothes. However, it was with even greater happiness that I accepted her invitation to the *Se'udat Hodaya* (thanksgiving dinner) celebrating her birthday and the birthdays of the twins, all in the company of their friends and the medical team from Shaare Zedek.

Leah not only showed us how with God's help she remade herself, but also how she exemplified *hakarat ha'tov*, recognition of gratitude.

May she continue to go from strength to strength and realize the many aspects of her potential in all that she wishes to do.

Re: Elections 2006 in Israel

Like other times when national elections are held here, I am more of an observer than a participant.

In 2006, on the morning of Election Day at 9 a.m., I went to my local polling station to beat the rush/lines. The lines seemed shorter, a sign of the voters who were not enamored with the choices. Israelis seemed at best apathetic and at worst disgusted with the whole voting process. Less than 66 percent of the voters have exercised their democratic privilege – the lowest in Israeli election history.

A comic on TV wryly noted that there were more *hatraot* – warnings of terrorist threats – than people who voted. It seems untenable that we, whose enemies are vociferous and at our doorstep, cannot and do not take part in our destiny. The larger parties are the most affected by the poor voter turn-out. The smaller parties have the innate excitement of their supporters. Voters chose with their feet – taking them anywhere but to the polling stations. National zoos and parks were filled with the air of wafting BBQs.

A sad commentary was a pre-election vote at local universities. At Hebrew University, a generally leftist secular environment, the "winner" was the NRP – the modern Orthodox rightist party – meaning that the much more numerous secular community of college students did not bother to vote. Well that was an improvement – in my eyes at least – to the results of the same pre-election vote at Haifa University, where the winner was the Green Party, whose major plank is the legalization of hashish/marijuana!

A party which was an unexpected winner (a "grey" if not "dark horse") is the Pensioners Party. Their Hebrew acronym is *Zach* which means "aged" and it is used in the expression "aged wine" as a sign of excellence. Their popularity with the aging and especially with young Tel Avivians seems to be both a function of the sorry affects of the economic reforms on the weakest members of society – the children and the aged – and the sense of frustration at the offerings of the larger more established parties.

The ballot area is in a large classroom, five people are sitting at a table, and in front of them and to their side is a cardboard or particleboard tri-fold screen about five and a half feet high. A large bridge table was set up with a large two inch high multi-partitioned box. In each square (which looks a lot like the boxes of teas which are sold with multi-flavored teas), are piles of papers with the initials of the various parties' names in Hebrew.

When you walked into the room past the *de rigueur* guards who checked my handbag at the entrance to the building and room, one of the people at the table compared my ID number, picture and address against a list. Another person gave me a blue envelope. I went behind the partition and chose my piece of paper and put it in the envelope. I closed and licked the envelope (not required) and placed it in the slot of the cardboard ballot box which was on another card table in front of the observers.

I walk out and recall the evening and night that I sat on that observer table.

My son and some of his friends had established a party whose major planks were *Chen* – an acronym which stood for Education and Beautification, but itself formed the word that means sweetness and beauty in one. After months of politicking, advertising and creating a buzz about being an "Anglo-Saxon" Party, the Israeli way of describing anyone for whom English is his/her native tongue, Election Day arrived. Being the mother of Number Three of the four party members, I asked my son how I could help. "You understand English, Hebrew, some Arabic and Yiddish, don't you?" he said. "Would you agree to sit on the observers table to check that there is no monkey business during the ballot counting?"

What could happen in this day and age? I was requested to appear at 9:45 p.m., fifteen minutes before the ballot areas were closed. I arrived at 9:15, just in case. The polling station closed, the door was sealed. We were sequestered with water and sandwiches that were of the highest Kashrut level, also just in case. The person in charge declared that the envelopes could be counted. I sipped water. They were counted. They counted them again against the list of people who voted. Oops, the list of people that voted was different for the two main observers who represented different parties. I sipped some more water, trying to hide my smile. They were recounted and found that the number was really the same. Then they opened the envelopes and put the ballots in piles. They then counted the piles and were requested, by the In Charge person, to leave them in the original piles. It was now about two a.m. I drank some more water to fight exhaustion. And then, as I observed from the side, the piles were precariously swaying. I tried to make a sign as to the imminent fall of this "Tower of Pisa." I was chastised that any word or sign from me was against balloting rules. I sipped more water to hide my look of impeding horror. Within seconds the neat piles of ballots teetered and fell in a giant mess.

I couldn't drink another drop of water, and just put my face in my hands, as my body shook with laughter. *Oh my, we will be here forever*, I thought.

Fortunately, it only took another hour, to re-pile them in countable mounds of ten, which didn't teeter at all, and get the final count. At 3 a.m., our "leader" declared the deed done, and everyone took out their cell phones. All the observers reported to their individual parties the room's results. Well, how couldn't I call my son when everyone else was calling their party?

"You okay?" he asked in a concerned but exhausted voice. "You guys are the last to finish counting." I was there though; I wouldn't have missed this experience for anything. I was a supportive and observing, if not water-logged mother – to me that was what counted!

P.S. His party received two seats on the city council, shared by the four candidates.

When Will We Ever Learn . . . ?!?

W E LIVE HERE with many contradictions. In the month of May, for example, we have the juxtaposition of Yom HaShoah to commemorate the Jews who perished during the Holocaust, Yom HaZikaron (Memorial Day) for Soldiers of Israeli wars, and Yom HaAtzmaut, (Independence Day). This juxtaposition is always poignant.

In 2005, we were getting ready for The Disengagement, getting ready to leave lands and villages that all the previous governments have politically, financially and emotionally encouraged and supported.

At the time, what happened in the *enlightened* world? The Association of University Teachers (AUT) in Great Britain decided to adopt a boycott against two universities in Israel, Bar Ilan and Haifa. Who is it who writes the deciding letter, none other than a University of Haifa senior lecturer, a Jew and Israeli, citing our "occupation and endless brutal and callous oppression of the people of the West Bank and the Gaza Strip."

When will they ever learn?

Also in Britain, we saw a future king sporting a nazi costume, "cause what does one expect from a 20-year old." Maybe he can forget six million Jews, but what about the hundreds of thousands of his countrymen who were killed when London was bombed by those "costume-wearing" nazis. (My computer wants me to capitalize the *n* in "nazi," but I resist!)

England even has a Jewish woman, the child of a Jewish woman and an African-American, Oona King, who in 2005 was a Member of Parliament, running for re-election in her heavily Muslim district. She is rabidly anti-Israel and anti-Jewish, and was surprised when she was pelted with objects, *by Muslims,* when she was out campaigning.

The Stockholm Effect, coined after victims of a robbery in that city (in 1973), who were held hostage and threatened with being killed, protected the robbers with their bodies when the police came to the rescue. Indeed, two of the hostages became engaged to their captors! This behavior is not unknown throughout history: slaves defend their masters; prisoners of war feel sympathy for their jailors; prostitutes defend their pimps; incest and other abuse victims excuse the actions of their dominators. It is hard to believe that the Hungarian psychoanalyst, Sandor Ferenczi (1873–1933), originated the constructs of "identification with the aggressor," close to one hundred years before the Stockholm Effect was coined!

When will they ever learn?

Everybody (in the local and foreign press) is bending over backward portraying the Hitler Youth graduate – Pope Benedict XVI – of being as clean as White Smoke. Wasn't he just a teen or just twenty years old at the time?! The sight of seeing smoke decide the future of tens of millions of people around the world should not lose its irony on us!

When will they ever learn?

Leading up to the Disengagement, news commentators (read: radio, television, and newspapers) were gearing up the populace for a civil war. Ironically, the army generals were more optimistic, knowing who the country's REAL enemies are, and they certainly don't wear *kippot*!

When will they ever learn?

In the aftermath of a terror attack, as my "comrades in arms" on Shaare Zedek's ER Trauma Team finally waved, hugged, and kissed goodbye to the family of a slain young man, I had an awful association. In my mind, I heard the voice of a witness in the Ukrainian-born Ivan (The Terrible) Demjanjuk War Crimes trial. As the sound of another mother wailing inconsolably in the ER, hoping against hope that the fact that her son was in none of the Jerusalem hospitals meant that he was still alive someplace, rings in my ears. She didn't have to spell it out for us, we knew that leaving the last ER she searched all night, would mean he was dead and the only place to see what was left of him was Abu Kabir, the country's Pathology Unit. So we stayed with her, not being able to console, or even speak to her in her native language, but just be there until she was too tired to go on, as the family of the slain young man, finally had to go home.

My association was the radio interview with the War Crimes witness, who described his concentration camp "job." He had the train duty. This was funneling the people off the trains onto their "next and final stop." He described as each train spewed out our brethren how he heard the cries of parents looking for children, and children searching for parents. "Ruchi, Oma, Opa, Yisroel, Zaida, Chaim, Mottie, Bracha, Mamma, Tateh, and on and on." Each train, it seemed, had the same people, because the names were the same. Each time and time again the voices that cried were in reality different voices never to be heard again. And then there was another train.

How many times do we as a society have to live (if we are lucky) and see history repeat itself until we *see* the signs, and *interpret* them correctly?!?

Will *we* ever learn, before that next *train* comes?

A NEUROPSYCHOLOGIST'S CASEBOOK

Who Can Benefit from a Neuropsychological Evaluation?

A NEUROPSYCHOLOGICAL EVALUATION can benefit individuals with:

- Traumatic injury, including brain injury and concussion, post-concussion syndrome, including the synergistic effect of multiple concussions
- Seizure disorders, such as epilepsy
- Systemic disorders such as diabetes, stroke and chronic fatigue, which can lead to cognitive impairment
- Attention deficit disorder with or without hyperactivity (ADD/ADHD)
- Learning problems (including the gifted learning-disabled)
- Cognitive changes resulting from radiation therapy or chemotherapy
- Cognitive effects of premature birth or birth injuries
- Brain damage due to lead poisoning
- Problems with memory, attention and concentration, word-finding, calculation ability, organization and planning
- Developmental disabilities, such as Asperger's Syndrome, retardation and autism

HOW A NEUROPSYCHOLOGICAL EVALUATION DIFFERS FROM A TRADITIONAL PSYCHOLOGICAL OR DEVELOPMENTAL EVALUATION

A neuropsychological evaluation provides a deeper, broader understanding of cognitive difficulties, enabling design of a more effective treatment program. Neuropsychologists also have more experience and training in understanding difficulties caused by brain tumors, head traumas and other neurological and developmental conditions.

HELPING THE GIFTED PATIENT WHO IS LEARNING-DISABLED

Even gifted children can have ADD or other learning disabilities. This can be confusing or demoralizing to children who know that even though they are getting average or better than average grades, they are not performing as well as they should. Neuropsychological evaluation can determine if there are disabilities and pinpoint the areas of weakness so the gifted child can learn to succeed and work to his or her potential.

SPECIAL TRAINING IN NEUROPSYCHOLOGY

It is very important to be an informed consumer and carefully check credentials when selecting a professional. To be considered a psychologist, one must earn at least a Masters in psychology from an accredited university and be licensed for private practice. To be a neuropsychologist, one must also complete additional training in neuroanatomy, neurophysiology and neurological disease. Pediatric neuropsychologists must also study neurodevelopment. Psychologists are required to have two years full time (four years part-time) of post-thesis (Masters) supervised clinical internship, with at least one year in a formal neuropsychology fieldwork.

Dr. Guedalia and the Neuropsychology Unit is recognized to fulfill the internship requirements by the Ministry of Health Psychological Department (*Moetzet Ha'Psychologi*) in Rehabilitation and Developmental Psychology. Yeshiva University's Ferkauf Graduate School of Psychology has recognized the Unit for the internship and clinical requirements of its doctoral level students.

Tissue, I Hardly Know You

Tʜɪs ᴘʟᴀʏ ᴏɴ ᴡᴏʀᴅs was a favorite of Mr. Simon Solomon, *z"l*, my Chumash-Torah teacher during my elementary school years. I guess with today's sensitivity to abuse, he would never have said it at all!

That said, it popped into my mind when a patient asked for a tissue. We in the helping profession touch the emotions of our patients. We are also touched by their narratives. In my work as a neuropsychologist, when a diagnosis is hypothesized or presented, there have been many occasions where tears of happiness, relief, anger or sadness have flowed.

I have some tissues in my handbag and unused luncheon napkins in my desk. What I don't have in my office, is a box of tissues. I really never thought about the absence of *the* Tissue Box until the following incident. A patient started to cry profusely. When her personal stock was depleted, I searched my bag for tissues, when they too were exhausted, out came the unused luncheon napkins. The crying subsided before the napkins were finished. At the height of her tears, the patient looked at me and tears streaming said: "How can you call yourself a psychologist if you don't even have a tissue box?!" Then more stridently: "Aren't you allowed to cry here!" I answered that I guess I'm not "that sort of psychologist," and thought, *no, we don't have time to cry here.*

I have since thought about The Tissue Box situation. Why do I still not have a tissue box in my office? Firstly, the answer might lie in the difference between the practice of neuropsychology and clinical/psychotherapy psychology.

Neuropsychology is the science of brain-behavior relationships. Clinical neuropsychologists focus on understanding how brain processes affects one's ability to function at work, home and school. It is no less important to know what normal cognitive and social development is, as to know how to diagnose dysfunction.

Neuropsychological examinations provide a broad overview of neuro-cognitive and emotional functioning, including sensation, perception, basic motor functions, language, attention and concentration, memory, academic achievement, global intelligence. Higher integrative functions which are today described as Executive Functions include: self-regulation, self-monitoring and impulse control. They can shed light on the underlying causes of behavior problems, discriminating between emotional and cognitive roots.

One of the most important benefits of such examinations is to document cognitive strengths which can be used to compensate for areas of weakness. Repeated assessment can document resolution, stabilization or deterioration of neurocognitive deficits and neurological disease. Combined with personality testing, it can also help to differentiate between psychological and physical problems (e.g., parathyroid disorder versus anxiety/moodiness).

Proper evaluation can also help the consulting physician make decisions on medication, such as which medications may be contraindicated from a functional viewpoint (for example a child diagnosed with ADHD and Tourette Syndrome).

Neuropsychological evaluations can pinpoint specific weaknesses that interfere with an individual's ability to function, so that an effective remedial program can be initiated.

What is psychology? One of the many definitions is: The study of an organism's thoughts, feelings, and behavior and how these processes are affected by the environment, physical states, and mental states.

How is crying defined? Demanding or requiring action or attention, as in "a crying need." Abominable; reprehensible, as in "a crying shame." Compelling immediate attention: burning, dire, emergent, exigent, imperative, instant, pressing, urgent.

On the other hand, what did I respond to: crying, as the process of shedding tears, the watery secretion of the lacrimal gland, which is located at the outer corner of the eye socket immediately above the eyeball. Tearing, or lacrimation, is a continuous and largely involuntary process stimulated by the autonomic nervous system. Fluid is secreted into the lacrimal lake, the area between the eyeball and the upper eyelid, and spread across the surface of the eye by blinking. Tears serve to bathe and lubricate the cornea, the sensitive outer covering of the eyeball. Typically, the fluid either evaporates or is drained off through tiny canals at the inner corner of the eye, but in times of excessive tearing the apparatus is overwhelmed and tears overflow the eyes.

In the case at hand, once the lacrimation seemed to be abating, I felt we could get down to the business of working on understanding strengths and weakness in order to use the strengths to compensate or even bypass the weakness and reach our goal of optimal functioning. This thought process, I guess, defines not only the field of neuropsychology but also my *Weltanschauung* (and probably the true answer to my question of The Tissue Box). As a developmental, rehabilitation, and medical psychologist, I work with people whose "differences" are obvious to the eye, or if not outwardly so, then obvious to Theodor Reik's Third Ear (listening with the third ear is to perceive what people really are trying to say). Using my poetic license, I am wont to say that neuropsychologists also diagnose seeing with the Third Eye. As I work with people with all kinds of "special abilities," most of them not obvious, my credo is "this is what IS, now let's get on with life." So, away with tissue boxes, and maximize *Avodat Hashem*, God's work.

May we all live our lives to the fullest potential. *L'Chaim ve'Briut* – to Life and Health.

Listening with the Third Ear

"Hello, is this Dr. Guedalia?"

When I answered in the affirmative the woman on the other end of the phone began to cry. I just held on to the phone. "Are you still there?" she gasped.

"Yes, I'd sing Muzak [elevator music] if I knew how, but as things stand now you would cry harder." That elicited a little auditory smile. "In what way do you think I can help you?" I asked.

"I don't really want to say, but the good cry I had with someone on the other end was enough. Thank you so much for being there," she said and hung up.

The Conflict Research Consortium of the University of Colorado describes active listening:[1]

> Active listening is a way of listening and responding to another person that improves mutual understanding. Often when people talk to each other, they don't listen attentively. They are often distracted, half listening, half thinking about something else. When people are engaged in a conflict, they are often busy formulating a response to what is being said. They assume that they have heard what their opponent is saying many times before, so rather than paying attention, they focus on how they can respond to win the argument.
>
> Active listening is a structured form of listening and responding that focuses the attention on the speaker. The listener must take care to attend to the speaker fully, and then repeats, in the listener's own words, what he or she thinks the speaker has said. The listener does not have to agree with the speaker – he or she must simply state what they think the speaker said. This enables the speaker to find out whether the listener really understood. If the listener did not, the speaker can explain some more.
>
> . . . Active listening has several benefits. First, it forces people to listen attentively to others. Second, it avoids misunderstandings, as people have to confirm that they do really understand what another

---

1. www.colorado.edu/conflict/peace/treatment/activel.htm.

person has said. Third, it tends to open people up, to get them to say more.

When years ago, Dr. S. noticed bruises on women too scared to cry or complain, she began what was then an uphill battle of giving a voice to those who had none. Rabbi Abraham J. Twerski, M.D. went on to write a book about spousal abuse in the *frum* (religious) community (*The Shame Borne in Silence: Spouse Abuse in the Jewish Community*), which was subsequently banned as being too provocative and a source of *Hilul Hashem* (a desecration of God's name)!

Some people felt that if you don't mention it, it won't proliferate; just the opposite has been proven true. By allowing the abused a voice and an ear, the *frum* world is taking its rightful place as the moral compass of our society.

Between those two pioneers and many other courageous souls like them who understood spousal abuse for the damage that it does, be it physical, verbal or emotional, this horrific crime, which can even exist in the *frum* community, has been brought to public attention.

The Beth Israel Medical Center, New York City, has received a grant to reach out to various culturally unique communities to help identify and treat those who are suffering in silence.

Yes, there are many helplines – open phone lines for people to talk anonymously about many topics – some specifically targeting: children, teens, depression, alcoholism and much more. Research done into the numbers of calls and the topics raised (without names or specifics) has shown that the specificity of the helpline assists those calling, even before they begin speaking with a real live person.

It seems that just knowing that the person answering knows *why* one is calling, relieves some of the anxiety. It is as if, at least, one is spared *that* bit of the conversation and can begin the healing and intervention immediately.

For this reason the SOVRI Helpline has come into existence. SOVRI stands for Support for Orthodox Victims of Rape and Incest. This includes any form of abuse and molestation. Staffed by volunteers who undergo intensive training by professionals to field the phone calls, the training encompasses over twenty-six hours of theory and practical information in both a workshop and role-playing format.

The success of this project doesn't just require putting one foot in front of the other, but rather to paraphrase Theodore Reik: to be effective you have "to learn how one mind speaks to another beyond words" – or using the Third Ear.[2]

---

2. Theodore Reik's *Listening with the Third Ear* (1948) takes this phrase from Nietzche, *Beyond Good and Evil*, Part VIII, 246.

Depression and Help from Our Friends King Saul, King David, Job and Others

Oᴠᴇʀʜᴇᴀʀᴅ:

– I'm so depressed I gained five pounds over the last holiday!
– The economic situation struck so hard, I'm down to cleaning help just once a week. I'm feeling really depressed.
– My so-called boyfriend has not called me in over a week, I'm really depressed.
– Recession is when your friend loses his job. Depression is when you lose yours.
– Did you see that woman shopping? It's not for me to say, but doesn't she look like she's in a depression?

When I relay these remarks to Jenny, she almost jumps out of her chair as she exclaims:

"Depressed Depression! People who use language with total disregard to its meaning make me want to explode."

Jenny S., who is blind from birth but doesn't consider it a handicap, has been plagued by extreme dizziness from seemingly neurological issues. This condition has caused her difficulties with balance which has impacted on her independence and landed her here, in my office. We write this together.

Over the years, we have had a revolving door relationship. We met for a time when she was twelve years old, and now when she feels the need to talk, she schedules an appointment. Jenny is a very unique individual; she has an innate skill and joy when it comes to learning and using language. She reads and writes in Braille, as well as in Hebrew, English and Arabic all of which she also speaks fluently. "Of cause no one can speak Braille!"

She continues: "I have an annoying case of 'where to go'!"

Catching that on the first bounce, I say: "'Vertigo,' a great Hitchcock classic." "Talking about classics, I think Umm Kulthum's song is the best," and she begins singing it in Arabic, deftly using all the quarter notes that I am used to hearing on the radio channels as I surf for Israeli music! For my sake, she translates the title and main theme: "Patience Has Limits."

I am quiet and she says: "Don't go all *psychologist* on me." Not a chance. I'm just thinking of my two favorite "get me through it" songs: "You'll Never Walk Alone" from the Rodgers and Hammerstein musical "Carousel," and Simon and Garfunkel's "Bridge Over Troubled Waters."

She knows those songs too and begins to hum and sing. But then she stops. "They're okay, but as far as I am concerned still don't capture depression with a capital *D*."

Jenny loves to turn a phrase and so she metaphors on: "Even when the storm ends, the sea is still not calm. I feel that the Big *D* is more akin to being at sea on a small craft, even when beached on *terra firma* one never feels stable. In spite of having a raincoat, the anxiety/fear that not only will the storm return, but also maybe the weather conditions will become even worse, persists. The next storm might catch this little flimsy boat at sea and not on dry land!"

She breaks her train of thought, raises her head and looks at me. "After going through feelings such as I just described, there are no suggestions from the outside that help. Sure family and friends say (and worse yet, *think*) 'what you need is something inspirational, uplifting and then you'll be on the road to getting over it.' This I feel is the biggest difference between depression and sadness. Sadness is to depression what a cold is to cancer.

"Anyone who tries to cheer up a depressed person by telling them how bad someone else's life is, shouldn't be surprised if the person they are trying to help gets furiously angry."

"Furiously angry sounds like emotional energy that may be not too far from the surface," I say.

"Let me advise friends and family of the depressed, don't help unless you are asked. Don't assume the person needs help. Never make a depressed person feel guilty for his depression. Never let him feel 'bad' or 'broken'."

"What can they do when they see their loved one in so much pain?" I ask.

"Even though it may seem drastic to family and friends, going to a psychiatrist and getting a proper diagnosis and medication may be the best and most economical and therapeutic path to follow. I am not a professional, but have gained my experience the hard way. I was clinically depressed! I saw so many people during my journey and many drastic measures were taken to help me. In the end, the lifting of my depression came from changing my neurological situation and being significantly helped by psychiatric meds. No one should be ashamed of saying any of those words. Depression is an illness that can be overcome. Hashem created the people who developed the medicine that truly saved my life.

"Another reason to go straight to a shrink is because you can't speak to depression and you can't reason with it. The meds make you available to think. I liken the experience to being able to survive in the stormy sea without a life jacket. Even if you know how to swim under normal circumstances, you can't in a stormy sea, and don't forget one can't reason with the waves."

I ask her what she thinks about Talking Therapy.

"Again, from personal experience, it may be helpful after the person has been stabilized by the medication. There are side effects to medications. However, there may be side effects from the therapy that are not so obvious as well.

"Side effects from a 'bad' therapist may include exacerbated feelings of defenselessness. I'm still troubled by some of the therapists who said: 'you are hiding something that is keeping you from getting well.' I didn't have the energy to even whisper that it is not true, but I still felt like a 'criminal,' denied the ability to speak for myself, just because I was depressed."

I told her that music as she mentioned before helps. Whenever the evil spirit (dark mood) came upon Saul, the King of Israel, David would take the harp and play it (I Samuel). Saul would become refreshed and be well, and the evil spirit would depart from him. Who else do we have that we can learn from? Iyov or Job comes to mind, but he seems to be in deep mourning rather than depressed.

"Iyov, hmmm," she says, "that reminds me of Eeyore, quite a depressed character."

Eeyore is a favorite for most admirers of Winnie the Pooh characters, a loveable donkey who is mostly gloomy. Eeyore, who is about 18 inches in height and 27 inches in length, resides in an area marked as "Eeyore's Gloomy Place: Rather Boggy and Sad." His favorite food is thistles. Eeyore doesn't expect much of himself and remains quiet for most of the time. Eeyore has few expectations from his friends and always expects the worst whenever they come to help him. Here is where his friends come in handy; they dismiss his gloomy thoughts, which cause him to feel grateful to them. Eeyore's biggest problem is his tail falling off, which happens frequently. Looking for it and then reattaching it is where his friends help him the most.

Job is the quintessential icon for loss. In fact many of our *minhagim* or customs regarding *shiva*, (the first seven days of mourning) come from the Book of Job. However much he has lost, in the end Job has a new family and has learned from the experience about humility, loss and man's place in God's majestic world.

Maybe we too can learn how to do *bikur cholim* when we are with a depressed person. We should learn to not expect much in the way of conversation from them; rather we should be there for them as an anchor attached to the bottom of the sea, helping them re-enter the world slowly. This too is a part of the *shiva* process, which can give us signposts as to how to act in the presence of such pain.

In a small voice, Jenny says, "I do appreciate those around me more now that I was so close to losing not only a piece of myself, my 'Eeyore tail,' but also my whole Self."

Hang In There:
Metamorphosizing to
Functioning Adults

METAMORPHOSIS IS A biological process by which an animal physically develops after birth or hatching, involving a conspicuous and relatively abrupt change in the animal's form or structure through cell growth and differentiation ... Scientific usage of the term is exclusive, and is not applied to general aspects of cell growth, including rapid growth spurts. References to "metamorphosis" in mammals are imprecise and only colloquial.

Larva stage: During the larva stage, mealworms will undergo repeated molting between bouts of eating various vegetation or dead insects. During its last molt, it loses its carapace before curling into its *pupal* form.

Pupa stage: The pupa starts a creamy white color and changes slowly to brown during its pupation stage. In this stage it is said that they look a bit like "aliens."

Adult stage: The newly emerged mealworm beetle will sit still as its wings unfold and dry. It will appear a creamy color, stop moving, and will slowly turn brown over a period of 2–7 days. Once the mealworm beetle has turned brown they will become more mature and begin to look for a mate. (Wikipedia)

Some kids are just so difficult. They're called "at risk" or are actually off the precipice, in a lost valley. Sometimes *chas v'shalom* – Heaven forfend – seen as a *rodef* (pursuer) by and to their families. Maybe giving them up for lost is the right way for the family (and therapist) to survive. They suck your blood like a vampire bat; they spit on those who feed and care for them as do camels. Metamorphosis? Become butterflies!? These beautify our world; pollinate our flowers; bring the flavor of honey to all – what a dream!

I guess I looked at this chance meeting as a Round Table meeting, similar to those I read about among the *Algonquin crowd.*[1] A number of independent

1. The Algonquin Round Table was a celebrated group of New York City writers, critics,

thinking "artists" sitting around and shooting the breeze on a lot of topics on which they have pondered. As the *repartée* and topics hovered about the four of us, we each brought our histories to the table: historical, personal, professional, religious, and academic.

I enjoyed the excitement of scintillating conversation around a table between people passionate about taking amorphous basics such as primary colors and making them into something unique and indelibly their own.

I thought of how a painting takes shape when the palate is full of ideas and each artist holds his or her own paintbrush to the blank sheet. Does one sitting around a table use one sheet of paper, with each one, allotted a space? Does the paint of the one broach the boundaries of the other? Are these skirmishes across another's space seen as intrusive, as interference, as welcome cross-pollination? Is the end result, the *end* result? Is there a greater whole that comes of the pieces?

I wondered about the *chavruta* experience of those who spend years in *Batei Midrashim* hammering out ideas/thoughts of those before them, their teachers and their own nascent thoughts, in order to develop experienced learning styles. Many of the people (mostly men) I poled for this unstructured study, felt that any time they tried hammering out ideas with more than two people in a *chavruta*, it was less than successful, as compared to when the points were labored on over time, in the age-old way of the two-man *chavruta*.

And yet, here we were – four strangers who sat about a table with Diet Coke and water, touching on our historical narratives, our educational and professional selves, our belief systems of the past and present and our evolved personae of this moment.

The topic settled on was the FFB/BT (*frum* from birth/*baal teshuvah*) time continuum, of when and how in life these epiphany-laden altering changes occurred.

Only moments were relegated to them: sort of a shorthand "yes, the Shabbat moment thing"; "oh, the boy-girl thing"; "the Truth versus the expedient thing."

I felt as an insider and outsider – at the same time. My life, I felt, was so boring by comparison. In observance, thoughts and activities, I am not much different from my mother, grandmothers, and great-grandmothers and even great-great grandmothers (we are fortunate to have pictures and stories of them all). Once you have changed the scenery to take into account that *this* play was happening in the twenty-first century and not the eighteenth century.

Another topic was (for a short minute) what is referred to as "at risk" teens behavior. A code word for behavior that bespeaks teens' developmental issues, whether they may be hormonal, a burgeoning need to break away and assert

---

actors and wits that gathered for lunch each day at the Algonquin Hotel from 1919 until roughly 1929.

independence of thought and behavior, albeit under the watchful/non-watchful all-seeing/unseeing eye and roof of parents/Rebbes/Rebbetzins, and the sociology of friends .

So here we are at a defining moment. An avatar (a computer user's representation of him/herself or alter ego, Wikipedia) has been created in the center of the table depicting one such at risk/off the *derech*/loose cannon/lonely/sad/love-starved/love sated/hormonally erratic/religiously confused/ignorant/naively knowledgeable 13- to 19-year old.

This persona fits the requirement of someone who we've all seen many times, and whose unique diatribe is eerily familiar; in a sense we know the music and the words before s/he opens his/her mouth to speak.

What now? Where are we in this "as if" meeting? Where does transference/ narcissism/skill/professional maturity/counter-transference/the poetry and dance of psychotherapeutic contact meet and do its transmigration work/magic?

Opening moves/styles are as finite and yet as different as Bobby Fisher, the late chess *"ilui,"* (genius) demonstrated, but our proverbial avatar is standing in the center of the table waiting to be fixed. Behind the scenes there are many that pray for and at the same time pray against the overall price and energy this change will exact. "Fixed/change" may and does impact on the IP – Identified Patient – the whole family constellation, the school, and even our combined universe.

The voices around the table speak. They are not one voice. The "art" they will bring forth looks like it will take place on separate parts of the community canvas.

Interestingly, once the veneer of each voice is neutralized, what seems to remain is not so much their right/left/modern/FFB/BT-ness but rather the aura/ mist/cloud-like envelope of their unstated and seemingly forgotten, "graduated from" metamorphosed selves.

I went home thinking that I hope we all use, bless and recognize the good-bad-ugly-glorious generations of experiences in a reparative way when we delve into ourselves to help others.

Don't think for a minute that what you have been "created" – in formal schools and the informal school of life – can be better than that created in the Seven Days of Creation. In attempting to do so, we risk throwing out the proverbial baby that Hashem created in Gan Eden along with our historic bathwater.

Parents, Teachers and Mental Health Professionals, let's get out the elbow grease and help that avatar polish the gold *Pintele Yid* – that little spark of Jewishness that remains alive and indestructible inside. In order to do that, one has to connect with one's own self and that glow will point you and your charges in the right direction.

The Fear of Isaac, but
What about Abraham?

W HEN MY KIDS were younger, I used to say, "My sons keep me in stitches," meaning that they were great fun, and also frequently needed to get sewn up after their various exploits. One particularly harrowing time, the nurse at their school called very apologetically to say that one of my sons had been injured at school while the other had been injured on a school outing. They were at two different ERs with two different teachers.

As soon as I found out it was only stitches, I was sort of okay. This of course only happened (as all things of this sort) when my husband was out of town. I took the baby with me and went to the younger of the two boys, called the other teacher at the ER (pre-cell phone days) and said I'd be there in twenty minutes. Then, with two in hand, went to the second ER for the stitching there.

The nurse said, "No children allowed in the room."

"Fine," I said. "Here, take these two and I'll handle my son in the ER." Needless to say, the rules were bent and after finding more rubber gloves to blow up into little balloons, we got down to the business at hand – so to speak – and helping my second son through the ordeal of shots to anesthetize the area and then stitches.

Not every parent should or does attend when a child gets stitches, but I knew from previous experience that my sons would be better patients if I could take care of their heads, while the doctor took care of their stitches.

Attending children who need to undergo medical procedures, no matter how minor, is always difficult for parents. When children undergo psychological evaluations at the Neuropsychology Unit, I usually have the parents in the room for a few minutes, and then I try to go it alone with the child. This is for both the parents' sense of calm as well as the children's.

Most of the tests require finding a basal score – lowest level at which the examinee succeeds, and a ceiling score, level of first consistent set of failure. The fact is, though, parents do not know what the average performance on the specific test is, and may see any failure as meaning their child (who I might add they brought in because of some problem) is worse off than they had thought. It is very hard for a parent to watch his/her child not perform as well as they had hoped.

This whole long introduction is to Yitzchak and his father Avraham. These are not their real names, but the choice of these names will be apparent. They are garnered from the Bible.

They came for assessment of Yitzchak's cognitive level after over a year of severe intractable epileptic seizures. An estimated two million Americans of all ages have epilepsy, and most of them are successfully treated with medications that keep their seizures well-controlled. As many as 35 percent of epileptic patients are termed drug-resistant, experiencing frequent, sometimes disabling seizures.

As the medical history unfolded (both in the many papers that were brought and the almost robotic repetition of dates and procedures endured), I understood that this had been a period of severe "dis-control." Not only the unending seizures, but also visits to specialists, more and more tests, more and more medications – all of which did not produce the sought after relief. I sensed that both father and son were joined in a knot of fear, helplessness, anxiety, frustration and pain.

I had magical hopes that this knot would lend itself to unraveling or cutting in a helpful fashion, similar to the Gordian Knot, which is a legend associated with Alexander the Great. The Gordian Knot is often used as a metaphor for an intractable problem, solved by a bold stroke – as in "cutting the Gordian knot" (Wikipedia).

Now they were in my office – medically things had calmed down somewhat – to "only" a few dozen seizures a day, down from a hundred or more!

They came in and sat opposite me. I did my standard interview of Yitzchak, trying to get a read on his cognitive, expressive and receptive language, and abstract reasoning abilities. I was watching how father and son related with each other and with me. What seemed obvious was they were both in need of help. I placed Yitzchak, the boy, in front of our portable sand box with soldiers and tanks, and the father in a seat opposite me.

As I started to engage Avraham, the father, in conversation, I noticed Yitzchak's body becoming less stiff and his work with the soldiers in the sandbox taking shape. Avraham, on the other hand, began to be more and more agitated. "What are you doing just talking to me? Shouldn't you be talking to Yitzchak? Why are you sitting here near me and not next to him?"

As he spoke, Yitzchak's back (which was facing me) became stiff and he seemed to hold his hand above the sand and wait.

"I am thinking how difficult this year has been for you – all those hospitalizations. Winston Churchill is quoted as saying, 'They also serve who sit and wait,' and you certainly didn't sit, you were an active participant in your son's journey to better health. I am watching Yitzchak play with the soldiers, he too is a fighter and won many battles, and you fought side by side with him."

Out of the corner of my eye, I see Yitzchak's hand return to the sand and move a tank up a hill he fashioned.

"Why do you speak to me? I am not the patient here!"

"You know," I say, "in English the word for *savlanut* is 'patience,' and it is a homophone – sounds the same even though it is spelled differently – as the word 'patients'."

I sense the father's anger. Yitzchak is again holding his hand above the sand. I try a different tack.

"When Avraham had his biggest test of faith, he had to hold his beloved son down on the Holy Altar. Yitzchak was an extremely pure and faithful son, he knew how hard it was for his father to do what had to be done, and he helped in every way he could. I see that your son is very sensitive to you, too. He is sitting here and letting us speak, not interrupting."

Yitzchak's shoulders dropped a bit from the high alert position they were in, just seconds before.

"This is not working. I don't think you are doing the job I brought my son here for you to do. I think this meeting is over and I don't think we will be back."

Though there is quite a lot in the commentaries about Yitzchak's fears and behavior after his almost sacrifice, we know that Sarah, his mother, died upon hearing about it. Avraham's emotional state is not discussed. Yes, he seemed to continue on with his life, in fact he started anew, remarried (Ketura), and fathered five more sons. But what were his scars from the thwarted *Akedah* (sacrifice)?

As they left the room, Yitzchak gave one last longing look at the sandbox. Maybe this battle was over for now, but the siege and war were still raging.

I felt I had messed-up an opportunity to help them both. Sadly, I made a mental note to call the following month in order to find out how things were going and if they would like a referral to someone else, or would possibly return to where we had left off.

On Weddings and Children . . .

W<small>E WERE AT</small> a wedding, when a woman whom I didn't know asked me if I would talk with her husband. I thought about what a friend who is a physician says when people ask him medical questions at weddings, Bar Mitzvah celebrations or the like. He says: "No problem, but as I take your questions seriously, please disrobe so I can be thorough, or I can give you an appointment at my office tomorrow." He rarely (I should say never) has had a "patient" disrobe for an examination at a wedding.

As a psychologist, however, I obviously could not use this strategy. So I said: "Sure."

She brought her husband over and stood discreetly in the background.

"I can't handle it. How could he do this to me and to my mother, z"l? Sure he was widowed two years ago, but what is an 85-year old man doing, getting remarried?"

"Was your father living with you since your mom died?" I asked.

"No, he was living in a senior citizen hotel in another country."

What was this all about, I wondered. It seemed as if it was all about the son and nothing about the father.

What I then said to him was that he seemed to be suffering a lot, at a great distance from his dad. He said he was protecting his mother's good name. I noted that this was a serious problem, because not only was he in pain, but his obvious difficulty was also affecting his wife and possibly his children, as well – not to mention his father. I thought that therapy would be helpful and said that I could give him a referral to someone else or set up an appointment with me for two days hence.

Preparing for the appointment, I sought out secular professional articles, and as we have our own wealth of resources, I also perused Torah and Rabbinic literature.

According to the 1990 U.S. Census, 10 percent of the women and 2.5 percent of men had lost a spouse (unfortunately, this specific information was not collected for the 2000 Census). About 300,000 remarriages in the United States each year involve previously widowed brides or grooms.

Some questions may be left unasked by widows/widowers: "How long is it proper to wait before dating or considering remarriage?"

Little research has been conducted on remarriage after the death of a spouse as opposed to divorce. Existing research, however, suggests that only about 25 percent of widowed men and 5 percent of widowed women remarry, and they take one to two years longer to remarry than do divorced individuals. One reason that widowed individuals have lower rates of remarriage is that they are usually much older than divorced individuals. Given that fact, we find that there are fewer people in their age bracket to remarry, and there is less incentive to do so.

According to U.S. Census figures, widowers generally remarry within three years of a wife's death, and widows within five years of a husband's death. Generally, people who have been caregivers for terminally ill spouses have grieved long before the actual death. This process may shorten the period before they consider remarriage. Also, older people may believe that they have less time left and may desire to marry again, more quickly.

According to Halacha (Jewish Law), a widower may remarry after the *shloshim* (thirty-day mourning period). A widow may have to wait three months, in case she is pregnant and, as such, to validate the paternity of the child; a nursing mother/widow should ask her rabbi. Unfortunately, in Israel we have quite a lot of young widows and Rabbinic response may vary depending on each case.

If I fall in love again, does that mean I wasn't in love with my deceased spouse?

After the numbness of loss has passed, many widows and widowers think they'll never be able to love the same way again. The reality is that people who've had good marriages are often eager to resume married life. Sharing their life with another is important to them. Many previous widows and widowers have dealt with those concerns by viewing their new marriage as a tribute to the first.

AM I MARRYING FOR THE RIGHT REASONS?

People marry for many reasons. For widows or widowers, these reasons can be complex. It's common for widowed spouses to consider marriage because they feel:

Overwhelmed: New responsibilities placed on widows or widowers can be daunting. Those who face sole responsibility for parenthood may suddenly realize they're doing the work of two. These feelings can propel some to rush into marriage to relieve their stressful situations.

Lonely: It's difficult to adjust to being alone. People who were happily married suffer a great deal. They lost a partner, friend and confidant.

Remarriage can relieve these problems, and in some cases, ease the grief. Although these feelings are common, they're not good reasons to remarry. Secular statistics report that 60 percent of all remarriages fail.

CHILDREN OF WIDOWS OR WIDOWERS

Children of widows or widowers, of any age, have their own concerns regarding their parents' new marriage.

They often have idealistic impressions of their parents' marriage and find it difficult to understand how their widowed parent can move on to a new marriage.

Even though they may spend a lifetime grieving for a lost parent, children also need to remember that as much as they try to comfort their surviving parent, a child isn't a replacement for a loving spouse.

In addition, young children may be afraid of what the new family will mean to them. Do they have to give up memories of their deceased parent? Will they have to call the new stepparent "Dad" or "Mom?" Young children also may fear that there may not be a place for them in their new family.

In some secular and non-Jewish weddings, the stepchildren are included and given a medal, to symbolize that the stepparent is also making a commitment to them, not just to their parent. This service, developed by Roger Coleman, a chaplain at Pilgrim Chapel in Kansas City, Missouri, helps children adjust to their new family and feel that they're an important part of their new family's life.

There is a strong *minhag* that children are not present at the *chuppah* (marriage ceremony) of their parent.

HEALTH ISSUES

Studies have shown that only 10 percent of elderly men live alone, as compared with 32 percent of older women. Nonetheless, the survival curves demonstrate that up to the age of 80 years, women living alone experienced lower mortality than those living with partners. In an Italian study, the results suggest that being married provides a protective role against mortality in later life only for men. It is possible that elderly women, who take care of a husband or relatives, do not care for themselves (or their health), as do older women who live alone.

I didn't find any research about remarriage of widows or widowers in Jewish societies, though I recalled a story, which sounded a bit familiar, regarding a widowed father remarrying.

The Bible tells us (Genesis 25:1–2) that after Sarah's death: "Abraham took another wife, whose name was Ketura. She bore him Zimran, Jokshan, Medan, Midian, Ishbak, and Shua."

WHO WAS KETURA?

Rabbi Judah says in the Midrash (*Beraishit Rabbah* 61:4): "She is Hagar." This is the opinion of the *Zohar* (133b) and of *Targum Yonatan*, as well. Rashi agrees with them.

WHO ARRANGED ABRAHAM'S MATCH?

This is barely touched on in the text (unlike the detailed description of Isaac's *shadchan*, marriage broker, Eliezer). But the Aggadah tells us that it was his son Isaac who brought Abraham and Ketura together, as Rashi says in his comment on the verse: "Isaac had just come back from the vicinity of Be'er Lachai Ro'ie" (Genesis 24:61) – "to where he went to bring Hagar to Abraham his father that he might wed her" [the well of Lachai Ro'ie is the spot to which Hagar wandered after being cast out by Abraham (and Sarah), see 16:14].

Now I know that this is not a full account of all the midrashic, halachic and Torah commentaries, but I hoped to use them in the therapy hour to present biblical scenarios and open conversations, in light of the issues that seemed so contemporary, but indeed were centuries old.

As usual the Torah has it all. Hopefully, the son in question will be able to learn an important lesson from Abraham's son, Isaac.

FOR FURTHER READING:

T. Weathersby, *Getting Married After a Spouse Dies*, August 19, 2002.

K. McQuillan, "Family Composition and Remarriage in Alsace," *The Journal of Interdisciplinary History*, Spring 2003, 33:4, 547–567.

B. Foley Wilson, S. Cunningham Clarke, "Remarriages: A demographic profile," *Journal of Family Issues*, 1992, 13, 123–141.

We Have All Been in School at One Time or Another

I N SCHOOL, WE were all aware of who was known as the "class clown," the "one the teacher hated," and "the teacher's pet." In my day, there was the "*lishka*-boy." Usually in a boys' or co-ed school, this referred to the boy who could not stay still and was put in charge of office (*lishka*) jobs. He had keys jangling and a clipboard. He may have collected the attendance sheets from all the teachers or had some other job. Today he might be diagnosed as having ADHD and be on medication or not. He may currently be a multimillionaire who, once out of school, could put to use his multitasking abilities for professional advancement.

I was thrown back to this earlier (high school) period of my life when I sat down in an off the trendy track café for a quiet cappuccino. Who did I spot out of the corner of my eye but the teacher's pet! Whoosh, I was back in class hearing effusive compliments for none other than her. Well, certainly never me! I smiled to myself at the power of our minds and especially of memory, for today I might need to write down where I placed the car keys, but yet can recall demonstrative compliments given to someone else – scores of years ago, no less.

In these few seconds, I was also reminded of the following case. On the phone, she sounded like just like another seminary student away from home for the first time. That was until she began crying hysterically when the rebbetzin in her Halacha class said that she couldn't marry a Kohen, and shouldn't even contemplate a *shidduch* date with one. The tears were so bitter and sad. "Wait a minute," I said. "Did the rebbetzin catch you being assaulted by a *goy*, a non-Jew?"

All the while I was thinking about some of the axioms that get me through my professional day until I can get further "supervision." One is a legal term in Jewish law: *Ein adam maseem atzmo rasha* – a person cannot implicate himself as evil. Another is *tinok she'nishba* – a child who was coerced. Yet another adage I hold is that you can say almost anything in your first interview with a patient, but afterward there are civilities that need to be observed. There are still other axioms that pop to the fore on a need-to-use basis.

She gave a loud "*chas v'shalom.*" Then I asked if she thought she could wait for an appointment in three days hence, hoping that by not responding to her emergency-sounding voice or tears in the same tone, I would help calm her down a bit until we met.

When we met, she related a story about a relationship with her young, dynamic teacher in seminary school. This teacher became more than just a teacher; she became her mentor and close friend. So close, that this young woman had started questioning her own sexual identity.

After the summer months of being home and going out on a few *shidduch* dates, she decided that she definitely wanted to rejoin other young women her age, and that she indeed did have interest in getting married. She returned to Israel to a different seminary, and when the rebbetzin gave her talk to the prospective *kallot* (brides), she panicked at the thought that her "relationship" with her previous mentor made her *pasul* (unacceptable) to marry a Kohen.

My throwaway line to her let her feel that maybe there were other halachic ways of seeing the issue – as indeed there are.

All these memories passed before my eyes as I sat with my coffee.

A little time went by, and my erstwhile classmate walked over to my table. "You may not remember me," she began, "but I remember you. I'm a psychologist now too, and have been reading your articles in Nefesh Israel ListServ and *The Jewish Press*."

Now it was my turn. "Oh, but I do remember you. You haven't changed a bit. I thought that it might be you when I walked in, but then again, I have this hard and fast rule that I never say hello to anyone first, as many people don't want it 'out' that they know me or vice versa. I'm pleased that you did come over."

We spoke for a while, and she confided that though she is no longer *frum* she feels a reawakening of her inherent, spiritual soul and came to Israel for the year to work on herself. She added that she holds her experience with a certain teacher as responsible for years of self-doubt, and her anger at "the religious and religion."

Whoa, I thought, *and this is without even sharing my cappuccino!*

I was later to understand that after years of soul-searching and what she described as "good therapy," she is in a "different place." Though nothing untoward had taken place between them, this teacher's pet and her teacher had a close relationship for years, which seemingly caused her to question her sexual identity and never allowed her to connect with the opposite sex in a healthy way. (Similar cases have been coming out into the open in Europe, the U.S., Australia, and Israel.)

King Solomon said, "There is nothing new under the sun." As students, parents, educators and professionals, we must be aware that we and our teens may be susceptible to mentors who, although seemingly religious and charismatic, are indeed odious. Their interest is not in our children, but in their own narcissistic selves.

May the Gates of Heaven Connect to Our Bridges of Beseechings

Coming into Jerusalem is always a thrilling experience, even for veteran Jerusalemites, but since the opening of the Jerusalem Chords Bridge, designed by Spanish architect, Santiago-Calatrava, Jerusalem has another way of communicating with its inhabitants and visitors.

At the beginning of October 2008, the bridge's evening lights were turned on and they were PINK! This was in unison with many other inanimate objects throughout the world's capitals, signifying a global kick-start of October 2008 being designated Breast Cancer Awareness Month.

I have met many people who in their daily lives demonstrate *chesed*. One in particular is Gail. (She has permitted use of her full name, but I have decided to just use her first name.) Gail was honored at the annual Shaare Zedek Women's Organization Luncheon in the United States. She didn't want to accept the honor, but was told that the only way she could disseminate her story was for her to speak herself, and the only way to do that was to accept the duly deserved honor.

Keeping lifesaving information for herself alone is not Gail's way. She is a consummate researcher of getting to the bottom of information and then uses it to get to the top. Here is her story – in her words:

Before I tell you my story, I would like to mention some of the cutting-edge research and actual clinical work that is being done under the leadership of Prof. Ephrat Levy-Lahad, MD of Shaare Zedek's Medical Genetics Institute, which she helped found, and is committed to all aspects of clinical care in genetics, as well as performing groundbreaking research.

I will briefly discuss some work in three areas which I believe you will find of particular interest: prenatal, stem cell, and breast cancer.

Firstly, the Medical Genetics Institute has Israel's largest lab for Pre-implantation Genetic Diagnosis (PGD). In this lab, embryos obtained by In Vitro Fertilization, or IVF, in couples at risk for genetic diseases, are tested, and only healthy embryos are returned to the womb. Additionally, it is literally only one of a handful of labs in the world that can perform PGD on the egg rather than on the embryo, and this minimal manipulation results in higher pregnancy rates.

Thanks to the generosity of Rabbi David and Mrs. Anita Fuld, even a woman who has no insurance can have PGD. There are never any out-of-pocket costs to either patient or hospital. Since its inception in 2004, over fifty-three healthy babies have been born to couples at risk for devastating genetic illnesses, with another eleven on the way.

Secondly, again under Dr. Levy-Lahad's guidance, Shaare Zedek has opened a Stem Cell Research lab. What I particularly find exciting is that stem cell lines will be created from the diseased embryos obtained by PGD. Shaare Zedek's Stem Cell Research Lab intends to provide a unique global resource for studying human disease in human cells – as these lines will be made available to researchers outside of Shaare Zedek. This means that researchers – anywhere in the world – will have access to these stem cell lines.

Now, I will tell you about some of Shaare Zedek's work in breast cancer research. Within the Medical Genetics Institute, Dr. Levy-Lahad has pioneered Israel's first specialized Cancer Genetics Clinic, which enables genetic analysis of families with multiple cases of cancer. An outgrowth of these studies was the realization of the cancer risks in Ashkenazi BRCA1 and BRCA2 carriers.

In addition, in 2000, Shaare Zedek's Medical Genetic Institute became the first foreign institution to be chosen for support of breast cancer research by the prestigious Breast Cancer Research Foundation – and they are funding a study which includes over 8,000 participants to determine if it would be justified to offer BRCA1 and BRCA2 testing to all women.

Dr. Levy-Lahad also collaborates with the scientist, known as the "mother" of breast cancer genetics and a member of our board, Dr. Mary Claire King, who is based at the University of Washington. It was Dr. King who discovered and named the BRCA1 gene. I asked Ephrat if she was involved in this. Her response was, "No. I was busy discovering a gene for Alzheimer's at the time." However, it was their collaboration that established the importance of another Jewish mutation; this one, in the CHEK2 gene and this is where my story begins.

In 1979, my beloved sister, Marsha Dane Stern, of blessed memory, lost a five-year battle with breast cancer. She was only thirty-six. Then, in 1980, my mother, of blessed memory, found a lump. Thank God, she survived cancer-free and only passed away last year.

All was quiet within our family until 1992, when I, too, was diagnosed with breast cancer – bilateral – both breasts with three primary sites and, as with many other pre-menopausal women – nothing showing on a mammogram. By the way, in my family, pre-menopausal women have sonograms, or more recently, some are having MRIs, in addition to mammograms.

My case was a little unusual. It was the topic of Grand Rounds at Mt. Sinai

Medical Center in New York. I spoke with Drs. Larry Norton and Susan Love, names that many of you know. My records were reviewed at Harvard, NIH, and the Milan Institute and a course of treatment was decided.

Subsequently, one of my doctors presented my history to a Congressional Committee in an effort to get increased Congressional breast cancer research funding. Remember, it was around the time of my sister Marsha's cancer discovery that First Lady Betty Ford had her very public battle with breast cancer. Up until then, many women still considered breast cancer a taboo subject, too fearful or even shameful to be discussed openly.

Unfortunately, my family learned the hard way how truly important it is to know one's family's medical history. My sister's lump was not taken seriously because of her young age and it wasn't until my own cancer that I was shocked to learn that I was one of eight acknowledged breast cancer cases in my family, dating back through my paternal grandfather to my great-grandmother.

I had easily accepted that I had cancer – with the breast cancer probability in the female population being what it was. I had thought, "why not me?" However, after I learned about my family statistic, I asked, "Why my family?" As those who know me well know, I am a doer, so I started searching for an explanation.

I called the big guy himself, Dr. Frances S. Collins, who had not, as yet, announced that he was leaving the University of Michigan to succeed James Watson and become director of the National Human Genome Research Institute and overseer of the International Human Genome Sequencing Consortium. That group that has been responsible for mapping and sequencing all of the human DNA.

Yes, I started big time. My family was accepted in Dr. Collins's study, which was later taken over by Dr. Barbara Weber and moved to the University of Pennsylvania. In addition, we were accepted in studies at Mt. Sinai Hospital and Memorial Sloan Kettering.

Finally, in 2002, Dr. Weber told me I had a CHEK2 mutation which no other family members tested had, and a finding other institutions could not replicate.

In 2004, I again had breast cancer – in a muscle in the chest – an impossibility, one would have thought, after bilateral mastectomies. Not surprisingly, the number of known family members, with at least one instance of breast cancer, had risen to twelve.

It was at the last Shaare Zedek luncheon that I first heard of the work being done by Prof. Ephrat Levy-Lahad in collaboration with Dr. Mary Claire King. My family became part of their study. In October, I learned that Dr. Barbara Weber had been right – I have a CHEK2 mutation. However, I have another CHEK2 mutation which was recently discovered in the King lab by a post-doc originally from Shaare Zedek, Dr. Avraham Shaag. Until my case, these two

CHEK2 mutations had never been seen in the same individual. It has been ascertained that my sister Marsha shared this dubious honor.

The first CHEK2 mutation is found in populations of northern European ancestry, including Ashkenazi Jews. The second mutation is specific to Ashkenazi Jews. These mutations increase breast cancer risk by a factor of two to three and Prof. Levy-Lahad says additional gene mutations will be forthcoming. As a result of these findings, one of my relatives who has a CHEK2 mutation, as well as BRCA2, and has had breast cancer twice, recently had a prophylactic hysterectomy. Another relative, because she has the newly discovered mutation, is planning on having prophylactic mastectomies.

Dr. Larry Norton once told me that my family might be the Rosetta Stone for breast cancer. I don't know if we are, but, I do know that the work of Shaare Zedek's Prof. Ephrat Levy-Lahad, M.D. will save many women from this dreaded disease and has had a major impact on my own family – for which I will be eternally grateful.

So, thank you, Shaare Zedek, for this honor and for allowing me to speak.

Is Ice Meaty or Dairy?

Late one afternoon, my secretary, Tova, told me that I really had to take the call *urgently*, as the woman on the other end of the phone kept saying, "This is an emergency." I picked up the phone and noticed that as Tova left the room she had an odd smile on her face, not at all in keeping with the word "emergency."

"Please help me; I am not religious but I was told you might be able to help me. Is ice meaty or dairy?"

I wasn't sure whether to be sad or glad for this type of referral. Someone felt that notwithstanding the fact of my being religious, I would help someone who wasn't. How could anyone assume that you have to be of the same religion, let alone level of observance, to ask for or receive help from a professional? I find even the existence of this perception appalling!

Instead of lashing out and haughtily listing rabbinic literature, which permits desecrating the Shabbat to save the life of *anyone*, I just replied, "Maybe you should start from the beginning. On second thought, let's start at the end."

"My daughter is newly religious and when I tried to put ice in my baby grandson's soup to cool it down, she said that I couldn't because I don't have separate meaty and dairy ice-cube trays. Is ice *fleishig* (meaty) or *milchig* (dairy)?"

I decided to handle this question in the age-old Talmudic fashion, answering a question with another question. "I think this is more complicated than it would appear at first blush. Would your daughter be prepared to come in and speak to me herself?"

Within a few days, the daughter called and said she knew her mother had spoken to me, and that she is only making an appointment because her mother is so upset and crying all the time.

An intake/first appointment is usually scheduled for between an hour and a half to two hours. In that time, we chat, trying to know one another. A kind of first date, it allows the therapist a chance to get a "feel for the patient." Many first appointments can last for four or more visits.

The daughter (I'll call her Dianne) came at the appointed time with her infant son. We started talking and I had the immediate impression that Dianne was a highly intelligent, well-spoken person. She attended to her baby during the course of the meeting, fussing with him, nursing him and checking his diaper when appropriate. She had also brought along a sheaf of papers. "I Googled you," she said proudly. In the years that the Internet and especially Google have become household words and all sorts of information are literally at one's fingertips, I have had many patients who have similarly looked me up. They have also frequently Googled the information regarding their diagnosis, treatments and everything in-between.

I know many of my colleagues in the hospital find this, at best, annoying and, at worst, threatening. I know that I would have probably done (and have done) the same thing. What most of my previous patients and I would *not* do is bring the papers – specifically on my research of the doctor – into the office with us.

During the course of the interview/meeting, Dianne frequently referred to comments I made in articles I wrote or that were written about me to punctuate her points. As if to give further credence to her statements, she quoted *me* to me! She also noted pointedly personal information that she had culled from the Internet, and asked me if the other people listed with the same last name were my husband or children. As she asked the last question, Dianne looked at me with her eyes lowered, head tilted to one side, and a smile that seemed more like a smirk on her face. My association from her facial expression was, "gotcha."

I frequently teach my students that how we feel during the interview is of the utmost importance to note. My mantra is, "pay attention to your visceral reaction – immediately."

Transference, first described by Sigmund Freud in relationship to psychoanalysis, has been written about *ad infinitum*. Here it is just defined as an unconscious redirection of feelings for one person to another, feelings that probably originated in childhood. And the counter-transference is not *only* – but *also* – the psychologist's response to these "redirected feelings."

Patients have a right to know my professional credentials. So what was my visceral reaction? In cases like this, I see their search not as a genuine need to have information about the professional to whom they are planning to share their issues. This time I felt stalked and my privacy invaded. She had crossed Internet etiquette. There was something aggressively intrusive about her hunt for information about me.

I ask her where most of her friends live. "That's a funny thing to ask," she replies. She looks at me and says that she "never really had any friends – even before I became a *baalat teshuvah*."

"What about your relationship with your siblings?" I ask. "We still fight like cats and dogs even though we are all in our thirties already. Actually they get along together, they just don't get along with me, and never did for that matter. Now that I am religious it is more of the same."

I tell her that I really respected the fact that she came in to speak to me, when it was her mother who had asked her to come. "*Kibbud em* (honor thy mother)," she says. "Still, it speaks well of you." Then she smiles – genuinely – for the first time. I feel relieved that there was some sign of genuine emotional resonance. Her diagnosis, treatment and prognosis might be more optimistic than I had first thought.

Over one hour had gone by, and I was trying to formulate some form of game plan that for me meant trying out a hunch vis-à-vis a preliminary diagnosis. I asked myself what would make someone need to know information that belonged to someone else? How and why would having information relieve someone's anxiety to such an extent that, in this case, for example, it then allowed the person to relax sufficiently in order to accept a compliment?

I went back to my original impression that once Dianne had the info on me, I perceived her looking down her nose and smirking – as if to say, "gotcha." If she got me, was that a way of pre-empting my getting her? Was she girded/armed with the information about me as a protection against attack?

I turned to Dianne and told her my feelings of her having "gotcha-ed" me, and that I felt she had crossed the line from appropriate to invasive. I said that I am now going to ask her an off-the-wall question that she didn't have to answer if she felt it was too intrusive. "I am asking myself what happened to you very early on in your life that would make you wary of being attacked?"

Quiet for a long time, she then answers, "I have many allergies, starting with Lactose Intolerance that was diagnosed when I was two months old. My whole life I have had to be careful about the food I ate and places I went."

I thought that had I been Sherlock Holmes, I would take out my pipe now and smile contentedly. Her behavior – her "gotcha" with the personal information and the meaty and milky ice – spoke of severe anxiety, defensiveness and even paranoia. Instead of dealing with the anxiety as an internal experience, I might propose a treatment plan externalizing the basis of her anxiety by trying to understand the "siege" she has been under by her Lactose Intolerance and allergies.

Being Orthodox can mean "separate," but can also be a way of joining and including others without the constant anxiety about being harmed, devalued and embarrassed. I would try to posit that being a new mother might have triggered the fact that she might not be able to protect her son from pain and noxious foods in his environment – as her own mother could – and did not know that while being nurtured with a bottle of milk, her mother may have been perceived by infant Dianne as someone "out to get her." When a child is born with Congenital Lactase Deficiency, a genetic disorder that prevents enzymatic production of lactase, the child may experience severe stomach cramps and gaseous – full but empty – feelings until diagnosed and treated.

In her seminal book, *Psychoanalytic Diagnosis: Understanding Personality Structure in the Clinical Process*, Nancy McWilliams writes: "The main polarity in the self-representations of paranoid people is an impotent, humiliated and despised image of self versus an omnipotent, vindicated, triumphant one." Further in the chapter, she states, "They [paranoid individuals] never feel fully safe and spend an inordinate amount of their emotional energy scanning the environment for dangers."

As Dianne leaves the office, I ask her if ice is *fleishig* or *milchig*. She smiles and says, "I'll tell my Mom ice is *pareve*, [not meaty or dairy]."

Don't I Have the Right to Love and Be Loved?

It was an unusual request for an appointment. A phone call from a Rav who is a well-known popular *posek* (decides on halachic issues) for married couples, requesting an appointment to come and speak with me about something personal.

Sure, I said, sensing that this was as unusual a request for him to make, as it was for me to receive.

At the appointed time, he arrived and sensing on the phone how uncomfortable he was, as the *helper going for help*, I had prepared a tea/coffee tray as well as cookies. I felt that this might help to level the playing field when the mountain, so to speak, traveled to Mohamed.

Dressed in traditional Haredi garb, the Rav sat looking intently at the wall where, for all intents and purposes, he saw some sort of deflected image of me in a picture frame glass. After years of working with the ultra-Orthodox community of males, I understand and respect this for what it is: eye-contact in a permissible format.

After we finish the coffee/tea, he says: "Thank you for seeing me on such short notice, I know you are very busy."

"We are all busy," I counter, "and there is a saying that 'if you want something done, ask a busy person,' so I guess we're going to get something done."

He smiles an inscrutable smile. I wait.

"A person, a married man in his early forties, came to me with a question. He knows I work with young couples and help them with *shalom bayit* issues at the beginning of their marriage." (I have learned over the years that the term "*shalom bayit*" usually refers to anything but *peace in the home*!)

He goes on: "I asked him how I could help. We spoke of his learning, his family of origin, his children, his wife, and the stress of worrying about how to make ends meet. All this was conversation, but I knew he wasn't getting to the point, getting to the reason he came to see me. I started to tell him our time was almost up, whereupon the man began to cry.

"I was so taken aback because it hadn't seemed as if our conversation had touched on anything emotionally meaningful. Then he asked me the question

139

that brought me here, to your office, Dr. Guedalia. He asked: 'Don't I deserve to be happy too, don't I deserve an opportunity in life to love and be loved?' He was quietly sobbing, and I didn't know what to do; this had never happened to me before.

"Certainly, people who have come to me have cried and showed their emotions, but this was the first time anyone had posed this particular question to me, and it was the first time I felt hit-between-the-eyes like this. I've thought about his question and what followed for weeks, before making the appointment to come and talk with you."

At this point, I still had not been told what the reason for his referral was, but it was clear that the question the Rav had been asked touched a chord in him that resonated in ways other *shealot* (halachic queries) have not. I thought that the conversation he relayed and his reaction might have had more to do with the word "deserve" than even the word "love." I'm not sure what made me think so, but he might have emphasized the word in a way that was different from the other words in his narrative.

In life, we all have periods where we feel we are in a certain groove (I guess that vinyl record metaphor dates me!). At any rate, there is routine that is comforting and helps put order in our lives, and yet, sometimes, the thought of breaking-out is a tantalizing one.

I remember when we first moved to Israel there were *sherut*/jitney stands up and down Jaffa Road, with their drivers shouting out different destinations, cities and towns all over the country as they attempted to fill their taxis before they left. I remember wondering what it would be like to just say: Okay, I'll go to Kiryat Ono (I'm not even sure where it is today!) and then reality would hit, and I'd know that I had a stroller in my hand with some little person with needs and wishes; my husband would be home for dinner, which needed to be cooked; a *shiur* to attend, planned for the evening; school work to do, etc.

I've often thought about a song: "Stop the World – I Want to Get Off" from the 1960s musical of the same name by Leslie Bricusse and Anthony Newley. In the story, the hero felt caught up in an empty lifestyle, and what turned out to be a success early in his life, that he didn't appreciate. Not only that; he also felt trapped and wanted "off the carousel."

It usually takes less than a nanosecond of thought and I would think of how fortunate I was to have a carousel at all; a life that God gave me with all the responsibilities of being a Jew and how the feeling of needing – *deserving* – time off was only possible because I had so many things pulling on me and my time, even with the "freedom" of not being required to do positive *mitzvot*, which were time dependent!

These thoughts passed through my mind as the Rav continued his story. The man who came to him was someone who was grappling with sexual desires that were against Halacha in its most basic sense. The question of *deserving love* was tainted by that fact.

The Rav clearly had knowledge and opinions steeped in Halacha and would surely be able to help this religious man do the right thing. But he came to me, someone perceived as a secular thinking person (a psychologist) who was *frum*, as someone who could possibly offer a different perspective. He asks if I felt – psychologically speaking – that the terms "deserve" and "love" could be validated, though they were contra to what he believed in so strongly?

I think a bit; not too long, because my "psychological" mind and soul are inexorably intertwined with my *frum* self and so, I ask the Rav a question. "What if this troubled person had asked instead: 'Don't I deserve to live my life with love' – then I wait a second and say – 'with my neighbor's wife'?"

"Ahh, I know both the problem and its solution," says the Rav, with a smile on his lips and a twinkle in his eye, sagely touching his beard. "It is I who has been influenced by the world around me, not you, the 'modern' *frum* psychologist."

A Tale of Two Cities
and Life's Passages

I<small>F YOU ARE</small> "sane" enough to say you are crazy, you are not insane enough to be taken seriously (as in Joseph Heller's *Catch 22*).

Two parallel existences go on. The inhabitants of both "cities" project their hopes and dreams on one another.

Another axiom is that of passages. In our lives, if we are fortunate, there are many passages. The importance of passages was highlighted most dramatically during the Exodus from Egypt. At the behest of Hashem, Moses instructed his people to mark the lintels of their home with the blood of a sacrificed animal. The passage from Egypt into the Promised Land was "marked."

Parents of children with special needs are experts in finding doors and portals through which their children may pass, sometimes well-girded for the next passage, other times, less able to take an equal place with their peers. As each passage in life begins to appear on the horizon, it is as if a parent is "stabbed in the heart" yet again, with a painful reality. "My child is different than others his/her age"; "I thought that *this* time we had finally *made it*" – the entry into the "good-enough" if not perfect life.

These "Two Cities" do not have to be in a geographical divide, rather they exist in the same time and place, yet a different dimension. Yet though they may co-exist, they rarely intersect, establishing is a constant Push Me Pull You between what might be and what is.

When an advertisement for a special yeshiva for a year of study in Israel appeared in the local Jewish newspaper, Mrs. Lahav was thrilled. Her son Gadi would be able to attend a yeshiva abroad, just as his age-mates would be doing.

Gadi was diagnosed as having psychiatric problems from age eight. His parents noticed difficulties with his development from age five and over the years have done everything in their power to provide him with the special medical attention and environment that would allow him to take his place among healthy children his age. There were some better years and some years that painfully required hospitalization.

Now at nineteen years of age he was pretty aware of his limitations, yet dreamt of taking his place among his friends and neighbors who were going to

Eretz Yisrael for a year of study, before going on to learning Torah, college or work. The ad in the paper was the opening of one such window.

Under "rabbinical" and "professional" supervision, young men with mental health issues were invited to submit their applications for acceptance to a one-year program. It was costly, more than other such yeshiva programs, but this was a small special needs group. Mr. and Mrs. Lahav were cautiously elated at the opportunity.

What transpired was every parent's nightmare.

Once he had arrived at his "yeshiva," Mrs. Lahav was in contact by phone with Gadi at least once daily. After a few weeks, it tapered to twice weekly. He was so happy in Israel, in general, and in the "yeshiva," in particular. He sounded homesick but the "rabbi" in charge said this was to be expected and that he was doing quite well.

Mrs. Lahav felt there was some hesitation creeping up in Gadi's voice. It seemed that he was always tired or sleeping, but kept hoping that his homesickness would soon be resolved. She asked friends whose sons had been in Israel for the year and found that this was not an unusual reaction – off on their own, up until all hours, new freedom – all sounded plausible.

When he didn't call at the appointed time, she felt he was really getting into learning, and things were moving along well. She tried to reach the "rabbi," after Gadi missed two phone calls, to check on what was going on. The report was positive and she was pleased.

Ten days later she began to be concerned. When she finally spoke to him, he sounded confused and anxious. She decided that maybe Israel was too far away for someone with his history, and began looking into options in the New York area. The environment, which she felt would be optimal, required a current neuropsychological evaluation, and they referred her to me in Jerusalem. She decided she would fly over to see Gadi and also accompany him for the assessment which usually takes about six to ten hours over two or three days.

Gadi presented as a well-groomed and attractive older adolescent. He did show some facial and motor tics and as the initial interview continued began to behave somewhat erratically. As I took a history from the mother, my colleague went into another room with Gadi to continue with further neuropsychological testing. When I rejoined Gadi, the tics and recurring thoughts had become more pervasive. And, added to that, were as I feared, early signs of psychosis that was affecting his cognitive ability.

I recommended that we take a break in the testing, and consulted with Mrs. Hinda Schryber, a psychiatric social worker and the director of Ohr LeNefesh. Ohr LeNefesh is an organization that provides services for the mentally ill in Jerusalem, and Mrs. Schryber is a native English speaker. After speaking with Mrs. Lahav, and impressing upon her the urgency of a psychiatric consultation (it wasn't hard to do given that Gadi's state seemed to be deteriorating before our eyes), she arranged to take a taxi to Ohr L'Nefesh.

What transpired afterward was the following:

In subsequent hours, Gadi's medical/psychiatric condition further deteriorated. Mrs. Schryber referred them to Eitanim Child and Adolescent Psychiatric Hospital where he was checked by a physician who found signs of physical abuse on his body. It seems as though there had been ongoing physical injury and that he may have also been sexually abused. Though he was unable to communicate clearly, it seemed as though his recurring thoughts and anxiety stemmed from the nightmare he had lived. Further, there was another young man in the same hospital with similar signs who had attended the same "yeshiva"!

Contrary to the glowing references in the advertisement, the "rabbi's" name was already connected to similar cases. No professionals were employed by the "yeshiva"; the "yeshiva" was not licensed by the State of Israel to operate a "psychiatric" residential environment. Neighbors later reported hearing screams coming from the apartments connected with the "yeshiva," but did not report what they heard to the authorities.

The police were called in and revealed that they had already had complaints of similar cases regarding the "rabbi" and "yeshiva." When they went to investigate, they found hand restraints on the beds and the "rabbi" was missing. He has yet to be found by the police, and it is thought that he fled to England or Canada.

Gadi received requisite psychiatric and medical care and within a few weeks was able to make the trip home with his mother.

The "yeshiva," which is in fact, a few apartments in a religious town outside Jerusalem, lies empty; the "rabbi" has not, as far as I know, returned to Israel.

This horrible story ends on a more positive note vis-à-vis Gadi. His mother reports that he has recovered from this harrowing experience and is doing well in a *frum* residential facility in the States and has begun taking courses at a local college.

Please consult with organizations such as Nefesh Israel (www.nefeshisrael. com), the Israeli branch of Nefesh International (www.nefesh.org). We *may* be able to make contact with various individuals and organizations and will *try* to use due diligence in researching special institutions in Israel. But as always, *Caveat Emptor* – Let the Buyer Beware.

On Crying and Genetics

Sнe came in with two children; a 6-year old girl and an infant boy in a stroller. Batya, the elder of the two children, was to be assessed. At age six, she had been held back in kindergarten for a year to help her mature. When Mrs. L. began to explain the reason for bringing her daughter, she mentioned that she seemed to have difficulties in attention and learning. After already repeating kindergarten, the *gannenet* (kindergarten teacher) recommended that she undergo a developmental neuropsychological evaluation.

An assessment begins with the first phone call and the basic information the parent provides regarding the referral. In the case of children, when the parent or parents bring the child, even without speaking, they also provide important information, which is part of the evaluation. Do both parents accompany their child? How do they relate to each other? What information about their educational and intellectual skills does their expressive language say about them?

Mrs. L. came without her husband; she gave the impression of being well educated and articulate as well as presenting as an attractive mother in her early thirties. She was also smiling uncomfortably which isn't unusual when someone brings a child to be assessed by a neuropsychologist, but what I remember the most about this mom was that although she was not crying at all, her eyes were swollen and red as if from crying. I had this odd association of Leah, wife of Jacob, our forefather's wife number one.

The Bible refers to Leah's soft, tender, reddened eyes. Rashi comments that, as Laban's oldest daughter, she cried all the time at the prospect of having to marry Esau, Rebeccah's oldest son (Genesis 29:16–17). According to the Midrash, she was crying because of the inescapable nature of the proscribed *shidduch*. At the outset, she thought she'd have no choice but to follow the societal norm, yet Hashem had different plans for her and she became Jacob's wife, not his twin brother Esau's. (I am not relating to alternative primogeniture issues here.)

I pushed this spontaneous association aside and continued to take the anamnesis, medical history. Batya had been born by breech delivery. Developmental milestones including language were delayed.

I was watching Batya as her mother spoke. I noticed that Batya had blotchy skin tone, her hands seemed puffy and red, her gait seemed clumsy and un-steady and, when I touched her hands, they were ice cold even though it was warm in the room.

As her mother was speaking to me, Batya was playing with some toys, which I had put out. All of a sudden she stumbled and fell. She began to cry. Her mother went over to console her, but Batya continued crying. What became obvious was that though she was crying, no tears were coming out of her eyes.

I had a glimmer of an idea as to why her mother could not stop crying.

I begin to ask some specific questions. Mrs. L. looks aghast as she answers each question, one by one. "You guessed, didn't you!" she exclaims sadly.

"I'm not sure," I answer, "but has she been tested by a geneticist?"

The mother starts to cry and mumble. "You don't understand, *it* shouldn't have happened. We were each married to someone else and for different reasons divorced and were given this *shidduch*. We married and were so happy and thrilled when Batya was born. Then the problems began, but before we understood what was happening we had another child. Then the doctors suggested that we have tests to tell if the next baby would be okay or not. We are religious, we went to our Rav, and he said try again. We did and the baby has *it*, too," she wails.

What Batya and her siblings have is Familial Dysautonomia (FD).

FD is a genetic disease present at birth in male and female Jewish babies which primarily causes dysfunction of the autonomic and sensory nervous systems. These systems control bodily functions that are often taken for granted such as:

– Overflow tears when we cry
– Breathing when there isn't enough oxygen
– Regulation of blood pressure and body temperatures
– Normal swallowing and digestion
– Safe responses to stress
– The sensory nervous system, which regulates:
    Protective reactions to pain
    Perceptions of hot and cold
    Taste

The prognosis of the disorder depends on early detection, severity of symp-toms, and the individual response to therapeutic treatment for this disorder. Supportive treatment can enhance quality of life and promote better survival.

The lack of tears is the landmark symptom of FD. Specifically, children with FD have an absence of overflow tears with emotional crying.

FD children are usually of normal intelligence. There has been an increased frequency of learning disabilities in FD children, however. Early intervention and aggressive therapy in areas of language and learning have been extremely successful in prevention of greater variances between non-affected peers and treatment.

FD is inherited. It is estimated that one in 27 individuals of Eastern European Jewish (Ashkenazi) ancestry is a carrier of the gene for FD. All parents of children with FD are carriers of the defective recessive gene that transmits the disorder. A parent has no symptoms or warning signs of being a carrier. The first clue for most individuals that they are carriers is the birth of a child with FD.

Today there are tests done by geneticists that can identify the gene (as with Tay-Sachs, Cystic Fibrosis and others).

In regard to Tay-Sachs Disease, another more infamous Jewish genetic disorder, Rabbi Moshe Feinstein, z"tl, was asked whether or not it is advisable for a boy or girl to be screened for it, and if it is proper, at what age the test should be performed. His answer was:

> ... It is advisable for one preparing to be married, to have himself tested. It is also proper to publicize the fact, via newspapers and other media, that such a test is available. It is clear and certain that absolute secrecy must be maintained to prevent anyone from learning the result of such a test performed on another. The physician must not reveal these to anyone ... these tests must be performed in private, and, consequently, it is not proper to schedule these tests in large groups as, for example, in Yeshivas, schools, or other similar situations. (*Responsa: Even HaEzer* 4:10)

Dor Yeshorim Organization in the U.S. and Israel does pre-marital (pre-*shidduch*) screening.

Sadly, the mother went on to tell me that she felt so alone in her pain, as they hadn't told anyone in either family. She had siblings that were still unmarried, she explained, and was afraid to harm their *shidduch* prospects.

I could only think of how many more red, swollen-eyed mothers were in harm's way. I requested that she come in with her husband to talk about these issues. Later, after we had met, I gave them the name and phone number of a Rav who is also a physician who could speak with their Rav in a common rabbinic language.

The story of biblical Leah and her "soft red swollen" eyes, teaches us that Hashem works to change what might be thought of as inevitable. In this case, it truly resonated in the words of Mrs. L. when she said: "*It* shouldn't have happened!"

FOR FURTHER READING:

http://www.ninds.nih.gov/disorders/dysautonomia/dysautonomia.htm.
http://www.jewishvirtuallibrary.org/jsource/Judaism/genetic.html#5.

The Miracles of PGD

Oｎｅ ｏｆ ｔｈｅ ｂｅｎｅｆｉｔｓ of working in the same place for close to twenty years is receiving surprise guests. Not infrequently, people who happen to find themselves at Shaare Zedek, and specifically on the fifth floor, pop in to say hello years after our having met professionally. One such guest was an attractively dressed woman in her early 30s. She knocked on the door, and as I opened it I had a flashback of my first days on the job. I had been asked to see a 13-year old girl in Pediatrics who was crying softly to herself for, what the nurses felt, was an inordinate amount of time.

Now, hospitalized children are generally not in the ward for "happy" reasons, so when a pediatric nurse is concerned about a patient crying for an extra long time, I know it is out of the ordinary. What I saw was a young girl – I will call her Malka – with her arms and legs in casts and traction. The first thing that popped into my mind was that this child was in what I could best describe with the phrase a "bed made in Sodom."

The men of Sodom were notorious for placing a guest on a bed, and if his length exceeded that of the bed they cut off his feet, yet if the man was shorter than the bed, he was stretched (Greek legend of Procrustes). Asked to lie in the bed, Eliezer, our forefather Abraham's devoted servant, replied that at the death of his mother he had vowed never to sleep in a bed (*Pirkei D'Rabbi Eliezer* 16).

This young girl had inherited the bone growth disorder Achondroplasia (a form of Dwarfism). Specifically the cartilage in her developing body did not form the long bones of her arms and legs. So that her head and trunk grew age appropriately, while her legs and arms did not. All people with this genetic make-up have short stature (the average height of an adult male with Achondroplasia is 131 centimeters – 4 feet, 4 inches, and the average height for adult females is 124 centimeters – 4 feet, 1 inch). People with Achondroplasia are generally of normal intelligence even though there are other physical anomalies of the head.

Achondroplasia is the most common type of short-limbed dwarfism. The condition occurs in one in 15,000 to 40,000 newborns. Mutations in the FGFR3 gene cause Achondroplasia. Achondroplasia is inherited in an autosomal

dominant pattern, which means one copy of the altered gene in each cell is sufficient to cause the disorder. About 80 percent of people with Achondroplasia
have average-size parents; these cases result from a new mutation in the FGFR3
gene. In the remaining cases, people with Achondroplasia have inherited an
altered FGFR3 gene from one or two affected parents. Individuals who inherit
two altered copies of this gene typically have very severe problems with bone
growth, and are usually stillborn or die shortly after birth from respiratory failure. Unfortunately, there is no treatment that can cure this condition. Surgery
is sometimes needed to correct specific skeletal deformities. For example, in
patients with severe knock-knee or bowed legs, the pediatric orthopedic surgeon can perform an osteotomy in which he or she cuts the bones of the leg and
allows them to heal in a more correct anatomical position.

The straightening surgery deals with the bowing of the bones and as a result
may add a few inches of height to the patient.

Malka had had this surgery. We spoke a number of times during her hospitalization and I came to understand that her quiet tears were both of pain and
hope against hope that the few inches would be more than a "few," and make
a significant difference in her future height. Though I had thought about her
over the years – she was released to rehabilitation out of the hospital – that was
the last time we met until she saw my name on the door, remembered me, and
knocked. I was so pleased to see her as an adult, and commented to her about
how well she looked. She beamed and proudly told me that she has a job as a
Front Office receptionist.

I would not have recalled the whole incident had I not read about the birth of
a baby boy at Shaare Zedek, born Achondroplasia free. This is the first time ever
that a woman with this type of dwarfism delivered a healthy child following
diagnosis of the embryo before pregnancy (PGD).

The pregnancy was achieved using In Vitro Fertilization, IVF and followed
by PGD, both conducted at the Zohar PGD Unit at Shaare Zedek donated by
Rabbi David and Anita Fuld (of Jerusalem and New York). Rabbi Fuld saw a
need and tirelessly worked to find a way to allow Shaare Zedek the ability to
offer parents with genetic issues a means to overcome the pain of not having
healthy children. The methods used are halachic and accepted by a broad range
of great Torah scholars.

In this particular case, an older sibling had been born with Achondroplasia
several years earlier, and genetic testing found that the mother carried the gene.
Director of Medical Genetics, Prof. Ephrat Levy-Lahad says that the expertise of
the PGD and IVF staff at Shaare Zedek enabled this success.

When performed via the polar body method, as it is at Shaare Zedek and only
a handful of other facilities in the world, PGD has an extremely high degree of
accuracy, thus ensuring that an embryo deemed healthy via the procedure will

in fact be born as a healthy and non-affected child. The "polar body" refers to a tiny attachment that extends from the egg, which contains all of the relevant genetic material; it can be analyzed without the need to touch the embryo. Since PGD was introduced at Shaare Zedek in 2005, over 35 babies have been born to parents without the genetic diseases carried by the mother, father, or both. A list of over 22 chromosome-identified disorders (Familial Dysautonomia, Cystic Fibrosis, Gaucher, Neurofibromatosis are just a few examples), have been isolated and healthy children have been born to parents who might otherwise have remained childless. Medicine, as well as everything else in Hashem's Universe, is evolving every minute. Who knows what miracles He will bring, and the "vessels" He chooses by which to deliver these miracles. It is of paramount importance that we not look at children or adults with genetic disorders as the "un-altered" cases. May we be available to the greatness and sure of His wisdom as He guides us all.

FOR FURTHER READING:

http://www.hopkinsmedicine.org/orthopedicsurgery/achondroplasia.htm.

Who Moved My Chocolate Cake?

Levi is a 26-year old Chassidic young man. At age twenty, he was hit by a car. Over five years later, after many hospitalizations and then rehabilitation, he functions pretty well physically. But cognitively he has some problems and serious issues with short-term memory.

He lives with a family as a boarder, has a life coach who is with him throughout the day, and a job that recognizes his unique abilities in recalling what he used to know – cold. He is well versed in three languages (Hebrew, Yiddish and English). Levi was referred to me to see if I could help develop a rehab schedule to advance him further in his recovery.

It took a while for him to feel comfortable with me – a woman – and a *non-Chassidic* one, as well!

When we would meet he would say that he doesn't recall anything from the last meeting. I take this at face value and each visit I try to create a learning experience as well as an opportunity to discuss issues that bother him.

Over the months, he has learned to make note of occurrences in his diary. We also try to hook a memory with an emotion, as emotions are stored in a different place in the brain than verbal memories.

When he went home for a fairly long visit, I called, and he did remember me. I joke with him that his recall of me throws his "no short-term memory" diagnosis into the garbage can. He laughs and requests that I ask him anything else other than who is speaking to him, and he insists he will not remember. He partially grins at that comment himself.

During an appointment, for the first time, he told me a dream he remembered. He said it was a question that bothered him, and he thought maybe he had dreamt it. I waited with bated breath to hear the question.

"You are a psychologist doctor, right? What kind of person would do this? I have my favorite type of cake in front of me – chocolate. I leave it on my plate and go to wash. When I come back, someone has eaten it, and there are barely any crumbs on the plate. Who would do that?" he plaintively asks.

I am ecstatic! This is really a breakthrough! "You know," I say, "you have just told me a very interesting and special story!"

I recall the book, *Who Moved My Cheese? An Amazing Way to Deal with Change in Your Work and in Your Life*. It is a motivational book by Spencer Johnson that uses parables to describe change in one's work and life. And then he gives four typical reactions to said change, with two mice, two "little people."

Who Moved My Cheese? was a *New York Times* business bestseller since release. It remained on the list for almost five years. Also, it has spent over 200 weeks on *Publishers Weekly*'s hardcover, nonfiction list.

This is a brief (very thin book) tale of two mice and two humans who live in a maze and one day are faced with change: someone moves their cheese. Reactions vary from quick adjustment to waiting for the situation to change by itself to suit their needs.

This story is about adjusting attitudes toward change in life, especially at work. Change occurs whether a person is ready or not, but the author affirms that it can be positive. His principles are to anticipate change, let go of the old, and act the way you would if you were not afraid. Listeners are still left with questions about making his/her own specific personal changes.

I look at Levi and say, "Five years ago, you had a wonderful life. You knew you were an *ilui* who knew so much. You got up and went outside, and when you came back, there were only crumbs of your former life, your 'chocolate cake' on your plate."

Levi looks at me very pensively. "I see what you are saying."

"But this isn't the end," I continue. "What is your next favorite cake or cookie?"

Levi thinks a minute and says his usual: "I don't think I remember."

"How about chocolate chip cookies?"

"Yes, I do like them."

We planned to meet in two days. I prepared chocolate chip cookie batter at home in the morning, put it in a very thick plastic bag and put the chocolate chips in another bag.

When Levi came for his appointment I ask him to remind me of the cake story. He repeats the whole story with the same sadness and amazement that someone would do such a despicable act.

I show him the batter and ask him to knead in the chocolate chips. We then place the batter in little foil cupcake tins, and I put them in the toaster oven we keep in the office. With the wonderful smell wafting through the hospital corridor, people knock on my door and ask what is going on.

I used this opportunity to give the *nimshal* (parable's meaning). I say that there are other kinds of cookies and cakes waiting for you to make and eat. Many people think that a new "chocolate chip cookie" is wonderful. You have a new and different life now, no question about it. But it looks, smells and tastes pretty good!

I tell him what I read in a book, but know from life: "Things change. They always have changed and always will change. And while there's no single way to deal with change, the consequence of pretending change won't happen is always the same: The cakes/cookies run out" (Lou Schuler).

We say the *bracha* (blessing) on the cookies. Levi has the first one. He smiles and says: "Pretty good."

I pray we have found the recipe for success.

A Plane Story: A Holocaust Story

I PRIDE MYSELF ON *not* being a creature of habit. Well, except when I fly as a passenger, which I do a bit. I have developed a pattern of sorts. I have my flying outfit, which not only includes the clothes and sweater (not too warm, not too light) I carry, but also my own earphones, my music – bland, and doesn't get interrupted by the cockpit telling me that thousands of feet below me we are passing over Greece or somewhere else. I also have my neck pillow, so my sleeping head (I'm optimistic I will sleep) will not loll afar, and eyeshades to block out visual interference, both "booty" from the rare time(s) I was upgraded to the ever-civilized Business Class.

I'm sure I am not unique, but people do seem to end up speaking to me, and by "speaking" I mean confiding. My husband jokes that I am the only one who can say: "Please pass the salt" at a dinner party, and end up with the person crying: "I know I have a bad relationship with my father." (I'm not joking, this has indeed happened!) Long transatlantic flights seem to have a loosening of lips effect on many people. So once ensconced in my space aloft, I try to be as uncommunicative as possible. At any rate, I politely say hello to my immediate neighbor (I hope for a window seat, so that I only have one neighbor), and soon put on my paraphernalia which is decidedly non-conducive to chatting.

Once I was traveling around the time of Yom HaShoah, Holocaust Memorial Day. My neighbor started crying soon after take-off. How could I sit there, eye-masked and neck-pillowed and not say a word?! In no time at all, she told me that she was on her way to Israel to say goodbye to the man she loved. This was not an obvious case of the vicissitudes of young love – she was young looking, but in her early seventies, and he, she told me, was in his eighties.

Both had been divorced over fifteen years before, both had had children, both had lost a child, she had two more, he had none. They had met on a cruise and had fallen in love as youngsters might, and had courted one another for over a year. During his last visit to her in the States, he had bought her an engagement ring. This was supposed to be the trip when they would have been married, she cried.

The story really began in the Holocaust, she told me. He was away from his

154

home when the nazis (a word I refuse to capitalize!!) rounded up the Jewish inhabitants, killed the men and boys and took the women away. He was blond and didn't look Jewish, and had heard about it from villagers in the town where he was studying. He refused to believe the horrible news, and went back to the village under cover of darkness. A young non-Jewish teenage girl whom he knew grabbed him and told him he had to hide, as the local villagers, his "friends" and neighbors were searching for any Jews who had gotten away and were either turning them in or killing them outright. Again he was too stunned to do anything, but to continue on to his home. It was only when he saw other people squatting in that home, did the awful truth sink in. She, this young girl, had gone with him and now was beseeching him to go to her home to hide. Her parents were away for a few days and no one would know.

She hid him in the area around the hearth. There were loose bricks and her family had constructed a very small space to hold firewood and other items for the hearth. For two years, he hid there. She brought him food and water in the middle of the night, and she removed his excrement at the same time. They left that eastern European country after the war, and married. No, they had never really been in love, but how could he not marry the person who had saved his life?

He had done financially well in his adopted country. They might even have been considered wealthy. They had a son. When his son, an avid aviator, was twenty-one years old, he had bought him a plane. On one of his son's maiden flights, the plane crashed, he was killed. The marriage didn't survive this tragedy. The couple separated and later divorced. He emigrated to Israel. Fifteen years later, he went on a cruise and met her, my neighbor on the plane.

"We were all set to get married, when he called and crying on the phone, he said I needed to come to Israel, so that he could say goodbye in person. I couldn't believe my ears – goodbye – what are you talking about, I shrieked. We're getting married!"

"No, he said we couldn't. His ex-wife had called, the first time in years, to say that she was diagnosed with terminal cancer. How could I not go and be with her, and tend to her needs in these last months or years as she had once done for me. At my age, this must be my last marriage."

What was there to say, here was yet another Shoah tragedy, haunting its victims to the end.

Sometimes the Diagnosis Is as Clear as the Nose on Your Face

She came into the office with her mother. They sat down. The mother, facing me on an angle, her back towards her daughter; the daughter, on the other, hand was facing me, but her shoulder was defensively up against her mom. *Well,* I say to myself, *they are both here together; that's one step in the right direction.*

She was a compact 14-year old; her brown hair neatly combed and pulled back, twisted and pinned to the back of her head with a clip that looks like the jaws of an uncompromising barracuda (or shark). I imagine it painfully clenched in the back of her head. Personally, those clips hurt me when they get their teeth firmly around any wisps of hair of my *pe'ah* (wig head covering). To do its job, the clip has to attach itself not only to my hair but also to some of my scalp, and I go through the day feeling no *kalut rosh* (lightheaded) for sure, but rather I get a painful reminder that I'm being held up by outside forces. I think of this when I look across my table at my new patient and her mom.

These associations and the feelings they have engendered in me are interesting. Why am I suddenly having visceral reactions to the back of her head? *Hum,* I think, *transferential and counter-transferential feelings. Associations to the back of the head of the 14-year old girl who is in reality sitting in front of me?! What am I avoiding?*

This is probably another example of counter-transference. (See above "Is Ice Meaty or Dairy" on counter-transference.) I take a more directive and less associative (or Freudian) approach to this "first impression" meeting with a girl and her mom. Essentially the intake is an opportunity for us all to meet and interview each other – me, her and she, me. And so, I take another look at her, and see what cues/clues ease across the table in the nanoseconds that our senses: visual, auditory, haptic (touch), olfactory search to make cognitive sense from this moment in time and create a pathway for a brain/behavior (neuropsychological) response.

Her eyes are staring right at me, almost challenging me to *do something.* I look again at the area around the challenging eyes and get a glimmer of understanding as to why my first conscious (or semi-conscious) thoughts were directed to the back of her head.

Hemda was staring out of her eyes, her eyebrows had a metal post with a ball at either end pierced through them – like two mini dumbbells that a weight-lifter might hold. Her cheekbones on both sides had a metal button, more like cylinders going through them. She had a a nose ring in each nostril. Her mouth had a stud on the lower lip, and her ears were rivulets of metal on the helix (outside of her ear).

I ask her name and age. I always ask questions that the person can answer, without making them an issue, and once we began talking, we were having a conversation. I scan the rest of her face and hands. "Any more piercings that I can't see right now?" Her mother begins to cry, silent tears running down their own rivers on her face. Hemda looks into my eyes and says two on either side of her chest. As she says this, I notice a slight lisp, and look more closely at her mouth and see something glistening on her tongue, another stud.

I say, because I am not just curious, but also interested: "Do you have pierc-ing in the same places that Michael Jackson had?" (To my modest assessment, Jackson was "The Poster Boy/Man," or The USA "role model" for dysfunctional child/adolescent/adult behavior – *big time*! Anyway, to be somewhat *au courante* for my patients, I read *Harry Potter*, *The News*, etc., and am not totally oblivious to what happens in the non-*frum* world. I try to temper this quest for informa-tion with *shiurim* and learning of *our* material.)

At any rate, Hemda's eyes open wide, she stares at my *pe'ah*, and says: "You *knew* Michael Jackson?"

"Well, he didn't *daven* in my *shul* (synagogue), but I *have* heard of him," I answer, somewhat tongue in cheek. She thought that this was quite funny (so did I). Her mother was still crying, but now she stares at me, wondering, what in the world was going on here. How could her daughter and I be sharing a joke! This, after all, was a crying matter!

I certainly agreed, but Hemda would never have opened up to me had I not "joined" with her a bit, and had she not recognized that I was trying to find a *modus vivendi*, a "place we could meet" in this conversation without being judgmental.

I ask Hemda to have patience with me, and say that almost every person who has piercing does them in a sequence. I ask her if we could take some time now and make a list of the sequence of these "events." I took out a ruler, colored pencils and paper, and with great care, enlisted her help to keep the lines and columns straight. After a few minutes, we had a chart. Each column had a head-ing that represented date, time, place on body of piercing, location of the shop that provided the service, and who was with her at the "event."

– What struck me at first was that Hemda had been alone each time she had a piercing. Usually there is peer pressure, or peer support for this type of acting out. As noted, Hemda had been alone for each of these painful occurrences.

– Secondly, the sequence of events began three months prior to our visit, in

November. Until then, she had only one hole pierced in each ear, done in early childhood and in her mother's presence.

– The ear studs were both made of silver and gold metals.

– The sequence of piercing was: lip/mouth; eyes; many more in the ears; and finally the tongue. The chest was the final two piercings. She told her mother about them and it immediately precipitated the visit to a host of psychologists, who didn't "click" with Hemda. And now, they came to me, a neuropsychologist, thinking that perhaps a visit to someone in this field would have a different result/diagnosis.

The chart laid it all out in front of us. I stop in my tracks. I say to her: "You've already figured out, that I am a 'little different' than the other psychologists your mother has brought you to see. I also really want to tell you how much I respect your *ometz* – which means 'bravery' and also 'guts.' You must also be the most loyal and respectful person I know." Now both she and her mother just stare at me, with their mouths ajar!

(This happens not infrequently in my office, when I kind of have that effect on people!)

I then ask them both what had happened in November. They look at each other and say nothing. I sit and wait. "Nothing, really, except my nephew's Bar Mitzvah." I sit and wait. Mother answers: "We all went away for a weekend to a kibbutz – the whole family, with all the children, cousins and everyone. It was a very special Shabbat."

I say: "When did he hurt you, Hemda?"

Whispering, with tears rolling down her face, she says: "In the morning, before anyone else was up."

"Was it the Bar Mitzvah boy?"

"No, another cousin."

She looked at me, relieved but still crying. Her mother was dumbfounded, crying and then crooning. She took her daughter to her breast, hugged, and rocked her.

My hypothesis was that Hemda was calling out for help, and no one had heard her speechless terror, nor did they see that she had been violated. Her trust in her family had been punctured in ways she could not discuss. Her family saw the changes in her personality, the signs that were right out there "as clear as the nose on her face." But no one was able to even imagine her horror. My clue was of course from the Book of Psalms:

> For the Lord will judge the cause of his people, and he will relent concerning his servants. The idols of the nations are silver and gold, the work of men's hands. They have mouths, but they do not speak; they have eyes, but they do not see; They have ears, but they do not hear;

and in their mouths there is no breath. May they who make them become like them, and every one who trusts in them! Bless the Lord, O house of Israel! Bless the Lord, O house of Aaron. Bless the Lord, O house of Levi! O, you who fear the Lord, bless the Lord. Blessed be the Lord from Zion, he who dwells at Jerusalem! Hallelujah! (Psalms 135:14–21)

No more words were needed. I said that they should call me the next day to decide how to go on from here. They thanked me, and left, holding onto each other.

FOR FURTHER READING:

P. A. Dewald, (1971), *Psychotherapy: A Dynamic Approach.* (New York: Basic Books, 1971).

L. Epstein, "The therapeutic function of hate in the counter-transference." *Contemporary Psychoanalysis,* 1977, 442–461.

S. Freud (1933), *New Introductory Lectures on Psychoanalysis. Standard Edition,* 22:5–182. (London: Hogarth Press, 1964).

J. Gardner, "Supervision of trainees: Tending the professional self," *Clinical Social Work Journal,* 1995, 23:271–286.

I've Got to Hand It to You:
Pre-Operative Intervention

An ARTICLE IN the *Journal of Medical Genetics* brought Leah to mind. Though it was years earlier, I remembered her very clearly.

It was late afternoon on a Thursday. The Neuropsychology Unit I head is in the same quadrant of the hospital as the Pre-Operative Clinic. As Friday is the "Sunday morning" of Israel, elective or scheduled surgeries do not take place on Friday mornings, so by early Thursday afternoon the Pre-Operative Clinic is empty.

I had a 4 p.m. appointment with a woman who was referred to me by the Genetics Department. From what I had read in the consultant's request (filled out by the geneticist with the patient's approval), her mother, aunt and sister had died of breast cancer. She and another sister had been found to have the BRCA1 mutation. This sister lived abroad and was in the process of having prophylactic treatment to avoid being a BRCA1 statistic. A third sister had been tested and found free of the genetic mutation.

I digress with some information about these mutations. Women with BRCA1 or BRCA2 mutations have a very high risk of developing breast and ovarian cancer – possibly as high as 70%.

Women with the mutation have options to reduce their risk of cancer including prophylactic mastectomy, prophylactic salpingo-oophorectomy (removal of ovaries) and chemo-prevention.

Prophylactic salpingo-oophorectomy offers both a breast cancer and ovarian cancer risk reduction. As a matter of fact, this surgery is associated with an almost 50 percent reduction in risk of breast cancer. However, there are side effects associated with the surgery that need to be considered.

In a July 2001 article,[1] it was reported that "among women of Ashkenazi Jewish (Eastern European) descent, carriers of one of the three most common BRCA1/2 mutations have a 40–73% chance of breast cancer by the age of 70 and a 6–28% chance of ovarian cancer. Few options exist for primary prevention of these cancers other than prophylactic surgical removal of noncancerous organs

---

1. K. Hurley; W. Redd, "Decision-Making Regarding Prophylactic Mastectomy and Oophorectomy in Ashkenazi Jewish Women Seeking Genetic Testing for BRCA1/BRCA2 Mutations," Mt. Sinai School of Medicine. See http://www.stormingmedia.us/85/8556/A855693.html.

in order to prevent occurrence of the disease. The primary aim of the study is to describe the levels of intention to undergo prophylactic mastectomy and/ or oophorectomy among Ashkenazi Jewish women seeking genetic testing for inherited founder BRCA1 and BRCA2 mutations, and to identify factors that influence decision-making about prophylactic surgery. To achieve these aims, 611 women undergoing genetic counseling and testing for inherited breast ovarian cancer risk will be assessed before their first genetic counseling session and three times in the year following notification of their genetic test results. Major accomplishments during the past year include establishing collaboration with parent study, completing all pre-recruitment tasks, and publishing a peer-reviewed article and abstracts related to the study."

The results of recent research of a large international study by Eisen et al. on BRCA1 and BRCA2 mutation carriers studied the age at oophorectomy and its association with breast cancer risk reduction. Women who underwent oophorectomy before the age of 40 years gained the greatest breast cancer risk reduction of 67%. Having the preventive surgery between the ages of 41 and 50 years also offered a significant breast cancer risk reduction; having the surgery after the age of 50 years did not significantly reduce a woman's breast cancer risk.

At our meeting, Leah started out by saying that I should not be insulted but she only had half an hour to speak with me. She did not feel she needed any help, her mind was made up, she was having the surgery.

"Okay, why don't you start at the end." I usually say this to new patients. Starting at the beginning is what they expect to be asked and I like to shake up the "homeostasis" so that the response I get is not something they have rehearsed or told many times to a bunch of professionals.

Here was a woman in her forties, a mother of teen children, who was prepared to be operated on, have a double mastectomy and oophorectomy. She elected to have re-constructive surgery at the same time. She had done her homework and knew that this was going to be a long operation and recovery. She was prepared. She didn't understand why the geneticist thought she needed to see a psychologist at all.

I agree. "You're right, it's a done deal. Maybe your doctor should have come instead. She might have issues with being the cause of your decision to break what is healthy now and then fix what wasn't broken!"

She looks at me askance. "You really think it could be her problem?"

I nod.

"Well it certainly isn't her fault! My sister, mother and aunt dying of breast cancer wasn't their fault. Once my sister was tested and found out that she was genetically predestined to get *it*, her dying wish was that no more of us should die of breast or ovarian cancer, we should *do* something. I'm *fine* with this decision, I haven't told my kids as I don't want to lay it on them and there is nothing they can do until many years hence if they *do* have the gene. You should just know my husband is *fine* with the decision, too."

There was something in how she said *"fine."* It was in her tone of voice giving me the perception that she was saying this through clenched teeth.

"I'm going to ask you a strange question. Do you have a picture of your family with you? Do you have a separate picture of your husband?"

"Not such a strange question, I do have both."

"You have a lovely family, may you have a lot of *nachat* (contentment) from them, but I haven't asked my strange question yet. Okay," I say taking a deep breath, "here comes the strange question: What part of your husband do you love the most?"

I was not quite sure where I was going with this; her answer would predicate my next step.

"You're right, that is a strange question, but the answer is quite easy for me – his hands. From the minute I met him, I have loved his hands."

"Are you familiar with a computer program called Photoshop®?"

"Yes, that is the program that you can take pictures and 'fool around with them,' isn't it?"

"Okay, looking at your husband's pictures here, I would like you to visualize him clearly in your mind, especially his hands. Okay?"

She nods.

"Ok, now Photoshop his hands to his shoulders."

She looks at me askance, a bit horrified, but as she closes her eyes "using Photoshop with her mind," a small smile appears on her lips.

"Okay, now move his hands to where his ears are; take a few seconds and 're-attach' his hands to his knees. Okay, now his elbows."

Smiling, with her eyes closed she says: "You have *no* idea where I'm moving them now, and I'm not telling you!"

I let a few minutes go by. Then I say: "Do you love him any less? Look into his eyes, how does he look?"

Leah looks at *me* hard. She is smiling now with a kind of "I can't believe this whole thing" look.

"Just *fine!*" Laughing now she gets up from her chair, shakes my hand and as she holds the door open, she says: "You know, I thought I was completely calm with my decision to do the surgery, and in a big way I was. As I said to you in the beginning of our meeting I didn't think I needed to speak to a psychologist at all." Smiling she says, "I have to *hand* it to you, though, you helped me a lot, thank you for that."

I smile gratefully and wish her good luck: *"B'Hatzlacha!"*

P.S. Years after the surgery, and Leah is *fine*.

FOR FURTHER READING:

"Risk reducing mastectomy: outcomes in 10 European centres." Published Online First: 7 November 2008. *Journal of Medical Genetics* 2009; 46:254–258.

"Oophorectomy for Breast Cancer Prevention in Women with BRCA1/-2 Mutations: Prophylactic Salpingo-oophorectomy" http://www.medscape.com/viewarticle/585896_3.

J. Gahm, G. Jurell, A. Edsander-Nord, M. Wickman, "Patient satisfaction with aesthetic outcome after bilateral prophylactic mastectomy and immediate reconstruction with implants," *Journal of Plastic, Reconstructive & Aesthetic Surgery* 2010; 63:2, 332–338.

The Case of the Soldier
Who Couldn't Whisper

T HEY WERE AFRAID, afraid for him and afraid for themselves.
He, let's call him Lochesh (Hebrew for "whisper"), could not whisper. When
they are out on dangerous missions, their faces painted in camouflage colors,
their uniforms and helmets adorned with branches, their life is dependent on
counting on each other. Having among them a soldier-in-arms who couldn't
whisper was life threatening.

The soldiers with whom he was posted went to their senior officer, who in
turn went to the medic who went to his supervisor. Eventually, Lochesh was
referred to me by the doctor of the army unit in which he was serving after he
had been checked by an ENT doctor and neurologists for muscle disorders such
as Dystonia that can affect the vocal cords. All of these more medical tests came
back WNL, which is medicalese for Within Normal Limits.

The army doctor referred him for a Neuropsychological Assessment, to see
if we could find the source of his problem in the intersect of neurology and
psychology.

After speaking with the referring physician, I thought of different types
of language or neuropsychology disorders that might cause this "not being
able to whisper" problem. Our method of problem solving is known as the
hypothesis-testing-branching-approach. We begin with a tree trunk of basic
tests and we use the resulting data to branch upward and outward as we hy-
pothesize what the problem might be, at each branch we go further out (using
specialized tests and subtests) to refine our thinking, onto the twigs. The goal,
to paraphrase an early mentor of mine, is that the data has to make neuropsychological sense.

There are many aspects of spoken language: Phonetics – the study of the
sounds of human speech, is concerned with the physical properties of speech
sounds (phones), and their physiological production, auditory perception and
neurophysiologic status; Prosody – the systematic use of sound to encode meaning; Morphology – the identification, analysis and description of the structure of
words; Syntax – the study of the principles and rules for constructing sentences
in natural languages.

Neuropsychologists are familiar with people who after a brain injury (or children with specific developmental disorders) cannot modulate their tone of voice or have difficulties with prosody. Psychiatry journals report cases of hysterical inability to speak (aphonia). After researching, I could not find another case of an inability to whisper.

Anticipating his visit, I had prepared the literature and the test protocol based on projected hypothesis. I must admit I was both curious and excited.

He walked in and sat down. Observing him, I must say that outwardly he looked just like most of the young soldiers that inhabit our world here and fill us with pride, anxiety and hope.

During the hour and a half intake he told me about the different sorts of doctors he had seen, how many days of service he missed and what he does for enjoyment – he loves solitary hiking and sharp shooting. I had a queasy feeling in the pit of my stomach. There is no objective test that I have studied or bought that produces this specific gut result, however years of experience and the differential diagnosis that usually explains this specific type of queasiness is scientific data to me. I guess that this gut form of diagnostics is part of the reason I became a neuropsychologist.

I ask him: "What do you hear when someone says 'whisper'?"

He replies: "I hear the voices louder and if I'll whisper I won't be able to drown them out!!"

"What do 'they' [the voices] say?"

"'Kill yourself!'"

"I am very grateful that you shared this with me. Now I'm going to tell you something that is just between us: If you listen to those voices you'll ruin my good record. No one kills themselves when they are my patients!"

That was some conversation stopper! He looks at me and just stares.

"You're a nice guy," I continue, "and I'm really serious about this. I promise I will get you help, the voices will stop and you will be okay again. But no guns, no *tiyulim* on dangerous terrain, and no walks by yourself. I'll speak to your folks and we'll work together to get you help, even by tonight.

"But promise me, and I trust you to keep your promise, nothing dangerous and especially NO whispering. You must speak loudly and clearly, no listening to those awful voices in your head, and NO killing yourself! Do we have a deal? Let's shake on it."

We did.

Psychosis is a condition in which a person isn't in contact with reality. Psychosis can take many forms, including:

- Sensing things that aren't really there (called hallucinations)
- Having beliefs that aren't based on reality (called delusions)

- Problems in thinking clearly (e.g., thought insertion, withdrawal, block, broadcasting)
- Not realizing that there is anything wrong with themselves (called lack of insight)

In Psychiatry, there are a number of disorders that come under the general title of the psychoses. They all differ in symptoms, but all are joined in that the person is in some way not experiencing reality like most people.

What causes psychosis? No one really knows. However, some popular theories include:

- Genetics
- A wiring problem in the brain
- A chemical imbalance in the brain/body
- Too much anxiety to stress
- It's a psychological defense mechanism
- Any combination of the above

Sometimes psychosis can be brought on by:

- Using illegal drugs (e.g., cannabis, LSD)
- Infections (e.g., Meningitis)
- Brain tumors (cancer)
- Epilepsy
- Head injuries

It is imperative to ask about hallucinations and the risk of self-harm and of harm to others. These may be closely related when command hallucinations instruct the person to commit self harm or harm others. Suicide is the chief cause of premature death among people with schizophrenia, with 4–13% of such people committing suicide and 25–50% making a suicide attempt.

Do people recover? Some people who experience a psychosis may only experience it once throughout their whole life (this is called a single episode); other people may have problems with it for the rest of their lives.

In Lochesh's presence, I called his parents and asked them to come to the office immediately. I called to find out which of the psychiatrists I knew would be available to see a new patient that very evening. I called and postponed my other appointments.

I kept my end of the deal and he kept his. He recovered from this Single Episode psychotic break.

I whisper thanks to Hashem that I have not heard anything new.

FOR FURTHER READING:

J. A. Ogden, *Fractured Minds: A Case-Study Approach to Clinical Neuropsychology*, (Oxford University Press, 2005).

D. E. Everhart, H. A. Demaree, A. J. Shipley "Perception of Emotional Prosody: Moving Toward a Model That Incorporates Sex-Related Differences," *Behavioral and Cognitive Neuroscience Reviews*, (2006) 5:2, 92–102.

L. M. Black and J. P. van Santen, "Expressive and Receptive Prosody in Autism." Presentation at the Child Development & Rehabilitation Center, OHSU, Portland, Oregon, May, 2005.

A. F. Hurstal, A. Wilson Gill, "Hysterical Aphonia (inability to speak) in Soldiers," *The Journal of Laryngology, Rhinology, and Otology*, 34:189–200 (Cambridge University Press, 1919).

http://easyweb.easynet.co.uk/simplepsych/psychosis.html.

When the Mouth Can't Speak

"I can't believe I finally reached you," says the harried voice at the other end of the phone. "I have been trying to call you for months."

"Trying to call me for months? I usually have a pretty good 'call back return' time," I answer.

"Oh no," she says, "I didn't leave any messages, nor did I reach anyone in your office. I meant I have been *meaning* to call you for months."

She went on to describe that her son was having social problems at home and at school. He was also in trouble with most of his teachers.

The first intervention with a patient occurs with the first phone call or, sometimes though rarely, with a letter requesting an appointment. Much information can be culled from a phone conversation – information that can be expanded upon during the first formal intake meeting.

So, I asked her to describe "social problems," which can be anything on the neuropsychological radar screen – from Frontal Lobe injury, to stroke, to Right Hemispheric Disorder, to Non-Verbal Learning Disabilities, to Autistic Spectrum, or anywhere else on the brain-behavior continuum. She answered that he had issues with personal cleanliness. I waited. He is *encopretic*. She began to explain the word. I told her I was familiar with the diagnosis.

According to the DSM-IV-TR®, 531 Elimination Disorders – and specifically Encopresis – appear in the following forms: With Constipation and Overflow Incontinence, and Without Constipation and Overflow Incontinence.[1] It is not to be confused with Enuresis (also an Elimination Disorder). Interestingly, Encopresis does not generally/normally occur at night.

Encopresis is diagnosed when:

- Accidentally or purposely, the patient repeatedly passes feces into inappropriate places, i.e., clothing, the floor.
- For at least three months, this has happened at least once per month.
- The patient is at least four years old (or the developmental equivalent).

---

1. *Diagnostic and Statistical Manual of Mental Disorders*, Fourth Edition; Text Revision, American Psychiatric Publishing, Inc. / Jaypee; 4th Edition, June 2000.

– This behavior is not caused solely by substance use (such as laxatives) or by a general medical condition, but through some mechanism that involves constipation. (Mechanisms that involve constipation could include hypothyroidism, side effects of medication, and a febrile illness that causes dehydration.)

Enuresis is diagnosed when:

– Accidentally or purposely, the patient repeatedly urinates into clothing or the bed. The clinical importance of this behavior is shown by either of the following: (a) It occurs at least twice a week for at least three consecutive months, or (b) It causes clinically important distress or impairs work (scholastic), social or personal functioning
– The patient is at least five years old (or the developmental equivalent).
– This behavior is not directly caused by a general medical condition (such as diabetes, seizures, or *spina bifida*) or by the use of a substance (such as a diuretic). It is described as Nocturnal Only; Diurnal Only; and Nocturnal and Diurnal.

Over the years, I have seen many different children with Encopresis, and many more with Enuresis. What amazes me still is how long it takes the parents, and truly the child, to get help.

One case in particular comes to mind. The father came first by himself. "You don't have to see my wife to understand the problem," he said. The child would "retain" for weeks, and have stomach cramps. They would give him stool softeners, and he would finally be convinced to go to the toilet. Once there, he pressured his parents to empty the room, i.e., take out the towels, soap, toothbrushes and anything else around. Then he would close the door to the toilet. Upon reentering they would find feces smeared all over the toilet bowl, bathtub and other surfaces.

"How long has this been going on?" I asked, assuming the answer to be days or weeks. "Six or seven months," said the father. *Astounding*, I thought, *and how sad that this poor child and his parents have had to suffer for such a long time.*

Generally speaking, in my experience with psychological intervention, the symptom should be gone within a month or so. After the first month, accidents may happen over the next three months. Once the cause/underlying issue is resolved, the behavior/symptom does not persist.

Back to the case at hand: At the appointed time, I invited Sara and Moses Banai and their 12-year old son Zvi into my office. They came in and all three moved their chairs so that they each sat at some distance from one another. *Umm*, I muse to myself, *three islands near each other; is that an archipelago*? But it might be a sign of communication difficulties between the family members.

I ask Zvi why he came. He put his hands to his ears to block out sounds and says in a quiet voice, "Ask them." I had a lot of information already, so I ask Zvi if he would mind sitting in the waiting room while I speak with his parents. A huge smile appears on his face. He held his hand out wordlessly toward his father who placed a seriously gadgetized cell phone in his son's outstretched hand, and he was out of the room.

His parents then began telling their story, which ran the gamut from embarrassment, shame and blame, to anger, tears and frustration – and other emotions in between. They began speaking at the same time and either echoed or disapproved of the other's remarks.

"Okay, it's my turn to talk now," I say. "I understand this part of the family story. Can you each tell me a bit about your families of origin?" I ask Moses to tell me about his wife's. That was a surprise. He began slowly, measuring his words so as not to wound with his usually verbal, explosive manner of speaking. Sara voicelessly looked at her husband with appreciative eyes, as if to thank him for not saying everything there was to say and for saying what he did with kindness.

I turn to Sara and say, "Your turn to tell me about Moses's side." As she spoke, he sat wordlessly. She spoke softly and no longer in the shrill tones I had heard when she was describing what went on at home. She was especially supportive of her husband when she described how hard his childhood was, and how hard it must have been (and still is today) for him to live in close proximity to his intransigent and overly strict parents.

Then I ask them to call Zvi on the cell phone, and ask him to come in.

I thanked him for letting me have this time with his parents and for being so patient. He seemingly ignored me and brashly told his father that he wants the same cell phone. "It's not fair that you have such a good one and I have a rotten piece of junk."

His parents look at each other and at me, shocked and embarrassed. I smile and think, *now we're cooking with gas*. Instead, I say, "Almost everything is negotiable. But you just have to learn how to ask, and especially how to speak with respect to the people from whom you want a favor."

"What did you talk about for such a long time?" he asks. I answer that we talked about his parents growing up, his grandparents, and things that are going on at home that are difficult for them all.

"Tell *him* to speak to me with respect first; tell *him* not to hit me; tell *him* not to scream; tell *her* not to cry and tell on me." Then he starts to cry.

Our time is up, but one very important thing came out of this meeting. I say, "Zvi, whatever you do until our next appointment in three days, do not stop leaking – please don't stop."

I got up from my chair. An hour and a half had gone by, and my next patient would be arriving any moment. When the family left my office, they were somewhat shell-shocked by what had transpired.

Three days later we met again.

By then, I had done some homework and printed out the *bracha*, the blessing of *Asher Yatzar* as well as drawn a mouth on a piece of paper.

When they arrive, I just speak to Zvi, telling him: "I have thought about our visit and the things you said, and I give you a lot of credit." All six eyes are on me. "Yes," I go on, "you are a very strong and powerful young man." He shows his arm muscles. "I know you think I am being sarcastic but I'm serious. Very few people would be strong enough to do what you do on a day-to-day basis. I hope I am able to give you some time off and help you out.

"But first I want to say, I know why it is so hard for you to talk about yourself and your problem. How can the mouth (I point to my picture of the mouth) talk when it is busy saying *Asher Yatzar* all day long!"

I take out the four copies of the *bracha* and give one to each of the parties in the room, myself included:

> Blessed are You, Hashem, our God, King of the universe, Who formed man with wisdom and created within him many openings and many hollows (cavities). It is obvious and known before Your Throne of Glory that if but one of them were to be ruptured or if one of them were to be blocked, it would be impossible to survive and to stand before You (even for a short period of time). Blessed are You, Hashem, Who heals all flesh and acts wondrously.

"Yes, of course your mouth can't talk and speak about the things that are troubling you, it is busy. It won't be easy, but I am sure, *B"H* (with God's help), we can help you out."

"That would be magic!" the father quips.

"Funny that you say that; but some people may agree with you that I am a 'magician/witch'." (In Hebrew, the word for a female Witch is a *very* uncomplimentary curse word!) Smiles and snickers from Zvi, and an embarrassed look for my reading the shade of aggression that Moses painted into his "that would be magic" comment.

"As a matter of fact, I have something I call 'Magic' that will help you out. But you have to have your parents' permission and help to be able to get the full benefit." Six eyes with question marks stare at me.

Over the years, I have developed a protocol for working with children/families where Encopresis is the presenting problem. It is a multi-pronged approach using metaphors; changing the nexus of control or agency – of who *owns* the symptom and therefore can *control IT*; by refocusing muscles; connecting or re-connecting the identified patient with their same sex parent; moving the conversation out of the toilet into a more socially acceptable and less personal room of the house; and a few more cognitive behavioral tools of the trade.

An important aspect of the whole enchilada is wearing a day-liner. In

Hebrew and Yiddish "day-liner" translates to "something white to keep the whites white" and in 1950s English it would be the same. In today's American vernacular, I might say (to boys): "It's Mr. Clean®."

"No," I pre-empt the Mom who is especially aghast. "He will *never* be the husband that 'has' the children. It is what I call 'Magic' and it *will* work."

I don't want to give the impression that therapy or psychological interventions are effortless, easy, fast working or even successful. Hashem and His way, our wonderful *berachot* and *halachot* are integrated into our personal and professional lives. I've had many teachers and to just cite two, the theoretical and clinical lessons of Salvador Minuchin and Milton Erickson are part of the *cholent* (stew) that has become my clinical toolbox.

This family helped themselves; they were just more ready to do so than earlier in their lives together. My seemingly *laissez faire* attitude allowed them to use their energy in a *goal-directed* and *empowering* way. Metaphors are neuropsychologically powerful tools as they *engage* and *enlist* many areas of the brain simultaneously.

I met Zvi with his parents three times, and the parents alone, three times. We also spoke on the phone, intermittently. Within a few weeks the symptom significantly decreased – Zvi was using the Magic and *it* was working. At the three-month mark, he and his father have worked out together to gain strength and muscles in the right places; the parents are instituting clearer boundaries vis-à-vis "what mouths say"; Zvi has begun to receive specific help in schoolwork and building social skills. There are still rough spots, but not any of the other sort.

The Third Star Had Just
Begun to Twinkle

It was just about Motzei Shabbat. The third star, of the three required to signify the end of Shabbat, was barely twinkling when I received a phone call. Thinking this must be from a family member, telling me something happened over the past twenty-six hours when we were out of communication, I answered, greeting the caller with a good week: "*Shavua Tov*, what happened?" I didn't expect to hear the voice of a somber Rav, who identified himself as a leader of a specific ultra-Orthodox group. He had previously consulted me by telephone over a case of a very troubled adolescent young man. My guess was that he was calling about a similar situation.

Would I be able to see a 9-year old girl right now!? This is an emergency. As I've written above, there are really no neuropsychological or even psychological emergencies. "No, no," he insisted. "The Rebbe agreed, you should see the child tonight." I tried to convince him that I was not trying to shirk responsibility, but rather direct them to the truly correct address. Would he be able to give me a run-down on what happened that made this such an emergency?

And so unfolded what was to be a twenty-six hour marathon case.

On Thursday afternoon, after school, this 9-year old was feeling ill. The family doctor's clinic was in the basement of the building in which they lived and the mother was comfortable in sending her down to wait on line for an appointment to see the doctor. She would follow soon. One thing led to another, with seven other children to take care of, the mother did not start going downstairs until about thirty minutes later, when she met her daughter walking up the steps. Her behavior seemed a little odd; she was kind of skipping and singing to herself, no signs of the earache she had been complaining about.

By dinner time, the young girl, who we will call Malca, was talking about the doctor's appointment she had, and how Refael (let's say that this was the doctor's first name) was a great man, and liked her a lot too, more than anyone else. The mother became very suspicious. What was this, her daughter speaking of a relative stranger, using his first name, and a doctor at that! As night approached, Malca was whispering to her sister that Refael had given her a gift. The mother overheard this and questioned what this gift was. "He put a

173

ring on me." (In Hebrew, that sentence can have two meanings. Both utilize the word *"tabaat,"* ring: one can mean placing a ring such as a wedding ring, and the other, a "ring" usually internally placed by a specialist in female medicine.) The mother looked at the girl's hand and saw no ring.

That is when the mother got really frightened. She started to scream and cry. She called her husband to come home immediately as they had a major tragedy on their hands. He came home and went to his Rav, and by three o'clock in the morning they had arrived at a plan. They would send Malca to the local hospital to be checked (with ultra-sound) by a female doctor to see if indeed any sign of a "ring" could be found. This appointment was scheduled for 9 a.m.

An hour earlier, at 8 a.m., the doctor (Dr. Refael) arrived in his office without knowing anything about what was going on with Malca, or by now, the community of rabbis who were consulted. At about 8:30, a group of four or five Haredi men appeared in Dr. Refael's small office. They barged in past the waiting room, and began to beat him up! They were from *Mishmeret HaTzniut*, literally, the "watchers of modesty," and they were punishing him for his dastardly deed. He had no idea what this was all about. They accused him of denying it and hit him harder. He dropped everything and ran out of the office. He managed to put together some of the story and called the Rav of the community to beg for assistance in this terrible miscarriage of "justice." The medical examination and ultra-sound revealed nothing was in the child.

It was close to Shabbat and all decided to wait until after Shabbat to continue.

"So, you have to help us," said the Rav, as he spoke to me in the male plural form of grammar, for modesty sake. By now it was close to 11 p.m., Saturday night. I called another Rav I know who works with troubled teen girls to meet with the father. I wondered how a 9-year old Haredi girl would think in terms that would be unfamiliar to many a seminary girl. I wondered if this hyper-arousal or hyper-informativeness could be a result of being exposed to an unhealthy environment at home. Maybe Malca may have said "doctor" when possibly her father was being untoward to her. I felt that in a meeting with the person I sent them to, the father's relationship with his daughter would be assessed. I gave them an appointment to come to the clinic (at the hospital) at 8:30 a.m.

By 7 a.m., I was told that the father seemed fine and very normally concerned with his daughter and this situation.

The parents and Malca came on time. I spoke to them for a short time together, and then told Malca that I understood she had an earache and saw the doctor, and then had another visit with another doctor on Friday. I was a different sort of doctor and wouldn't be touching her at all, but rather we would draw pictures, speak and tell stories and work with blocks and other things. She seemed relieved, and let her parents leave without as much as a goodbye. In light of her past three days, I found that this, her being able to part with them so easily a little odd, to say the least. I did my psychological and neuropsychological assessments and in the course of the next few hours began to get a more and more disturbing picture of this young girl. The behavior I was seeing could be signs of some neurological disorder or (unfortunately, more likely) fragmenting of her emotional state – a sign of psychosis. Childhood psychosis is uncommon, but not rare. As a last ditch effort to explain the behavior in neurological and not psychiatric terms, I spoke to the pediatric neurology department about doing an electroencephalogram (EEG) which is a test to detect abnormalities in the electrical activity of the brain. Maybe what I was seeing could be some form of epileptic seizure and not delusions. By this time, the father had gone home, and the mother had not come with enough cash or a referral to do this examination that would be covered by their medical insurance. I was concerned that if they left, they wouldn't come back and that Malca's situation would deteriorate further without proper medical attention. I took out my checkbook and paid for the EEG, and the father later repaid me.

The neurologist looked at me after reading the EEG results, and said: "This is one for you, not me."

I set up an appointment with a child psychiatrist for the next morning. If she confirmed the psychiatric diagnosis, she would be able to begin treatment to stabilize Malca. I sent them home and wrote up a report, it was now close to 7:30 p.m. on Sunday. I called the Rav who had referred the case to me. By this time I had the parents' signatures on a confidentiality release, so that I could speak to him about their daughter. He told me that they were getting a Beit Din together that evening to exonerate Dr. Refael.

At close to midnight, I received a phone call, the Rav who interviewed the father was called to appear before the Beit Din to give his testimony. Was there something I wanted to add? "Yes," I said, "not only should they prepare a letter clearing the doctor's name, but they should also 'slap' the proverbial hands of the *Mishmeret HaTzniut*, for taking the law into their own hands, or fists should I say!"

"One more thing," I added.

"Yes?" he anxiously said.

"Why didn't they want to interview me?"

"Oh, Dr. G.," he said with exasperation, "when will you ever learn!?"

Moli's Story: The Heroism and Optimism of a 15-Year Old and Her Mother

SHE WAS A cute teenager of fifteen from a development town in the southern part of Israel. She couldn't believe that her usually strict Moroccan-born father and French-born, chic but very protective mother, had allowed her to go on a three-day trip to Tiberias with friends.

Sitting at the bus stop, she had a strange sensation around her mouth. It almost felt as if her mouth was being pulled to the right. Her friends were off buying last minute candies for the trip, and when they returned she didn't bother to say anything because her mouth had returned to itself.

She returned home and she just forgot about the whole thing, enjoyed herself, her friends, the trip and life in general.

What she didn't know then, was that this would be the end of her carefree life, and to a great extent, the end of her childhood – her teenage years.

Less than a week later, the strange feeling around her mouth returned. She went to show her mother, to see if her feeling that her mouth was being pulled up to the right, on the inside, was noticeable on the outside, too. As she was telling her mother, she lost consciousness, shook, trembled and collapsed in her mother's arms. She had what was later described to her as her first epileptic seizure.

Her life, and her family's life, had irrevocably changed in that moment.

The next eighteen months included repeated seizures, diagnoses as epileptic, as well as a non responsive/negativistic patient, who was held responsible for the fact that the medication prescribed did not seem to work. It was implied to both Moli and her mother that had Moli taken the medication as prescribed, she would not be having these recurring seizures. As the months progressed, Moli gained a lot of weight which seemed to be a side affect of the medication. This fact did not enamor Moli to the medication, as one might expect of any normal 15-year old.

As the months progressed, Moli began to withdraw from her school and social set. As time went on, Moli's "body integrity" continued to dissipate. Eighteen months after the initial attack, Moli's right arm was somewhat paralyzed as was her leg.

On yet another hospitalization in a noted Tel Aviv medical center for evaluation of medication failure, her regular neurologist was ill. In the course of Grand Rounds, a visiting neurologist with a whole entourage of medical students introduced "this case" as a Brain Tumor. For Moli's mom, who understood just a little English, this was the first time someone had used the word "tumor" in describing her daughter. Then both mother and daughter asked questions and told the doctor this fact. He was surprised, as to him it seemed obvious that a Brain Tumor was the diagnosis.

What about her MRI, she was asked. What MRI, Moli had never had a MRI, though she had undergone CT scans, which were inconclusive.

Mom was told to get Moli a MRI as soon as possible. This was not as easy as one might expect. Moli's Mom was told that there was at least a two-week wait for emergency MRIs. But she was told, that she was nice, and if she asked the overworked MRI staff nicely, they might accommodate her. With eighteen months behind her, she had just a minimal amount of energy left to cajole the MRI staff. But Moli is blessed with an optimistic, resilient, and persistent mother. She told them of her daughter's plight, the year and a half, without knowing that a Tumor may be at the base of the difficulties, the progressive loss of motor functions, hand and foot. They agreed, and Moli had her MRI by the end of that day.

The tumor was identified as 3 × 4 cm.

A date for surgery was made. The parents, through the help of Rabbi Elimelech Firer, the founder and head of Ezra LeMarpeh, a non-profit organization that helps the sick, had researched the hospital and surgeon they wished. Within a week, they had an appointment. Moli was prepared and ready to go. With nervous anticipation, they waited for ten o'clock, the time designated for the surgery. However, at close to three o'clock that day, the neurosurgeon told them that he had had an emergency, and could not operate on her that day. Another date was given.

Who can even find words for the frustration and disappointment Moli and her family felt. To know a tumor was present, to have found a neurosurgeon, to have a date, time, to prepare oneself for the worst, and then to be postponed. What a crushing experience!

A new time and date was given for the surgery. Though Moli felt like bolting yet again, she was unable to do so, and two days after the initial date, she underwent her operation. The tumor that was removed had grown further, and was 4 × 4 cm. when it was removed.

Within a relatively short period of time, she was almost back to her physical self. Moli had gone a great distance. She was in another place and time as compared to her peers. She was not the same person. She did not want to go back and pick up the pieces of her life before the surgery. She did not wish to continue a "life interrupted." She wanted to start a new life, a newborn life, not an interrupted life.

This course was one that she acted out. Rather than expressing in words these feelings, she acted in a fashion that isolated her from her peers, and created situations that caused the school to ask her to leave.

When she found another high school, she was told that she had missed a lot of material (school work), and would have to redo the grade again. An embarrassment and yet another attack to her sense of self, but one which she was prepared to withstand in order to continue her education. She knew that her future, now medically assured, would not be realized if she did not complete at least her high school and Bagrut – the National Matriculation examinations.

The new school was prepared to grant her special dispensations for tests. However, the Ministry of Education required that she undergo a neuropsychological evaluation in order to verify that she indeed required the extra help which she and the school's guidance counselor were asking for.

It was as if having had seizures for eighteen months, receiving medication that did not help the medical situation, gaining weight because of negative reaction to the medications, withdrawing in shame from friends, school and family, having the surgery, the crushing fear of pre-operation brain surgery, and then the conflict of disappointment tinged with relief when the surgery was unceremoniously postponed. All the while knowing that your life was at stake. After recovery from a trauma most of us will never come into contact with, Moli who has overcome so many adversarial situations accepted the embarrassment of being forced to repeat a year in a grade.

Now the Ministry of Education was requiring this teenager to undergo a full neuropsychological evaluation to prove that she is "damaged." Could the Ministry of Education possibly see this as an educational response? Could they fathom the opening of psychic scars that a "damaged" diagnosis could cause?

Instead of using the neuropsychological assessment as another assault against this heroic teenager, we tried to reframe the referral question. The object being, not to emphasize past problems, but rather, the future – by relating to the positive results. The assessment would help Moli, evaluate her strengths to circumvent her weaknesses, in an effort to emphasize her options for achieving education and professional goals.

I B, Ther4 I M – But Wht 'bout Me 2?!@?!

Note: *"HE" AND "SHE"* here are a conglomeration of quite a number of similar yet different cases.

He called and said he was having terrible headaches; the headaches felt as though there were stones in and on top of his head. I ask if he'd already been to a physician to rule out medical/neurological diagnosis. *He* says, ". . . the neurologist was the doctor who referred me to you."

"Okay," I respond, as my son would say, "let's meet once in a row."

I generally find that people feel that "a meeting" with a psychologist is necessarily many, if not endless appointments. This doesn't fit my *Weltanschauung* – worldview. What if the chemistry is all wrong on both sides of the table? What if this is an issue I know *nothing* about – dentistry or ophthalmology, for example, or don't feel I have enough experience to do a reasonable, "Good-Enough" (neuro) psychology.

So *He* comes at the appointed time. *He* says: "I brought *Her* too, but I'd like to start with you first." *"Her"* turns out to be his wife. Well, she could have been his mother, grandmother or friend (among other possibilities).

Okay, let's chat. After about half an hour. *He* takes a breath. I say something like this:

"Correct me if I am wrong. If I understood you correctly . . . may I call you Rip or Honi?" (Referring, of course, to Rip van Winkle, or in our culture, Honi HaMaagel, both of whom, according to the stories related to them, are reported to have slept for over seventy years.)

"At any rate, sometime about two/three/four months and/or years ago you went into a 'deep sleep' and just woke up with a mammoth headache. You looked around your bedroom and it didn't look like your bedroom at all. No carpets, No familiar furniture and lots of stuff that you don't remember buying. Maybe even a baby crib or two. Where were you, how did you get here and more importantly . . ."

He interrupts: "The nightmare I woke up into is worse than the one I had sleeping."

"Wow," *He* says, "My headache seems to be lightening. It feels like some of the stones are coming off."

"Do you recall with whom you came to this office?" I ask gingerly, afraid of any answer besides "Yes." Mercifully, *He* answers in the affirmative.

He brings *Her* in. It is *Her* turn to speak. *She* looks at him with a mixture of frustration, pity and anger. *Her* time *here in Israel* (this sounds like a jail sentence, I say to myself) was first spent going to *shiurim*, calling on the phone and meeting new and old friends. Then it was spent going to doctors, pre-pregnancy and if they were fortunate, after she was pregnant. They also went back and forth to *"home"* (fill in a country name anywhere in the globe other than Israel).

She will have/or did have a baby. Now there are few, if any, *shiurim*. Much less time spent (or any sort of time spent) with the "Learning/Not Learning *Him*," and a lot of time spent doing laundry. For the most part, aside from the pain of childbirth (they must have skipped that part of the Book of Genesis at seminary/high school), that is the single biggest secret her mother/*kallah* teacher forgot to tell her. Basically, she has one enormous child – *Him*, and a few smaller one(s), all of them crying for her attention.

She, too, is wondering why, if she did everything right – including having the best engagement story/picture on www.onlysimchas.com – is she not having the "happily ever after" life promised to those who do "everything right?!" But, *She* is in *no way* complaining, only wondering. I notice that they both speak *at* me and *at* each other.

We agree to meet another time this week, as we are clearly not done with intake.

As I don't see many couples in my work, I have only heard a variant of this story from someone with physical/neuropsychological symptoms. I have, though, consulted with colleagues at Nefesh Conferences. The resounding answer to my perplexing queries was, *yes*, they too, have seen many "Hims and Hers."

What is happening? Any answer is too facile.

It is a very complex, sociological/religious/pragmatic/psychological/educational issue. What *answer* could cover all this ground? What *test* could render a *diagnosis*? What experimental paradigm has been used to statistically prove this is (a) a phenomenon; (b) a problem; (c) even exists?

So, let's go with the hypothesis *that this situation is just a figment of my imagination.* Let's say it has been true of *all* previous generations. For, who gets married "older and wiser?" The majority does not. If we all did wait for that sort of age and wisdom, the world would be inhabited by many fewer people, not just for the reason that fertility is directly related to timing, but also we would all be paralyzed into inaction because we "pondered too much."

What can we do now? How is it that today this seems to have created (this is a figment of *my* imagination) plague-like invalids. Why now, why here?

This is too easy a response, I know, but here is what I recommend to *Him* and *Her*.

"Do you want to stay married to each other?"

They bashfully look at me and at one another; clearly this is a topic that has come up before.

"Yes," they answer, "we do."

(I smile at the first-time use of the word "we.")

"I'm not sure, but I may be able to help you. You will have to see me a few times a month and other professionals including rabbis and rebbetzins, all of whom have more experience than I do working with couples."

A few seconds go by, "Okay," He/Him and She/Her answer, after nodding to one another. I have come to understand this as: "His mom will pay/your dad will pay/my dad/mom will pay."

"Now for setting up your contract with me; I won't work with you unless you agree to the following *immediately*:

"(1) Get rid of your iPod."

Horror on their faces, "What about *shiurim*?" they ask in unison. I note that this is the first time they agree on something!

"(2) Get rid of the iPod with podcasts."

They look amazed at how "in" I am.

"(3) Get rid of text messaging on your cell phones."

Now they are both screaming at me. "What if there is an emergency?!"

"Call each other on the phone, the cell or landline phone. *No*, and I mean *no* text messaging to each other or to anyone!

"(4) Close down your separate email accounts – you can write an 'away' message or 'Gone Fishing' for all I care, but close them down.

"(5) Open a combined email account; you can call it by your former last names hyphenated, or any fish or animal that is kosher." (This saves Barracuda, Shark, etc. for nameless other individuals.)

They are staring numbly at me.

"(6) Internet browsing is for a specific hour and a half of the day, in which *both* of you are present *together*, and sharing the time."

Now they are more alive, but silent. There *is* a life-line *out*.

I add:

"(7) No YouTube or Facebook."

They look like they are sitting *shiva*, mourning for a loved one (or loved-many).

"(8) Visits to onlysimchas.com are only during the proscribed 1.5 hours of *together* browsing time.

"See you in two days." They silently gather their stuff and leave.

Later, my secretary says she is a bit embarrassed but would like to tell me something: "Please, please, please, don't be insulted, but do you realize that more people than *you* could ever imagine leave your office smiling and saying, '*She* is *really* the one who is crazy'?"

Another success, I smile to myself. If we are lucky, they will not become a statistic of early divorce for *they have no idea why* because *they are from a good family* and *they really liked one another* and seemed to be *so in love* and *enjoyed being together.*

Out "Darn" Spot

In shakespeare's macbeth, Lady Macbeth, plagued by guilt for her part in the killing of Duncan, utters the famous line "Out, Out ['Darn'] Spot!" while in a state of almost manic sleepwalking. "The king and queen persist in imagining that physical actions can root out psychological demons, but the play is an exposition of how wrong they are" (*Brush Up Your Shakespeare*, Michael Macrone).

She was referred to assess if EMDR might help with her nightmares and fears.

When she arrived, there was no way of knowing or understanding the depth of her seemingly irrational fear of elevators.

Other psychologists using dynamic and traditional modes of psychotherapy helped her understand that what she felt was an irrational fear might really be her unresolved and repressed feelings of guilt surrounding her mother's recent death.

These therapists explained that people, who lose a significant love object, frequently go through a period of suffering from guilt. Consequently the nightmares they develop of being entombed in an elevator could be seen as part of the process of empathizing with the person who died. This perspective of her difficulties was helpful for a while, she reported, but the feelings of choking and gasping for air soon returned to what they had been prior to therapy.

"How do you think I might be able to help you?"

"I was just at the pulmonologist for my belabored breathing and he suggested I speak to you as my lungs are as clear as a whistle," she smiles ironically, all the while breathing with great gasps. "Can you help me get rid of this feeling?

"A psychiatrist, Dr. X, also referred me to you, but, if you don't mind, I won't use his name because I'm about to quote his *lashon hara* about you. He wasn't very sure you could help me. He says that, though you are a senior level psychologist, you don't follow the accepted ways of doing things." (My ears perk up, because, for the first time in the conversation, I detected a respectful tone in this *wannabe* patient.)

"Also," she goes on, "my grandson helped me Google you, and I really do think that the psychiatrist is wrong and you might be the very person to help me. I feel as though I am gasping for air and yet afraid to open my mouth to let the air in.

"Do you see this spot on my neck – it may be hard to see today – at times it is a lot larger than other times. When I look in the mirror and see it, I get a panic attack. I've been to dermatologists and plastic surgeons and they say 'it is all in my head,' a statement which makes me cry in frustration, anger and, most of all, embarrassment."

My ears perk up at the word "embarrassment."

"I want to leave my room in the senior citizens hotel. Sometimes I do. But I can never leave the building alone," says this fashionably dressed and well-coiffed septuagenarian.

This said, she sat back and waited to see if I would pick up the gauntlet. She gave the impression that not only was she an intelligent woman, but one who could see the ironies of life and especially the peccadilloes (slight faults) of others. I assumed that was the case, considering that I do like to be intellectually stimulated by a challenge.

As she was relaying her story, I kept asking myself what is the neuropsychology here? What type of standard neuropsychological assessment might unleash the answers to her behavioral/medical responses? Her responses to elevators seemed to relate more to be post-traumatic stress reactions than standard, unresolved mourning, or survivor guilt – though life has taught me that there is no "standard/normal" – only many single cases!

I ask her if she would bear with me and walk to the elevator bank further down the hallway from the Neuropsychology Unit, which is on the fifth floor at Shaare Zedek. She gives me a long, hard stare, and smiles: "Dr. X was right, you don't do anything anyone else does! Okay, let's go."

As we walked to the elevator, she was breathing loudly, all the while, answering my questions about her visit to Israel. I told her that we would wait for an empty elevator, and that I would press the stop button at any point she felt she couldn't breathe, and that we would only go down one floor.

When the elevator arrived, she looks at me and grasps her neck with her hand, much like choking herself and, in a very small voice, says: "I can't do it, I can't even go in." I say "Fine," and we walk back to my office. I did notice, though, that she had finger marks on her neck. When we got back she took out her compact from her bag, and as she was re-fixing her face. Looking at her neck, she says: "See, here are the marks again." She obviously had not recalled that she had squeezed her neck herself. *Hmmm, this sounds very promising*, I think to myself.

Our time was up and we made another appointment for two days hence. I ask her to pay attention to any daydreams, night dreams or nightmares she may have and jot them down till we would meet again.

She came to our appointment on time, again looking very well-dressed in a coordinating outfit of dress, shoes, hat, and handbag. She was also carrying a small notebook.

She smiles, and proudly says: "I did my homework, I wrote down all my dreams, day and night, and though I am somewhat scared, I am also very excited about this meeting."

I explain EMDR and set up a Safe Place for her to imagine when any thoughts that came up might be difficult. I ask her to choose one of the dreams from the notebook as a focus of what would be our first EMDR session.

She describes an image of being in an elevator going to a wedding hall. There were other people in the elevator and it was a little crowded. She felt that she was being pushed into a corner. She begins to breathe in a labored fashion. I continue to do the bilateral movements. All of a sudden, she stops and says that something very odd happened. The elevator changed into her bedroom in her old house and the man next to her changed into her ex-husband.

"Go with that," (pretty standard EMDR statement when things look like a breakthough is about to happen).

"I am upstairs, in the laundry room, I feel I am being pushed against the wall."

Silence, then I whisper: "Go with that."

She continues: "And all of a sudden, I see my ex-husband with his hands around my throat. He is trying to strangle me!"

She is perspiring profusely and breathing very heavily. Her tone of voice though is strong, giving the impression that she is both surprised and angry.

"How dare he put his hand around my neck! You know what, I'm not so scared – I'm really angry with him for being drunk again. I had called the police the last time, but look what good it did! As soon as I realized he was drunk, and I was more angry than scared, I stepped on his foot really, *really* hard and ran out of the small laundry room to my bedroom and locked the door. I didn't want to scream and wake up the kids.

"I knew in a few hours he'd come out of it and begin knocking on the door, crying that he was so sorry and that I should forgive him.

"That night, before he woke up, I called the police and they helped me leave the house with the kids."

She opens her eyes, looks at me with resolve and says: "You know, I haven't thought about that in thirty years, I put it out of my head. I felt I needed to move on. The police had taken pictures of the scene and the marks on my neck and testified in court for me. I got full custody of my children and moved on, until the breathing problems began."

"Can you recall when the breathing difficulties began again?"

"Yes, I was at a family wedding and my ex-husband's cousin who looks a lot like him walked into the elevator.

"Oh my, the laundry room in my old house wasn't much bigger than an elevator!"

Once again, I am in awe of the power of Hashem's creations, the strength of this woman to save herself and her children, in more than one way, in order to survive. Now, in her new home in Israel, she was starting life over again, feeling good about her independence and joining her children and grandchildren who had previously made Aliya.

Her "declaration of independence" was achieved in a "breath-taking" moment. On the brink of a different independence, living in a new country – a new beginning, the circumstance of being in the elevator and seeing her ex's cousin, brought the buried – or I would say, "safe deposit" – memories out into the open.

We had a few more sessions, essentially consolidating what was achieved. At the last one, she brought me a plant, which she had nursed to health and it was now flourishing, transplanted in a beautifully decorated pot.

I Heard You Like a Challenge

MY PRIVATE NUMBER at the office rang. Now I am quite reachable, most people have my number. I don't answer phones during work hours (or I'd just be answering phones all day and not working). The exception to the last point is my nuclear family.

So I answered the phone, thinking it *was* a family member. It wasn't. Instead it was a medical doctor who had convinced the hospital switchboard operator that this was indeed a neuropsychological Emergency (with a capital *E*), and she needed to let the call go through immediately.

The doctor apologized profusely upon hearing my worried "hello," and then my very cool "yes." But he really had an emergency on his hands, and then said the magic words, "I heard you like a challenge." We then arranged a time to talk.

Okay, so what is the challenge? His patient, Bracha, was a 54-year old woman who had been diagnosed as having neurofibromatosis (NF2) at age of 14, and over the past forty years had undergone many brain surgeries to remove the continually growing tumors. These lifesaving surgeries (as the tumors were space occupying and threatened her life and cognitive abilities) were not without their own complications. Today, she was hemi-paretic (paralyzed on one side of her body), deaf, and severely vision-impaired.

"But that's not the emergency," he said. "She has been living with her widowed father, and now he is unable to care for himself and for her, and is going into a senior citizens' residence/convalescent hospital." I knew more information was coming and just waited quietly at my end of the conversation. "Our problem is that Social Services doesn't know where to place Bracha, and that maybe a neuropsychological evaluation could give us information. The emergency is that there is now a place for her father and we can't hold it open for more than a week – and we have no spot for Bracha!

He was right. He had ignited the challenge area of my brain, and certainly gotten my attention.

In preparation for Bracha's visit, I did some research. What is Neurofibromatosis? To begin, it is a synonym for Von Recklinghausen's Disease, a nerve disorder often leading to tumors on the nerves and now divided in two geneti-cally different forms: NF1 and NF2, with different clinical features.

Friedrich Daniel Von Recklinghausen (1833–1910) was a German patholo-gist. Neurofibromatosis was first described in 1768 by Mark Akenside, later in 1793 by Wilhelm Gottlieb Tilesius von Tilenau, in 1849 by Professor Robert William Smith of the University of Dublin, and by Rudolf Virchow in 1863. Recklinghausen's detailed description was of the autopsy findings in a 55-year old female and a 47-year old male, and so the disorder is named for him.

Some of you may have read or heard about Joseph Carey Merrick (1862–1890), known as "The Elephant Man." Leading authorities at the time stated he suffered from *elephantiasis*. This is a disorder of the lymphatic system that causes parts of the body to swell to a huge size. In 1976 a doctor postulated that Merrick suffered from neurofibromatosis, a rare disorder that causes tumors to grow on the nervous system. Photos of Merrick, however, do not show the brown skin spots characteristic of the disorder. Also, his disfigurement came not from tumors but from bone and skin overgrowth. Unfortunately, even today people still (wrongly) call neurofibromatosis the "Elephant Man disease."

The 1980 movie "The Elephant Man" portrays how at first a doctor and then others (including royalty) came to see the intelligent, sensitive man behind the grotesque deformities. The universal message of tolerance of difference found in Joseph Merrick's story touched and moved those who saw it. But what most people don't know is that it took one hundred years for doctors to correctly identify his medical condition.

It wasn't until 1996 that the answer to the mystery of what affected Mer-rick was found. A radiologist, Amita Sharma of the U.S. National Institutes of Health, examined x-rays and CT scans of Merrick's skeleton (kept at the Royal London Hospital since his death). Dr. Sharma determined that Merrick had Proteus syndrome, an extremely rare disorder that was only identified in 1979.

WHAT IS NEUROFIBROMATOSIS?

The neurofibromatoses are genetic disorders of the nervous system that primar-ily affect the development and growth of neural (nerve) cell tissues. These disor-ders cause tumors to grow on nerves and produce other abnormalities, such as skin changes and bone deformities. Although many affected persons inherit the disorder, between 30 and 50 percent of new cases arise spontaneously through mutation (change) in an individual's genes. Once this change has taken place, the mutant gene can be passed on to succeeding generations.

Scientists have classified the disorders as neurofibromatosis type 1 (NF1) and neurofibromatosis type 2 (NF2). NF1 is the more common type of the neurofibromatoses. In diagnosing NF1, a physician looks for changes in skin appearance, tumors or bone abnormalities, and/or a parent, sibling or child with NF1. Symptoms of NF1, particularly those on the skin, are often evident at birth or during infancy and almost always by the time a child is about ten years old. NF2 is less common. NF2 is characterized by bilateral (occurring on both sides of the body) tumors on the eighth cranial nerve.

The tumors cause pressure damage to neighboring nerves. To determine whether an individual has NF2, a physician looks for bilateral eighth nerve tumors, and similar signs and symptoms in a parent, sibling or child. Affected individuals may notice hearing loss as early as the teen years. Other early symptoms may include tinnitus (ringing noise in the ear) and poor balance. Headache, facial pain, or facial numbness caused by pressure from the tumors may also occur. NF2 is the type that Bracha was diagnosed as having.

IS THERE ANY TREATMENT?

Treatments for both NF1 and NF2 are presently aimed at controlling symptoms. Surgery can help some NF1 bone malformations and remove painful or disfiguring tumors; however, there is a chance that the tumors may grow back and in greater numbers. In the rare instances when tumors become malignant (three to five percent of all cases) treatment may include surgery, radiation or chemotherapy.

For NF2, improved diagnostic technologies (such as MRI) can reveal tumors as small as a few millimeters in diameter, thus allowing early treatment. Surgery to remove tumors completely is one option but may result in hearing loss. Other options include partial removal of tumors, radiation and, if the tumors are not progressing rapidly, the conservative approach of watchful waiting. Genetic testing is available for families with documented cases of NF1 and NF2.

WHAT IS THE PROGNOSIS?

In most cases, symptoms of NF1 are mild, and patients live normal and productive lives. In some cases, however, NF1 can be severely debilitating. In some cases of NF2, the damage to nearby vital structures, such as other cranial nerves and the brainstem, can be life-threatening.

So when Bracha arrived, I thought I was prepared. I had typed questions to some of the basic tests, and had enlarged them as much as possible so as to make reading and communicating with her easier. I had planned on using the computer to write to her, and she would answer me directly, as she had no problem speaking. However, a bit of a problem was anticipated as a result of the possible facial paralysis. What I was not prepared for was Bracha herself.

As I noted before, she was fifty-four years old. She was also highly intelligent, well-read, a ballet aficionado and a host of other things that came to light in the hour *she* interviewed *me*, and told me about some of her life experiences! The "interview" began with her asking me questions about NF2 and grading my answers. I passed, she told me, because I was interested in learning and had obviously done my homework. And most important, I had begun the visit by telling her that *she* was the expert on her case. The two and a half hours with this fascinating woman flew by. At its conclusion, I told her I'd have to let all the information she gave me settle in, and I'd be in touch with her through her father the next day.

All night, I thought about her, and the dilemma of what place to recommend for her. In the morning, I came up with a thought. I called the doctor, and asked, "Why not place her with her father in the same facility?" I went on: "She is not 'culturally deaf/hearing /physically impaired' as a result of her motor problems; she doesn't know and can't learn how to Sign (Israeli Sign Language); she was only recently visually impaired; and the paralyses were also relatively new conditions. So she probably won't fit in with a group residential arrangement with others who have had a lifetime to prepare."

There was silence on the other end of the phone. Among the ideas being considered was a residence for the visually impaired; the deaf and physically handicapped were descriptive of the conditions Bracha had. No one had suggested the senior citizens' option. Finally, "Why separate her from her dad? As a bonus, the others in the senior citizens' home would love having such a 'young,' stimulating person around."

"We'll do it! See?" he said, "I knew you'd like the challenge."

FOR FURTHER READING:

www.ninds.nih.gov/disorders/neurofibromatosis.
Wikipedia – Volker Paech, M.D., and Claudio Crisci.
http://www.wrongdiagnosis.com/medical/von_recklinghausen_s_disease.htm.

Two Is Better than One, and the Cord of Three Strands . . .

Written with Chaim K., Jenny S. and Mimi N.

I WAS NERVOUS. This was going to be my first group in a very long time. How would I segue to a foursome from a *"sicha b'arba einaim"* – literally, four-eyed conversation – the vernacular for the French *tête-à-tête*, "head to head," or in English: a private conversation between two persons?

Group therapy is different from individual therapy in a number of ways, with the most obvious difference being the number of people in the room with the psychologist. Originally, group therapy was used as a cost-saving measure, in institutional settings where many people needed psychological treatment and there were too few psychologists to provide the treatment. However, in conducting research on the effectiveness of therapy groups, psychologists discovered that the group experience benefited people in many ways that were not always addressed in individual psychotherapy. Likewise, it was also discovered that some people did not benefit from individual therapy.

In group therapy, you learn that you are not alone in experiencing psychological adjustment problems, and you can experiment with trying to relate to people differently in a safe environment, with a psychologist present to assist, as needed.

Additionally, group therapy allows you to learn from the experiences of others with similar problems and also allows you to better understand how people very different from yourself view the world and interact with people. Of course, there are many other differences between group therapy and individual psychotherapy. Many people are anxious about participating in group therapy, because they don't want other people (in addition to the psychologist) to know about their problems. Group members are told not to discuss information shared in the group with others. Usually the need for mutual confidentiality preserves the privacy of the information.

Jenny S. is congenitally blind, so she doesn't see blindness as a major problem requiring the help of a psychologist or anybody else, for that matter. However, today, she has a dizziness that has defied medical diagnosis, but which has made her almost totally bedridden.

Mimi N. has a Cervical Spinal Injury (CSI). She and I met about two hours after the injury. The accident was result of a five-minute motorcycle spin around the block, late in the evening of Yom HaAtzmaut a year and a half before our meeting.

Chaim K. has a CSI, too; he was hit by a car in the early hours of the morning a few years before. I knew all three of them individually, but this was going to be the first time they met each other, and that we would be creating a new entity: The Group. How would I begin? How would they get along together and with me – now a facilitator/member of The Group?

The Group was Jenny's idea. There seemed to be no young adult group of this *sort*. What *sort*, you might ask? I guess it kind of defies definition, and since we, The Group, agreed to write a piece, together, I'll let them talk for themselves.

Before they begin, let me describe The First Meeting. I knew that they had all met psychologists before and were none too enthralled. So, with the help of my son, I downloaded some *Ketzarim* – short video clips – of a four-person comedy team that does skits, poking fun at many different subjects. Psychologists are one of their favorites. I chose one clip about the first session of group therapy for people with imaginary friends. Every one in *our* group is fluent in both languages, and Jenny does a fine job "seeing" with her ears, i.e., listening to the nuances in the video. As I had hoped, they all thought the video clip was funny, and it gave us a chance to size each other up.

"Without further ado, let's introduce ourselves." This went without a hitch. Then I ask each one to say how someone who didn't know them would describe them. Jenny says they would say she is blind. For Chaim, this is the first time in his life – well, in the years since he has been a quadriplegic – that his condition is not obvious to someone he had just met. He says he is in a wheelchair; so too says Mimi.

"Okay," I say, "now, how would I, Judi, introduce you?"

"Oh," say Jenny, "Judi would say I was smart, witty and I'm not using all my intelligence and blah blah blah." Chaim starts to laugh.

"What's so funny?" I ask. "She would say the same thing about me," Chaim answers. Mimi smiles too. That was our first meeting.

By now we are on our fifth and The Group is somewhat more familiar with the extent of each other's medical situation, which they each had just mildly alluded to and significantly minimized that first meeting.

At some point, Chaim's articles with me were discussed, along with the fact that he receives mail (email and snail-mail), proving "that *even* someone as handicapped as I am, can have an effect on others." He also told about going to give out candies and cakes to families waiting outside of critical care units. Mimi was very impressed with this gesture.

In most situations, with five years under his belt so to speak, Chaim is an experienced handicapped person. Well, sort of, until he met Jenny, someone who is congenitally blind but only considers herself handicapped for a year and a half, since her dizziness began. Mimi's entry into this world is relatively new. All three though, have developed a sixth sense in relation to assessing the people with whom they come into contact.

They decided to work on a topic for me to write up. How do they size up the people they meet for the first time?

Jenny says she pays attention to the content of the language the person uses. Examples she gives of the difference are: passive voice, "It will be taken care of," rather than the active voice, "I will take care of it." Jenny feels that people who use this grammatical formulation are controlling and patronizing, two *really* nasty words in Jenny's lexicon.

"Being blind makes people feel that they can tell you what to do: 'cross here,' 'let me take your hand,' and many such intrusions," she says with feeling. "Can you imagine that *more than once* have people shouted at me, thinking that blind means deaf?"

Chaim and Mimi burst out laughing and so does Jenny. They have personal experience with people who are trying "to help" but end up hurting them, instead.

Chaim has developed a series of *questions* he asks others and waits to see their reactions, both verbal and non-verbal. A keen observer, his questions are laser sharp and more indirect. So, in a relatively short period of time he can zero in on his quarry without them even being aware of the *meta*-conversation that is going on with this smiling person in a wheelchair.

Mimi is speaking for herself: "I pay attention to what the person is looking at. I used to think that someone checking me out was flattering, but now it's become something intrusive. I wonder if people are listening to *me* or are trying to figure out 'how she works,' as if I am some odd object, not a person like they are.

""I often feel like they are zooming in on my hands; I am unable to move my fingers, and they are permanently in a bent, contracted position. Sometimes, I have muscle spasms in my legs and arms, which also make me feel self-conscious. Someone once saw my leg spasm and thought that I had moved it willingly.

"But, then again, people who know me tell me that they don't even notice that I'm in a wheelchair anymore."

As The Group disperses after our sessions, I leave feeling uplifted and in awe of their individual and combined strength.

Truly an example of the saying: "Two are better than one . . . and the triple twisted cord can never be torn asunder" (Ecclesiastes 4:9–12).

Phantom Tickets

HE KNOCKED ON THE DOOR. He was early and I asked him to wait in the waiting area. He paced back and forth. He knocked again. And again. All I could think of as I opened the door was Mr. Hare (The Mad Hatter, actually) from *Alice in Wonderland* singing:

> *I'm late; I'm late for a very important date.*
> *No time to say hello, good-bye,*
> *I'm late, I'm late, I'm late.*
> *I'm late and when I wave, I lose the time I save.*
> (From "I'm Late" lyrics, Disney's cartoon
feature, "Alice in Wonderland")

It was five minutes to our appointed time. Hearing the urgent knocking, the patient in the room was rising. I ushered Levi into my office.

Levi was in a car accident six years before, when he was twenty and an *ilui* – a brilliant Talmudic student at a Chassidic yeshiva. He went out for a break in the beautiful Jerusalem winter sunshine and the next thing anyone knew he was on the ground, not breathing. He showed no physical injuries, but by the time the ambulances came he had not been breathing for over ten minutes.

They revived him, but other major complications arose during his hospitalization. Suffice it to say, he was left with severe physical and cognitive problems.

Miraculously, and through very hard work and *emunah*, faith, Levi today, is not the same person who was released from months of rehabilitation. Today he speaks, thinks, walks and does many other day-to-day behaviors we all take for granted, but he had to relearn all that he lost.

Levi is back in yeshiva and works part-time, and if you saw him in Meah Shearim you would not see any differences between him and the thousands of other *bachurim* who learn in yeshiva there.

There are problems, though, with his short-term memory. Whereas, he may not recall specifics of what we speak about, he does remember me, even after relatively long absences.

Here he was, though, very agitated and exhibiting a disquiet that I had not seen in the eight months we have known each other. "I am late, have to leave today; I have to go to the airport."

What seems to have occurred was that Levi's brother came to Israel for a visit and was returning home later that day. It was never in the plan that Levi would accompany him on this trip; it was clearly wishful thinking – or was it?

Levi kept insisting that he was told that he was leaving today. "Do you have tickets?" I ask. He searches his pockets and asks his flat-mate who was present. No tickets. "I may not have tickets but I know I am supposed to leave soon for the airport. Maybe my brother has my tickets?"

All of a sudden, another idea percolates in my head: "Phantom tickets," maybe *"phantom self."*

Phantom limb pain has been recorded almost as long as people have been losing limbs and surviving. As we can see on the motor cortex of the brain, specific areas function to map out specific parts of the body. Losing a part of the body doesn't necessarily stop the cortex from continuing to map the missing part.

While not all amputees will experience phantom limb pain, there is evidence to suggest that the majority will, at least initially, continue to perceive the body part as still being present in some form.

In the late 1980s, Vilayanur S. Ramachandran, the neuroscientist who was born in India, educated in England and living and teaching in the United States, turned his attention to Behavioral Neurology. Ramachandran is best known for his work on neurological syndromes such as phantom limbs, specifically his invention of The Mirror Box.

Previous attempts at eliminating the phantom pains involved surgery to remove another inch or two from the affected limb/stump or even cutting through the relevant nerve root emerging from the spinal cord. These methods are very rarely found to be effective and generally end up with a surgical "game without end" in a manner described by Ramachandran as "chasing the phantom."

He describes in detail, the behavior of phantom limbs that might not necessarily hurt, but will gesture, itch, twitch or even try to pick things up. He also describes that some people's representations of their limbs don't actually match what they should be, for example, one patient reported that her phantom arm was about "six inches too short."

In order to alleviate phantom limb pain, Ramachandran developed The Mirror Box, in which patients place their good limb and the amputated limb, and imagine making mirror symmetric movements. Due to the visual feedback, patients feel their limbs to be moving which helps alleviate phantom limb pain.

Neuroimaging studies suggest that this may be a result of reversing the remapping that leads to phantom limb pain.

Sitting opposite Levi, I have an idea. Maybe I could use a variation of The Mirror Box to help him out. I ask him if he looks like his brother. He replies that he does. I ask if his voice and that of his brother's are similar. Again, he replies that they are. I toke a mirror out of my bag and show it to him. "Does the image in the mirror look like your brother?" I asked. "It does," he answered.

I went on, "We both know how much you want to go home. We also know how much you and your brother look alike and sound alike. Could you now look at the reflection in the mirror and say: 'I have to rush today, because I am late to go to the airport? I am going home today'."

Levi asked, "Do you want me to say my brother's words in the mirror to me?" "Yes," I said enthusiastically. He did this a few times. It was hard for him to humor me, but he did do it.

"You see," I said, "I think that your *neshamah* knows how much you want to go home and so it 'convinced' your brain that your brother's words were your words."

At that moment, his brother called from the plane to say goodbye. With tears rolling down his face he wished his brother a *Nesia Tova* (good journey). He left the office slowly; he was no longer in a rush. My heart ached for him as I thought that frequently, achieving reality isn't a race we wish to win.

FOR FURTHER READING:

V. S. Ramachandran, S. Blakeslee, *Phantoms in the Brain*, (Quill William Morrow, 1999).

O. Sacks, *The Man Who Mistook His Wife for a Hat*, (Touchstone, 1998).

A Bonnet Lass

SHE IS EIGHT YEARS OLD and was referred for neuropsychological assessment consequent to being in a car accident when she was only a few months old. By age eight, both sides of the lawsuit had waited a sufficient amount of time (according to the pediatric neurologist) to evaluate the effects of the accident.

Everything was going along as expected. She was completing the testing in various modalities, which would give us insight into her strengths and weaknesses in varied domains. These included: intelligence, perception, motor, language, learning, memory and achievement. All of a sudden, she said: "That purple light and those little men are back again." I asked her to repeat what she had just said, as I wasn't sure I understood her. Again she noted, quite rationally, "The purple light and those little men are back again." This time she added: "Well I'm pretty sure you don't see them; nobody does, but I do."

Here was a seemingly perfectly normal child of eight, completing over an hour-and-a-half of testing with no odd behavior noted. There hadn't been any signs of emotional fragmentation, and now these delusions came up in the course of the evaluation. When asked about her visions and if this was the first time she experienced them, she answered no. She had seen them many times and had even told her mother about them. Her mother, she noted, had told her that many children had imaginary friends and fantasies and left it at that.

I checked and re-checked the subtests for signs of perceptual difficulties and found the results to be in the normal range.

Delusions, hallucinations, illusions – what is the difference? "An illusion is a perceptual disturbance, while a delusion is a belief disturbance" (David A. Gershaw, Ph.D., 1994).

People with a mental illness have trouble telling the difference between their fantasies and reality and will often come up with complicated explanations for the things they are seeing (sometimes called a delusion). An illusion is a misleading perception, usually visual. You see something, but you consistently misjudge its length, shape, motion or direction.

In their extreme form, delusions and hallucinations are symptoms of people who are psychotic; they cannot clearly distinguish what is real, from what is not. With psychotic disorders, hallucinations are most frequently auditory – like hearing voices.

I then began researching under what circumstances might someone have hallucinations, delusions or illusions without obvious psychosis, and found a fascinating disorder: Charles Bonnet Syndrome (CBS).

This syndrome generally affects older individuals with diminishing eyesight. However, the literature does note that it may occur in children.[1]

WHAT IS CHARLES BONNET SYNDROME?

A Swiss philosopher named Charles Bonnet first described this condition in 1760 when he noticed his grandfather, who was blinded by cataracts, describing how he saw birds and buildings, which were not there. Although the condition was described very early, it is still largely unknown by ordinary doctors and nurses. This is partly because of a lack of knowledge about the syndrome, and partly because people experiencing it don't talk about their problems out of fear of being thought of as mental health difficulties.

At the moment, little is known about how the brain stores the information it gets from the eyes and how we use this information to help us create the pictures we see. There is some research that shows that all this constant seeing actually stops the brain from creating its own pictures.

People with CBS (or Bonnet-people) are otherwise mentally sound. The "beings" appear when the Bonnet-people's vision deteriorates as a result of eye diseases such as age-related macular degeneration – or when patients have had both eyes removed. Though there have been reported cases in children, Charles Bonnet Syndrome is more common in older people with a high level of education.

IS THERE A CURE FOR CHARLES BONNET SYNDROME?

Unfortunately at the moment, there is no known cure or treatment for CBS. However, just knowing that it is poor vision and not mental illness that causes these problems often helps people come to terms with them. Generally, these experiences will disappear after about a year or eighteen months, but of course, this will not happen for everyone with this problem.

Doctors are unfamiliar with the syndrome as a possible diagnosis. Near-misses have been reported, in which patients were almost confined to mental

---

1. *J AAPOS* Oct. 1998; 2(5):310–3; T. L. Schwartz, L. Vahgei, 26506–9193, USA; *BMJ* 2004; 328:1552–1554 (June 26), doi: 10.1136/bmj.328.7455.1552.

health institutions. Given the prevalence of partial visual impairment, the number of people in the community – especially elderly people, who do not report the symptoms for fear of being labeled as mentally unwell or demented – must be substantial.

Clinicians must, therefore, be aware and ask elderly people with visual impairment whether they have hallucinations. Firm reassurance that the syndrome is not related to mental illness is in itself a major relief to an elderly person already burdened with failing vision, social isolation and other medical problems.

I recommended that my patient be seen by a pediatric retinal specialist and a psychiatrist to help make a differential diagnosis. The specific outcome notwithstanding, I feel that this case and awareness of Charles Bonnet Syndrome may help many elderly people in our midst with failing sight, especially those who are having "hallucinations" and are frightened that they may be thought of as mentally disturbed. We need to reassure them that they may be Bonnet/ Bonnie people.

A Schnitzel in Time
. . . Saves Lives!

"WE NEED A CONSULT," said the voice on the other side of the phone. A quick look at the LED read-out on my smart-phone anchored the caller to the Pediatric Nephrology Department. "She is eleven years old and refuses to comply with the dietary requirements of her ESRD."

ESRD stands for End Stage Renal Disease. This is a condition of total or nearly total and permanent kidney failure. People with ESRD must undergo dialysis or kidney transplantation to stay alive. Following a diet is crucial to the various forms of treatment for ESRD.

Shaare Zedek is one of the only medical centers in Israel to have separate adults and children dialysis departments. They were a forerunner of separate dialysis units since the late 1970s, over thirty years ago.

One visit to the sixth floor dialysis rooms, when they are in full swing, is worth a thousand words. In one room, adults sit hooked up to dialysis machines. Some are weary, uncomfortable, nauseous, and clearly unhappy; many are sitting there alone.

One connecting door away, the brightly decorated pediatric dialysis room is abuzz. Sure the kids and young adolescents who are having their blood "laundered" are less than comfortable for the most part. But their developmental needs are being met with the help of the constant team of teachers (Hebrew-, Arabic- and English-speaking), art and music therapists, as well as an occasional medical clown. In addition, there are teens volunteering to cheer them up and bring them normalcy from outside.

Dialysis patients must be hooked up three times a week for about three to four hours each time to the machine that exchanges and purifies their blood, as their kidneys have stopped doing so.

Hemodialysis and a proper diet help reduce the amount of wastes, which accumulate in the blood. A dietitian can help plan each patient's meals according to the doctors' orders. When choosing foods, one should remember to:

- Eat balanced amounts of foods high in protein such as meat and chicken.
- Watch the amount of potassium eaten. Potassium is a mineral found in

salt substitutes, some fruits, vegetables, milk, chocolate and nuts. Too much or too little potassium can be harmful to the heart.
- Fluid intake must be limited. Fluids build up quickly in the body when the kidneys aren't working. Too much fluid makes body tissues swell. It also can cause high blood pressure and heart trouble.
- Avoid salt. Salty foods make one thirsty and cause the body to retain water.
- Phosphorous intake needs to be limited. Foods such as milk, cheese, nuts, dried beans and soft drinks contain the mineral phosphorus. Too much phosphorus in the blood causes calcium to be pulled from bones.
- Calcium helps keep bones strong and healthy. To prevent bone problems, your doctor may give you special medicines. You must take these medicines every day as directed.

There are other options for treatment of ESRD: Peritoneal Dialysis is a type of dialysis that uses the lining of the abdomen to filter blood. This lining is called the peritoneal membrane.

TYPES OF PERITONEAL DIALYSIS

(1) Continuous Ambulatory Peritoneal Dialysis (CAPD) is the most common type of peritoneal dialysis. It needs no machine. It can be done in any clean, well-lit place.

(2) Continuous Cyclic Peritoneal Dialysis (CCPD) is like CAPD, except that a machine, which connects to the catheter, automatically fills and drains the dialysate from the abdomen. The machine does this at night while the patient is asleep.

(3) Intermittent Peritoneal Dialysis (IPD) uses the same type of machine as CCPD to add and drain the dialysate. IPD can be done at home, but it's usually done in the hospital. IPD treatments take longer than CCPD.

Not everyone with ESRD has the option of choosing which form of dialysis that they may use.

Diet for peritoneal dialysis is slightly different than diet for hemodialysis. One may be able to have more salt and fluids; eat more protein; have different potassium restrictions; may need to cut back on the number of calories eaten. The calorie limitation is because of the sugar in the dialysate that may cause the patient to dangerously gain weight.

The final option for ESRD is Kidney Transplantation, which is a procedure that places a healthy kidney from another person (or cadaver) into the patient's body. This one new kidney does all the work that the two failed kidneys cannot do.

A surgeon places the new kidney inside the body between the upper thigh and abdomen. The new kidney may start working right away or may take up to a few weeks to make urine. The original kidneys are left where they are, unless they are causing infection or high blood pressure. Here too, diet plays an important role. However, for transplant patients, it is less limiting than it is for dialysis patients. The diet probably will change as medicines, blood values, weight, and blood pressure change.

Again, transplantation is not a possibility for all (or even most) ESRD patients.

I went up to meet the young girl who "wasn't cooperative" with the life-saving dialysis stratagem. Alexandra is a twin. Her sister has normally functioning kidneys, which makes the three times weekly visits and serious discomfort especially difficult for Alexandra. She would never wish this disease on anyone, least of all her sister, but it just doesn't seem fair! To add insult to injury, she cannot abide the special menu she has to eat. Especially no chips (as french-fried potatoes are known here) and other fried foods.

"What," I ask her, "is the best thing about coming here to the hospital? I know that the dialysis and stuff is the worst."

She looks at me a moment and grudgingly tells me: "The Chicken Schnitzel."

I glance over her head in the direction of the nurse, and discover that Alexandra may eat this fried, breaded, fatty protein food only when on dialysis, as then her blood is cleansed as she eats it. The nurse goes on to say that Alexandra is spoiled because she only wants that food every time she comes and refuses to eat anything else – this too is also not "good" for the dialysis recipient.

Ever a solutions person, I ask if she could bring the schnitzel from home and have it while on dialysis. "That's also a problem," I was told in almost unison by Alexandra and the nurse. (The rabbi would have to okay the Kashrut, which is another issue, but not one that I was going to attempt to tackle.)

"What's the primary difficulty?" I asked.

Alexandra has tried to get her mother to make the SZS (Shaare Zedek Schnitzel) and it never comes out the same as the one made in the hospital commissary, and worse than that, no one can figure out the secret recipe.

"This is a very difficult problem," I say. "Will you give me a week to see if I can solve the problem? Alexandra, you have to promise you will eat properly, at least until I fail at my job. Give me a chance to succeed. Will you do that?"

She looks at me solemnly, and pronounces: "Four days, not a whole week."

"It's a deal; let's shake on it," I answer.

We have a life and death issue here. I know my limitations as a neuropsychologist. Who cares what her cognitive ability is when her life will indeed be at risk if she won't eat a proper diet?

I call the director of the kitchen. We have a life and death case on our hands.

I have his attention. I tell him that there is an 11-year old who is "dying for your schnitzel" (in Hebrew it is a double entendre, *"he meta al ha'schnitzel shelcha"* means "she's crazy about it").

"What's the problem?" he asks, "I'll send some up."

"No, that will not be good enough. Can we have an appointment to discuss this with you?"

"You mean bring the patient down to the kitchen?" he asks in amazement.

"Yes, that's what I have in mind."

He gives us an appointment a half an hour before she is scheduled to begin her dialysis.

I phone her to say it is imperative that she must arrive early for dialysis. (This is akin to going to the dentist early to have your teeth pulled; early, so as not to miss out on any of the fun!) I remind her that she has given me one chance to "not fail" and she owes me, because "we shook on it." Reluctantly, she agrees.

At the appointed time I meet her at the dialysis unit. We go down to the bowels of the ship, as it were, the kitchen which is on the first floor of this ten-story building; the third floor and below are all underground.

Waiting to greet us is the head of the kitchen, Mr. Rudel, and his chief chef. They have never had a request such as this, nor had they ever been so complimented as to have a patient want to meet them and discuss their schnitzel.

Wonderfully, they have prepared a demonstration and a tour of the kitchen. First, we take the chicken out of this massive fridge, then it goes to this spot where it is dredged in flour and specially spiced breading mix and then it is lightly fried.

Not only do we get a show in keeping with a Julia Child demonstration, but also a sample of the breading mix, and the "secret" recipe! The pièce de la résistance was that they had prepared a few portions for Alexandra to eat then and there, and later while she was on dialysis.

Glowing, she hunkered down to the feast. Then, with recipe and extra portions in hand, we went up to meet the thrice-weekly dialysis, head on.

We arrived and the nurses see crumbs on her face as well as the dish laden with schnitzel. "What is all this?" they ask with a mixture of awe and a tinge of jealousy. When Alexandra tells them about our appointment they ask to see the recipe and just taste the spice mixture.

"Sorry," says Alexandra, "I promised not to reveal the secret recipe."

"I'm sure you might make an exception," I murmur, as I exit "stage left," the nurses glaring at me.

Well, you can't win them all, I say to myself, as I return to the safety of my office.

Doing "The Right Thing"

T HE PEDIATRIC HEMATOLOGY Department referred her to me. I was told that she had severe anemia and needed to be developmentally assessed prior to receiving a bone marrow transplant in a European country.

She came with her mother. What was most obvious about her was her short stature and Arachnodactyly (long fingers). This nomenclature is derived from the words "arachnoid" (any of a class of arthropods comprising chiefly terrestrial invertebrates, including spiders, scorpions, mites and ticks, and having a segmented body divided into two regions of which the anterior bears four pairs of legs but no antennae), and "dactyl" (from Latin word "*dactylus*," literally, finger).

Arachnodactyly is a physical condition in which the fingers are long, slender and curved, resembling a spider's legs. I read about it and saw photos in textbooks, but never observed it close-up. Long, slender fingers can be a normal variation and not associated with any medical problems. However, in some cases, the tendency to develop spider fingers can indicate an underlying hereditary disorder. The inherited Fanconi's Anemia (FA) is one such disorder.

FA is an autosomal recessive disease in more than 99% of patients. In the U.S., the carrier frequency is estimated to be approximately one per 300 people, leading to an expected birth rate of approximately one per 360,000 people. FA has been reported in all races, although founder effects exist, which result in higher carrier frequencies in Ashkenazi Jews and Afrikaners. Among Ashkenazi Jews, the carrier frequency is approximately one per 90 people, with a projected birth rate of one per 30,000 people. Internationally, the carrier frequencies are similar to those in the U.S., depending on the population. It is classically diagnosed between the ages of 2 and 15.[1]

---

1. Research for this article included: S. Seal, R. Barfoot, *et al.*, Evaluation of Fanconi Anemia Genes in Familial Breast Cancer Predisposition; "Breast Cancer Susceptibility Collaboration" Harvard Gazette; Updated 7/29/2005. Updated by William Matsui, MD, assistant professor of Oncology, Division of Hematologic Malignancies, The Sidney Kimmel Comprehensive Cancer Center at Johns Hopkins, Baltimore, MD. Review provided by VeriMed Healthcare NetworkMedline.

MORTALITY/MORBIDITY

The major cause of death in FA is bone marrow failure, followed by other fatal situations. Though the mortality rate has been extended in its most severe form (patients do not live beyond the age of 40), many die earlier. Bone marrow failure usually presents itself in childhood, with bruising and hemorrhages, along with pallor and fatigue from the anemia, punctuating the young life. Developmental delays, learning disabilities and retardation are among the cognitive problems.

PHYSICAL

About 75% of patients with FA have birth defects, such as altered skin pigmentation and/or café au lait spots (50%), short stature (50%), thumb or thumb and radial anomalies (40%), abnormal male gonads (30%), microcephaly/small head (25%), eye anomalies (20%), structural renal defects (20%), low birth weight (10%), developmental delay (10%) and abnormal ears or hearing (10%).

FA is distinct from Fanconi's syndrome, a rare kidney disorder in which nutrients are lost through the urine.

The disease is caused by a genetic defect that prevents cells from fixing damaged DNA or removing toxic, oxygen free radicals that damage cells. Patients may be suspected of having the disease if they have particular birth defects or develop decreased blood counts.

FA is primarily an autosomal recessive genetic condition, as this gene is on the X chromosome. For an autosomal recessive disorder, both parents must be carriers in order for a child to inherit the condition. If both parents are carriers, there is a 25% risk, with each pregnancy for the mother to have an affected child. Genetic counseling and genetic testing is recommended for families that may be carriers of Fanconi Anemia.

PROGNOSIS

Patients who have had a successful bone marrow transplant and, thus, are cured of the blood problem associated with FA still must have regular examinations to watch for signs of cancer.

TREATMENT

Bone marrow transplantation can cure the blood count problems associated with Fanconi's Anemia. An HLA-matched sibling is the best donor source, although umbilical cord blood cells and unrelated bone marrow can also be used. This therapy is very effective, and although there are associated toxicities, there has been improvement in the care of Fanconi patients during the transplant. There is approximately a 70% success rate for those patients fortunate enough to have a well-matched donor.

So why am I presenting a modest genetics course? This little 8-year old girl had been adopted, and when her adoptive parents (who knew she had some physiological problems and was therefore given up for adoption) found out about her disease, they tried to reach the biological parents to have her blood-siblings tested for a match of bone marrow. They were summarily turned down and told that the biological parents did not want their other children to know about this child or her illness because among other things, they didn't want to *fashtair* (spoil) their children's *shidduchim* (marriageability). They were insistent on doing "the right thing" for the majority of their children. Their decision of not permitting an ideal biologically-matched donor significantly reduced her chances of long-term survival.

I hadn't thought about this case in a long time. But then I came upon an article that discussed an amazing finding that occurred in the past ten years. The discovery that the Fanconi's Anemia gene and BRCA1 and BRCA2 gene for inherited breast cancer are intertwined. So much so, that under the microscope they are hard to tell apart.

Women today can be tested for this form of inherited breast cancer, which is more common in Jewish Ashkenazi women.

And here is the connection. The biological parents have unwittingly put their other children at risk. For if these children know that their family genetics include Fanconi's Anemia, they would be able to check for BRCA1 and BRCA2. They would then be able to alter their statistical chance of getting this form of breast cancer from 70% down to 30% (which is similar to the general non-inherited statistics). It is important to note that men with an inherited altered BRCA1 or BRCA2 gene also have an increased risk of breast cancer (primarily if the alteration is in BRCA2), and possibly prostate cancer as well.

May Hashem grant us the wisdom to "do the right thing."

Do You Have a Moment to Discuss Something with Me?

It was late in the afternoon – well, early in the evening, and my last patient had canceled. I am grateful that I love my work, but also relish those "found" hours when someone needs to cancel, and the spot is not filled.

I was sitting in the office peacefully getting some paperwork out of the way when the phone rang. "Do you have a moment to discuss something with me?" And without waiting for my response, she said: "My 7-year old has been thrown out of school, I need an emergency appointment as they won't take him back without an evaluation."

What could a 7-year old have done to cause such consternation and dire response?

So this is where I made my first mistake in this conversation. I asked what happened to make the school so angry with him. A bit on the defensive, the mother said he had a fight with another boy. Too much anxiety and sniffles about a "fight with another boy." So I ventured further (continuing error of blithe conversation too late in the afternoon). "What got broken?" I asked in an easy-going manner. More tears and whimpering on the other side of the phone when she said: "A chair and the other boy's skull and nose."

Oops, I said to myself, *looks like you got in too deep too soon. Let's try to get some distance from the present* (i.e., get away from this immediate event and get a broader picture).

Taking what I thought was a different tack, I asked, "Do you have any experience with anyone else in the family, whose behavior resembles your son's?" Now she was frightened, "How do you mean?" she asked. I ventured, "Letting anger get out of control and responding physically." She was quiet a moment and I took this as a positive sign that the conversation was becoming more rational, when she let out a primal wrenching cry. "My nephew murdered my sister a few years ago."

Whoa, this mild-mannered conversation has become a downright stampede of fears and emotions. "How old was he at the time?" "Fourteen years old," she answered, breathing heavily and painfully over the phone.

"Okay," I said with a bit more levity than I felt, "We have at least six years to

207

get your son help. And that's if he is as problematic as your nephew, which in all probability he is not." (So, I may have lied, but I'm not a *neviya* [prophetess] and a little modesty was in order!)

I suggested that she call her husband, and I'd wait for them at the office, so that we could talk about the school situation of her 7-year old without infecting the conversation with a horrible tragedy.

Within a half an hour the couple was in my office. I used that time to go down to the cafeteria to get some juice and cakes, hoping to reduce cathexis from the "space" (psychoanalytic term relating to great concentration of emotional energy on one particular person, thing or idea.)

What seemed to have happened, was a confluence of events which made the mother very vulnerable from the start; the phone call after hours contributed to my being overly relaxed, asking questions without any means of seeing or understanding the person's reactions, and the outcome had led to the slippery slope with leaked information that needed to be collected, so that the couple could leave with a measure of strength and dignity to get useful help in the near future.

This would be different from the situation now, where we all got into a horribly traumatic topic too deeply and too quickly to make the experience anything but painful, destructive and devoid of therapeutic purpose.

I gave them the name of a male colleague and suggested they go together first and discuss ways of their taking charge of helping their only son resolve some of his issues.

We shook hands, and they left the office. Whew, I breathed a sigh of relief, and called my husband and said that I needed to go out for dinner to give myself some space before going home. I said I had had a difficult meeting, and since this was a rare event, he readily acquiesced.

We agreed to meet at a restaurant near our house. Just as we were being shown to our table, I heard a familiar gasp. I turned and saw *that* couple. They looked at me beseechingly, and I said to my husband that I had changed my mind and preferred to eat at home. He looked perplexed, but then he saw my resolute expression, and we left for the quiet safety of home.

The Happy Non-Dyslexic

AVRAHAM CAME IN with his mother. My previous patient took longer than expected, and I had gone into the waiting room to tell them of the delay. The waiting room is a large area that the Neuropsychology Unit shares with the Pre-Operative Clinic.

I asked a harried-looking mother of a boy who was walking around if she was waiting for me. She was, and as I apologized for the delay, I couldn't take my eyes off of the smiling boy as he walked, well, pranced around the large waiting area. There was an odd stiffness to his gait that first caught my attention.

I went back to my office to finish up with the previous patient and then called them in. I have to admit, though I was concentrating on finishing up, I was also trying to recall if I had ever seen anyone walk as that boy did.

When they entered the room, his wide gait and smile were the two features that I continued to notice. We began chatting; the mother had read an article in which I described a case relating to dyslexia (Latin for difficulty in reading). After reading this article, she was very concerned about her son and felt that I was the address to answer her question: "Did he have this dreaded disorder of dyslexia?"

It is not infrequent today that people call for appointments after having read something on the Internet. This woman did not have Internet nor was the crumpled article she showed me – in fact, it was probably over three years old.

I started to speak to them to get an anamnesis. Avraham, an only child, was ten years old (he looked a bit short for his age I thought); birth history was normal but he was hyper-kinetic as an infant. His motor movements were also jerky. This gave me an opening to ask if he had physical therapy or any other therapy.

All of a sudden, Avraham began to laugh; a full and loud laugh. Nothing had been said that was at all funny, and though I do often try to engage my patients with humor, I had not done so yet. However, I did have a glimmer of a hypothesis. I started to ask other questions.

She looked at me a bit annoyed. Why was I asking so many questions? Couldn't I just give an answer to her question?

I explained that this preliminary conversation was important so that I could tailor the testing appropriately. I proceeded with my questions. "Avraham," I asked, "do you enjoy recess?" Avraham was fidgety the whole time, and though he seemed to understand my questions, he was slow to answer. He nodded instead. His mother noted that he doesn't speak a lot.

I was thinking: early history of hyperkinesis, spontaneous laughter, stiff and jerky wide-gait walk, poor expressive speech with reasonable receptive language. Might Avraham have Angelman's Syndrome? In 1965, Dr. Harry Angelman, a British physician, saw three unrelated young children with the type of behaviors I was observing in Avraham. He describes how he formulated a new diagnosis, as follows:

"It was purely by chance that nearly thirty years ago three handicapped children were admitted at various times to my children's ward in England. When on holiday in Italy, I happened to see an oil painting in the Castelvecchio Museum in Verona, called a Boy with a Puppet. The boy's laughing face and the fact that my patients exhibited jerky movements gave me the idea of writing an article about the three children with a title of Puppet Children. It was not a name that pleased all parents, but it served as a means of combining the three little patients into a single group. Later the name was changed to Angelman's Syndrome."

After some initial interest, this article lay almost forgotten until the early 1980s. In fact, many doctors denied that such a condition existed. In the past ten years, American and English doctors have placed the syndrome on a firm footing with the ability to establish the diagnosis beyond doubt.

The fact that laughter is so frequent in Angelman's Syndrome (AS) is not understood even today. Laughter per se, in normal individuals, is not well understood. Studies of the brain in AS, using MRI or CT scans have not shown any defect suggesting a site for a laughter-inducing abnormality. Although there is a type of seizure associated with laughter, termed Gelastic Epilepsy, this is not what occurs in AS. The laughter in AS seems mostly to be an expressive motor event.

As a result of the tentative diagnosis, I tested Avraham's ability to understand language and not rely on his poor expressive language skills to "muddy the waters" of an assessment of his cognitive abilities. He functioned in the low average range for being able to make a sentence with a series of pictures, and even to understand a code and be able to apply it. These were positive signs for being able to communicate and learn by reading, or at least benefit from augmentative language therapy.

By the end of the session, I was sure that Mrs. L. was very cognizant of Avraham's problems. Although she may not have been given a diagnosis (tentative diagnosis), she was doing all she could for her son. What was also obvious was that she loved her son the way he was and provided him with a lot of supplementary help. This is what brought her to my office in the first place. She had read an article about dyslexia and wanted to know if she could help him further.

I recommended that Avraham, who was quite social, would benefit from language therapy emphasizing complementary means of communication. An after-school program in theatre and especially "miming" might also increase his skills in communicating.

I also referred Avraham for further testing (neurological and genetic) of the possible Angelman's hypothesis. With this diagnosis they would probably be able to apply for a stipend, which would defray some of the costs of therapy. Finally, I gave Avraham's mother an answer to her initial question. No, Avraham does not have dyslexia. She stood up, shook my hand vigorously and said: "*Baruch Hashem* and thank you."

FOR FURTHER READING:

H. Angelman, "Puppet Children: A report on three cases." Developmental Medicine and Child Neurolology, 1965, vol. 7, 681–688.

http://www.angelman.org.

http://www.geneclinics.org/profiles/angelman.

Confusing and Converting Symptoms

I HAD ALREADY RECEIVED four different phone messages referring this child for assessment. The parents, the Talmud Torah Rebbe, and the Rav they consulted. The fourth call was from an *askan*. In the ultra-Orthodox world, he is an interlocutor between the professional world and the lay members of the community. Would I please see this child who has difficulty reading, possibly suffering from an odd form of Dyslexia. *Okay,* I thought, *that isn't so unusual here in the Neuropsychology Unit.*

To paraphrase the words of the Haggadah, "Why is this dyslexic different than all other dyslexics?" What's the rush and why can't he wait for his turn on the patient list? Experience has taught me that, this many and varied a group exercising *protexia* (use of "pull") connotes a case where there is more than meets the eye.

They, both parents and their 10-year old child, arrive on time. I set out three chairs and wait to see who sits where. The father sits down first, nearest to my side of the desk, the son sits next to him and the mother, looking a bit lost, chooses the final seat and sits with her left arm to the wall. *Hum,* I think, *this is already unusual. No one has spoken and she seems a little out of the loop.* I ask some basic getting to know you questions, and ask the mother to fill out a form. The father takes the form, says her hand hurts her, and begins to fill out the form (about pregnancy and delivery of this child). *Not very respectful to his wife,* I think.

I turn to Moshe and ask him why his parents brought him. He looks at me, then at his father and then at me again. "Well if you don't know and I don't know why you are here, we are really in trouble," I say. "He has trouble reading," his father says. "But not always," pipes up Moshe.

"Could you explain this?"

"Well, some days I can read and some days I can't."

I felt he was being earnest and sincere, even though the premise was preposterous. One cannot be a "some time dyslexic." You are either dyslexic or not.

After doing a full intake, it turned out that the days that Moshe "was dyslexic" were days that his father slept away from home. He had taken to doing this while he was considering divorcing his wife. Moshe's odd condition, which was not in his conscious control, served as a means of bringing his father home to help solve the problem.

I referred the parents to couples' counseling to see if the marriage could be saved. A short time later I was informed that Moshe's "dyslexia" disappeared.

CASE NO. 2

About two months after the Disengagement from Gaza, I received a phone call from an anxious mother. "My son, Yossi's behavior is frightening us. Since he returned home from three weeks of actively protesting in Gush Katif (Gaza Jewish settlements), his physical and mental condition is deteriorating. He has stopped speaking and using his right hand."

This was right before the holidays when Israel closes down for a month – from Rosh Hashanah until after Sukkot. I needed to be assured that the medical realm, where emergency conditions can exist be looked into, before I would see him. I insisted that they consult a neurologist and also a psychiatrist. A neurologist would assess his neurological functioning to rule out a physiologi-cal condition that may be putting pressure on the neurological systems that may cause the paralysis his mother was describing. The psychiatrist would rule out psychosis, a break with reality. If both these physicians would rule out pathology, I would see them, the parents and Yossi immediately following the holidays.

As we were talking about Yossi's condition, an hypothesis, more like an odd association, came to mind.

As I noted above, Yossi's mother described his symptoms as "not speaking and loosing the use of his right hand." I thought of Psalm 137:

> By the waters of Babylon – there we sat and also wept when we re-membered Zion ... And we vowed: If I forget you, O Jerusalem, let my right hand forget its skill. Let my tongue adhere to my palate if I fail to recall you, if I fail to elevate Jerusalem above my foremost joy. (Psalms 137:1, 5–6).

Wasn't Yossi "mourning" the loss of Gush Katif?

I related my somewhat off-the-wall association regarding Yossi's symptoms to his mother, and asked her to share it with both the neurologist and the psy-chiatrist.

Immediately after Sukkot, Yossi's mother called me and said that both physi-cians said there was no pathology. Also, though Yossi was still not using his right hand, he was speaking again. Could they please have an appointment?

When Yossi and his parents were sitting in my office, Yossi's first comment to me was: "What you told my mother about the Psalm was 60 percent correct." I told him that for psychology, at best an inexact science, 60 percent was a terrific 'grade!'

*

The defense that the minds of both boys, Moshe and Yossi, were exhibiting is known as "Conversion Disorder" (once known as Hysterical Paralysis).

Conversion Disorder:

Conversion symptoms suggest a physical disorder but are the result of psychological factors. According to the psychodynamic model, the symptoms are a consequence of emotional conflict, with the repression of conflict into the unconscious.

It has been postulated that the patient derives primary and secondary gain. With primary gain, the symptoms allow the patient to express the conflict that has been suppressed unconsciously. With secondary gain, symptoms allow the patient to avoid unpleasant situations or garner support from friends, family, and the medical system that would otherwise be non-obtainable.

I know I am preaching to the converted when I share my awe with the divine and wondrous workings of the mind and body to aid the soul.

FOR FURTHER READING:

American Psychiatric Association, "Somatoform disorders," *Diagnostic and Statistical Manual of Mental Disorders*. 4th ed. (Washington, DC: APA Press, 1994: 452–7.) A. B. Carter, "The prognosis of certain hysterical symptoms," *British Medical Journal*, 1949; 1: 1076–9.

R. Gould, B. L. Miller, M. A. Goldberg, D. F. Benson: "The validity of hysterical signs and symptoms," *J Nerv Ment Dis* 1986 Oct; 174(10): 593–7 [Medline]. H. Stevens, "Is it organic or is it functional. Is it hysteria or malingering?" *Psychiatric Clinics of North America*, 1986 June; 9(2): 241–54 [Medline].

Empathy Pre-Birth:
Response to Family Stress

The referral was from Social Services. In their words, ". . . the family was known to Social Services." I have learned over the years that this can mean anything from: the parents are both felons in jail to extreme social, psychiatric and fiscal reasons that they came to the attention of Social Services. In this case, nine of the children where living outside the original biologic family home as the parents' problems left them unable to care for their brood.

The 16-year old sitting opposite me, let's call him "Daniel," presented a conundrum to the psycho/social staff who assessed him in hope of placing him in an appropriate hostel. They were unsure if his problem was emotional, psychiatric, learning related and/or social.

At the outset he was very polite. Darkly handsome and well groomed. Once he started speaking there were gaps in the flow of information. Sometimes this type of gappy speech flow can be a result of many situations, among them extreme psychological stress (Thought Disorder; Blocking) and sometimes it can be a sign of a seizure disorder (Petit Mal). As our conversation progressed, his thoughts raced from topic to topic which seemed tangentially related.

Here, I recalled an early professor of mine who would say that concerning me and my (schizophrenic) patients, the conversations were always "Folie a Deux" (a shared psychosis, a psychiatric syndrome in which symptoms of a delusional belief are transmitted from one individual to another). In other words, the professor commented on the fact that I *could* carry on a conversation and understand the mental gymnastics of my psychotic patients. Not only that, but I would feel that it "made sense"!

While one of my neuropsychology interns looked on, glazed eyes in wonder and exhaustion of trying to keep the pace, Daniel and I continued our conversation which had started with his humming a melody that I recognized from the *Selichot* (prayers during the month of Elul and the Days of Awe). We spoke of *paytanim* (poets), Sephardic Rosh Hashanah and Yom Kippur melodies, menus of various holidays, the differences between Sephardic/Eastern woman and Ashkenazi/European/Russian women, motherhood, childbirth, child raising, fatherhood, living in Israel, terrorist actions, and more.

I tried to join the dots and found a common thread in all these. Okay, the professor wasn't all wrong! I told him he had a wonderful ear for music and wondered if he inherited it from his mother or his father. I also asked him could he tell me something about his mother and father and terrorists.

There were a few minutes of silence. Then he said, "My father." He added: "There is a big difference between Ashkenazi women and Sephardic mothers."

Here I felt that the leap wasn't too far, as sitting opposite this very dark-eyed individual, was me, a blond, fair-eyed woman.

"Ashkenazi women talk a lot and let things out; Sephardic women keep things inside. My mother was pregnant with me when the terrorists blew up the bus where she was mildly injured and my father blinded. I was inside her then."

Always in search of an opportunity to reframe, I said: "You were there, too, and probably all the extra 'insulation' of you in her stomach protected her from the bomb."

"She never spoke about all the worry. She just kept it inside, all the bad stuff. I was born with feces in my lungs."

And this disclosure, I really did understand his diagnosis better. He was a MAS newborn. He had been born with Meconium Aspiration Syndrome, a medical condition which occurs when meconium is present in a newborn's lungs during or before delivery. Meconium is the first stool of an infant, composed of materials ingested during the time the infant spends in the uterus. If meconium, which is normally stored in the infant's intestines until after birth, is ingested by the fetus, this is often in response to fetal distress. It is expelled into the amniotic fluid prior to birth, or during labor. If the baby inhales the contaminated fluid, respiratory problems may occur by the material blocking the airways leading to poor oxygenation to the brain and consequent cognitive and medical disabilities. (See Wikipedia.)

Neuropsychologically, the basis of his learning problems and "stickiness of thinking" became more apparent. His test results pointed up similarities to children with autistic spectrum disorder. This diagnosis would help him receive help in placement and rehabilitation. Psychologically, there would be a map with signposts for therapists to follow and not breach. For here was a 16-year old, young/old man, who felt that his ailment had a purpose. He was given the *zechut*, the honor, to be the repository of the anguish his mother kept in. So deep was his empathy, even prenatally, that he "consumed the feces" of his mother's experience. So great was this act of selflessness, that even though it resulted in the detriment of his own cognitive development, he had given his mother a "gift."

Nursing a Grudge

LEAH ABRAMOWITZ, M.S.W. (co-founder of Melabev, a leader in Alzheimer's care in Israel) and I were so affected by our experience at a Nefesh International Conference that we returned to Israel and initiated Nefesh Israel, the largest branch of the Nefesh International Family.

Understanding the cultural and religious background of our patients gives us a chance to save much time and effort when diagnosing and treating. Nefesh has given countless Torah observant professionals an opportunity to bounce ideas around and learn strategies from one another.

The following case brought my gratitude to Nefesh to mind:

They are an ultra-Orthodox Sephardic family. Her father was very critical of her when she was a child and even as an adolescent. To add insult to injury he himself was alcoholic, and verbally and physically abusive to her mother. He also gambled. His losses caused financial hardship on his family but especially on her mother who had to work to support the family, and so had little time or energy left for her many children when she returned home. The family tried to keep all this quiet until he was once so drunk that he made a pass at another woman – on Shabbat – in front of their entire community.

She had originally come to the Neuropsychology Unit with her daughter who she feared was autistic. As it turned out, her daughter was actually socially immature based on a severe problem in the area of Attachment. In essence, I felt we had two generations of Attachment problems in the room. Over two years of dyadic therapy and using the mother as my co-therapist to help the daughter, the girl was placed in a regular class and is now doing well in third grade.

So what's the problem? She has come in after the birth of her fourth child, her second son. She cannot understand why she is so angry with him. He is just a newborn baby. Being my co-therapist for two years taught her that there might be something underlying this strange anger that she feels toward him, so she called for an appointment. I tell her to come in with him.

He looks like an adorable newborn. She scowls. When he starts to fuss I watch them together. She takes a thin cloth blanket and throws it over her shoulder.

She grabs him out of the stroller and puts him under half the blanket and begins to nurse him.

"I think I understand the problem," I say to her. "How many names does he have?" "Just one," she answers. "I think you are going to need to see your Rav and ask him if you can add a name."

She is silent for a while. She begins to look at him a little more maternally and beginning to smile she says: "He really is a good boy, you know."

"I know," I answer. It isn't his fault that in Sephardic families, the second son is named for the mother's father.

She leaves and I begin to understand the meaning of the old adage: Nursing a Grudge.

Consultation across a
Seemingly Great Divide

THERE WAS A request from both the nurses and social workers of Pediatric Oncology to see a patient. The patient was a 9-year old girl, but the person "we *really* need help with, is the brother!"

Since each department has a social worker assigned to it, and having experience that our specific services are generally requested when all else has been tried, this referral, to see a young patient "but more so, her brother," piqued my curiosity. I also know that going in and acting as: *hakol yachol*, or "know it all," was sure to backfire. This consultation would need to be handled in a discrete fashion so that we would not be an excuse for failure, but rather, the tools for success.

We are a 500-bed medical center that services Jerusalem and its environs, so that our patient population reflects the cultural, religious, and political diversity that is day-to-day reality in Israel. In this case, as I went upstairs, to the Pediatric Oncology Unit with an intern, I did not know who we were going to meet. Certainly, I had the facts: Patient's name: Wafa, aged 9; address: a small village near Jericho; citizenship: Israeli; religion: Arab Moslem (all identifying information has been changed). Those are obvious starting points, but who was I really going to be seeing?

On entering the room, I observed the following *tableau*. Mom in traditional Moslem garb; father, no beard but unshaven in secular jeans; son, early twenties in traditional garb, very hirsute and unkempt, beard, mustache, a lot of head hair and a large knitted white kippa, or as it is known in Arabic: "*kufi*," skullcap. And there, almost forgotten on the upper far corner of the bed, lay a small 9-year old girl. She had a distinct pallor, brown rings under her eyes, and little wisps of hair peeking out of the triangular fabric wrapped around her almost bald head. Wafa's body was held in an almost fetal position, she looked sad, with a far-away gaze which I had seen in the past with so many other young oncology patients. Though the room was full of people, her pose said: "I am alone, and there is no one to protect me."

Just before I entered the room, the social worker for the unit pulled me aside and said: "The brother goes to a *madressa* ("yeshiva" for Moslems) and seems to be ruling the roost with the family. I tried to work with them, but they were unresponsive."

Though I can speak enough Arabic to make a patient feel as though I am trying, I do not do therapy in Arabic. Luckily, one of the psychology interns also includes an Arab student of psychology. Abdel (not his real name) is Israeli-born, and doing graduate work in a European university. I have been impressed with his knowledge of psychology and especially his willingness to learn during his first few weeks of his internship at the Neuropsychology Unit. As we walked up to the sixth floor, to the Pediatrics Department, he was expectably anxious and excited at the same time. This would be his first patient and his reactions were appropriate, too much confidence would not have portended well, vis-à-vis my perception of an optimal learning infrastructure. A little anxiety is a good motivator for learning and achieving, too high a comfort level, generally signifies a student who will miss important clues/information because of over-confidence.

On the way upstairs, I notice Abdel putting the cross he wears around his neck, into his undershirt. He notices that I notice, and says: "If the son is in *madressa*, I don't need to begin by showing that I not a Moslem, but rather a Christian Arab." (His sensitivity and preparedness make him go up another notch in my estimation!)

We were introduced to the family just as big brother, aged 19 years, was reading to his sister, and the parents were looking morose in their chairs. "What are you reading?" I asked curiously, big brother looking downward and trying not to make eye-contact with me (for modesty reasons), answers: "poetry." There was an overall mood in the room that didn't compute with what I expected "reading poetry" in a patient's room would evince. We talked about "cabbages and kings" (nothing really, the view, the food, the pictures of beautiful photographed flowers which are hanging on the walls). In this fashion, they have an opportunity to meet/see us, and we them, as well as give them a heads-up that we'll be back. We haven't intruded too much, and we have given them a measure of control regarding contact with us. It also gave me an opportunity to check out what poetry they were reading.

I found out that the "poetry" was about death and the sacrifice of the dead for the holiness of the rest of the family. It seems that Brother required that the whole family be present whilst he read these "poems" to his 9-year old sister, both at home and in the hospital. Further, the brother was newly ardently religious, having been somewhat of a problem child in the past (cutting school, possible drug abuse and other non-conformist behaviors).

There was something very familiar about the scene. I recalled a case where a Jewish teen was severely injured in a terrorist attack. The brother blamed himself for his sister's injuries. Had he been more religious, then his sister wouldn't have needed to suffer for his sins. With each passing day in the ward, the brother thought of another act of piety the patient should take on to clear herself of the punishment.

The similarities between the cases helped me formulate a plan. I decided that the Mom would be our "therapist" and that Abdel would use Gerald Caplan's Consultee Centered Psychotherapy/Intervention (Model of Mental Health Consultation, 1973, 1994). Caplan developed a model where he would elevate the professionalism of caregivers which in turn, created an attitudinal shift among them leading toward their establishing a professional identity and a sense of newfound abilities. Collaboration among child care center staff appeared to support professional growth, while empowerment surfaced as an important part of this process involving increased competency among caregivers (Schien, 1997).

In my professional life, especially that of working in a multi-cultural environment, I try to seek the similarities rather than differences in observing human behavior. I attempt to enlist the strengths and abilities of all those concerned to further our goals. In this case, adding the spice of understanding of the effect of behaviors on family dynamics that the re-entry of a "prodigal son" might cause, we were able to enhance the active understanding and empathy of the parents, nurses and social workers. Not being misled by obvious cultural differences, but instead using our combined across cultures experiences, we were able to construct change in how the parents related to their son and daughter. In supervision with Abdel, I was able to help him reframe and translate the brother's feelings of misplaced responsibility for his sister's illness as he co-opted the Mom to be the family's "therapist."

Most of all, we were able to engender trust and mutual respect and help our patient, 9-year old Wafa.

But I Just Drank Two
Piña-Coladas a Week!

OVER THE PAST DECADE, the shelves of wine in my *makolet* and the regular supermarket have spread. Gone are the days where sweet red, syrupy *Kiddush* wine was all you could buy. Standing shoulder to shoulder are kosher wines from Israel, but also from countries as far away as Chile, France, Spain, Portugal, Australia, South Africa and too many more to note. Kosher wine-tasting parties, with lectures by connoisseurs, have made their way from adult birthday parties to *tzedakah* (charity) events. Spittoons have replaced the kibbutz *kolbo* (literally, everything in) "centerpieces" for getting rid of remnants of a taste, in order to make room for another few ounces of the multi bottles of wine at these "academic" introductions to Wine (with a capital *W*).

Please don't get me wrong. I enjoy a nice glass of Cabernet or Merlot as much as the next person. And anyway, doesn't research show there are medicinal benefits to drinking red wine? So what's my point? Here I wish to introduce you to another case in my Neuropsychologist's Journal.

Pinchas Cohen, age 14, was referred for a neuropsychological assessment by his tutor. He had been having trouble with schoolwork and social connections since the beginning of elementary school. Mr. and Mrs. Cohen accompanied their son to his appointment. At first blush, Pinchas looked a bit different than his folks. They were tall and he was much shorter and seemed to have a completely different body build. (According to the anamnesis-intake/history form he was their biological child.) As we sat and talked, I noticed some other differences. His head seemed a bit smaller than his body size would suggest. He was friendly and affable and seemed even more communicative than most adolescents, who can be downright surly when schlepped to a "shrink for yet another test." Also, there was something different about his smile, but I couldn't put my finger on what was bothering me.

As I noted above, he had had difficulties in learning, reading came late and arithmetic never "came." He was socially isolated from his peers though he, according to his mother, was friendly and loyal to a fault. "He just 'doesn't get it' in social situations," she said, in contrast to his much younger siblings who had no problems in this area. Pinchas was very chatty, but as the interview progressed, I was impressed by how superficial and concrete his comments were. Also, he tended to repeat himself often and didn't seem to pay attention to either of his parents' non-verbal (body language) communications, which signaled that he slow down and let someone else speak.

As Pinchas and his parents came from out of town, it was decided to do both the interview and the testing in a two-day, marathon session. (Usually, if the commuting distance is under two hours, the assessment process may be anywhere from two to four visits over a period of a month.) So Pinchas went to another room with another psychologist to begin this aspect of the assessment while I continued the intake with his folks.

We had been chatting for close to an hour and Mr. Cohen had not said a word. I noticed that he was sitting with arms crossed in front of him, seeming to be both reserved and angry at the same time. I asked some basic questions about their academic background and family history, but I felt that the father was holding back. "What am I missing?" I asked aloud.

Mrs. Cohen looked at her husband and then at me and candidly said, "You don't recognize my husband, do you? Well you are religious and probably don't go to nightclubs." I nodded in agreement. "He is a well-known comedian, and before we came he was concerned that you would recognize him. Now that you don't," she said with a sardonic smile, "he's surprised, too." I apologized for the slight, he pooh-poohed it, and after that, he sheepishly began to relate his feelings. "I am embarrassed to say that Pinchas's behavior in public often causes me to feel uncomfortable. Not only doesn't he get my jokes, but he becomes too friendly with people, even on the bus. He'll begin talking with anyone, and it is not only embarrassing, but I'm also worried about his safety."

They went off to tour Jerusalem, and I observed Pinchas as he was being tested. The hours passed, he was very cooperative and we adjourned until the next morning to finish up. (He and his parents were going to stay at the hospital's "hotel." Shaare Zedek has a number of rooms with amenities, a communal kitchenette and a living room set up for patients' families to stay.)

At the end of the second day, I sat with the parents. The written report would follow, but based on the neuropsychological testing battery results and the clinical observations, I had some more questions before I could supply answers.

Aside from the cognitive and social deficits that the parents described, the data seemed to point up to what we call in the trade, Nonverbal Learning Disorder. Also seemingly highlighted was a specific pattern of strengths and weaknesses that we see in children with White Matter Disorder (such as those suffering from Williams Syndrome).

White matter is one of the two main solid components of the central nervous system. It is composed of myelinated nerve cell processes, or axons, which connect various grey matter areas (the locations of nerve cell bodies) of the brain to each other and carry nerve impulses between neurons. Cerebral and spinal white matter do not contain dendrites, which can only be found in grey matter along with neural cell bodies and shorter axons.

Generally, white matter can be understood as the parts of the brain and spinal cord responsible for information transmission, whereas grey matter is mainly responsible for information processing. White matter injuries (axonal shearing) may be reversible, while grey matter regeneration is less likely.

White matter forms the bulk of the deep parts of the brain and the superficial parts of the spinal cord.

Grey matter is the major part of the nervous system in which the nerve impulses for all kinds of mental functions are produced and then sent away, to be carried to their target organs by white matter.

Pinchas's developmental/medical history also showed that he had:
- Low birth weight
- FTT – Failure to thrive (eat and grow well)
- An exaggerated startle response
- Poor wake and sleep patterns
- Hyperactivity, distractibility and attention deficits
- Impulsiveness
- Temper tantrums

The school history (as well as the testing) noted:
- Poor social skills
- Poor abstracting abilities
- Serious Dyscalculia (arithmetic disability)
- "Cocktail Speech" (superficial speech)

Clinical observation:
- Small head size
- Short stature
- Wide spread of eyes
- Flattened nose-bridge

And I finally figured out what bothered me about his smile: He seemed to have a very thin upper lip and a flattened *philtrum*. (The *philtrum* is the "dimple" under the nose that, according to Midrash, is the place the angel touches babies about to be born; so that even though they know the whole Torah and Judaism's laws in their mother's womb, they "forget" upon birth and spend a lifetime regaining that knowledge.)

I had one question left to the mother. Did she drink alcohol? "No. Well, not really; only socially, and then never a lot." Maybe not lately, but could she recall fifteen years ago, when she was pregnant with Pinchas?

She became thoughtful. "When we were first married and when my husband used to perform, I would accompany him to the nightclubs twice a week. I remember having a Piña Colada (pineapple juice, rum, coconut-cream *pareve* mixed drink). But only two drinks a week, and after I knew I was pregnant, I stopped even that."

The hypothesized diagnosis was Fetal Alcohol Effects (FAE). I would send them to the geneticist before making a final diagnosis. Fetal Alcohol Syndrome (FAS) and FAE are relatively rare in Israel, though a few cases have been reported, as the drinking habits of Israelis and *olim* from various populations – where alcohol consumption is more normative – have risen. I had read about it, both in professional literature and also in the seminal novel, *The Broken Cord* by Michael Dorris (1989), which was the first book to describe Fetal Alcohol Syndrome and Fetal Alcohol Effects for the general public. The author wrote about his experience in trying to find a diagnosis for Adam, his adopted Native American son, whose behavior and specific facial and body-size anomalies were as yet undiagnosed. I had never seen a case.

There are variables, which help determine whether a teratogen will have an effect upon the fetus. Which teratogen is used – alcohol, crack, heroin, nicotine (smoking), x-rays, etc. – also affects the type of damage one might see in a fetus. The dosage of the exposure is very important. The more minimal the exposure, the better off the fetus will usually be. In fetal development, when the teratogenic exposure occurs is of vital importance. Is it one short exposure time or was the exposure on a daily or hourly basis?

A mother's nutritional status and physical well-being might also play roles of varying significance in determining whether an infant is affected (and to what degree) by the prenatal exposure to alcohol. A great deal more research is necessary to determine the reason that some developing fetuses are more vulnerable than others to prenatal exposure to alcohol. The knowledge base in this arena needs to be greatly expanded. The individual factors of the mother and child are also vitally important. That is the reason why professionals cannot tell a pregnant woman how much would be safe to drink.

Since these individual factors cannot be determined, the only way to prevent FAS and FAE is for a pregnant woman to abstain from the use of alcoholic beverages during her entire pregnancy. (The USA's surgeon general's warning in this regard states pregnant women, but the crucial time may be before a woman herself knows she is pregnant. Ironically, during childbearing years, *frum* women have their *niddah* schedule, knowing when they are definitely not pregnant. So they know when the time is "safe" for wine tasting.)

This was a very unusual situation. In this case, the mother drank only two alcoholic drinks a week and she stopped as soon as she knew she was pregnant (about eight weeks into her pregnancy). After consulting with an internationally known specialist in the field of FAS and FAE, I learned that there is both a critical time and critical mass of alcohol involved in FAS/FAE. The unfortunate set of circumstances in this situation dealt with the mother's nutritional make-up and the timing (first weeks of pregnancy). The confluence of these factors was more crucial than the relatively small amount of alcohol she consumed.

My point is that FAE and FAS is a completely preventable disorder with life-long affects. Keep both timing and amount in mind. To paraphrase the words of *Kohelet* (Ecclesiastes 3:1), "Everything has its season, and there is a time for everything under the heaven."

A toast *l'Chaim* and *l'Briut* (to life and to health) to you and yours.

How We Deal with Something that Frustrates Our Success

THE MOTHER SPOKE to me with tears in her voice. "We are having a lot of difficulty with my daughter in school. She is eight years old, a very good girl and is trying, but the teachers are angry at her and keep saying that she isn't paying attention. We have been to neurologists, psychologists and special education teachers who have all said she is fine. We even tried medication for ADHD – which didn't help, and now they say it's all in *my* head!"

Both the "angry at her" and "in my head" intrigued me. One of my axioms is that there is no child that has a mother who wants to see a problem in her child. It goes without saying, that if that child's mother does want to see a problem, then the child *really* needs help! (An example thereof is Munchausen's by proxy.)

When Tikva, the cute 8-year old, came in for neuropsychological assessment, it was hard to imagine that she made her teachers angry at her. Maybe frustrated was a better word. Another of my basic axioms in life is that: we are all trying our best to succeed. That goes for *all* of us – children, parents, teachers, doctors, etc. So when that success eludes us, we respond in different fashions depending on our personalities and our life history of dealing with success and failure. Many people respond to a student's inability as a thwarting of their own success. The converse example is seen in the famous Pygmalion Effect, where teachers were told that specific students were "gifted," when in reality they were average. When these children achieved results that were only average or even poorer than that, the teachers understood the gap in expectation and result as their fault and attempted to teach them in a different fashion, sometimes even giving supplemental classes on their own time. The end result was the children achieved higher scores than their average peers.

So I looked at Tikva's condition, and especially the behavior she elicited from her teachers, as one of a stumbling block to the teachers' success.

How did her neuropsychological scores and the mother's and teachers' description differ and how were they the same – that was my challenge, since we were all seeing the same child, and we all wanted to succeed.

When communicating with Tikva, and hearing her responses, one got the impression that she wasn't paying attention. Well, the tests for attentional abilities came out WNL (Within Normal Limits). "She responds to a different question than the one asked." Both her expressive vocabulary (naming pictures and concepts) and receptive vocabulary (understanding and pointing to the correct picture that described a word or concept) were very much below average. Maybe she just wasn't intelligent? Her IQ subtest scores were very disparate, showed strong (average to above average) abilities in tests that required abstract non-verbal abilities and very poor scores (on the impaired level) in sequencing and some language and short-term memory encoding skills.

But they also reported that: "Tikva acts as though she doesn't understand what is being said." When asked to respond to a task where there was background noise, Tikva's function dropped significantly. When told a story and asked to repeat it, and later retell it and answer questions about it, she couldn't recall it, and what she did recall did not make sense in relationship to the questions she was asked. When questioned about the specifics, Tikva responded that the whole story she was told didn't make sense to her at the time either. "You mean that was a story? It just sounded like a jumble of words and sentences."

During the testing sessions, I also noted that Tikva:

- Says "huh" or "what" frequently
- Inconsistent responses to auditory stimuli
- Often misunderstands what is said
- Requests that information be repeated
- Poor auditory attention
- Difficulty following oral instructions
- Difficulty listening in the presence of background noise
- Difficulty with phonics and speech sound discrimination
- Poor auditory memory span
- Poor sequencing skills
- Poor receptive and expressive language skills
- Slow or delayed response to verbal requests and instructions
- Reading, spelling and other academic problems
- Learns poorly through the auditory channel
- Exhibits behavior problems – especially when she perceived she had gotten something wrong.

I began to get a glimmer of a hypothesis. We did some more testing in the area of phonetic ability. And the picture became clearer. Maybe she had CAPD, Central Auditory Processing Disorder, which is a type of physical hearing impairment, a form of developmental aphasia. "Aphasia is any language impairment caused by brain damage, which is characterized by complete or partial impairment of language comprehension, formulation, and use; excludes disorders associated with primary sensory deficits, general mental deterioration, or psychiatric disorders. Partial impairment is often referred to as *dysphasia*."[1] Aphasia, which does not show up as a hearing loss on routine screenings or an audiogram, affects the hearing system beyond the ear, whose job it is to separate a meaningful message from non-essential background sound and deliver that information with good clarity to the intellectual centers of the brain (the central nervous system). When we receive distorted or incomplete auditory messages, we lose one of our most vital links with the world and other people.

These "short circuits in the wiring" sometimes run in families or result from a difficult birth, just like any learning disability (LD). In some cases, the disorder is acquired from a head injury or severe illness. Often the exact cause is not known (it is also not a common disorder and so could easily be mistaken for other things that "go bump in the night," though speech and language therapists and neuropsychologists may be more familiar with aphasic disorders than other helping professionals).

Tikva was sent for further testing to an audiologist and speech and language therapist who concurred with the diagnosis. She, her parents, and teachers were taught about CAPD, and though she still is having some problems in the academic sphere (and may always be challenged in group learning situations), she and those around her understand the reason for her difficulties; specifically they know that they are all trying to succeed, and that they are complementing/ complimenting each other's strengths and not blaming difficulties on the weaknesses, and especially not responding as though each is out to "fail" the other.

Sometimes, the most we can do when attempting to fix a problem which is out of our hands is to identify it, and help all concerned understand behavioral responses that may be responses to frustration of success.

---

1. L. Nicolosi, E. Harryman, and J. Kresheck. *Terminology of Communication Disorders, Speech-Language-Hearing*, Third Edition.

He Is Blind but He Can See

"We'd like you to come up to see a young boy," said Dr. A, the then pediatric chief resident. "We have a patient here, an 8-year old boy from a small Bedouin village, he is blind but he can see."

That immediately caught my attention. Here was an obvious example of the doctor reporting his own cognitive dissonance. Cognitive dissonance can be defined as a psychological phenomenon which refers to the discomfort felt at a discrepancy between what you already know or believe, and new information or interpretation. There is a need to accommodate new ideas. In this situation, it occurred when the blind patient could really "see."

When I told the floor nurse who I was looking for, she said she had seen something different about his behavior, too. She told me that as opposed to other children in the unit, he did not show fear when they came to take blood, or inject him with antibiotic. In general, she said, "his affect was flat."

Hum, I asked in my most professional manner, where I could find him. She told me that he was in the school. Every large hospital in Israel also has a school, a one-room schoolhouse, under the auspices of the Ministry of Education. The teachers are in contact with the inpatients' school so that a hospitalized child can keep up with homework and curriculum. At Shaare Zedek, we have both Hebrew- and Arabic-speaking teachers who teach the relevant curriculum.

Fuad had been hospitalized for severe diarrhea, diagnosed with Shigellosis. He was being treated; one morning his worried parents told the doctor that he didn't recognize them. When I saw him, Fuad was being pushed in a wheelchair by his father. *Marchaba* (Hello), *sho ismac*? (what is your name), I said in Arabic. He looked in my general direction and said his name. I asked him to imitate some hand signals. He did so, but at the same time he moved his pinky and eyebrow. I did some more, and noticed that these seemingly peripheral movements continued. As it happened, his back was toward the wall and I was standing facing a mirror which was hanging in the play area of the school. As I recorded his odd eye and pinky movements, I suddenly noticed that he was imitating my eyebrow and small finger moving. Interesting, I thought, he is attending to extraneous movements in his field of vision.

I gave him a cup of water to drink. I had wanted to see if he noticed the cup coming at him and wondered what he would do. He moved his mouth to the cup I held, and started to lap it up, as a cat might lap up milk in a dish.

Then quite unexpectedly, he sneezed. I gave him a tissue; he ate the tissue.

To make a long story short, the intern and I looked at each other disbelievingly. In graduate school, especially in the field of neurology, the professors always bring up these "weird" cases that you think in a million years you'll never see yourself (most of the time that is correct). With the exception of odd sexual behavior – which one wouldn't have expected seeing in a 9-year old anyway, little Fuad seemed to demonstrate the criteria of Kluver-Bucy Syndrome (KBS).

The syndrome is named for Henrich Kluver and Paul Bucy, who in 1939 bilaterally removed the temporal lobes in rhesus monkeys, in an attempt to determine their function. This caused the monkeys to develop psychic blindness (visual agnosia), emotional changes, altered sexual behavior, hypermetamorphosis and oral tendencies. People with lesions in their temporal lobes show similar behaviors. They may display oral or tactile exploratory behavior (socially inappropriate licking or touching); hypersexuality, bulimia, memory disorders, flattened emotions (placidity), and an inability to recognize objects or to recognize faces (prosopagnosia or "face blindness"). They also show signs of visual agnosia or psychic blindness, i.e., an inability to visually recognize objects.

Further research in the hospital's medical library turned up a few cases of KBS in humans with trauma to their temporal lobes. After a CT Scan and EEG, it seemed that Fuad did indeed have some unusual activity in the temporal areas of his brain, probably related to seizures he had had as a younger child and Shigellosis which is a bacterial infection affecting the intestinal tract. We hypothesized that the Shigellosis (causing temporary metabolic deficiencies and high fever) may have created a transient form of bilateral temporal dysfunction, which in turn produced the symptoms of KBS. His condition improved over a week, which made it unusual for science, as KBS is rarely transient.

I love the dynamism of the field of neuropsychology: it is like solving a mystery. One never knows for sure what the day's patient list will present. I guess among the skills the field teaches is being able to see and understand clues when they are presented to you. We wrote it up and published it in an international neuropsychological journal as an unusual case of transient Kluver-Bucy Syndrome.

"I Am My Brother's Keeper"

Written with Jeff C.

This is not our first appointment – he has been here before. We are writing this together, Jeff (nom de plume) and I. He was referred to me with a possible neuropsychological problem which keeps him from actualizing his full potential. Some of what has been said about him: "He's a wonderful child"; "He can't get along with authority"; "He's well-meaning with a heart of gold"; "He's chutzpadik to his parents and teachers"; "He's self-destructive"; "Oppositional Defiant Disorder, but not exactly."

After reviewing his previous assessment and incorporating my clinical evaluation of his behavior, I feel that there is something else going on. His higher cognitive ability is fine. This means that he does not have a specific learning disability of a measurable kind. Though he had been in school, he has not learned in an organized fashion for a long time, practically since sixth grade. Why, when everything measurable by tests seems to function well, is his life in such a mess?

The purpose of his second appointment was to address what I instinctively felt was the something-else. The stated purpose however was to teach him the neurology and neuropsychology of Pre-verbal Trauma. The almost in passing notation in his previous assessment is that he was born with a broken clavicle, a physical trauma not unusual to natural/normal birth. However, I am saddened to think of this infant being in pain for much of the early bonding time between mother and child and the physically painful connections that would exist between this essential dyad during nursing and being held. Could this possibly be the basis of Pre-Verbal Trauma that is seen in children, adolescents and adults?

After that meeting, he decides on his own to come and work on this issue; this truant/oppositional child is always on time, always polite and cooperative. We – him and I – are on a mission to help find, and hopefully begin to allay, the source of his black hole, a sense of unfeelingness that his evermore risky behavior does not seem to fill.

I sit in my office opposite a very handsome and charming 16-year old. His pleasant disposition and looks belie the fact that he's been out of the organized Haredi school system since fourth grade, bounced to a time and again less demanding religious and academic educational environment until here he is with me, parallel to his being in a rehab center for drug misuse, a hair's-breadth from juvenile detention.

He has spoken about his younger brothers, who idolize him, their oldest brother. His concern is palpable as he sees them going in his path.

He's sad, dejected and close to hopelessness. Almost as a pre-programmed robot he relates his next step goals – getting his high school diploma, going to college in the States and then law school. Even before this mantra of a plan leaves his mouth, he doesn't exhibit a minimum of optimism. Basically, even before he says it, he feels that it is not realistic or even possible. I am not sure what is sadder for me to see and hear – his present state or his plan for the future.

What I say and believe is: "I think you have something special to offer your brothers and other people's brothers as well."

He looks at me askance and is surprised. He asks me to repeat what I just said.

"I really do think you have the voice of experience, and since you brought it up, when you mentioned how you fear your brothers will go your way, I think you have something to say. So much so, I would like to work with you and write it up together and see if we can get it printed."

It was post-Purim, a holiday which in Israel takes up the better part of a week, well maybe a month if we start counting since the beginning of Adar, at Rosh Chodesh Adar. Kids of every stripe are mal-educated to believe that *ad d'lo yada* is an open license for lascivious behavior, be it smoking whatever, drinking or doing whatever. (*Ad d'lo yada* – until one doesn't know – indicates the extent that drinking wine makes one unable to differentiate between "Blessed be Mordechai" and "Cursed be Haman," two central characters in Megillat Esther.)

So we begin to talk about his letter to his brothers:

"Well, we are all our brothers' keepers. My little brother who is eleven years old is beginning to hang out with a bad crowd. He was smoking even before Purim."

"At 11?" I ask.

"Sure, even before this year, when he was ten years old. When do you think I started smoking? I recall finding a half smoked cigarette, taking matches from home and smoking it with a friend, barfing too! That was the beginning.

"I won't talk about drugs because he doesn't know a thing about them yet! I would say to him:

- Stay in school
- Don't start smoking
- Believe in God
- You don't have to learn everything the hard way."

Dashed, he says: "Nothing I can say that will really make a difference, but I'll try. I went to everyone on the face of the earth, every social worker and person. Like that – see what good it did?"

I ask: "What would *you* say to yourself at ten or eleven years of age, if you were sitting with the young you?"

"I have no idea, can't look at time like that."

Not giving up on my own pride in this "wonderful image" I construed, I say: "Well, you have siblings, let's look at them like as if in a flashback."

"When I was 14, I thought I knew everything, didn't listen to anybody, thought I knew it all. That was the dumbest thing to think. When I was 11, I was just opening my eyes."

"Okay," I say. "What did you see?"

"At that age, you are not a baby anymore and just beginning to realize stuff. Kids have minds; they understand stuff."

"Yes, you are correct," I answer. "They understand enough which is why your brothers could and would learn from you."

He thinks a moment and says: "I wouldn't bother; trying to help kids is, well, setting yourself up for failure. Truthfully, I think you can only bribe them."

"What will happen to them the next time, bribery sounds like it is a one time solution of sorts, not an educational moment," I ask.

"What about the next time, it's really the friends that they meet. Kids today are stubborn and awful."

"Boy, you sound like a dejected and rejected parent! You know, I don't agree with what you said, I don't believe kids are bad."

"I don't think kids are bad either, really. Stuff that you do can be bad. Stuff they do can define them."

"Boy, that's what Dumbledore said to Harry Potter. Maybe we can even understand the saying: *Zeh lo hakankan ela ma she'b'tocho*, it's not the kettle but what is inside. Wait a minute, in the story of Cain and Abel, Hashem understood what Abel's *kavana* was – his intention, not specifically the sacrifice itself. This is something Cain did not understand at all.

"To me," he says, "maybe it is like when you open your eyes and see something new, a new store in the mall. It seems interesting and better than all the other boring stores. You are always going to find something new. I discovered this in Jerusalem, smoking and hanging out with friends. When I was eleven, I was smoking cigarettes, but I never thought I'd be doing drugs."

What happened?

"I found a cigarette one of the Arab workers had left behind. I made a 20 *shekel* bet that I would smoke it, took a package of Listerine and deodorant spray out of the house and I smoked two puffs and sprayed myself.

"And that was the beginning. There is nothing that protects kids from when they see something new that isn't good."

I look at him as the fountain of youthful information, the *mayim* (water) should and could have been Torah, but instead something happened along the way and today he has the wizened words of an old man, not a 16-year old who is bright and should have the whole world in the palm of his hand.

I ask this *zaken*, this wise old man: "What's the difference between the kids who did see it – did they see the new and didn't get sucked in, versus the ones who couldn't keep from falling into the trap?"

"I have a friend who did all the bad stuff and he went one way and I went another. I also thought he'd end up like me. He's a really good kid now; we are still friends. He experienced a personal tragedy before high school. I was sure he would be my buddy on this trip, thought he was coming with me, but he changed paths, he took a fork in the road and ended up a good kid, and I . . ." his voice trails on.

Thinking of his floundering away, a fish out of water, hanging with a bad crowd I feel he *is* his own tragedy.

"Maybe you need a personal tragedy, too," I say.

But his demeanor and answer showed me this was too flip and too fast.

"I know kids who took their tragedies in a totally opposite reaction, too." Meaning they *really* went down a terrible path.

I couldn't check my next remark, it just popped out: "I don't believe that."

"Yeah, I don't believe, Tupac is dead – huh?"

"You know the first Rapper."

"He's hiding out with Michael Jackson, and the Lubavitcher Rebbe," feeling this would really get a rise out of me.

"Now, if you said Elvis, I'd have a hard time arguing with you."

"I'm just joking," I say.

"Yeah, I know that," and left unsaid, was that I wished he was too.

We make an appointment for the following week.

*

Eight weeks have passed quickly. We did some EMDR, but mainly we spoke. He taught me many things. At our last meeting before his case goes to court to decide what happens next, he wrote me a Rap Song. He asked that I not share it with you, so I won't. But he is calmer, more resigned to be helped in rehab, and hopefully gleaned a sense of purpose to be his brother's keeper.

FOR FURTHER READING:

A. Becker-Weidman, "Treatment for Children with Trauma-Attachment Disorders: Dyadic Developmental Psychotherapy," *Child and Adolescent Social Work Journal*, 23:2, April 2006, 144–171.

Dr. Bruce Perry's work: www.ChildTrauma.org.

Being Too Frightened
to Stop Running

H AVE YOU EVER felt these signs when in acute stress?

– Heart beating out of control
– Flushing and/or paling of our face
– Butterflies in our stomach
– Sometimes, in dire situations, release of our sphincters
– Loss of hearing – "Everything became quiet"
– Uncontrollably shaking

What is going on neuropsychologically, or in other words, with your brain/behavior relationship?

When a person is in a calm, unstimulated state his/her neurons don't fire in what one might call "trauma alertness specific areas" (I refrain from using specific neuroanatomical names, and leave the neurologically curious among you to do your own further research). However, when a new stimulus is perceived – visually, aurally, by smell, etc. – as dangerous, it is relayed from the area of the brain responsible for senses to one that is deeper and more basic or primary in the brain's development.

The person becomes attentive and hyper-alert to their environment. S/he will, in all likelihood, neurophysiologically go into automatic pilot and begin to act in behaviors that are meant to lead to survival, such as fight and flight. The success of the action leads to a neuro-chemical reverse of the condition until the person is sure that s/he is safe and calm.

Males and females, even as children, tend to respond differently. Males generally, but not always, go into the fight (aggressive) modality, whereas women and children may do flight or play-dead (dissociate).

Once the response to the threat is successful, the person slowly but surely returns to a normal state of calm and necessary alertness.

*

THE CASE

He came having been referred by his psychiatrist. He couldn't sleep; he was jumpy and couldn't concentrate. He was screaming at his family all the time. Even though the majority of my trauma cases are terrorist- or abuse-related, this referral was different.

He was a doctor for one thing (let's call him Dr. Refael). Second, what happened to him had not taken place in the hospital. He had been walking home and saw someone on the ground, so he put out his hand to help the man get up. What happened next was part of the reason he was sitting in my office. As he put his hand out to help this man, the man lifted a bag at his side and whacked Dr. Refael in the face!

Dr. Refael was left with a very sore jaw, beginning of swelling in his eye and a whopping red mark on half his face. He went to work as if nothing had happened. However, as his face was very raw, people asked him what happened. After he told his story, someone joked, "What you really need is a mark on the other side as well," and then proceeded to slap him on the other side of his face!

Refael tells me, "He smiled after he did this, as if he was pleased with himself for balancing me out."

I am not sure what caused more shock and trauma, the first smack or the second. However, there is no question that what I saw as I sat opposite him was a man in extreme anguish and replaying everything that happened, over and over again.

"Get over it, people tell me," he continues. "I know I should; it was a stupid prank; the person who did it apologized many times since and sent a beautiful flower arrangement, as well as his wife's special potato *kugel* for Shabbat.

"But I can't. It is as if I'm on a gerbil's treadmill inside a cage. I have to keep running around the loop."

"What would the worst thing be for the gerbil if he stopped?" I ask.

He looks me straight in the eye and says in a low voice: "He will die there."

Good, I think to myself, *now we are getting somewhere*. "Let me get this straight. Your gerbil is going crazy running around in the wheel, maybe a wheel of fortune and if he stops he will die. What happens if he continues?"

"He will die. He can't continue like this. There isn't a choice – either way it's death."

He seems so doomed, I think.

He continues, "Choice one: keep moving. If you stop, you die. Choice two: if you keep moving, you die."

As he is talking, I am visualizing this gerbil as Rafael's heart and soul. Too scared to stop running to safety, and at the same time, too busy running to be safe. All I could fearfully imagine is that both would only be stopped by a heart attack!

"Which do you recommend that he choose?" I ask.

He starts to cry – he is big, over six feet and full-bodied, though not fat. But sitting there crying in front of me, I see him just as small as his gerbil, heaving from the conundrum of this closed choice.

"Let's say that magically something or someone could appear and give the gerbil a tool or magic wand to help him. What do you suggest he might use? How?"

The words "magically appear" get him to stop a minute and think. This is out of the logical loop.

He looks ahead as if seeing the treadmill and racing gerbil clearly in front of his eyes.

"I guess the tool would be a spanner." (A "spanner" is the British English word for "wrench." "Putting a spanner in the works" is similar to "throwing in a wrench" – messing up the works.)

"Wait a minute," I almost shout with joy. "I think you are on to something very important!" He looks up at me, no doubt thinking I am nuts; I know that look well from many of my patients.

"Your inner gerbil," I tell him, "knows he doesn't want to remain a slave to the wheel which is going nowhere good. You have figured out that this requires a drastic measure. Throwing something into a continuum to stop what seems inevitable. You have figured it out, it's not even a magic wand, and it is a real tool which can help him!"

"Are you are saying that I can stop his running afraid and the gerbil won't die?" he asks.

"You gave me an idea, you have a tool to help him, and I might have a tool to help you help him."

What I say is something like this: "I'd like to see if we can offer this gerbil a safe place to go to in his thoughts while he is running around. When he is a bit relaxed in his thoughts, he can figure out how to live and be, when you put the spanner in the wheel and cause it to stop. I agree, he can't stop running just yet, but he needs to be able to run *and* think.

"Can you think of a place where, though he his running, you could hold his cage and be safe?"

As the beginning of trying to do the cognitive behavioral intervention EMDR, which is among the tools I use with traumatized patients, I tried to help him search through his memory for a place he himself felt safe and calm.

"The beach, a mountain view, your favorite spot at home, your childhood hide-a-way, what about your bed, in your room?" I suggest.

"I have to admit something," he responds, "even on Shabbat, when I am lying in my room for my rest, I put on earplugs to my radio, which I leave on all of Shabbat, and it makes me calmer."

I stop a moment, and looking right at him, ask him what happened to him the first time he felt the gerbil feeling.

He looks somewhat sad now, like here we go again. "No," he says, "I wasn't beaten by my father, certainly no more than anyone else, and no, though I was in active army service I never was in serious danger."

"It seems," I respond, "that you have been asked these history of trauma questions many times and have the answers all ready. But please bear with me; I am going to ask you a weird question now. Will that be okay with you?"

He looks at me expectantly.

"When did you die?"

He is silent for a moment, and then tells me of a *pigu'a*, during the Second Intifada, in 2002, that killed a number of people standing in front of and behind him, and didn't even leave a scratch on him. The blast had knocked him to the ground, his ears rang, his face was flushed, but he didn't have a scratch on him. As a doctor, he just got up and started to minister to the wounded and never told anyone. For the most part, people just thought that he was a passer-by after the fact, and that as a doctor, volunteered to help out.

"Nothing happened to me, you see, but at the moment when I was on the ground everything was white, quiet, I couldn't hear anything and I was sure I had died."

It was at this point, acknowledging the death that was not death, the safety of a quiet spot that was not safe, at which we could begin to help his gerbil find a safe place to hold onto while Refael put a "spanner in the works" to stop the wheel racing to and from death.

Stop and Smell the Flowers

THERE IS A saying in English, "Stop and smell the flowers," which loosely means to take time out and enjoy the beauty in life. In Shaare Zedek Medical Center, Jerusalem, one hardly sees people walking slowly and enjoying the framed pictures that decorate the walls. I too am always rushing from one place to another. However, there is one place that I do stop to enjoy a sense of peace.

The place is the halls of the fifth floor near the Hedi Steinberg Auditorium and not far from the Neuropsychological Unit I head. It is always a mixed and special experience for me. Hanging on the wall are framed photographs of flowers. They are each individual pictures of a flower; the colors are vibrant, reminiscent of early spring. They are alive yet still.

In a sense, they exemplify the attributes of their photographer, Edward Michael Adler, 1948–1979, my cousin, of blessed memory. Eddy's life was cut short by his attributes.

Growing up, I remember Eddy as one of the Adler boys. At family gatherings, with many boisterous children running about, he remains uniquely etched in my memory as a quiet boy.

He grew up to become a quiet dedicated man. Though not wealthy, he modestly supported many charities: Shaare Zedek was one of them. He was inducted into the imbroglio of the Vietnam War, which so many of his age group and middle class Orthodox Jewish upbringing easily avoided by staying in university or going into the clergy. He didn't. He went into the army, and as the human soul he was, could not shoot to kill anyone and so became a conscientious objector and was trained as a medic.

On returning home, he continued working in the public health field at Staten Island Hospital as a blood bank supervisor. It was there that he made his ultimate selfless contribution. He always ate his lunch alone in the parking lot of the hospital, in his car, so that afterward he could daven *Mincha* quietly and inconspicuously.

On the afternoon of November 29, 1979, from the safety of his car he noticed a youth armed with a knife force a female nurse in a van. To quote the Congressional Record:

> . . . without regard for his own safety, Adler got on to the van's rear bumper and began shouting and pounding on the roof.

As the assailant drove the van erratically around the parking lot, Adler fell off and suffered fatal head injuries. The nurse sustained lacerations before being thrown out of the van; she lived. Eddy was posthumously awarded the Carnagie Hero Fund Medal.

So when you come to Shaare Zedek, come to the fifth floor and join with the memory of a quiet brave man and *stop to look at the flowers.*

CURRENT EVENTS
IN ISRAEL

Beaufort and Me

At the nefesh israel Conference held in 2008, a woman gave two thumbs up, smiled and said, "'Beaufort' made it; we're on the short list." I knew her to be *his* mother, Mrs. Tzippi Cedar, an experienced psychodrama therapist in her own right and mother of Yossef Cedar. The son is the co-writer and director of the film "Beaufort" – an Academy Award nominee for Best Foreign Language Film. This was Israel's first such achievement in twenty-seven years.

In a televised interview, when he was awaiting the news from Hollywood, one saw a kippa-clad Cedar in a large book-filled room with numerous awards – many of them heavy in weight – safely placed high up on a bookcase, to keep them from being damaged and to protect his children from hurting themselves. "Heavy," as well, are the topics that Cedar raises in his eloquent films.

"Beaufort" is the story set in 2000, of a group of Israeli soldiers stationed in an outpost in Lebanon, prior to the withdrawal of forces. This is a film that evokes in the audience, an almost visceral experience of the idealism, fear, boredom, ardor, frustration, honor, bravery and zeal of Eretz Yisrael's young men. The film portrays the raw emotions of the soldiers amid existential questions that arise during the Friday night *Kabbalat Shabbat* service – taking place under fire – for those men who are *davening* and those who are not. The audience feels the charged atmosphere surrounding the soldiers as they endure the ever-present challenges they face while being deployed as the last Israeli presence on this Crusader-built fortification.

When I saw the film, I was reminded of my own visit to Beaufort during Sukkot of 1982, during a hiatus in the fighting, months after it was first captured by Israel during the First Lebanon War. It was one of the strangest road trips I had ever been on.

It all started in *shul* over the *chagim* period. My Dad, z"l, was chatting with some *minyan* buddies over the month-long *shul*-going time. Everyone was speaking about the War – Operation Shalom Hagalil – that has become known as the First Lebanon War. It began with the constant shelling of Kiryat Shmona and consequent entry into Lebanon by Israel in June of 1982. It was now October and Israel and its Lebanese ally, Tzadal – the South Lebanese Army, were in charge.

One of the several *shul*-buddies was from the Foreign Ministry, another from the Tourist Ministry, and the group of them decided that a tourist visit (in this case, American businessmen) to Lebanon to see what was really going on, would help the *Hasbara* – the explanation – of Israel's position regarding the war, that they could bring back with them when they returned to the States. "It was safe," they said and to prove it, they added, "You can even bring your wives."

My Mom didn't want to go, so once I was offered the extra seat, I said, "Sure, I'll go."

There were seven of us in a Ministry of Tourism car with the grapes symbol on it. The insignia of the Ministry of Tourism is a picture of two of the biblical advance investigative team, returning from their reconnaissance of the Promised Land, carrying a huge cluster of grapes on a stave of wood. We drove up the Jordan Valley road to Kiryat Shmona, slept overnight and went on in the morning. Our first stop on the Lebanon side was the Beaufort Crusader Fortress.

As a citizen of Israel, and not just an ordinary tourist, I knew about the fierce battle to capture Beaufort and the "psychological" effect this achievement was supposed to incur in the enemy. The ostensibly unattainable fortress flying an Israeli flag meant that the most difficult and fortified position was *ours*.

The fact that there was a tremendous amount of political and press machination, mainly the report that Beaufort was captured "without losses to our side" versus the true facts which later came out – the loss of six fighters among them the legendary commander of the top unit, the *Sayeret*, Major Goni Hernik – made seeing this fortress an emotional sight.

The matrix of tunnels, like a bitter honeycomb, rendered the description of the difficulty of clearing the spaces from hidden enemy a reality. We continued up to Baalbeck, to eastern Beirut, a beautiful if not lawless territory even then, and on down to Sidon and Tyre, then home to Rosh HaNikra. A number of images are etched in my mind.

- At each of the many roadblocks, it was hard to tell which of the soldiers were ours and which were Tzalalniks, as Israel provided the uniforms for both sides;

- The lawlessness was obvious by the fact that there were many expensive brands of cars with no license plates identifying them or their country of origin (we were told by our tour leader that the cars were probably stolen in their country of origin and driven overland through Turkey, sold on the way or in Lebanon);

- The sight of a 12- or 13-year old with two bandoliers crossing his little body, shooting birds as he stood next to us overlooking the valley of Baalbeck, and among the thoughts running through my mind, was that he could just as easily have shot us;

- Seeing a flatbed truck with a *sukkah* built on it and Lubavitch Chassidim offering Israeli soldiers at checkpoints an opportunity to eat in the *sukkah* and *bentch lulav*;

- More poignantly, seeing an army bus on its side and IDF soldiers putting on their helmets and flack-jackets going to help their comrades-in-arms who had been shot by snipers, and we, following the shouted orders of the officer, turning down the next street only to see another Israeli soldier totally oblivious to what had transpired, thumbing a lift;

- And then there was Beaufort, where its tunnels and stone walls echoed with the pain of so many that were lost for a "psychological" victory.

*

On February 24, 2008, Oscar Night in Hollywood, the co-writers Ron Leshem and director Yossef Cedar, were in the audience among the four nominees for Best Foreign Language Film. War is so complex; the least one can say is that it is, at the same time, awful and awe-inspiring. "Beaufort" captures this.

The Color of Water

Late one evening, I needed something from the supermarket. I walked over to the Supersol on Agron St., near King George St. This was not an easy task at the time as the construction of the Jerusalem light rail system was going on full steam. Evening and night are the peak periods of work. There were many stumbling blocks – literally – in the path, as well as fences and equipment and, of course, the ever-present traffic.

I made it there successfully and passed the flower stand opposite the market on my right and I was security checked by the two guards, one a kippa-wearing Ethiopian *oleh* (immigrant) and the other, an immigrant from the Former Soviet Union (his accent gave him away), and then began my shopping.

All of a sudden, the title of a book I had read more than ten years earlier came to mind. The book's title is: *The Color of Water*, by James McBride. As I was going through the store collecting the stuff on my shopping list, I was trying to understand this seemingly random association.

As a psychologist, I knew there must be some relationship between what I had just experienced and what came to mind. And then it dawned on me.

I recalled a story that was in the newspapers in the late 1960s about the flower sellers that owned and operated a small stand outside the then, newly built North American style supermarket established by former Canadians. The Jewish-born flower sellers had just re-converted back to Judaism.

It seemed as though none of the other shops on that street (including an internationally famous bank) had permitted them to use water. And so, desperate to not lose their livelihood, they went across the street to the Convent, a huge gated stone edifice adjacent to what is now the Jerusalem U.S. Consul's residence, and were given water to use for their flowers if they promised to convert to Christianity. Somehow, this event had become known. Once they understood this calamity, the Chief Rabbinate arranged for both the re-conversion and a water source.

The title of this book comes from a quotation of the author's mother, Mrs. Ruth McBride Jordan née Ruchel Dwarja Aylska Shilsky bat Fishel and Hudis, who was born in Poland on April 1, 1921. In the book, she describes her Tateh as being an Orthodox rabbi named Fishel Shilsky. Twice widowed, she brought up all twelve of her children, mostly in poverty, but always in deep faith, never even applying for welfare funding. All of her children went on to graduate from university and some of them have post-graduate degrees. Mr. McBride, a musician, reporter and college professor, was always troubled by questions regarding his identity. In this book, he finally persuades his mother to tell her story.

Ruth says, in an interview with her now adult son, that her father was as "hard as a rock." Her sweet-tempered mother, Hudis Shilsky, or Mameh to Ruth, wed Tateh in an arranged marriage. The story goes on to recount how her Mameh never felt love or affection from Tateh. Mameh was mild and meek, partly from having had polio, the effects of which she suffered her entire life. The family had migrated to America and finally settled in rural Virginia in a black community where they ran a grocery store. The black community, according to an Amazon.com review, was more accepting of Jews (well, at least less violent towards them) than the local white one!

When Mameh died, Ruth left her home and her father, whom she described as being "inappropriate" and abusive. She eventually married an African-American man (McBride's biological father). At one point during her hard life, she describes going to visit her mother's sister for help. She was turned away as an embarrassment to the family. She was widowed and later married another African-American man, Hunter Jordan. He raised the eight McBride children as his own and then the four children they had together.

Growing up in Harlem and other all-black neighborhoods, James McBride and his eleven siblings were always troubled due to the fact that their mother was white. He feared for her safety and had many unanswered questions regarding her identity as well as his own. She was a very religious woman who began her own Baptist church in her home. When her children would ask: "What color is God?" she would answer: "The color of water."

As I began to make sense of the association (water and the florist stand I had passed), I also thought about a headline news story in Israel regarding events in a religious elementary school for girls.

Yediot Ahronot reported that four Ethiopian first grade girls who had just moved from Haifa to Petah Tikva, enrolled in a Zionist Haredi (ultra-Orthodox) elementary school called Lamerchav. Once in this school, they were segregated into a classroom at the end of the hall, had a separate teacher, and had no contact with other students their age. Their recess periods were also at different times than the other children, and they were transported by taxi and not on the regular school bus. "As far as Principal Yishayahu Granwich was concerned, however, these new students could not be fully integrated into the school community. Ostensibly," as noted by municipality officials, this was because the girls were not observant enough, and did not belong to the Religious Zionist Movement as do all of the students at the school.

School officials also note that since the school only agreed to admit these

Ethiopian students at the municipality's insistence, they therefore were forced to relegate them to special classrooms where they could "catch up academically." Furthermore, the students in question also attended many lessons in regular classrooms along with their peers. The school staunchly denies the claims that the girls had separate recess hours, labeling the claim as "utterly false." Furthermore, school officials describe the cab rides home as a perk given to the Ethiopian students by the local municipality.

"Who wouldn't want to be chauffeured home in a cab?" they remarked, according to ynetnews.com.

Had this been an isolated incident of elitism and "separate and un-equal," one might have been able to explain it away. However, it is not a secret that many Haredi schools will not accept Ethiopian immigrants, though they do accept immigrants (read "white") from other countries whose families are not so observant and even include converts. Other seminaries and *yeshivot* do not accept *frum* Israeli children from eastern (read "Sephardic") backgrounds.

On this basis, Moses's children would not have been permitted to attend these schools. His wife was "of color" and she and his father-in-law Jethro were converts! Jethro is credited with helping Moses promulgate the Torah by teaching first tens, then having those tens teach others and so on. The Parsha (weekly reading) named for him is one of the two that contain the Ten Commandments.

On Pesach, we keep in mind the symbolism of the holiday, especially the Seder (known as the "*Haggadah*" to Sephardim), and especially the Four Cups of wine. We are entreated to remember that we were strangers in another land; we were oppressed and God heard our cries (especially those of the children). Using His mighty hand and outstretched arm He brought us out of Egypt (Deuteronomy 7:19). We drink the Four Cups that represent the four expressions of deliverance promised by God: "I will bring out," "I will deliver," "I will redeem," and "I will take" (Exodus 6:6–7).

The Abarbanel relates the cups to the four historical redemptions of the Jewish people: the choosing of Abraham, the Exodus from Egypt, the survival of the Jewish people throughout the exile, and the fourth which will happen at the end of days.

Today, our people who were "taken out" of Africa and the Former Soviet Union exemplify the trials and tribulations of our ancestors. We are enjoined to restate and replay their travail and deliverance every year, lest we forget whence we came and where we are ultimately to go in the "end of days."

We are all created in the image of God, and to quote Mrs. Ruth McBride Jordan, born Ruchel Dwarja Aylska Shilsky bat Fishel and Hudis, God is "the color of water."

Waiting to Exhale:
Israel, August 2006

W E SEE EACH OTHER in the *makolet* (local grocery), and though we have known one another from the neighborhood for over thirty years, we just nod. We look forlorn and use our hands and eyes, as we look heavenward to express "What can one do besides pray?" We can't talk because we are waiting to exhale.

There is no one here who doesn't have a close family member, relative, neighbor, or someone who knows someone, who is not either "In the North," or "Down there" (Gaza area). "In the North" can mean in the army or just living above Netanya. Rockets hit Hadera Friday night, "lowering the boom" (literally and figuratively) from more northern cities and villages.

You hear the collective intake of air when on a bus or just walking around as cell phones beep, buzz or just vibrate with a news update. We just don't exhale, as if by letting out air we will cause more casualties and horror stories in this new Lebanon war, to be called the "Second Lebanon War."

Boaz Ofri's song from 1986 "*Shtei Etzbaot Mi'Tzidon* – Two Fingers from Sidon" refers to the distance from Israel to Sidon in Lebanon on a map – just two fingers away, but one knows and feels that at the same time, it's so close and so yet so distant.

It never seems to stop amazing me that places that were considered dangerous (Jerusalem, Ashkelon and the West Bank, for example) are now deemed havens to the new northern refugees. I know of many Israeli inhabitants, who for years would not visit Jerusalem or Judea and Samaria (Efrat, for example). During the war, those communities and individual families took families into the safety of their homes, gave them physical shelter, clothing and food, as the "just for a day or two" goes into its third week (inhale here)!

On the news, a mother tells about how she text-messages (SMS) her son on his cell phone: "We're fine, how are things where you are?" "Fine!" he writes back. They both know that they are lying to each other, but at least they are communicating. As she talks to the news reporter, she gulps in more air.

With God's help, she, and the rest of us, were finally able to exhale.

Tragedy at the Dentist's Office

Our hearts go out on hearing about the tragic case of the death of 2-year old Yair Lupoliansky, the grandson of the former Mayor of Jerusalem, Uri Lupolianski and his wife, Michal, during a dental treatment. The toddler died on his birthday.

The experienced pediatric dentist who works both in the Hadassah Hospital dental clinic and sees young patients in a private clinic, seems to have done everything according "to the book" – to quote from Prof. Shapira, the head of Hadassah Medical Center's Dental Clinic.

Yair, z"l, was under mild sedation, a common procedure for treating very young dental patients. At two years of age he needed four root canals crowns.

I am writing this not to blame anyone, but rather, we as mental health professionals are going to need our skills to calm parents and children facing similar treatment. Not treating rotten teeth can lead to serious infection to the mouth, body and of course the nearby, brain.

WHAT CAN BE DONE AS PREVENTION?

We all know about sweets, but everyone needs to be educated that putting a child, of any age, to bed with a bottle causes bottle rot – rotting teeth that are being bathed in sweet fluid. "Sweet fluid" refers to any liquid other than water! So that mother's milk, diluted apple juice, etc. are all potentially carcinogenic – causes of tooth decay. Think of it, the infant and child's mouth is sitting for hours as the child is sleeping, and even during the day, this is a tooth-rotting environment. Infants should have their first tooth brushed by a parent with a little amount of toothpaste before bedtime. A child should be seen by a Pediatric Dentist – a dentist who is board certified in treating children's teeth and mouths, a half-a-year after the eruption of his/her first tooth, at around one year of age.

I am not a dentist, but both my brother-in-law and son-in-law are, and I have heard stories of serious dental problems among young children for years.

Prevention is the best medicine.

May Yair ben Yaacov and Leah, z"l, find *menuchat olam*, eternal peace, and may Hashem grant his family *nechama*, comsolation with the Mourners of Zion and Jerusalem.

On Motherhood and Punishment

A COMPLEX CAPTURE INVOLVED the Argentine and Israeli police, Interpol, and the assistance of the local Jewish community. About five months before, while on weekend leave from prison, a young man named Ben-Ivgi managed to skip the country (Israel). He was apparently working overseas for the Abergil crime family, who helped him escape. The Abergil family is a known crime family in Israel, purported to be involved in many gangster activities and murders.

In September 1994, two 14-year old boys, Ben-Ivgi and Aloni, were arrested for murder. We were all shocked. As more and more information became known about the case, Israeli society (all of it!) became revolted and then frightened. These two young classmates, from "good families" (read: wealthy and professional) decided to kill someone for a "thrill." They had well planned this horrible crime, and had gun in hand, when poor unsuspecting Derek Roth, z"l, picked them up in his taxi. They shot and murdered him.

What had gone wrong? Their parents were professionals; they lived in Herzliya and had everything going for them. Yes, one seemed weaker, maybe even motherless, as his mother had left the family to live with someone else, but divorce is not so unusual. Everyone kept murmuring ". . . they are only children." They were sentenced to prison; their names were not publicized until they were on a furlough four years later. During that weekend off, they committed an armed robbery! Their lawyers said: ". . . they are only children," but the court held otherwise and all at once their names and privacy were no longer protected.

Their case reminded me of another that seemed too similar to ignore. In that one, two 19-year old American Jews, one motherless and the other sadistic and manipulative of his friend, kidnapped and murdered a 14-year old boy (also Jewish). They did this for the "thrill" of committing the perfect crime. This case took place well before I was born, but as I was always interested in human behavior I had delved into it as a child.

On May 21, 1924, Nathan Leopold, Jr. and Richard Loeb, two wealthy Jewish students (infamously known as Leopold and Loeb) murdered Bobby

Franks. Similar to Ben-Ivgi and Aloni, they believed themselves to be so clever, respectable, and talented that they could commit and profit from a kidnapping and murder without fear of punishment. The body was found and alongside it glasses belonging to Leopold. They were quickly arrested and fully implicated each other.

Their lawyer was the famous Clarence Darrow who was hired to defend the boys against the capital charges of murder and kidnap. They were expected to plead not guilty by reason of insanity. Darrow surprised everyone by having them both plead guilty. In this way, he avoided a jury trial which due to the strong public sentiment would certainly have resulted in a pair of hangings. Instead, he was able to argue before a single judge pleading for the lives of his clients. Darrow gave a two-hour speech which has justifiably been called the finest of his career. In the end, the judge sentenced Leopold and Loeb to life in prison for the murder, and 99 years for the kidnapping. Loeb died in a prison fight and Leopold was released on parole in 1958, after 33 years in prison. He died of a heart attack at age 66 in 1971.

What about Judaism? We believe in the death sentence. In the Torah, we read about the *ben sorer u'moreh*, the incorrigible and intransigent child. He is over Bar Mitzvah and not yet a man; his parents bring him to the Beit Din, when they feel they cannot handle him. Rashi suggests that his parents may have been the soldier and the beautiful woman whom he vanquished and then married (referred to in Parshat Ki Tezei, just before *ben sorer u'moreh* is mentioned). She is a woman without her own voice – the Gemara notes that she and her husband speak in the same voice, not only in words but in the same timbre. Their child, whom they cannot control, then goes through a process of being warned and then if he continues in his ways, is punished by death. According to the commentaries, he is killed for what he will do in the future and not necessarily for what he has done in the past and present.

I am in no way suggesting that this is what we should do when our children do not listen to us, and are not controllable. But what we may learn from all these extreme cases is the middle road. A mother needs to be heard and her presence and humanity needs to be expressed in the bringing up and chastisement of her children. The commentators also say there has never been a case of *ben sorer u'moreh*. One wonders if that is because the parents and society has always said: ". . . but they are only children."

Bringing on the Redemption
via Southeast Asia

In december 2004, the Trauma Team of Shaare Zedek Medical Center was informed of an upcoming drill with the Home Front (similar to the U.S. Dept. of Home Security). We were supposed to update the ER response to potential chemical/gas warfare. Over the years, we have had many such drills. During previous drills, the male soldiers were given parts to play in a script; they might play a child or woman who was injured by chemical or gas warfare. We were informed as to what the code for the drill would be on our beepers or cell phones, and mentally prepared for the event.

The drill was cancelled because a natural disaster, the tsunami, a tidal wave following an earthquake, happened in Southeast Asia. How, you might ask, did this tragic event for so many affect a national drill at a Jerusalem hospital?

The answer is the Home Front had mobilized its team to go to predominantly Moslem Sri Lanka and Indonesia. Hatzalah Yosh, the Emergency Medical Response Team for Judea and Samaria, acronym YOSH, is there too. This organization was established in October 2000, following the outbreak of the Second Intifada. The predominantly kippa wearing volunteer medical group operates in order to save lives, provides first aid, and acts as additional medical forces in security areas in Israel. The organization acts in full cooperation with the IDF, security services and civil representatives. Representatives from ZAKA, the Haredi organization whose volunteers work identifying the dead and collecting body parts for that purpose also went. Many other traumatologists (specialists in the field of trauma, both medical and psychological) that I know personally also left on this mission.

Why, you might ask, did they go? Why would Israelis go to areas where they are not wanted (the local government of Indonesia at first rebuffed Israel's offer of aid), and might be in physical danger not only from the post-tsunami conditions of crumbling buildings and disease, but also from local anti-Israeli militants?

The answer may be found in the stateament of the Chief Rabbi of Israel, Rabbi Yona Metzger. He felt that the Jewish nation held a moral obligation that could not be overlooked, and this was to aid the helpless people. The Hatzalah

Yosh delegation was given the added blessings of the former Chief Rabbi Mordechai Eliyahu.

What about the money and manpower this costs? What about the time away from other local jobs? I imagine that if one life is saved in Israel or around the world by outsiders observing the selflessness and *firgun* of Israel, then it is indeed *hatzalat nefashot* – saving lives – which transcends any other mitzvah and brings forth the *Geulah*/Redemption. May it be so.

Mirror, Mirror on the "Cell Wall?"

F ORMER MEMBER OF KNESSET and former Prisoner of Zion Natan Sharansky is said to have kibitzed that he seems to have been the only Knesset member who had the distinction of having sat in jail *before* he was elected.

He was referring to the spate of investigations, arrests and indictments that have plagued Israel's army, elected officials and public servants from "top to toe."

A number of Knesset members are under investigation; a civil servant is shown on television with his head covered by a coat (hiding his face, so as not to reveal his identity, even as his name has been released to the press); and a trusted head of the tax department is jailed while being investigated for taking bribes, nepotism, and what I best describe as all-around misuse of power.

In 2006, nearly 85 percent of the Israeli public thinks the country's leadership is corrupt, while more than half said that all Israeli political party leaders are tainted by corruption, according to a survey released by the Center for Management and Public Policy at Haifa University. Ninety four percent of the public believes that corruption weakens the state, while 71 percent of those polled said that corruption by the nation's leadership leads to corruption in the general public.

An outright majority, 52 percent, said there was no political party in Israel whose leaders were not tainted by corruption. Seven percent said that the leaders of the far-right National Union-National Religious Party were not corrupt, while an equal percentage believes that the leadership of the far-left Meretz Party is untainted by corruption. Five percent said that Avigdor Lieberman's Yisrael Beiteinu Party was not corrupt, while an equal percentage said the same about the leaders of the Pensioners Party.

Only three percent said the leaders of the Labor Party were not corrupt, while a mere one percent said the leaders of the Kadima Party were not tainted by corruption, the survey found. Sixty-five percent of those polled said that the bribery suspicions involving senior tax authority officials are well-founded, while 18 percent said the opposite.

Aside from the obvious distaste for this abuse of the law and, no less so, our misplaced trust in our leaders to do their jobs effectively and efficiently, how else are we, the public, affected?

An interesting phenomenon in which to understand our general distaste and possible fear of the non-trustworthy may be gleaned from research in the area of neuroscience. In this area of brain-behavior research, scientists are studying the emergent area of Mirror Neurons, or to use Sandra Blakeslee's article titled, "Cells That Read Minds."[1]

This discovery happened like many others – accidentally. But the persons seeing the behavior were neuroscientists, who were prescient enough to understand that what they were observing was a key to understanding human behavior. It helped them understand, for example, empathy, philosophy, language, imitation, autism and even psychotherapy.

One summer day fifteen years earlier in Parma, Italy, a monkey sat in a special laboratory chair waiting for researchers to return from lunch. Thin wires had been implanted in the region of its brain involved in planning and carrying out movements.

A graduate student entered the lab with an ice cream cone in his hand. The monkey stared at him. Then, something amazing happened. When the student raised the cone to his lips, the monitor sounded; and even though the monkey had not moved but had simply observed the student grasping the cone and moving it to his mouth, the area of its brain responsible for these actions "mirrored" them, as if the monkey himself had an ice cream cone in its hand.

Iaccomo Rizzolati and Vittorio Gallasse discovered mirror neurons. They found that neurons in the ventral pre-motor area of macaque monkeys will fire any time a monkey performs a complex action, such as reaching for a peanut, pulling a lever, pushing a door, etc. Different neurons fire for different actions. Most of these neurons control motor skills, originally discovered by Vernon Mountcastle in the 1960s. A subset of them, the Italians found, will fire even when the monkey watches another monkey perform the same action. In essence, the neuron is part of a network that allows you to see the world "from the other person's point of view." Hence the name, "mirror neuron."

"It took us several years to believe what we were seeing," Dr. Rizzolati related in an interview. The monkey brain contains a special class of cells, called mirror neurons, that fire when the animal sees or hears an action, and when the animal carries out the same action on its own. But if the findings, published in 1996, surprised most scientists, recent research has left them flabbergasted. Humans, it turns out, have mirror neurons that are far smarter.

He continued, "Mirror neurons allow us to grasp the minds of others, not

---

1. See *The New York Times*, January 10, 2006.

through conceptual reasoning but through direct simulation. By feeling, not by thinking."

Everyday experiences are also being viewed in a new light. Mirror neurons reveal how children learn, why people respond to certain types of sports, dance, music and art, and why watching media violence may be harmful.

Mirror neurons are found in several areas of the brain – including the pre-motor cortex, the posterior parietal lobe, the superior temporal *sulcus* and the *insula* – and they fire in response to chains of actions linked to intentions.

Researchers at UCLA found that cells in the human anterior *cingulate*, which normally fire when you poke the patient with a needle (pain neurons), will also fire when the patient watches another patient being poked.

"I call them *empathy neurons*," leading neuroscientist V. S. Ramachandran is quoted as saying. "Intriguingly, in 2000, Eric Altschuller, Jamie Pineda and I were able to show (using EEG recordings) that autistic children *lack* the mirror neuron system. And we pointed out that this deficit may help explain the very symptoms that are unique to autism: lack of empathy, theory of other minds, language skills, and imitation." Although initially contested, several groups – including UCLA, spearheaded in part by Lindsey Oberman in Ramachandran's lab – have now confirmed this discovery of the neural basis of autism.

Mirror neurons also deal a deathblow to the nature versus nurture debate, for it shows how human nature depends crucially on *learnability* that is partly facilitated by these very circuits.

Ramachandran's pronouncement that "mirror neurons will do for psychology what DNA did for biology," is a prophecy which is already starting to come true. In fact, he noted, "When I saw Rizzollati at a meeting recently he complained, jokingly, that my off-the-wall remark is now quoted more often than all his original papers!"

So I guess we can only pray that our Mirror Neurons will gain their learnability from the *yetzer hatov* (positive inclinations). And may we be worthy of the trust of the Almighty.

FOR FURTHER READING:

M. Iacoboni, I. Molnar-Szakacs, V. Gallese, G. Buccino, J. C. Mazziotta, et al. "Grasping the Intentions of Others with One's Own Mirror Neuron System," *PLoS Biol* 3(3): e79 (2005).

V. S. Ramachandran, "Mirror Neurons and imitation learning as the driving force behind 'the great leap forward' in human evolution," *Edge*, no. 69, May 29, 2000.

E. Altschuler, J. Pineda, and V. S. Ramachandran, Abstracts of the Annual Meeting of the Society for Neuroscience, 2000.

A Sad Tale of Four Sons

During january 2007, I saw the telecast of a horrible car accident on the Arava road to Eilat, where two people were killed and five wounded. It was announced that the driver was Ami Popper, who was convicted of murdering seven Arabs sixteen years before. The announcement went on to say that his wife, Sarah (née Goldberg), 42, and their 6-year old son, Shimshon, were the individuals killed.

The police informed the press that, "The initial investigation suggests that the three Popper children were sitting in the back seat without seat belts. Police said they believed that Ami Popper had been distracted by his children, causing him to veer into oncoming traffic (Josh Brannon and *The Jerusalem Post* staff)." Popper's driver's license had expired in 1999, police said. Popper and his surviving sons, ages nine and eleven, were injured.

Ami Popper's shooting rampage had rocked the nation and still resonated sixteen years later. Popper, 21 at the time, arrived at the Rose Garden Junction between Rishon LeZion and Ness Ziona with an IDF-issued rifle that he had stolen from his younger brother. He lined up Arab workers at the junction, stopped a car with West Bank plates, and made the passengers join the lineup. He then went on his shooting spree, stopping several times to reload.

Following his arrest, Popper told police he shot the men after his girlfriend left him, only to say later that he was raped by an Arab during his childhood and had acted out of shame and a desire for revenge. He was sentenced to several life terms in prison, which was later commuted to forty years with monthly furloughs as the result of his wife's work on his behalf. He became a *baal teshuvah* and married Sarah, z"l, while already in prison.

The complicated feelings for the poor children, now motherless with a father who is a convicted murderer, abounded. The police and newspaper reports inflamed feelings further by stating that the boys were not wearing safety belts. Later, I was informed that the release letter from the hospital states clearly that the boys' injuries were directly caused by the seat belts that they *were* wearing.

As a person who studies human behavior, I wondered what caused the police to blame the victims. What may have transpired was that here was a person whose name is well-known in Israel as a result of the murder of seven unarmed men who were waiting to go to work. Even though Israel is a regular country with thieves and the like, any person – and a Jewish one at that – who commits such an incomprehensible deed becomes a pariah within his own community, be he religious or not.

The case at hand reminded me of another one, in which two boys of approximately the same age as the Popper boys were left motherless and fatherless due to the father's actions.

Michael and Robert (Rosenberg) Meeropol were about ten and six years old in June 1953 when their parents, Ethel and Julius Rosenberg, were executed after being convicted of conspiracy to commit espionage on behalf of the Soviet Union – at the height of the McCarthy era.

The Rosenbergs left their young sons a legacy that was a burden and a gift, as well as an aching emotional void. Both Michael, a college professor, and especially Robert – who in 1990 founded the Rosenberg Fund for Children, a nonprofit foundation which provides support for children whose parents are Leftist activists involved in a court case – credit their adoptive parents with giving them a loving, stable upbringing. Notwithstanding, they grew up torn between the need to pursue liberal political values and intense fear that personal exposure might subject them and their families to violence or even death.

When originally secret – but later released – information came to light, it seemed that Julius Rosenberg was in all probability a spy, but that his wife Ethel was not (Verona Papers).

Ethel was executed as a direct result of her brother being *moser* (giving false testimony) against her. In an interview with *The Guardian* (Michael Ellison, December 6, 2001) and CBS's "60 Minutes" television program, David Greenglass, aged 79 at the time, said, "As a spy who turned his family in, I don't care. I sleep very well. I would not sacrifice my wife and my children for my sister."

Greenglass, who lives under an assumed identity, was sentenced to fifteen years and released from prison in 1960. He said he gave false testimony because he feared that his wife Ruth might be charged, and that he was encouraged by the prosecution to lie.

Julius and Ethel died, rather than give up any names of their family or friends. Both claimed complete innocence until the very end. They are the only U.S. citizens ever to be executed for conspiracy to commit espionage. The government alleged that the couple, along with friend Morton Sobell, helped the Soviet Union acquire the secret to the atomic bomb.

Ivy Meeropol, daughter of Ethel's oldest son, Michael, made the film, "Heir to an Execution," which was released on June 14, 2004 – fifty years to the day after the execution of her grandparents. (After their parents were executed, as no relatives dared adopt them for fear of ostracism or worse, Michael and

Robert were adopted by the New York songwriter Abel Meeropol and his wife Anne – non-Jews originally from the Netherlands.)

Many of the friends of Ivy's grandparents speak with her on film, including Harry Steingart, 103 years old at the time Ivy interviewed him. Like Steingart, most of the Rosenberg friends were trade unionists and/or members of the American Communist Party. And every single one of them – Miriam Moskowitz, Abe Osheroff, Morton Sobell, etc. – was Jewish.

Their families are another matter. We learn that Ethel Greenglass had three brothers, one being the infamous David Greenglass, and Julius Rosenberg was one of five children. But to this day neither family – even after more than a half century – wants anything to do with the Meeropols. Ivy Meeropol does her best to track down her cousins and solicit their participation, but to no avail. In her film, she shows herself on the phone working from two hand-drawn family trees, but never shows us any of the names or tells us exactly whom she is talking to at any one time.

Finally, one early middle-aged man agrees to see her. She identifies him verbally as "Baron Roberts," son of Julius's brother, David. He is astonished when she tells him that none of the other cousins will speak with her, even off camera. He cries and she comforts him. Although the triggering events happened long before any of them were born, Ivy and Baron share a moment of sorrow for all the relatives who still live with their conflicted feelings.

*

Today in Israel, recognizing the importance for continuity in the lives of the two Popper boys, the philanthropic family that is taking care of them made a connected apartment available for their *heder* Rebbe, his wife and young children. Though their uncle, Lenny Goldberg, will be "in the picture with his nephews," this family – with a multitude of their own children – will be their foster family.

Today, *Baruch Hashem*, we have our own country, which has its laws and jurisprudence. But it is especially blessed to be the home of a community of Jews who are strong enough to do the right thing, namely to find a home and provide love for children whose father – a convicted murderer – is responsible for the unintended death of their mother and 6-year old brother. May these innocent boys, as they become adults, look forward (as well as back on their family and community), while holding their heads high.

MY PERSONAL JOURNEY

Revisiting Germany

The area I was raised in was then known as "The Gilded Ghetto." Today it is called the Upper West Side. Apartments were on and off the Avenues. We lived on the Avenue, Central Park West. I was fortunate to have parents and grandparents, uncles and aunts and cousins in close or reasonable walking distance from us all the years.

This may sound weird, but because my family was out of Germany during World War II and was fortunate to have not lost close family members, the old Bensheim homestead and the plaza in front of it, was a picture that hung in my parents' house, actually near my father's closet and dressing room, for much of my life. He would regale us with how he painted the coal-filled bed warmers with shoe polish and was thoroughly punished by his dour grandfather when he was discovered!

"GERMANY," SHE SHOUTED, as if I could have heard her here in Jerusalem through the open window. "The line is awful tonight. I thought I heard you say you are going to Germany." I told her that she had heard correctly.

My paternal grandfather, z"l, was born in Germany and left for England and then the U.S. before WWI. His wife, my grandmother, was born in the U.S. (about 120 years ago). My maternal grandfather was from Germany as well. According to family lore, he met my maternal grandmother, a registered nurse in the Jewish Hospital in Holland, on a train in Holland. My mother was born and educated in Amsterdam until they immigrated to Canada, just before WWII broke out. As a matter of fact, they arrived in Southampton, England to meet the boat just as the German's invaded Holland. So, my childhood experiences of the Holocaust are very different from most of the Jews I know. (As an aside, my husband's parents, grandparents, and great-grandparents were all American born, many of them were Spanish and Portuguese and not Ashkenazi).

It's important to understand that I grew up seeing and hearing native German people, be they Jewish or not (my Dad had German clients). Being a very curious kid, I learned to understand and speak it (albeit a not very grammatical version).

I received an email from a very distant cousin (I'll call him Nathan). Nathan's mother, z"l, was my grandfather's first cousin. Since the late 1940s, he and his family have lived in San Francisco. He called to tell me that the city of Bensheim had invited him and his (our) family, who were the only Jews of the town, to attend a special occasion. It seems the town had decided to name a Platz (Plaza) in memory of our ancestor (his great-grandfather and my great-great-grandfather's father) Heinrich Roteheim (not his real name). I immediately asked to be counted in.

Cousin Nathan had been born in the family *haus*, which had been inhabited by the only Jewish family in the town since 1597. The Jewish cemetery (Aisbach-Bickenbach) dates from 1300. He grew up and went to elementary school there, leaving only when his father, an engineer by education and trade, was "let go" from his job because of nazi (I won't capitalize this word) rules. Nathan, a brother, and their parents were in Auschwitz; the eldest brother escaped to Palestine. Though he and his parents survived the concentration camp, his brother was killed. The eldest brother, who went to Israel, joined the army and was killed in service to our country. After the war, Nathan, and his parents went to Holland, then France, before finally settling in the U.S.

The fact that Nathan, a spry 82-year old, returns to Germany regularly to see old friends (most of whom are not Jewish) and gives lectures for teens on his experience as a young child in the Holocaust, was a definite incentive to go on this trip. We were being hosted by the Bürgermeister of the city. You see, our ancestors had been very involved in the Jewish community, and as it grew, over hundreds of years, remained so. Cousin Nathan waxed poetic about the parsimonious locals hosting us, and how they seemed to be *ganz bauch-gepinzeled* about our coming. ("*Ganz bauch-gepinzeled*" was one of my Dad's favorite German descriptions. It means being pleased with oneself. Its literal translation is belly-scratched, a behavior seen in "very pleased" monkeys). I told him we were excited to be coming, but to remember we wouldn't be eating anything our hosts prepared. "What about the *Weisse Spargel*, the white asparagus, and fresh strawberries, one cannot visit Germany in this season and do without?" he practically cried.

And so along with the clothes, paper plates, plastic flatware, aluminum foil, and the vacuum-packed tuna, we packed the asparagus cooker I had ordered from Amazon.com.

My attitude about international travel is that Hashem did not give us *mitzvot* that cannot be adhered to under *all* circumstances, and that in *all* places in His world, planning and strategizing is the key.

We arrived at the airport, rented a car and drove to Worms, a city near the "home-town." My sister and her husband met us there, rounding out the Kosher Israeli Family. We went to Rashi's *Beis Medrash* and *shul*, and saw the *mikveh* (ritual bath), which was filled by a natural underground well. We visited the cemetery with graves dating back from 1011, among them Rav Meir, the Maharam of Rothenburg (c. 1215–1293). Rav Meir, was a German rabbi, poet, and a major author of the Tosafot on Rashi's commentary of the Talmud. He was kidnapped and held for ransom in about 1286, during the time of King Rudolf I. There had been an edict instituted to persecute the Jews and use them as cash reserves. Tradition has it that the amount of 23,000 marks silver was raised, by the Rosh, to ransom him, but Rav Meir refused, fearing it would encourage the imprisonment of other rabbis. He died in prison having been held captive for seven years. Fourteen years after his death, a ransom was paid for his body by Alexander ben Shlomo (Susskind) Wimpfen, who was subsequently laid to rest in Worms beside him.

Coming from Israel where we can date cities and artifacts to the time of our forefathers, experiencing "sensate" history is not a big deal. However, for those of us who came from America, first inhabited by Jews in 1654, being able to visit the headstone of a *gadol* (great Torah scholar) from 1293 was indeed a special *zechut*.

On the day the Platz was to be named, we gathered at 9:45 (*pünktlich*), for the 10:00 a.m. beginning. The Bürgermeister spoke for the city and Nathan spoke for the family, all in German. Both my sister and I were amazed how much we understood.

Interestingly, when discussing the destruction of the town's synagogue, the word "*geschichte*" was used, as in "the town's synagogue was destroyed at the beginning of the *geschichte* on the Night of the Broken Glass." The word does mean "history," but we knew it also means "yarn" or "tale," as in admonishing a child by saying: "I don't want to hear about your *geschichte*; you need to go to bed *now!*" Psychologically speaking, this double entendre may be an example of the subtle attempts of distancing the Germans from the events of the war, used by the Germans.

From the Platz naming, we took a short walk to our mutual "homestead." It is used today as a women and children's clinic of the Heiliger Geist (Holy Ghost) Hospital – the nomenclature has its own black humor!

Lunch, paid for by the city, was next. The quaint manor house in which it was to be held had been set up for *komish* (odd) me. I had spoken to them previously and emailed them a picture of my new *Spargel* (asparagus) pot. My sister was staying in the manor house, so all the paper goods and stuff we needed were readily available in her room. One of the gentile guests whispered to my sister, "This is a restaurant, you don't have to cook or clean," but we just did our thing with the *Spargel* and had fresh strawberries for dessert!

From there we went to the cemetery where our family is buried and were admitted by the man who has the key (on a previous visit thirty-seven years previously, my husband the kids and I climbed over the fence!). Our families are Kohanim and as such are buried around the periphery of cemeteries so that they can be visited without their family members getting too near. The oldest graves were from 1300. My husband said a *Hashkava* (Sephardic version of prayer for the dead) at the gates before we washed our hands with water from a nearby *Spargel* stand, where we bought a kilo of *Weisse Spargel* to bring home to my Mom.

In a nearby town we visited a small quaint one-room synagogue. It seems as though the *shul* was in use over 150 years ago. Its remains were found in the early 1990s during the construction of an office building, and the city spent thousands of dollars reconstructing it. There is a balcony for women, and chairs were set up in front of a lectern. As it turned out, that night at 8 p.m. there was to be a monthly lecture on "The Jewish Ritual of *Mikveh*."

Of course we went. The local priest and the head of the Education Department welcomed us; we were old friends, having met in the morning at the Platz naming ceremony. What was *amazing* was that the audience, who was seated by 7:45(!), numbered close to sixty! The lecture was all in German with the gentile professor showing slides he took at Masada and other more modern *mikveh* locations (such as Frankfort), using many citations in Hebrew from the Torah, Mishnah and *Shulhan Arukh*! He noted that the main source of a *mikveh* is *Mayim Chayim* – Living Water. He went on to say that if they leave just having learned that there is a difference between *sauber* (clean) and *rein* (clean/pure) then he taught them a lot.

I *had* to speak up at the end! I thanked them all for the day and said that just like the Living Water, which as the wonderful professor demonstrated, is in use today all around the world, the city and this lecture brought to life my family in a very "living" fashion. *Od Avinu Chai* – Our Father Lives On!

In the morning we went back to our *real* home – Eretz Yisrael.

The Appointment Dress

It wasn't until I entered high school that I had a rude awakening. Not everyone grew up like I did and not everyone could relate to what I thought was normal. You see, I had been with the same group of people since age three, and they just accepted what came with being me.

Let me explain. One major pre-holiday experience for me was "the Appointment Dress." My paternal grandmother, Oma N., was quite a stylish lady. She always matched, always dressed tastefully and always wanted her granddaughters to do the same.

My maternal grandmother, who lived in a penthouse apartment in our building "on the Avenue" in Manhattan, was not into clothes in the same way. Oma S. had been a Registered Nurse in Holland in the early 1900s. She was the person you went to with medical needs. I recall getting very sunburned and having a fever – my mother sent me to Oma S.'s home. While she lived in the penthouse apartment and had help at home, she took great pride in the fact that she hand-sewed her own dresses. She took particular effort in attaching a lace collar and lapel to each of these dresses. My Oma N. would roll her eyes and not say a word when my Oma S. would show off her new creation and the matching pancake hat with lace tulle veil she had also made. My Oma N. would have her hats created by the milliners of note.

My Mom's idea of shopping, for her increasing brood, was to go to the local children's shop, and take home racks of clothing Saturday night. We would try on and choose and then first thing Monday morning all the racks and clothing, except for those we wanted, would be returned.

So when my Oma N. called to arrange for "the Appointment Dress" with *just* me it was really quite a to-do. Sam, Oma's black chauffer for many years, would come and pick me up with my Oma in the car. The car was a black limousine. I never thought this was a big deal, because it just was.

As I said, though, in high school it was a big deal! I remember begging my grandmother (and Sam) to pick me up around the corner from the school. I hated hearing the other girls saying: "Your car awaits you." I practically crawled into the car crying hysterically, as my grandmother said: "This is something to cry about?"

Yes, it was!

But that was many years later. In elementary school, it was just what was and off we would drive to Best & Company. The one dress I particularly remember with warmth was my robin's egg blue dress. "It matches your fair coloring and blue-green eyes," I was told. I had never seen a robin's egg, blue or any other color. I thought eggs were white and born in boxes! We did not leave the store without buying a straw Bretton hat and white gloves. With black patent leather shoes and white thin socks, I was on a roll.

Needless to say, my Oma N., Sam, the car and the lifestyle are long gone.

When the Haggadah is completed and we say L'shana ha'baah b'Yerushalayim, Next Year in Jerusalem, we who are already here are just onsite waiting for the Third Beit HaMikdash (Temple) to make its appearance. It is as if we are the advance party of this special Appointment Day. We feel blessed.

A Thanksgiving Day Story

I married the boy next door, literally. I lived on 70th Street on the Avenue, and my husband lived on West 70th Street! We met in shul *during the sermons, when we both opted out. The irony here was that eventually my husband would become a Rabbi there (and in other communities) and give the sermons!*

ONE OF THE HARDEST things for me to give up when moving to Israel from the States was not Sunday, but rather Thanksgiving.

Growing up in Manhattan meant waking up *very* early on Thanksgiving Day and watching the participants dress in their costumes and blow up the giant five-story balloons at the New York Planetarium. Then we would go to a service at Congregation Shearith Israel or The Spanish and Portuguese Synagogue (the S & P) commemorating the day. The congregation's first members arrived in New Amsterdam in 1654, so this is *serious* American Jewish history. After we saw The Parade on Central Park West, we had *the meal* of turkey, chestnut stuffing and cranberry sauce.

I am a third generation Yankee. My husband's family has the first *ketubah* (Jewish marriage contract) registered at The S & P in the late 1750s. So Thanksgiving was not only a national holiday, but a special family one too, where the family who lived not in walking distance, could join together.

Here is my Thanksgiving story.

We came to Israel in 1969 during the post Six-Day War Great American Aliya. It was 1972. I was pregnant and had uneasiness that I couldn't explain which started after the *Chagim* (September/October). I can only explain it as cravings for specific foods, day and night! Now you have to understand, I had *never* had cravings in any previous pregnancy and thought it was a lot of malarkey, until then!

Since then, I know that although there is no widely accepted explanation for food cravings, almost two-thirds of all pregnant women have them. A more serious type of craving, called pica, in which women crave non-food items, like dirt or laundry starch, can be dangerous and even fatal. Several theories have been proposed as to what causes pica, from a deficiency of calcium or iron, to the ability of certain non-food items to quell nausea and vomiting. However, there has never been any medical reason determined. Needless to say, cravings of this nature are not to be indulged.

My craving was very specific. I was dreaming, during the day and at night, about turkey, chestnut stuffing and cranberry sauce.

Israel then was a different place. If you wanted to make chocolate chip cookies, you had to cut the chocolate into chips, brown sugar was made by adding molasses to white sugar, and the main dietary stables were eggplant and oranges (apples were just beginning to be available, having grown in the Golan, a part of Israel since 1967).

As I was dreaming day and night, I was also working out ways to solve my problem – by then my husband's problem, too! Turkey was no problem; chestnuts, though very expensive, could be found, but not the cranberry sauce. I called the American PX (canteen/store for U.S. military and consulate workers). After finding out that they had kosher cranberry sauce, I begged to be allowed to buy it. Nope, if neither you or nor your husband are "in the Service," you cannot.

By early November, the Dan Hotel in Haifa advertised a complete American Thanksgiving Day Dinner. That was in Haifa, we were in Jerusalem! No problem, there was the *sherut* (jitney) service, that delivers packages, and after hearing my tale of woe, the hotel agreed to prepare take-out and give it to the *sherut* driver. Two weeks before Thanksgiving, the Tel Aviv Hilton had a similar offer. I canceled my order in Haifa, and got the Tel Aviv Hotel and *sherut* to do the same process, and started to relax. A week before Thanksgiving, a Jerusalem hotel offered the same deal. Canceled Tel Aviv and booked Jerusalem. We would go out for *the dinner*.

It was Thursday night; we went out, had the dinner with all the trimmings on our plate in front of us. I saw it on the plate, took a deep breath – my poor husband smiled and wearily thought, *Well, we are finally going to be done with this*! Whereupon I bolted from the table to the Ladies Room. Yes, I couldn't eat a thing, the smell was even too rich for me!

Fast forward thirty years. We were at a pre-Thanksgiving dinner Sunday evening at friends. We were invited to a wedding on Thursday, and *Sheva Berachot* (one of seven meals of the bride and groom after the wedding) Friday night, where the menu would be, you guessed it, turkey, chestnut stuffing and cranberry sauce. Just in case though, my freezer always has a ready supply of frozen whole cranberries we schlep back from trips to the U.S. (still unavailable in Israel).

Goodbye Mikveh

"Take room number two. The *miztvah* is bigger when the *mikveh* is cold, Luv." Even though as a new bride I was new to the whole experience, I knew that this couldn't be right. I waited, and waited and waited, two hours to be exact, and finally got the "Hot One" – actually "tepid" was an understatement.

That happened in London almost fifty years earlier and is the first of many *mikveh* stories I have amassed of the many years of my "dunking" life.

Gail Sheehy, in her bestseller, *Menopause: The Silent Passage*, doesn't mention the regularities and challenges of *mikveh*-going as one of the many states of perimenopause, nor for that matter the surprisingly nostalgic memories its cessation engenders. *Mikveh* ranks with doing homework with the kids, and teaching them to drive. Menopause is among topics that rank as: "Why didn't my mother prepare me?!"

There were the early years, when my "waiting-room friends" and I would reward ourselves with Carvel soft ice cream on the way home. We all had different ways of working through the complex feelings of going.

I wrote my Master's thesis on the relationship between the *mikveh* and body image, my way of dealing through intellectualization with a personal "bump in the road." I had cause to look for it and read it. No great scientific opus, but the research and defense of it to my Jesuit proctor got me through some of the *mikveh* issues at the same time as Women's Lib issues ("My Body My Self") were looming in the secular world of the Baby Boomer women coming of certain age.

To this day, when I meet congregants from my husband's first community, they remind me of the Mystery Bus Ride I took them on called the "Dry Run Bus Trip." The community was *mikveh*-phobic and misinformation prevailed. They had all heard the story of Leslie's grandmother who had drowned in the *mikveh*. The poor woman did indeed drown in the *mikveh*, when the ceiling of the dilapidated building fell on her. So through the good offices of the synagogue's Sisterhood organization we rented a bus, visited the *mikveh* some three towns away. I presented (in retrospect, a somewhat stuffy) historic and religious lecture on the way there, and joined the group singing camp songs on the way back. To end the outing we had quiche for "lupper" (lunch and early supper) at my home.

These were the OPEC Gas Rationing months of 1973–74. Back then, trips and errands were calculated by how much gas they would consume. It took a whole tank to go from the little city we were in to the Jewish "metropolis" of Hartford, Connecticut, so kids' carpools had to be arranged so that I would have cover for the three days wait it took to refill the car with gas!

As a rebbetzin in a small community, I took the brides to the *mikveh*. Once, I even took a groom who wanted the same special experience as his bride-to-be and go into the marriage "purified" (I guess I did a great sales job!). That was in the sensitive 1970s, not the "me" years of today.

There were other stories, including visits to *mikveh*s on vacations. One was the visit to Bournemouth, England, where the Jewish Travel Guide said the *mikveh* existed – but omitted to say it was out of commission for ten years. I certainly won't forget my attempt to "dunk" in the October English coast. To make a long freezing story short, I took the train up and back to London the next day, where "tepid" was steamy by comparison to the sea!

Another, was the hot summer evening, when again the local *mikveh* was in repair and I went to a *very* Haredi neighborhood on the seacoast of Israel. I asked a religious woman where the *mikveh* was. As far as I could see, everyone was out on their *mirpesset*, porch. The woman, who looked the epitome of demure and modest, let out a howl: "Bracha, *Od achat le'mikveh*" (Bracha, another one for the *mikveh*). A million eyes, or so it felt, were staring at me from on high!

I will not give the name of the place we traveled to, and where the *mikveh* was open and not in disrepair. "Yippee," I said to myself as I entered. As soon as the *balanit* (*mikveh* lady) turned on the lights the place became alive with cockroaches! There was even one in the *mikveh*! I whimpered that there is a roach in the water. "*Hu met, lo?*" (He's dead, isn't he?) Whereupon she took a net, caught him, and proudly, and haughtily I might add, said, "Is the *mikveh* now clean enough for you?!"

As one who looked forward to pregnancy as a respite from these experiences, I learned to enjoy my monthly "quiet time" – I added Dead Sea salts to my *mikveh* bag which till then held my scissors, combs and pumice stone.

I recommend you sit down with your daughters, at the proper time, and show them the lighter side of this awesome contract we have with our husbands, our future children and of course, Hashem.

On Wayfarers, Tabernacles and Tents

Each of our holidays has unique qualities – beyond food – that allow us to build special memories for our families and us. With the approach of the Intermediate Days or Chol Hamoed Sukkot I am always on the lookout for *tiyulim* – outings. The following experiences involve New York, São Paulo, Brazil and Israel, too, to balance things out.

We were in New York one summer with our grandchildren looking for something for every age and level of walking ability – from ten months to grandparenthood – that does not cost an arm and a leg.

We had a great day. We went to see the New York City Waterfalls! We started at 10:00 a.m. in Red Hook, Brooklyn. We discovered NYC's other "checkered cabs" – also yellow with black and white checks – water cabs which we found on the Internet.

The New York Water Taxi ran a free daily shuttle from Wall Street's Pier 11 in Manhattan to Brooklyn's Red Hook Ikea superstore and in the reverse direction, too. On this free ride we were able to see the Waterfalls under the Brooklyn Bridge, a view of the Verrazano-Narrows Bridge, the Statue of Liberty and many other views of Manhattan and Brooklyn, ending up at the South Street Sea Seaport. We later retraced our water trip, and found our car back at Ikea, which is a short distance from Borough Park with kosher eateries galore.

What we didn't expect was a free parking place for the day! We went looking for the pier (as foreigners we used Mapquest and landed on the wrong pier first). We ran, attempting to catch the "taxi" twist, *kippot* flying, and one or two scraped knees, but just missed it. So we decided to slow down and wait for the next one. All of a sudden, our group who had not eaten in more than eight minutes (!) smelled fresh popcorn. Maybe there was a movie theater around with a Kashrut *hashgacha* for the popcorn? This didn't seem at all possible near the port, nor the unmarked factory buildings in the vicinity. There were no signs around.

All of a sudden, a mirage appeared. Two men in black and white outfits, *tzizit* (garment with fringes), large *kippot* and Bluetooth® earphones (all signs of *frum* businessmen!) were standing next to the opening of what we previously thought was a brick wall. They were not speaking English, one of my grandchildren said. He then went into Hebrew and asked him a *landsmann* question. It didn't seem like he understood this either. I then used my fractured German. He responded in Yiddish and asked if I could speak English and we were "connected." Is it possible that there is anything kosher in the vicinity? We told him our tale of woe concerning our *tiyul* and the missed water taxi. Within seconds, he nodded and winked to the man standing next to him. Shortly thereafter little hands were laden with bags of kosher, delicious-smelling popcorn. I offered to pay and he demurred. It seems we had met both Ike and a relative of Sam's from "Ike and Sam's Kettlecorn."

*

Following New York, my husband and I headed for Sao Paulo, Brazil. We were invited by Nefesh Brazil to give lectures to Jewish mental health professionals, rabbis, teachers and parents on various topics in São Paulo. So this is a recommendation for a *tiyul* over Sukkot for visitors to São Paulo (where there are 70,000 Jews)!

The community kept us happily busy with lectures and *shiurim*. We had the opportunity to see many Jewish institutions and were so impressed with the level of *chesed* and *chinuch* (education) and especially *kabalat orchim* – this community truly embodies the lessons of our forefather Abraham, whose tent was open from every direction to wayfarers.

The week was chockablock full of lectures, but we did get a visit to an inner-city jungle, Parque do Morumbi, a national monument to the natural São Paulo of thousands of years before it became the third largest major city in the world! On entering, we said hello to one of the guards. It turned out he was the one in charge. When he found out we were from Israel, he insisted on taking us around himself! He told us that among his ancestors are many of the indigenous Indian tribes. "And now," he said, "I have met descendants of the most important tribe of all, the tribe of Abraham." We were dmbfounded, and that was before he parted with us saying: "*Shalom* and *Shana Tova!*" (It seems he moonlights as a guard for a Reform synagogue!)

*

And now to Israel, which encompasses every fiber of our minds, souls and hearts, but in reality is smaller than the smallest of Brazil's twenty-six states.

Over Chol Hamoed, the magnificently reconstructed Roman antiquities of Caesarea (including the uncovering of some of the ancient Jewish neighborhood) have wonderful activities for children of every age (grandparents are kids, too!). Beyond the wonderful seascape, viaduct and artifacts, are the interactive holographic conversations you can have with historical personalities and the riding academy's bi-annual presentation at the hippodrome. There is also a kosher restaurant with a *sukkah*.

So, wherever you put down your *sukkah*, or as "*tiyulers*" (wayfarers), you may not be obliged to eat in one at all (ask your rabbi). May you pitch your permanent tent here, in Eretz HaKodesh!

Any Port in a Storm . . .

T HE DOCTOR GAVE ME a list of blood tests I needed to take, but said: "We'll start the chemo next week and you'll get the tests all done in a week or two." That was on a Thursday during the last two weeks of August 2010 when everyone the world over (or so it felt) is on vacation. If you are Israeli, that means you were in Greece or Italy as Turkey is off the vacation list. The Turks for their part are surprised that Israelis have responded to their president and compatriots' constant diatribe against Israel, Jews and Israelis, by canceling their vacations to places that sing, "Kill the Jews/Israelis" as a refrain for all songs!

Anyway, I was *home*, my Shaare Zedek Medical Center, my home-away-from-home for 26 years. In less than a week, I had all the tests done. The one thing that took a bit of negotiation was the port.

Being, as I am, a graduate of four C-Sections, thyroidectomy, corrective plastic surgery, eye surgery and now hysterectomy and general roto-rooter – I knew in what terrible shape my veins were. During the summer, a doctor had to be called in to draw blood from my foot, as phlebotomists are not permitted to draw blood from a patient anywhere besides his or her arms, and my hand and arm veins had shut down.

I knew that a port (or portacath) was the answer. I had heard about a Pediatric Port as a smaller one, more flush than the grown-up one. So I located a Pediatric Surgeon who implants ports and asked if he would do it. He said he needed the permission of the surgeon who did adults. I told him that he was in Greece on holiday. So we set the time and place and he did it. A port, to the uninitiated, is a small medical appliance that is installed beneath the skin. Mine was installed under general anesthesia. As it turned out, this was a good idea as I bled a lot during the surgery and needed intervention. A catheter connects the port to a vein, in my case the Jugular Vein. Under the skin, the port has a septum through which drugs can be injected and blood samples can be drawn, usually with less discomfort to the patient than a more typical needle stick. I have a small bulge under my skin that looks like a small smooth topped bottle cap.

The area is very sensitive and I am frequently in serious discomfort. I use a local anesthetic when it is bad and take a pain killer. I had the port put on my left side, even though I am a lefty, as I didn't want the seat belt, on the passenger's side, to bother me all the time. I also knew I wasn't going to be driving so much.

What is the point of all of this information? No matter what your situation, no matter what your illness, know your body, its strengths and weaknesses and use this knowledge to allow your body to be successful, much like I advise those who come to me in my parallel life as a psychologist (not patient). Don't wait for your parent, spouse, child (his/her teachers) to fail and then go in to fix the problem – understand their strengths and weaknesses. We all want to succeed, so do what you can to engineer the environment so that it is welcoming and allows you (and them) to achieve this success.

Purim 2011: Cheering On Our Warriorettes and Warriors

I KNOW I'M TREADING on thin ice, but I can't help but see certain parallels between what's been happening during the hair-raising Arab Spring in the Middle East and the events leading to Purim so many years ago. Passing through the month of Adar Alef, comparisons between the many who rose against us, the small Jewish community of old Persia, and our current many Jew-hating and Israel-hating Arab neighbors seem obvious.

I am reminded of stories of the ancient Greek Amazon women who were touted as active warriorettes. The men and boys in their society must have paid a tremendous physical and psychological price.

Was Esther our Amazon? She definitely treated and was treated by men differently; she paid a high personal price and was rewarded by Hashem in many ways. There are some sources that connect her with the building of the Second Temple. Historically, Megillat Esther tells of events which took place just prior to the very first Feast of Purim – which may have taken place on March 7, 473 BCE, forty-three years after the Temple was completed (Esther 8:12). The Persian king she married, Achashverosh, is said to have been Xerxes I, who reigned from 485 to 465 BCE. He was the son of Darius the Mede.

The Persian king who gave Nechemiah permission to return to Jerusalem and rebuild the city walls in 445 BCE was Artaxerxes Longimonus (Nehemiah 2:1). He reigned from 465 to 424 BCE and was the son of Xerxes I, and some say the son of our Esther.

We women today are also warriorettes, though our menfolk only seem to note it on Friday night when they sing "Eishet Chayil," which literally translates as "Warrior Woman" (more commonly known as "Woman of Valor").

Thinking of that I am reminded of an "only in Israel" experience that took place in the late 1970s. An ultra-religious member of Knesset was bemoaning the fact that finally there was a good television program, one that would be a positive influence on the television watching public. He, of course, did not have a television at all, and never watched the show. What was he bemoaning? The program began airing before Shabbat was over. To what program was he referring, you might ask? "Eishet Chayil." Much to the muffled laughter in the

Knesset, this rabbinically clad member of Knesset did not know that this was the modern Hebrew translation of the TV show featuring the scantily, lycra-clad Wonder Woman!

So, what's the point? Queen Esther is the Persian version of every *Yiddishe Mama* – fighting for her direct and more global family, following the destiny Hashem has set for her.

But there are other unsung warriorettes among us. Do you know that in the U.S. in 2011, there were probably –

- About 21,880 new cases of ovarian cancer
- About 43,470 new cases of uterine cancer (most of these will be endometrial cancer which starts in the lining of the uterus)
- About 192,370 new cases of invasive breast cancer

These and other cancers which effect women, *rachmana l'zlan*, (God have mercy) will touch so many of our sisters, mothers, grandmothers and daughters – and our families as a whole. But the woman alone fights most of this battle – and it is the loneliest war a woman will ever face.

In a regular army of fighters, soldiers have whole battalions fighting in front of and behind them. They practice maneuvers, wear special uniforms and all sorts of gear to not only protect them from and to attack the enemy, but also to identify them as part of a team to cheer on. We are proud when we see our soldiers walk around, all the while trying not to think about the fear, anxieties, pain, mud and brambles they must endure.

What about these women warriors fighting the battle of cancer? They have no outward signs of or uniforms which might identify them. We don't read about Haman during their "*megillah*," booing and stamping our feet. The enemy is faceless and nameless, just another factor among the various challenges faced by these warriors.

Hashem has given scientists the means today to fight this war again and again. Whereas in previous years cancer was a disease no one spoke about, and people were seemingly embarrassed to acknowledge the suffering, today things are different. *Baruch Hashem*, we live in a generation of ever-newer treatments; research of even one year ago is dated. Information is shared by cancer centers world over; the Internet connects warriors throughout the four corners of the world, allowing them to share diagnostic and treatment information, anxieties, hopes and dreams.

What can we learn from our Queen Esther? Don't see the battle as a lonely one; involve those directly around you and your community as a whole. Share information. Not only you, but your family and the greater community as a whole will benefit. You never know who might be living in a "walled city," without access to the information you have.

May we all find joy and relief from oppression as we listen to the heroism in the face of seemingly impossible odds. As we hear the words of the *megillah*, let us not just boo the bad guys, but also cheer our warrior, Queen Esther, her uncle Mordechai and all those who were and are involved in saving the lives of our people.

A Life Lesson and
My New Reality

IN THE SPRING of 1998, Shaare Zedek's New York-based Women's Division, under the watchful direction of Lee Weinbach, chose me as the recipient of the Maimonides Award. I knew it was not only for my work at Shaare Zedek, but also as a first of many future recognitions of my late father's dreams and aspirations for this wonderful institution.

I saw that honor as an opportunity to share a life lesson, as I present below in "The Maimonides Award." It also showed my deep appreciation of my years of employment at the Shaare Zedek Medical Center. That, dear readers, was then. I would like to bring to you a new reality for me during 2010.

Today not only am I a Shaare Zedek employee with twenty years of seniority, but as I stepped over the threshold last week, I was a "new entity" – an oncology patient beginning chemotherapy.

My serious cancer came as a surprise. I had no symptoms, and though I was in a six-month follow-up of blood tests for my previous cancer (fifteen years earlier), nothing showed up.

In hindsight, regular gynecological check-ups, which I neglected for the past many years, *may* have found this endometrial cancer earlier, according to the surgeon who operated on me. But maybe not. In any case I hope and pray that even one person gets diagnosed sooner because of my situation.

I am realistic, but at the same time optimistic. I wouldn't be me if I didn't see the funny/odd side of things. For example, many people have sent me emails telling me how I must envision the chemo attacking and killing the cancer buggers wherever they are hiding. Think of the drugs coming through your veins as "Pacmen" gobbling up the "nasties."

Try as I might, I can't do it. Instead, my mind is full of many ideas for articles and essays.

Best wishes and prayers for health, happiness and living life to the fullest from me – Judith Sandra Bendheim Guedalia, also known as Sara Zipora *bat* Rivka *v'HeChaver* Chaim HaKohen, *z"l*.

LIFE-WIZENED CHAIM K.

Soaring Our Minds to Heights When Stuck on Earth

Almost all of the cases or people I see cause my brain to take flight and soar to points unknown. This statement may seem like I have finally "blown a fuse" myself, but the metaphor of "blown" set me thinking about the highs and lows of the experiences with Chaim K. (among others).[1]

I digress, for I am responding to my need to think/work outside the box and try to figure out/what is happening with a patient who has "highs" and "lows" which do not fit the diagnosis of Bipolar Disorder. This disorder is the "new flavor of the month" chosen by many people (laymen or others not licensed) who are wont to give diagnoses. All of a sudden, all sorts of people with varying behaviors are arriving at the doorsteps of professionals, saying they are sure they are Bipolar; my son/husband/wife/sister are Bipolar.

What is Bipolar Disorder? As the word sounds, the disorder involves behavior that is poles apart. At one end, Classic Bipolar disorder (Bipolar Disorder I) is characterized by episodes of mania and episodes of depression. In a manic state, a person may have extreme euphoria or optimism to the point of impairing judgment. She may be hyperactive and stay up all night, talk and move extremely fast, have increased sexual drive and decreased inhibition.

Seventy-five percent of manic episodes include delusions of some sort (most often delusions of grandeur). This is one of the reasons it is sometimes confused with schizophrenia. Untreated manic episodes can last for weeks or even months. Conversely, during a depressive episode, the person can feel hopeless and personally worthless. He may lose interest in his normal activities (including sex), have very little energy or motivation, be unable to concentrate, and have disturbances in sleep and eating habits.

Just feeling blue and just being overactive do not define a person suffering from Bipolar Disorder. While Depressed may be easier to define, Manic is only defined by the *Diagnostic and Statistical Manual of Mental Disorders (DSM) IV* criteria.

Chaim K.'s appointment provided an opportunity to discuss the "highs"

---

1. All essays in this section were co-written with Chaim K., a nom de plume.

and "lows." Our conversations and his mood seemed on an even keel. This, of course, made me wonder when things would change, as they usually do.

Who are the people in literature – others' and ours – who soared high and fell low? What can I learn from their stories and share with Chaim K.?

In Greek mythology, Icarus is the son of Daedalus and is commonly known for his attempt to escape Crete by flight, which ended in a fall to his death.

Daedalus fashioned a pair of wings of wax and feathers for himself and his son. Before they took off, Daedalus warned his son not to fly too close to the sun, or too close to the lake. Overcome by the high that flying lent him, Icarus soared through the sky, curiously, and in the process he came too close to the sun which melted his wings. Icarus died and fell into the sea (Wikipedia).

In our sources, I thought of the two sons of the Priest Aaron who felt above others and brought their own – forbidden – offering to the Holy Tabernacle. They were killed.

When does believing in oneself become deadly? Does optimism, to an extreme, mean becoming heretic? Can a certain type of self-belief create a new reality? Is optimism more narrow? Can it be defined as appreciating something or projecting hope on a thing that already exists and will impact positively, therefore being less "interfering" in God's world?[2]

In the Rabbinic story of the Pardes (literally, "the orchard," also understood to be Paradise), four famous scholars entered the Pardes: Ben Azzai, Ben Zoma, Acher and Rebi Akiva.

> Rebi Akiva told them, "When you come to the place of Pure Marble Stones, don't say, 'Water, water,' because it says: 'He who speaks falsehood will not stand before my eyes'" (Psalms 101:7).
>
> Ben Azzai gazed at the Divine Presence and died, and with respect to him, it says: "Difficult in the eyes of God is the death of His pious ones" (ibid., 116:15).
>
> Ben Zoma gazed and went mad – to him the following verse may be applied: "Have you found honey? Eat as much as is sufficient for you, so that you do not consume too much and have to vomit it . . ." (The Book of Proverbs, 25:16).
>
> Acher "cut off his plantings" [i.e., he became a heretic and his descendants were lost to Judaism].
>
> Rebi Akiva entered in peace and departed in peace. (Talmud *Chagigah* 14b)

I don't profess to understand this very difficult story, but the manifest meaning

---

2. Please see my hypothetical questions as heuristics. Commonly an informal method, heuristics is a tool to help solve a problem. Its use particularly is to rapidly come to a solution that is reasonably close to the best possible answer or "optimal solution."

seems to be that these very holy men entered a hallowed place and were warned to keep a low profile. Three did not heed the instructions and the results were devastating to all but the only one who did – Rebi Akiva. One might say it was a fall from their lofty positions.

Continuing my search for more ideas, my son pointed me in the direction of Elie Wiesel's Nobel Prize acceptance lecture. I present here an abridged version.[3] Elie Wiesel told this story:

> A Hasidic legend tells us that the great Rabbi Baal-Shem-Tov, Master of the Good Name, also known as the Besht, undertook an urgent and perilous mission: to hasten the coming of the Messiah. The Jewish People, [and] all humanity was suffering too much, beset by too many evils. They had to be saved, and swiftly. For having tried to meddle with history, the Besht was punished – banished along with his faithful servant to a distant island. In despair, the servant implored his master to exercise his mysterious powers in order to bring them both home.
>
> "Impossible," the Besht replied. "My powers have been taken from me."
>
> "Then, please, say a prayer, recite a litany, and work a miracle."
>
> "Impossible," the Master replied, "I have forgotten everything." They both fell to weeping.
>
> Suddenly the Master turned to his servant and asked: "Remind me of a prayer – any prayer."
>
> "If only I could," said the servant. "I too have forgotten everything."
>
> "Everything – absolutely everything?"
>
> "Yes, except –"
>
> "Except what?"
>
> "Except the alphabet."
>
> At that, the Besht cried out joyfully: "Then what are you waiting for? Begin reciting the alphabet and I shall repeat after you . . ." And together the two exiled men began to recite, at first in whispers, then more loudly: "*Aleph, beth, gimel, daled* . . ." And over again, each time more vigorously, more fervently; until, ultimately, the Besht regained his powers, having regained his memory.

Wiesel then told his own story of the Holocaust and added:

> The next question had to be, why go on? If memory continually brought us back to this, why build a home?

3. For the entire speech see: http://nobelprize.org/nobel_prizes/peace/laureates/1986/wiesel-lecture.html.

Of course, we could try to forget the past. Why not? Is it not natural for a human being to repress what causes him pain, what causes him shame? Like the body, memory protects its wounds. When day breaks after a sleepless night, one's ghosts must withdraw; the dead are ordered to their graves. But for the first time in history, we could not bury our dead. We bear their graves within ourselves. For us, forgetting was never an option.

Just as man cannot live without dreams, he cannot live without hope. If dreams reflect the past, hope summons the future. Does this mean that our future can be built on a rejection of the past? Surely, such a choice is not necessary. The two are not incompatible. The opposite of the past is not the future, but the absence of future; the opposite of the future is not the past, but the absence of past. The loss of one is equivalent to the sacrifice of the other.

When Chaim K. came in, he was indeed experiencing an extreme low. I mentioned to him that I was concerned about him to such an extent that I did some homework. I read all the pieces of my homework, crying as I read Elie Wiesel's words.

What I hoped he heard was: "Please don't forget how you feel now, but remember your life has meaning; you are the future of a lost generation; you give so much to the world and your family and those who know you. We all do what we can to deal with painful memories and feelings of loss of control, and as the story of the Besht teaches, we can get ahead, one letter at a time."

But what I said was: "Look what you did to me now, my eye make-up is all runny and my nose is red from crying!"

Chaim smiled, and we reconfirmed our appointment for the following week.

Sail on the Sea of Life

CHAIM K. ROLLS into the office with a focused look. After nearly three and a half years of almost weekly sessions, we read each other quite well!

"Okay," I say. I have my computer open, my fingers poised almost as a concert pianist. "Let's get down to business, you look pregnant with thought."

He looks at me with a peevish grin: "I thought you wouldn't notice the few pounds I put on, what with all the summer *mangelim* (BBQs), it is hard to keep my boyish figure."

And then he begins: "It is told of a Maggid, who presents lectures through stories, that when he was a boy he lived in a small port city. He used to love watching the boats set sail and come in. Once he noticed something odd at sea. He saw a large boat, unloading a lot of merchandise. Before it left again, the sailors filled the containers with sand and rocks. That looked very odd to him, so he gathered his courage and asked the captain what they were doing.

"The captain explained that when the boat is empty it can't sail properly in the rough ocean seas. There has to be a third of the ship weighted down in the water so that it will sail with stability. Usually when the boat comes to a big city, they empty their load and replace it with new and different merchandise to sell in their homeport. But this particular port was one of the smaller ones and they didn't have enough of a load to fill the necessary third of the hold.

"As the Maggid grew up, he understood this story to be an important lesson in life. As Hashem allows us to 'set sail' – go forth out into His world, our proverbial Sea of Life, we can't sail smoothly if our boat is empty. So we have two options: one, to fill our lives with Torah and *mitzvot*, or two, to fill our lives with unimportant information and silliness. It is our choice how to go through life and sail smoothly, for completely empty would lead to instability or bobbing on the sea as a vacuous cork."

As Chaim speaks, many flags, or to continue the sea metaphor, buoys, pop up in my mind. Here is a young man with overwhelming physical challenges. His body moves unexpectedly due to neurological and muscular spasms over which he has no control. It is he that is "bobbing about." Yet Chaim is, for the most part, one of the most positive thinking individuals I have ever met.

From his perspective, he has the benefit of viewing us from the crow's nest on top of the high mast. No one would fault him for not wishing to look out at the world passing him by, and remaining in his *dalet amot,* his "four cubits" of personal space, yet he has chosen to transform his motorized wheelchair into a vehicle to soar in time and space. Through his writings for *The Jewish Press,* he has had the opportunity to share his perceptions with readers across the amazing divide of borders and seas. He is thrilled with the emails he receives, proving that there are people out there who do read his ideas.

When I tell him how amazed I always am at his perspective, he gets upset. "Enough, about me personally," he admonishes me. "I have something to say from *Pirkei Avot,* The Sayings of Our Fathers (3:4). Hananiah ben Hakinai, a disciple of R. Akiva and R. Joshua, said: 'He who awakens by night and gives his heart to idle thoughts, or he who walks alone and gives his heart to idle (vain) thoughts, endangers his life'."

Looking into this Mishnah, I notice that the fifteenth century commentator Rav Ovadiah Bartenura, explains it as follows: "Nighttime is a dangerous time because of the *mazikim* – harmful destructive Spirits. Someone who walks by himself is in danger from marauders and these harmful spirits. Thinking of Torah while walking alone at night can save one from danger – physically, morally and spiritually."

These thoughts underline the fear and panic of those with sleep disorders. "People with two or more sleep symptoms were 2.6 times more likely to report a suicide attempt than those without any insomnia complaints."[1]

The most consistent link was seen in early morning awakenings, which was related to all suicidal behaviors. People with this problem were twice as likely as those with no sleep problems to have had suicidal thoughts. Also, those who had trouble sleeping through the night – waking up nearly every night and taking an hour or more to get back to sleep – were twice as likely to have thought of suicide in the last year, and were three times more likely to have attempted it, than those who had no sleep problems.

Can we posit that an antidote for such fears is the Torah? Idle thoughts will only lead to more fear. Maimonides actually teaches that the best time to learn, the time when a person is most likely to remember his studies, is at night.

> When you walk, they [the Torah] will lead you; when you lie down, they will watch over you; and when you awake they will talk with you. When you walk it shall lead you – in this world; when you sleep, it shall watch over you in the grave; and when you awake, it shall talk with you – in the world to come. (Proverbs 6:22)

---

1. M. Wojnar; Dept. of Psychiatry at the University of Michigan, Associate Professor of Psychiatry at the Dept. of Psychiatry at the Medical University of Warsaw in Poland.

"Very *lumdish* (learned) of you," Chaim adds. "Just to prove that I am not totally without knowledge myself, did you know that physicists and philosophers have been studying for years whether or not there is such a think as vacuum, nothingness."

"No question about it," I answer. "you definitely give me a run for my money. Now you force me to look up Quantum Physics!"

He grins from ear to ear! "If you take water out of a bottle, something else will come in, air. Nothing remains empty forever. So too our soul; if we take the Torah out of our souls then something else will enter. *Batalah* – wasting time – and boredom are dangerous forms of matter that fill empty space.

"Our wise men have taught that wasting time leads to boredom and boredom brings sin in its wake. Our minds are the ships which can sail smoothly forever if we fill them with Hashem's words."

Amen, is all that is left to say.

Sounds of Silence: Chaim K.
and His Old Friend Darkness

Hello darkness, my old friend; I've come to talk with you again
Because a vision softly creeping, left its seeds while I was sleeping
And the vision that was planted in my brain; still remains,
Within the sound of silence
                    (From Simon and Garfunkel "The Sounds of Silence," 1966)

I SENSED MY SADNESS and trepidation from the moment he rolled into the room. This time he didn't ask to be pushed by his aide, but rather maneuvered his massive wheelchair using his chin on the joystick control. I saw his unsmiling face; his lips sealed shut and his always twinkling eyes, glazed over.

I knew we were in for a difficult session. When Chaim K. doesn't have the energy or drive to open the session, I know something heavy is weighing on him. It is a week before Taanit Esther, one week before the *yahrzeit* of the cataclysmic event that changed his life forever.

As I sit with Chaim, I sense the deep pain the car's tires etched into his soul forever as it ran over him, while he was on his way home from his job of baking *matzot*. Yes, his life was saved many times over, and yes, *Baruch Hashem* and with God's help, his brain was not affected. Though he can neither breathe on his own, nor move – with the exception of his face and one finger on his right hand – nor can he feel much sensation on his body, he is generally optimistic and exudes a unique life force.

Chaim has been here many times before. By "here," I mean a place that is noiseless except for his whimpers of silent thoughts, dry except for his inner tears, whispers of anguish, and unmoving paroxysm of pain. It is a place to which he does not invite even his dearest friends and most loved family members. It is his *Taanit Dibbur* – Fast of Silence.

In the years since I began meeting with Chaim, we have experienced few such sessions; he has had some such others at home. That is to say, that though every nanosecond as a quadriplegic on a respirator is a lifetime of "what might have been" vs. "what is," to Chaim's immense strength and credit, and the love and support of his wonderful family, Chaim is a joy and inspiration to be with and learn from. Amidst this ineffable sorrow, the "every day outward" Chaim is always working to create an atmosphere of wholeness, which causes others to want to be with him out of joy and not *chesed* (kindness). His interactions with us "civilians" is the *chesed*.

When I see him sealed, closing himself from the environment, and especially to me, I try to give him space.

"Okay," I say after about 45 interminable minutes, "I feel your power, your energy, and your sadness. The article we wrote with Mimi and Jenny, 'Mind, Body, and Soul in 24 Hours,' was published in a special issue of *The Jewish Press*. You all discussed how the 24 hours in your new, since the accident existence, seems like years upon years long. The praying and wishing for time to go by and for *Geulah*, the Redemption, to take place, is interminable.

"I thank you for sharing this small window of these feelings with me. These 'sounds of silence' are noisily playing their cacophonic sounds in my head and heart. I know how lame this may sound to you, but your strength amidst the unplumbed pain is what shouts out and resonates within me in this quiet room. Thank you for sharing what must be so impossible to express in mere words."

Our time is up. I venture, "See you next week, the day before Taanit Esther."

Chaim hesitates and whispers with his parched voice, "We have nothing left to talk about, why return next week?"

"I don't agree. We spoke for the whole hour of this session." I look straight into his eyes and think I see them saying "thank you."

Don't Judge Anyone

CHAIM COMES ROLLING into the office, and no sooner has he parked his motorized wheelchair, he says: "'*Hevei dan et kol ha'adam l'kaf zechut.* Give everyone the benefit of the doubt.' Look it up and see what you can find on it, I will look, too."

Taanit Esther 2009 was the eighth *yahrzeit*, anniversary of the cataclysmic moment when Chaim K., then a 14-year old adolescent was run over by a car. He related to me when we had first started meeting what he knew about the accident from others, since he remembered nothing. "I had marks on my shoulders from the tires, almost all of my bones were broken – and of course, my neck, my spinal cord. I clinically died six times, but each time they succeeded to bring me back to life – to *this* life!"

The period before and immediately after the Fast of Esther is one fraught with conflicted feelings. Fortunately, we have a day of space between "the day the old me died" and Purim as we live in Jerusalem, a walled city since the times of Joshua. Jerusalem is one of about ten cities in the world where Megillat Esther is read on the 15th of the month of Adar, and not immediately after the Fast of Esther (Purim is the 14th of Adar).

We discussed the results of our research on the statement he cited from the Sayings of Our Fathers (*Pirkei Avot*) in our meetings. After giving me this "job," Chaim told his story:

"A year and a half before my accident, we were living in an integrated neighborhood of secular and religious. We had a neighbor, a young guy of 24 who started to become more religious and, as his family was secular, we had kind of 'adopted' him into our family. He joined us for Shabbat meals, went to *shul* with us on Shabbat and holidays, and ate in our *sukkah*. One day, that same person beat me up, not only hit me, he broke my ribs – really, he actually broke two of my ribs! He thought he had a reason to hit me, but nothing can justify such a beating of a 13-year old kid or anyone of any age, for that matter.

"After that, I didn't report it or complain to anyone, as he was a friend of the family. He said he was sorry, and my family smoothed it over as an isolated incident and pushed it out of their memory.

"I didn't forget. I was very angry with him and unable to forgive him even years after it happened. Every Yom Kippur, I forgave the person who ran me over and ruined my whole life. It was very hard, but in the end I said, 'Yes, I forgive him.'

"Yet, regarding the neighbor who beat me, I put on him a curse that he should never get married or have children. I felt that the flash of anger and uncontrolled physical aggression he showed me should stop with him and not be allowed to be passed on to his children.

"A few years went by, I matured and became more sophisticated in my thinking. He asked to be forgiven, yet again, and we did make peace. He told me then that when he beat me up he was under the influence of drugs – not prescription drugs! However, it was almost five years later that I forgave him and blessed him that he should find his *basherte* (intended spouse), and have a family.

"Last night, I was at his wedding! We danced, I in my wheelchair and he in his *hatan* (groom) outfit. He has come a very long way; he is fully religious, learns in a yeshiva all day, and is truly a changed man. I blessed him that he would have a son in a year. And he said to me that he only prays that he can come to my wedding in the near future. It was a very emotional moment."

I didn't understand the connection Chaim was making until I saw the following comments on the mishnaic statement quoted above. Rav Nachman (of Bratislava) is quoted as saying that the *manifest* meaning is obvious: give everyone the benefit of the doubt. The *latent* meaning is: giving even a guilty person the benefit of the doubt, or judge him/her in a neutral fashion.

"What made you change your mind?" I asked.

Chaim's response was: "I know he is really a good guy. I am happy he got married and that his explanation that he was under the influence of drugs, and his promise that it would never happen again, forced me to see him in this positive light. I don't think I am so powerful that my 'curse' had the effect of his not finding a woman to marry, but I do think that until he was ready to admit to himself and to me that he allowed drugs into his body and their effect on his actions and behavior, he was not really ready to become a responsible adult and be married and have children.

"I judged him without knowing that he wasn't fully responsible for his actions."

Don't you think someone who engages in legal or illegal substance abuse is at the very least responsible for taking the drugs? What do you mean he was not responsible?"

"He was a *tinok shenishba*.[1] This happens in any family, religious or not,

---

1. A *tinok shenishba* is literally a "captured infant" which is a Talmudic term that refers to an individual who sins inadvertently as a result of having been raised without an appreciation for the rules of Judaism, when s/he was able to fully understand the consequences.

Jewish and non-Jewish. The point here being that he *did* take responsibility and rehabilitated himself fully."

Our time is up, and as Chaim K. leaves the room, I feel that he too had the distance of time and experience to understand that while *critical thinking* opens the world to you, *critical judgment* poisons your mind and sours your soul. Maybe he is able to judge the driver of the car on that dark night years earlier, and almost more importantly, judge himself less critically. May we all benefit in such an altruist fashion from the Sayings of Our Fathers.

A Purim Toast with
God's Intervention

"Whᴇɴ ᴀ ᴘᴇʀsᴏɴ wakes up in the morning, opens his eyes and he's alive, he might think that this is the most natural thing, that [anything] can be. Well he's wrong!

"What he doesn't realize is that this is a *miracle*. That he woke up *BS"D*, with the help of God. Every day in a normal life is replete with times that are *BS"D*. One doesn't even notice [them].

"Since my accident, I started to pay attention to personal *BS"D* that Hashem gives me. I'll recount for you the most significant ones.

"The first one is that I am alive. I didn't die when the car hit me as I was walking home on Taanit Esther eight years ago.

"The second one is that even though a lot of bones in my body were crushed – my shoulders, legs, hands, and most importantly my neck was broken – but even so I can say, *BS"D*, my skull and brain were not injured. *B'zechut zeh* [due to this], I am sitting here and talking to Dr. G."

What was I hearing, weeks before the eighth anniversary of the accident that left Chaim K. CSI – a quadriplegic on a respirator? Is he really saying that sitting here in this massive electric wheelchair with the constant humming, never ceasing reminder of his dependence on the non-natural life – this mechanical air-supply – is a recognition of God's act of intervention in his favor?!

I am very concerned. I am worried about the rebound-effect of this positive "reframing." Sure, it demonstrates his intense belief in Hashem, but at the close of Taanit Esther as the Jewish world prepares for the letting it all hang out fun of *our* victory over the descendants of the Children of Israel's archenemy, Amalek, where will that leave Chaim?

If he is "fortunate," he will be in his wheelchair – not in a hospital or worse – with his respirator humming, joined by the communal heartbeat of his wonderful family. Another year in which each hour, minute, second and nanosecond, remind him of who he was, who he is and who he isn't anymore. As my mind asks these questions, he is continuing to tick off his list of *BS"D* – acts of mercy that God's intervention permitted.

Chaim continues: "Thirdly, the ambulance was very close to the site of the accident, it took him under two minutes to arrive. The paramedic found me on the street, not breathing. He immediately began to resuscitate me. If the ambulance had been more than those two minutes away, my brain would have been damaged from lack of oxygen. This is a huge *BS"D*.

"Fourthly, even though I am paralyzed in my whole body – from my neck down, the only thing I can move besides my face is my right thumb – I can see the *BS"D* here, too. The fact that having the use of both my face and my right thumb is very fortunate, because as a result, I can use that thumb to operate my computer. I use a special mouse that I rotate with my chin, which operates a keyboard, letter by letter, then I "click" another especially equipped button that works practically at a hair's-breadth of force, to "enter" the information.

"Fifthly, several times in the last seven years, I had problems with the respirator, meaning that for some reason or other it stopped breathing for me. Once, I recall, a nurse wasn't in the room and the tube disconnected. Even though it beeps to alert those around, no one heard it. *BS"D* my father came into the room at just that minute, and found me unconscious and saved my life before I was brain damaged, or even worse, dead.

"Sixthly, since the accident, my basic contact with the outside world is by computer. As you can imagine – as this is my only form of communication with the outside world – my computers wear out pretty quickly! In the last seven years, I've had four laptops, and I didn't have to pay for even one! The first one I got from my father's niece; the second one, I received from the Make-A-Wish Foundation; the third one, from Reb Chaim Miller, who was the assistant mayor of Jerusalem under [then Mayor] Ehud Olmert. The fourth computer is from a friend of my mother's in America. I am so grateful to Yehoshua and Fraidyl for their wonderful and thoughtful gift of 'connection.'

"I believe that God saved me for a reason. But now I am disappointed. Don't get me wrong; God helps me a lot in my day-to-day life. And this is the reason that I am so disappointed that my physical situation has not improved. I am God's friend; why am I still in this chair? I know that this decision is in His hands and we cannot use our mere minds to understand His ways. I'll give you an example: if two ants are put on the table and you try to explain the respective platforms of the Democratic or Republican parties, this would have the same result as our trying to understand God's judgment. Clearly though, I am disappointed and sad. Life is hard for me. But I believe in Hashem even in my darkest hours."

"How do you do it?" I ask. This time of year, when his "*yahrzeit*," as I call the date of the accident that changed his teenage and now adult life comes up, is a time of inestimable pain and mourning. To be "alive" for one's annual day of "death" sounds impossible. Yet eight years after the original "Chaim's" catastrophic accident, he is here, waiting for redemption. (The name Chaim

[life] was added to his given name, as is the *minhag*, custom, when someone is deathly ill. Some say it is to "fool" the Angel of Death who is seeking the person with the name given him at his *brit*, circumcision ceremony.)

Chaim K. continues: "Magic," he smiles. "Seriously though, books like *Mesillat Yesharim*, *Sifrei Mussar* and a little *l'Chaim*." He is using the double entendre of "*l'Chaim*," which in Hebrew means "*to Chaim*," and is what is said when you have a drink of wine or liquor.

"*BS"D*, I feel it is the mental strength with which I was fortunate enough to be born, that allows me to carry on."

I am in awe of his strength, "How can you teach and share with the rest of us, how we might access your strength in our own day-to-day lives with its disappointments?"

"To paraphrase the Midrash," he continues, "we arrived in this world against our will or without our permission; we will live in this world without anyone asking if that is our choice, and we'll die too, without our opinion being asked. If you *are* already here, try to make the most of it in any way you can. That is my credo.

"In the first chapter of *Mesillat Yesharim*, it talks about man's responsibility to God's world. These words of *Mussar* – exhortation – encourage one to understand that even though as an individual one might dwell on his/her own problems, one must never lose sight of the fact that we are on earth for one reason, to ensure and increase our position in the Future World (*Olam HaBa*), the world that is the complete and ultimate truth.

"So when I say I am disappointed in God, I think about it and try to reconnect to the *Mussar* and realize that this time here is only a stepping stone to infinite life in the most perfect, whole and holy place. *BS"D* may we all achieve that goal, to appreciate and not fear the world as we know it. From my vantage point I must believe that these eight years are just a narrow bridge to *Olam HaBa*."

I sit in his company; tears are running down my face – if not externally, internally.

Capped and Then Handi-capped

El maleh rachamim
He Who lives in the uppermost levels of the heavens

So BEGINS THE PRAYER for those who die; beseeching God to help them find full peace under the wings of the *Shechina*.

"On Taanit Esther, the Fast of Esther, when we fast to show our empathy with Persian Jews at the time of the Temple's destruction, and recount the miracle of Purim, I have a *yahrzeit*. My mourning for my before-self is a daily occurrence. When the official date arrives every year and is joined with the joy of Purim, I am able to mourn in a more public fashion. People may interpret my sadness as being for the fast, but really it is the day I lost myself; the day my body was smashed by a car.

"For my family, it might be the beginning of the miracle of Purim and Pesach combined, as I wasn't given a chance of survival. I went into cardiac arrest six times, meaning that I have died six times over. To my parents and doctors, the fact that I am here at all and cognizant of everything around me is a miracle in itself. They see this day as a form of *techiyat hametim* [revival of the dead, a fundamental belief in Judaism]. I see this day as the day I 'died.'

"This sounds awful and Dr. G. is almost crying. I tell her that I am not mourning myself *now*, I'm really mourning who I might have been as a person, if only the car arrived at the spot, two minutes earlier or later.

"Who do I feel I am today, and who might I have been otherwise? Obviously, I have changed. Before the accident I was hyperactive. I could never sit still – I was always active in martial arts, biking, and playing hooky from school and yeshiva regularly. But now I can't be hyperactive. Have you ever heard of a hyperactive person who is totally paralyzed and on a ventilator/respirator? I don't think so!" he says cynically.

"My personality hasn't changed, but my perspective on the world has. My article "Seeing Life as It Can Be – Not Accepting Life as It Is" was very upbeat. I really feel that way most of the time. I smile a lot, make jokes, and enjoy going out and doing things – most of all being with regular friends and people.

"However, I can't lie, and say that there aren't times that I am blue and sad. *Baruch Hashem*, they are not the majority of my days, though my nights are particularly long.

"I didn't want to write about this sadness, but the proximity to my *Yahrzeit* makes it impossible not to think about what might have been. Dr. G. convinces me that you should not think of me as a 'plastic' person, but as a real, live man.

"Sadness is also a part of life. Learning how to live with it is the *chochma*, the clever way. So how do I manage to do that?

"I allow myself to feel. I sometimes ask someone nearby to cover my head, so that I can't see. The good news of being on a respirator is that I can't get smothered by the blanket. The bad news is I block out everything and everybody. I can't see, smell or taste anything around me. This is how I can be on my own.

"When I'm in this down mode, my family understands and they let me have some space. They're right, because after a few hours, I really begin to miss those around me, and my life, as I know it now.

"When I met Jenny S., who is congenitally blind and was a member of our Group Therapy Sessions at Dr. G.'s Neuropsychology Unit, I began to see my hiding from life differently.

"I could block out those around me, temporarily. The word 'temporarily' is the key. Knowing someone who can never turn the world on or off at will changed my way of thinking. Ironically, Jenny says being blind is not a big deal, as she thinks seeing is highly overrated by those who can see. I feel her attitude stems from the fact that she never could see, so that she doesn't know what she's missing! She has developed many ways of compensating and 'sees' those who come into the room with her ears. She 'hears' their image using language in a way that I never can. Meeting her was important.

"But my situation is so different. I know what I lost, because until the age of fourteen, I was just like everyone else, I still remember every sense and feeling in my body, below my head and face, the feeling of walking and touching the ground, and that's why I think I am in a worse place than she is!

"So, the last time I felt down and covered myself up for hours, I was happy that I could get the blanket removed and see the world again. My world, which has obvious imperfections, is one that highlights what remains. People who are 'capped,' as opposed to 'handi-capped,' may not be aware of the joys of their abilities.

"When all is said and done, I guess I can't be *me* without being optimistic."

Seeing Life as It Can Be – Not Accepting Life as It Is!

"W HEN I FIRST came to Dr. Guedalia, I believed that my life was over, because I am paralyzed, because I can't do anything, because I can't breathe on my own, because I can't get married. But since then, my way of thinking changed, and I learned to look at life in relative not absolute terms.

"Alright, my situation is not the best, but relative to Stephen Hawking, my situation is very good, because I can talk and express myself and my feelings in my own words.

"It's correct that I can't walk or breathe on my own, but relative to someone who is in a coma, my situation is good. I can go out to a restaurant, I can eat, and I can enjoy the food. I can meet with my friends and enjoy talking to them. I can hear and enjoy a good song. I can see and enjoy a good movie. I can appreciate little things.

"All of you, the people reading this, if you think your life is bad, think again. As much as your life is difficult, it could be worse. Take the gift of the life you are given and make the most of it for as long as it lasts. Because one day it's going to be taken from you and only then you will realize what you have lost. That's how I feel.

"I see people and I feel bad. Why? Because they are wasting their lives and their time, they are not taking advantage of *life*.

"I see myself four years after the car that hit me left me with a spinal cord injury. That was before I started coming to Dr. G. I feel bad that then I didn't make the most of the gift that I was given in my current situation. But now I realize that I have to appreciate the things I *do* have and not mourn the things I don't have. Stop looking at what you don't have and start seeing what you do have. Enjoy the good things."

"To what do you attribute your optimism, when so many doctors are pessimistic and tell you not to hope?" I ask.

"Because I do not believe they are right. They told me I should have been dead many times over. And see, here I am. I am sure that one day I'm going to have children, because the 'old-fashioned way' is not the only way. When I see my nephews calling my name and crawling around my room, I just want it more and more, and I believe I will achieve this goal.

"This is not just an understanding that comes out of accepting my situation, but has become a way of life for me. I think, it's not only people who are *healthy* that need to think and act and 'be' [into] this attitude, but people who are ill or handicapped in any way, can also improve their outlook on life.

"I'm not saying that it is easy to make this 'mind switch,' but it *is* possible. Just take a look at me. I promise you that your life will be better after you change your perspective."

I sit agape and aware of monumental changes in Chaim K. Am I watching neuroplasticity in action?

Over the past two decades, an enormous amount of research has revealed that the brain never stops changing and adjusting. Learning, as defined by Tortora and Grabowski, is "The ability to acquire new knowledge or skills through instruction or experience. Memory is the process by which that knowledge is retained over time."[1]

The capacity of the brain to change with learning is called "plasticity." So how does the brain change with learning? According to Durbach, there appear to be at least two types of modifications that occur in the brain with learning: a change in the internal structure of the neurons, the most notable being in the area of the synapses, and specifically, an increase in the number of synapses between neurons.[2]

Neuroplasticity is the brain's ability to reorganize itself by forming new neural connections throughout life, based on new experiences. In order to learn or memorize a fact or skill, there must be persistent functional changes in the brain that represent the new knowledge.[3]

While Chaim K.'s cognitive ability should not necessarily have been affected by his spinal injury, he had to work on changing the nexus of this thinking and attitude to his present condition. He has proven this "new" neuro-scientific fact by his apparent switch. As such, he has possibly made new synapses, connecting to different parts of his brain, learning to use the information at hand differently, i.e., new learning.

With a smile on his lips and a twinkle in his eye, Chaim K. ends our session with this postscript: "Hey, Dr. G., don't forget to add that I am available to optimistic, like-minded young women who live in Israel for a *shidduch* (match)."

---

1. G. J. Tortora and S. R. Grabowski, *Principles of Anatomy and Physiology*, 8th edition, (NY: HarperCollins College, 1996).

2. D. Durbach, *The Brain Explained*, (Upper Saddle River, NJ: Prentice-Hall, Inc., 2000).

3. R. Kandel, J. H. Schwartz, and T. M. Jessell, *Principles of Neural Science*, 4th edition (McGraw-Hill Medical, 2000).

Counting-up Our Days and Hopes for the Future

O**NE OF THE HARDEST** things to do is the "count-up." Start at a point of extreme, almost ineffable sadness and pain, and start counting the seconds, minutes and hours for the relief, elimination or resolution of that pain. The destruction of the Temple provides a larger than life insight into what may be the only way a person can cope when so overwhelming a tragedy strikes us as individuals or as a community, when there doesn't seem to be a repair/resolution immediately available. How we respond and act on a community level may provide insight into the individual's coping options.

On Tisha B'Av, the Ninth of Av, in many synagogues, there is a *minhag* to do the count-up. Starting the counting with day one, from the destruction of the first of the two Holy Temples, the head of the community announces, "This Tisha B'Av is seven hundred and fifty seven thousand, seven hundred and forty (757,740) days since the destruction of the Holy Temple."

In a way, this horrifically large number and the act of counting up to the Redemption may make us ponder: how much longer must we suffer? Help is surely close at hand. With this concept of a community resolve to cope with defeat, sadness and loss, our *minhag* may be shining a light on how to deal with what may seem as endless despair.

Other outward community signs of mourning include: sitting low or on the floor in a room darkened, using candles or flashlights and the reading – from an unbound book or from leaflets, symbolizing the "temporary" status of the Destruction – of *Eicha*, Lamentations, which we mournfully chant.

So I am saddened, though not surprised, that Chaim K. is in a blue funk when I see him on a sweltering summer's day at the end of July before the Ninth of Av, when national mourning is palpable and may offer a moment to feel a part of – and not apart from – a communal experience.

He is a sensitive young man, no longer a teen at age twenty, and, had it not been for the car that hit him at age fourteen, he would be over six feet tall with shoulders and a chest span a football player would brag about. A quadriplegic, with his respirator breathing for him, his kind face and twinkling eyes send a different message, a lamentation all their own: "Oh, what might have been . . . Oh, what is . . ."

With the end of the fast we go on with our lives. The month of Elul is approaching. *Selichot* (prayers and psalms of repentance) prepare us for the Days of Awe – Rosh Hashanah and Yom Kippur, followed by Sukkot. But what if every day resembles the one before? And what if your hope of becoming independent and being able to care for yourself in the most basic of functions, like breathing, fade with every machine-assisted breath? How do you deal with "imposed" acts of mourning when nanoseconds of your life are spent silently wailing your loss of who you were and who you might have been?

Since we first met, I have found Chaim K.'s resilience nothing short of astounding, even miraculous. Holidays are when people who have many fewer apparent dysfunctions are blue; the newspapers are full of articles describing this phenomenon. However, in my opinion, it's the imposed days of mourning that are the hardest for Chaim K.

"I have so much to learn from you and need your help to interpret this talent to others through our writing and through teaching budding professionals," I tell him.

He looks at me askance. "Are you pulling my leg? It's not fair to tease the handicapped," his eyes twinkle.

"No," I say, "I'm very serious. We keep ourselves from buying something new, wearing leather shoes, swimming, even not eating for twenty-six hours and feel that we are victorious and should be rewarded for our success over frailty. You must be laughing at us and not the other way around."

Chaim invites me to approach his souped-up chair, to which he has added a Bluetooth-equipped earphone and cell phone which allow him to talk, answer and hear music on his phone wirelessly. "Disconnect the Bluetooth, I know you know how to do it. You're very high-tech for someone your age, and for a woman, too," he smiles. "Then push the following buttons on my phone."

He directs me to play a song on the MP3 application of his phone. We listen to it together. I then go to my computer and try to download the lyrics in order to discuss them. Together we try to figure out or "psych out," as Chaim says, the motivations of the songwriter and singer (and the listener who chooses which tune to save and play).

Chaim K. is not like most people who listen to a tune and let it go in one ear and out the other. He spends time really listening and trying to understand the lyrics in much the same way as he used to learn Talmud in "the old days."

"Many times I am inspired by the songs. I hear things in the *Goyish* as well as the Jewish songs that let me *think and feel*. Songs are a very powerful force and influence one's mood. For example, everyone has his/her personal song that makes him or her sad. I have 'tested' this hypothesis on those around me and have proven to myself that this is a truism.

"There are people for whom the song itself changes their mood significantly within seconds of hearing it. I am one of these people. I can hear a song and it can throw me into the depths of depression and sadness. Another time, I can be blue and hear a specific song and my heart feels like it is flying and soaring above my body."

Here are some of the lyrics of his favorite song that I put on paper to discuss with Chaim K.:

> *Dancing all night and having a blast to cure my condition*
> *My heart is in prison, I'm hoping and wishin'*
> *That I'm forgiven, Say yeah.*
> *'Cause every time you leave me I'm sad,*
> *The moment you're returning I'm glad,*
> *So let's not go forgetting what we had,*
> *'Cause it's bad so bad, yeah.*
> *We're loving each day as if it's the last,*
> *I need you here*
> *'Cause we're loving, and we're dreaming*
> *and we're hoping and we're dreaming.*
>
> (From Ronan Keating, "Lovin' Each Day")

He is quiet for a bit. "What do you think it is about?" he asks.

"Hum," I say in my most professional tone. "It is clearly about the Days of Awe: *Teshuvah*, *Yirah* and *Ahavat Hashem* – asking forgiveness by returning to the righteous path, and the awe and love of God."

He looks at me thoughtfully, and says something about how psychologists are really in great need of help. He calls for his pusher/aide and leaves smiling and humming the tune.

When Pigs Fly:
On the Days of Awe
and the Swine Flu

T HE DAYS OF AWE – the Yamim Noraim – are a time of introspection and renewal. Time is reviewed and time is projected. When Chaim K. came into my office during the month of Elul, the month that school reconvenes, we began a new "semester" as well. He, always the gentleman, asks about my summer vacation, and then drops a bombshell: he had been suffering from a serious bout of Swine Flu that he contracted from one of his aides! Shocked, all I could say is: *Baruch rofeh holim*, Blessed is He who heals the sick.

At the same time, I look at Chaim and see his eyes smiling. I say something like: Ain't that a kick in the head! The point being that he is certainly among the most vulnerable of people for serious complications to the Swine Flu, "serious" meaning death. We have had many sessions wondering about the meaning of life and death, particularly for one under his grave set of circumstances, and yet here he is at the beginning of our fourth year together, and after the dreaded Swine Flu, no less!

Not only did he survive, but also the main reason he did so, was his respirator's entry hole. As opposed to other healthier young people in Israel and abroad who died from the huge amount of infected mucosa that reached their lungs, it was the intubation port in his throat that saved him. This entry point was what allowed his caretakers to suction the mucus from his trachea and save his life.

"I am fortunate, more so than the rest of the People of Israel. People that have too much of a good life really have to worry, because Hashem cleanses our sins through trials and tribulations. It is written that a person who goes through forty days without any difficulties is receiving his reward in this life and will not receive benefits in the future life. But don't be worried, because the Gemara uses the following as an example of a trial: a person putting a hand in his pocket wanting to remove three coins and only finds two.

"Where we are most different is that you may be going into the Yamim Noraim praying but not knowing how Hashem will deal with your sins, or even if you have a purpose to your life. Hashem has answered my questions of life and death. I know He has plans for me. He wants me here on earth.

"I accept God's judgment on me with love, and all of what has happened to me is a result of my sins, and Hashem, who is the righteous judge who doesn't err when He makes His decisions. I pray that the torments that I am going through will erase my guilt and sins. I am fully aware as I 'sit' before the Almighty that I don't understand the extent of His decisions, and therefore I pray with all my heart that He will redeem my misdeeds and sins and sweeten all the injunctions against me and all of Bnei Yisrael."

Chaim has paraphrased from the book *Shomer Emunim – Hashgacha Pratit*, section 14, but these words reflect his deepest feelings especially since he is a survivor of the H1N1 – the Swine Flu.

I look at Chaim, nonplussed. He knows me by now and says: "Out with it."

"I am afraid of hurting your feelings. I am embarrassed," I say.

"Come on, we know each other so well by now, you can tell me."

"Okay, did you cough when you had the Swine Flu?"

"Yes, so what's your point?"

"Did your cough sound like: 'oink oink'?"

We both crack up and say goodbye until next time.

A Visit to "Angels on the Moon"

Do you dream, that the world will know your name
So tell me your name
Do you care, about all the little things or anything at all?
I wanna feel, all the chemicals inside I wanna feel
I wanna sunburn, just to know that I'm alive
To know I'm alive

(From "Angels on the Moon," lyrics by Thriving Ivory)

THE FIRST TIME Chaim K. played this song for me, it was on his mobile phone. Then we listened to it again on the computer so I was able to view the words. "The music I hear and the songs I choose are the way I speak volumes of the pent up feelings that words alone can't express," Chaim explains.

Some of his "dreams" have been fulfilled. A world of readers knows his name because of *The Jewish Press*. Wherever I go, when I am introduced, someone asks me if he is, in reality, the way he sounds in the articles we write together. My answer is always, emphatically: Yes!

The song continues:

Don't tell me if I'm dying, 'cause I don't wanna know
If I can't see the sun, maybe I should go
Don't wake me 'cause I'm dreaming, of angels on the moon
Where everyone you know, never leaves too soon

This song says a lot. Chaim wants to feel life's pains and joys even though he may not be able to sense them. Ironically, even before he heard the song, he had told me that last summer he *davka* went out to get a sunburn. He smiled through the stinging pain of the burn and peeling of his face, because this sensation told him that he was alive and could feel just as everyone else does.

The choice by the song's author, of the moon for the place where angels are found, struck me as very interesting. Since 1969 when Neil Armstrong not only landed, but walked on and then returned from the moon, proving impermanence to "leaving earth"; doing the up until then impossible, going to the moon and coming back!

"When I am dreaming," Chaim says, "I sometimes liken the experience to the floating weightlessness of being in space. I had a dream that I was in a gravity-free zone and was moving myself as if without the pull of the laws of gravity. I was singing – I can move of my own volition. Maybe signing up for a space shuttle trip is the answer for my dreams."

> *Do you believe, in the day that you were born,*
> *Tell me do you believe?*
> *Do you know, that every day's the first of the rest of your life*

This attitude is the one so many of my patients would love to acquire from Chaim K. They feel that every day is their last day, every day cannot be altered to bring them peace or serenity. Chaim does not feel that way. He feels as the song does – that we need to joyfully and festively accept our birth into this imperfect world with an unexpected future.

> *Don't tell me if I'm dying, 'cause I don't wanna know*
> *If I can't see the sun, maybe I should go*

"When you are standing on the dark side of the moon, you feel that the warmth of the sun will never come," says a life-wizened Chaim. "It requires so much faith that even when you can't see it, you must believe that there is hope on the horizon."

> *Don't wake me 'cause I'm dreaming, of angels on the moon*
> *Where everyone you know, never leaves too soon*

In his seminal work on Existential Psychology, Viktor Frankl (*Man's Search for Meaning*, 1946) relates that while in the concentration camps, someone who knew he was a psychiatrist approached him, asking that he help a fellow prisoner who was having horrible nightmares. Don't wake him, advised Frankl, the reality of day-to-day life here is a greater nightmare than the one in which a sleeping man exists.

> *You can tell me all your thoughts,*
> *about the stars that fill polluted skies*
> *And show me where you run to,*
> *when no one's left to take your side*
> *But don't tell me where the road ends,*
> *'cause I just don't wanna know,*
> *No I don't wanna know*

"Most people are afraid of death, I'm not," says Chaim. "The end of the road is something no one wants to know and yet from the moment we are born, we are on that road which ends. What I *do* know is that no matter how aware you are about how short life is, you must keep living as though the road will go on forever. That's what I wanna know!"

Pyramid of Needs and
Then Some . . .

W E HAVE MANY NEEDS. Sitting with Chaim K. as an annoying fly buzzes around, a *need* that is not on Maslow's iconic pyramid comes to mind. The specific *need* to which I am referring is the need to be able to brush a fly off your face or just scratch something that itches.

Abraham Maslow in his 1943 paper "A Theory of Human Motivation," described a hierarchy of needs – a theory in psychology that he subsequently extended to include his observations of humans' innate curiosity. Maslow studied a rarified segment of American society – the one percent of the U.S. college population. He came up with a hierarchy of modern psychological understanding of motivation, the most basic being Physiological, then Safety, Love/Belonging, Esteem and finally, at the pinnacle – Self-actualization.[1]

As the world has been suffering the effects of an economic tsunami, a new look at Maslow – and maybe through the eyes of someone seemingly as limited in his choices as Chaim K. – may be in order.

That said, one caveat of Maslow's hierarchy needs to be explained. The first lower level is being associated with physiological needs, while the top levels are termed growth needs associated with psychological needs. The higher needs come into focus when the lower needs in the pyramid are met. Once an individual has moved upwards to the next level, needs in the lower level will no longer be prioritized. If a lower set of needs is no longer being met, the individual will temporarily re-prioritize those needs by focusing attention on the unfulfilled needs, but s/he will not permanently regress to the lower level (Wikipedia).

I asked Chaim K. what levels would be represented on his pyramid. "What is your triangle of importance?"

"What is important is the dynamics. It is the same for me as for an Indian in the deep, darkest Amazon. It is important to me as my clothes, I need to be dressed."

"And you always dress well," I add.

---

1. See http://a-ok-site.com/maslow/images/hierarchy_of_needs.gif.

He smiles bashfully and goes on: "The Amazon can live like in the Garden of Eden; he doesn't feel uncomfortable as he is. But put him on Jaffa Road. If he can cross it without getting killed because of the construction of the light rail, he will be very out of place and uncomfortable.

"That's the reason the triangle cannot be a fixed concept; rather it is dynamic and influenced by our environment."

But what is your triangle?

"Schopenhauer," Chaim says, "has something to say about this."

"Schopenhauer?" I squeak in question, as I look at this "highbrow" with renewed respect. Chaim smiles. He has just watched the movie: "When Nietzsche Wept," a 2007 film starring Armand Assante, Ben Cross and Katheryn Winnick. The movie is based on a book of the same name by Dr. Irvin D. Yalom and was directed by Pinchas Perry. It is about a fictional relationship between Freud and Nietzsche.

Back to Schopenhauer (1788–1860) who was also a character mentioned in the movie. Chaim has Googled the characters since he saw the film and this conversation is a result of his erudition on the subject.

The World as Will and Representation emphasized the role of man's basic motivation, which he called "will." Schopenhauer's analysis of "will" led him to the conclusion that emotional, physical, and intimate desires can never be fulfilled. Consequently, Schopenhauer favored a lifestyle of negating human desires. Chaim K. continues: "There are three things that a person doesn't feel that are missing until they are taken from him: 1) Freedom; 2) Youth; 3) Health.

"I feel that all three have been taken from me. I always say that I am a prisoner in my body. No freedom to do what I want or anything. Also, youth has been taken from me – I am only twenty-two years old and have osteoporosis. And my health is taken from me."

"So what do you *have* and what didn't he say?"

Chaim goes on: "Nietzsche [Friedrich Wilhelm Nietzsche, 1844–1900] says: 'The weak person is in charge.' *Ha'chalash cholesh.*"

Nietzsche's style and radical questioning of the value and objectivity of truth raise considerable problems of interpretation, generating an extensive secondary literature in both continental and analytic philosophy (see Wikipedia). Nevertheless, some of his key ideas include interpreting tragedy as an affirmation of life and eternal recurrence.

In that vein, Chaim goes on: "If I say, 'bring me a drink,' they have to bring me something to drink, like a damsel in distress. I take advantage of my position. In the theater I use it, I always get in and a good seat, too! Whenever I can, I do."

"You paid for it," I murmur.

"Yes, I paid a heavy price for it. I would give anything to be okay and work at minimum wage for twenty hours a day. This is not my choice. All the doctors can explain what happened to me and how, but no one can explain *why* it happened to me. This is what is so frustrating.

"Belief-in-understanding is an important step in my hierarchy. We think we can understand the world until something as big as health is taken away from us.

"It is a paradox. If we had answers to everything, our lives would be bland. Just as it was in Gan Eden," he says with a wink. "I'm proud of myself that I can control my need to hide within myself."

Achieving the goals one set, and being proud of one's achievements are higher forms of Maslow's Self-actualization.

People need to feel a sense of belonging, respect and acceptance, whether it comes from a large social group, such as clubs, office culture, religious groups, professional organizations, sports teams, etc. They need to love and be loved (intimately and non-intimately) by others. In the absence of these elements, many people become susceptible to loneliness, social anxiety, and clinical depression. This need for belonging can often overcome the physiological and security needs, depending on the strength of the peer pressure. An anorexic, to use an over-simplification, may ignore the need to eat and the security of health possibly in a misguided search for a feeling of control and belonging.

I see many children who are in trouble in the education system or at home, frequently their stories reflect young people who don't receive the respect of others, their teachers being on the top of this house of cards. From this teetering edifice they see their parents' respect for them failing, not to speak of the respect of their peers. These self-same teachers then write in referral notes that the child lacks self-esteem, self-respect, and respect for others. From which bank is s/he supposed to withdraw this emotional currency?

More than ever, today, as the youngest and oldest in the workforce are being let go, and financial houses are failing, the community on the whole needs to redefine what is considered valuable and worthy of our respect. The signs of the past are going to need a new overhaul, as in all probability a 21st Century WPA – Works Progress Administration (renamed in 1939 the Work Projects Administration; WPA which was the largest New Deal agency) will take form.

"Change" is not a "six-letter word." Our preparation for change and ability to move up the pyramid is only limited by our ability to be flexible and redefine ourselves as needed so as to learn how to live within compromise of our basic needs. This I have learned from Chaim K.

Off the Path:
A Different Perspective

"Don't make me into some kind of *chaham ba'laila*." Chaim is using the figurative term for someone giving advice by happenstance, whose input isn't based on professional achievement, but rather, serendipity, and thus should not be given credence.

"How about just a clever, insightful person," I venture.

"I don't know anything everybody else doesn't know," responds Chaim K. as we are discussing the "off the *derech*" phenomenon, when *frum* Jews "stray off the path" of religious Judaism.

"As an observer, you can't be beat. I am truly convinced that the fact that you have been forced to sit in your wheelchair, so unrelentingly, has had at least one benefit. You have become a very keen observer of the world around you, both concretely – what you visually encode, and metaphorically – the information you intuit."

The holiday of Shavuot commemorates *Matan Torah* – when we should prepare ourselves for receiving the Holy Torah. We are in a mess, not unlike our Forefathers in the desert, after having won a miraculous battle against the Egyptians of old. The process of receiving the Torah lasts much longer than Moses "just" receiving it amid a "sound and light show" that is the dream of Hollywood's FX (special effects) aficionados.

On Shavuot, Moses received the Torah. He saw that the bedraggled group he brought forth under Hashem's miraculous aegis was painfully lacking in Faith, so much so that by forming the golden calf, they desecrated the first and second of the Ten Commandments – even before they had them in hand! Then, before all of the Children of Israel, he broke the Two Tablets signifying "the deal is off." The date is the Ninth of Av, a date – to quote President Franklin Delano Roosevelt (*l'havdil*) – "that will go down in infamy." The two Holy Temples were also destroyed on Tisha B'Av. The Spanish Expulsion of the Jews was on that fateful date, as well.[1]

After forty days of interceding, praying, fasting and doing *teshuvah*, Hashem

---

1. See Eliyahu Kitov, *Book of Our Heritage* (Feldheim Press, 1979).

gives us a second chance, and Moses comes down from Mt. Sinai with the Holy Laws, not on Shavuot, but rather on Yom Kippur.

More than sixty years since the establishment of the State of Israel, with international recognition and economic prosperity that the original Zionists would never have imagined, we are in a mess. The country is in turmoil both from within and without. Nowhere is this more obvious than in Jerusalem, where you can't go up or down a street without bumping into a demonstration of some sort.

City garbage bins are being burned on one block to express annoyance at something; people dressed in green bemoaning the erosion of our green spaces and the veritable air we breathe; a marching band of tourists is going down, another holding Israeli flags. Women dressed in black are mourning relatives killed in Lebanon, fearing more will be killed in Gaza.

Knitted-kippa clad and long-braided teens are dressed in orange, waving flags reminding us that they were uprooted from their homes in Gush Katif; secularists, many tattooed, pierced and heads shaven are shouting profanities on the side. Yet another group, under heavy police protection in an ultra-Orthodox neighborhood where they insist on conducting their march, carrying a rainbow of balloons and banners demanding that the community accept what the Torah considers utterly unacceptable – same-sex marriages, and worse!

We seem to be in a conundrum of what is right-is-wrong and wrong-is-right; left-is-wrong; right-is-right; the middle is really wrong, as compromise is denigrated, decried and generally opposed by every position on the spectrum.

And then, from the ridiculous to the sublime, there are the "black yarmulkes," which should just be a benign symbol of acceptance and responsibility to God's presence. But no – born is yet another new form of discrimination and division. Are the wearers concerned that their *black velvet kippot* have a fabric band on the binding, or, *davka* – not? Is the kippa *black leather* or *black knitted*?

So obvious is one's identity with a kippa that Chaim K. relates the following story: "A young man in my neighborhood was walking around with a kippa with a *seret* (ribbon-like piping or band), and one day an elderly neighbor saw him with a kippa without a band. He went up to the teen and said: 'You started to walk around with a kippa without a *seret*; soon you'll be going to a *seret* – without a kippa!' It was a prophetic remark, as soon afterward, the young man took off his kippa altogether." (*Seret* in Hebrew is a homophone for a movie and a ribbon.)

"How do you think this 'off the *derech*' behavior happens?" I ask. "You and I have seen it often, but how do you think this painful situation for both the family, and usually, the teens and young adult can be contained?"[2]

---

2. See Faranak Margolese, *Off the Derech: Why Observant Jews Leave Judaism; How to Respond to*

"All I can say is my family is very different. Even though my father is from a very *mechubad* Chassidic family, Friday night we *daven* in a Sephardic *shul*; Shabbat morning, Chassidic; Mincha could be Yemenite or wherever we find ourselves. My parents feel that going to *daven* with a *minyan* (quorum) of Jews supersedes *davening* alone. Some people we know will defer going to a *minyan* at all because they are only going to a synagogue where like-minded Ashkenazim pray. I feel that this makes the 'path' so narrow, that going off of it is not only possible, but also probable.

"From my vantage point – and I observe life from the sidelines – this view may be a little different from others my age and my background.

"However, again with the disclaimer for not knowing anything everyone else doesn't know, I have seen many instances where, when the parents of a child keep correcting him again and again, the child tends to rebel. Those that seem to engulf their child with love and acceptance, even when they may feel hurt and angry at their child for acting out, experimenting with alternative forms of behavior, they have a better chance of reaching their child on his way back.

"Clearly, there are things that children can do that are dangerous and parents need to protect them from harm. This is my humble opinion, and I'm not a psychologist or a *rebbe*, but rather someone who has been forced to spend the past eight years watching from outside the *derech* of 'normal' life.

"Children have a need to please their parents, but may end up doing so only after a period of rebellion. Those parents who know this truism, and can hang in there, will be rewarded by children who come back. I can't promise it, but I have seen it to be true.

"*Chevre* or friends can have both a seriously positive and negative impact on teens. On the other hand, no teen wants his parents to tell him whom his friends should or should not be. Here, too, one needs both *mazal* (luck) and *Siyata D'Shmaya* – the help of God.

"I don't feel competent to preach to parents or kids who are searching. I can only speak of my own experience. I was a young kid of 14, who was not such a good student; I could have behaved a whole lot better, well maybe or maybe not, and then, the car hit me. The life that was chosen for me was not one I would ever have searched for myself. No one would search for this! But I have learned a thing or two in the years of captivity in this chair and in *this* life.

"Look for the good in your child and in yourself. Look for the whole in someone who is incomplete. Look at complaining and arguing as positive activities. They allow you to be real and honest and most importantly – human.

the Challenge, (Jerusalem: Devora Publishing, 2005).

Everything has its proportion. Ice cream is a great treat; a diet of only ice cream can give you a stomachache." (I find myself smiling a "*qvellsome*" smile.)

"People who do complain or feel sad and unhappy about their present state are not being honest and challenging themselves. Not every challenge is bad. It allows you to do a *cheshbon nefesh*, soul-searching, and change. But people who only complain, get depressed and sad, are in the end non-functional.

"Some kids don't eat the crust of the bread, but in wartime the crust was the bread. In my state, you learn life isn't a picnic, but it can be an interesting enjoyable journey. That is what I try to do with what I have.

"Oh, Dr. G., do put in that I do enjoy picnics."

States and Traits

Since i've started writing *The Jewish Press* column, many Americans visiting Israel who once introduced to me would say something like the following:

How is Chaim K.?
We feel so spiritually uplifted by your writings, by *your*, we mean Chaim K. and you.
How does he do it?
Is he really as copasetic as he seems?
Is he really suffused with so much *firgun* for others?

To quote Greer Fay Cashman, the *Jerusalem Post* columnist: "*Firgun* is one of those Hebrew words that defy exact translation. The closest interpretation is 'not begrudging,' but in point of fact *firgun* derives from a Yiddish word *fargenigen* that means enjoyment. The Yiddish word was in turn derived from German. Thus *lefargen* is to take pleasure in someone else's achievement."[1]

But more than any question, the one stands out: "Where is his anger?!"

At one of our meetings, Chaim and I spoke about some of these questions, but spent more time on: "What does he do with anger?" This question was the one that most piqued my curiosity too, over the three years we have been meeting.

"I have thought about this from my perspective," he winks. The double entendre is that in his motorized wheelchair he is at a reclining angle all the time, so that his perspective both encompasses the angle at which he observes the world around him as well as the one he has as a CSI quadriplegic on a respirator.

He continues: "I could be a bitter person, but I live at home, with my family and anger would spoil my time – our time, together when we are trying to behave 'normally.' Anger is a defense mechanism that doesn't pay!"

"*Firgun*, on the other hand, means that I don't begrudge someone what

---

1. http://info.jpost.comC005/Supplements/5766/07.html.

he/she has, even if seeing someone walking or biking or anything does squeeze and pinch my heart. I let it go quickly, because it would only harm me if I held on to it.

"It isn't easy to *not* be angry; I have worked very hard on my *middot* (personality traits) to keep from being bitter, angry and jealous. I could look at teens and others my age, younger and older, moving-on with their lives and I could be very bitter and jealous, but where would that leave me? Would it help? Would I walk? Would I move? Would I feel anything other than green with envy and bitter?

"Don't write that I am so perfect. The other day a *frum* woman parked her car in a spot reserved for the handicapped and I was indeed furious at her. How could she be so selfish, so without *hesed*, a *frum* woman?! I even asked her, as she walked away. She turned from me and continued walking away from her car. But do you know something, I felt badly. I felt that the anger poisoned me and didn't budge her. So really there was no purpose in my feeling angry at her, rather I pitied her and her family that she was so rushed that she lost her *middot* compass and could not get back on the right path. How would she be able to give proper *chinuch* to her children?"

In essence, what Chaim K. has intuited over the seven long years of his situation is what Bruce D. Perry, M.D., Ph.D. of The Child Trauma Academy talks about in his seminal article: "The Neurodevelopmental Impact of Violence in Childhood." In other words, how "States" become "Traits." I might oversimplify and say: how the event – more precisely – the biological, chemical/physiological, cognitive and emotional or the consequences of a traumatic event, shapes the traits a person may have consequent to it in the present, and in turn, how these traits will go on to affect those around him/her, and physiologically change her/him and progeny, ever after.

These changes may be life saving for that individual at the "entry point," as they stem from the earliest part of our brain, the reptilian area which becomes the Limbic System. They are responsible for survival – Fight or Flight; Freeze or Feign Death. In psychological terms, one might say, become aggressive or escape – where escape may mean to dissociate/depersonalize and regress/repress.

When children are threatened they are likely to regress and display immature behavior – e.g., suck their thumb; bed-wet; need their old, discarded transitional object – "blanky" or teddy, for example. Regression, a retreat to a less mature style of functioning and behavior, is commonly observed in all of us when we are physically ill, sleep-deprived, hungry, fatigued or threatened.

During the regressive response to the real or perceived threat, less-complex brain areas (not the higher cortical or thinking part of our brain) mediate our behaviors. If a child has been raised in an environment of persisting threat, the child will have an altered baseline, such that the internal state of calm is rarely obtained (or only artificially obtained via alcohol or drug use). In addition, the traumatized child might have an over-sensitized alarm response, over-reading verbal and non-verbal cues as threatening. This increased reactivity will result in dramatic changes in behavior in the face of seemingly minor provocative cues.

All too often, this over-reading of threat will lead to a fight or flight reaction – and increase the probability of impulsive aggression/regression/dissociation. This hyper-reactivity to threat can, as the child becomes older, contribute to the transgenerational cycle of violence. Perry's article presents this accompanying table to help one visualize the hypothesized "causal"/ adaptive events:

Social-Environmental Pressures	Resource-surplus Predictable Stable/Safe	Resource-limited Unpredictable Novel	Resource-poor Inconsistent Threatening
Prevailing Cognitive Style	Abstract Creative	Concrete Superstitious	Reactive Regressive
Prevailing Affective 'Tone'	CALM	ANXIETY	TERROR
Systemic Solutions	INNOVATIVE	SIMPLISTIC	REACTIONARY
Focus of Solution	FUTURE	Immediate FUTURE	PRESENT
Rules, Regulations and Laws	Abstract Conceptual	Superstitious Intrusive	Restrictive Punitive
Childrearing Practices	Nurturing Flexible Enriching	Ambivalent Obsessive Controlling	Apathetic Oppressive Harsh

Table 13. *The continuum of adaptive responses to threat in a living group (family, organization, community or society).*

In summary, exposure to violence activates a set of threat-responses in the child's developing brain. In turn, excess activation of the neural systems involved in the threat responses can alter the developing brain. Finally, these alterations may manifest as functional changes in emotional, behavioral and cognitive functioning. The roots of violence-related problems, therefore, can be found in the adaptive responses to threat present during the violent experiences. The specific changes in neurodevelopment and function will depend upon the child's response to the threat, the specific nature of the violent experience(s) and a host of factors associated with the child, their family and community (Perry & Azad, 1999).

When I go over this research with Chaim for this article, he responds with concern about the children of Sderot, the Gaza periphery communities, and Ashkelon, the areas in southern Israel shelled multiple times daily for years! Again Chaim K. understands and interprets to the "here and now" this most neurobiological and behavioral study, as if he studied it inside out – which, I guess, one can say he did and does!

"What can be done to help them?" he asks.

Perry *et al.* continue: "The focus of the solution can be the future and the least powerful members of the living group (e.g., children and women), they can be treated with the most flexible, nurturing and enriching approaches."

Chaim K. has chosen to have his own apartment within his family's apartment. He has his own entrance but is clearly a part of a multi-generational home with weaker and stronger members in an ever-extending cycle of life of "flexible, nurturing and enriching environment."

By living in a normal environment not overloaded with newspapers, radio and television as well as other stressors, Chaim has mitigated these reactions and allowed himself to become a sensitive, creative and understanding member of society. He eschews violence/anger responses and reactions, seeing them as the enemies of healing, and "snuffers" of his burning light of wholeness and health.

May we all learn from his unique behavior and have the Traits to turn adversarial States into positive *middot*. The specific changes in neurodevelopment and function will depend upon the child's response to the threat.

Living and Learning from the Sayings of Our Fathers

Hillel says: "Do not separate from the community. And do not trust yourself until the day of your death. And don't judge your friend until you are in his place. And don't say something is impossible to hear because it will be heard in the end. And do not say that when I have time available I will study, lest no time will be availed." (*Pirkei Avot*, Sayings of Our Fathers, 2:4)

DURING ONE OF the meetings with Chaim K., our conversation wouldn't budge. He seemed a bit out of sorts, and when I asked how he was feeling he responded weakly "Okay."

In the course of our years of meeting, some sessions are better than others. "*Yom asal, yom basal*" – one day is honey, one day onions – as the Egyptian Arabic slang goes. But being a psychologist-type of person, as Chaim K. would say, I "make *tzimmes* (literally, a carrot/yam casserole, but in the vernacular, a big deal) out of what we do say and what we don't say!" So in keeping with that, I went over our conversation in my head and in my notes for a few days.

What was the reason for this significant non-flow of this specific session?

In all relationships there is an element of Transference that goes on. Psychologists are trained to identify these feelings when they surface in therapy sessions, and subsequently to work them through with their patient/client.

What is Transference? Roughly, Transference is a phenomenon in psychology characterized by unconscious redirection of feelings. One might also say it can be "a reproduction of emotions relating to repressed experiences, especially of childhood, and the substitution of another person – for the original object of the repressed impulses." Counter-transference refers to transferential reactions within the therapist, in conjunction with or without the patient's transferential behavior.

My investigation began by going over my session notes and the feelings and recollections engendered within me during our session, and continued with Chaim K. the next time we met. What events/feelings/experiences came before this specific meeting?

Some clues: We spoke about a *brit* he attended of a first child of a friend. He was joyful for his friend – the new father, the *abba* – and sorrowful, but also optimistic that this level of normalcy retreats into the area of not too realistic wishes from the field of dreams.

The heaviness that seeped into the room that day was possibly exacerbated by the headlines that week which focused on the Covenant of an Israeli baby boy – in this case, the newly circumcised son of Yigal Amir and his wife Larisa Trembovler Amir.

On Sunday, November 4, 2007, Yigal Amir's wife and family arrived at the Rimonim Prison for the circumcision of their son – twelve years to the day after Amir assassinated former Prime Minister Yitzhak Rabin in front of tens of thousands of people and National TV.

While in prison, Amir became engaged to Larisa Trembovler. Amir had met her years ago, when he was a teacher of Judaism sent by Israel to educate Russian Jews. Trembovler first started to visit Amir in jail with her [then] husband. Amir and Trembovler began exchanging letters and speaking on the phone, after she expressed ideological support for him. She left her husband and academic career because of her public personal ties with Amir (Wikipedia).

Essentially, a question that is always there in the room and in Chaim K.'s life, is what could he have "done" in his fourteen years, culminating in his accident, to receive the punishment of lifelong incarceration as a quadriplegic on a respirator. The expression to "sit in jail" is not far off in your mind when you see him sitting in a wheelchair.

He has said more than once: "Did I murder anyone?" And now, a man who was convicted of murdering someone and is "sitting in jail" for the rest of his life, nevertheless gets married and has a child and can "get up and go" (albeit in chains) to the *brit* of his own child and, to top it off, be honored as the *sandek* holding the baby during the *brit*. The painful irony is almost too much to bear.

None of this is said in the meeting I first described. What is whispered when we speak is about lost opportunities. And, especially that of the leftist political parties and the Rabin family at the commemoration on Saturday night, November 3 (*erev*, on the eve of the secular date of the assassination, and *erev* the *brit*) that is punctuated by the *fisfus*/missed opportunity to join the country. Instead, they emphasized the spilt between the Orthodox and secular by painting in black all the kippa-wearing and Orthodox youth, not sending buses to bring their youth groups (Bnei Akiva, Ezra and Orthodox Scouts) to join the over 100,000 youngsters (bused in representatives of the more leftist and secular groups – Hashomer Hatzair among others) at the Rabin Plaza in Tel Aviv, the site of the assassination.

When we finish our righteous indignation about opportunities missed, Chaim K. whispers: "I wouldn't trade places with him."

"You never could have been him," I say definitively. "You are a true believer and your judgment is intact; you would never murder someone even if egged on by fifth columnist such as Avishai Raviv and his 'handlers'," I countered.

"We pray to Hashem '*Al ha'malshinim*,' which was added to the eighteen benedictions of the *Shemona Esrei*, the *Amida* prayer. They, the *malshinim*, 'the slanderers (*mosrim, zeidim*) shall not have hope.'

"Hashem, not mere man, will mete out their justice. Even when your heart is crying out in pain over what seems to be ever more horrific political plans, and what someone did which ended him up 'sitting in jail,' your head and soul could not have done it. I know, as you do, when you say you 'would not trade places with him,' that you will have the *basherte* that is waiting for you, and not the end to be endured by a murderer."

Jealousy, Desire and Honor
Put a Man out of the World

"Last night, I went to a good friend's wedding, yet again. My friends seem to be dropping out of bachelorhood like flies," smiles Chaim K., through moist eyes. "I thought about the scene of our last dance together. We were in the center of the circle, music blaring and our eyes locked. Menachem [not his real name] was holding onto my hand and spinning my wheelchair around with him. We both knew that I was happy and envious at the same time. I knew too, that he was happy that I was alive, and sad that I was locked in this chair with my respirator."

"I guess you could call this positive envy." Chaim K. has developed many theories on human behavior since his accident. His world today includes his warm family and visitors – some friends and the many more professional visitors: physical therapists, doctors, nursing aides, and rabbis from the yeshiva he attends. When we sit together and Chaim talks about interpersonal relationships and human behavior, I am talking to a *very* educated layperson.

He continues: "There is destructive envy or jealousy. For example, there is the type of guy who sees his neighbor buy a new car, say a Porsche, when *he* is driving a Honda. So a person that has *positive envy* might say: 'Oh, I wish I'd also have such a nice car," but the man who has *destructive jealousy* would be saying to himself: 'I wish he'd crash his car into a tree and the car would be totaled'."

Chaim K. has a point: there is a difference between envy and jealousy. Webster's Dictionary defines "envy" as a painful or resentful awareness of an advantage enjoyed by another, joined with a desire to possess the same advantage. "Jealousy" is defined as: a disposition, attitude, or feeling, and is related to "zealous vigilance."

Jealousy typically refers to the thoughts, feelings, and behaviors that occur when a person believes that a rival is threatening a valued relationship. "I am not jealous or want the exclusivity of others' material possessions. But I have had to try very hard not to be envious of people who walk, breathe, and move on their own. I hope I have succeeded. I am happy for them and don't wish them ill. However, I would not be completely honest if I didn't say that seeing

328

their freedom of movement squeezes and pulls on my heart, but I seriously don't wish them any harm."

As a psychologist, I can't refrain from noting to myself that *Pirkei Avot* (Sayings of Our Fathers 4:21) goes on to mention desire and honor in the statement used for the title. A Rogerian psychologist might just say: "Umm," meaningfully. As I relate more with the Cognitive Behavioral School, I ask Chaim if he can tell me about the rest of the statement.

He smiles knowingly, and goes on: "Without *ta'avah*, desire or cupidity, mankind could not go forward. Without our hunger/desire for food, we would starve to death. Without our emotional and physical desires there would be no future generation.

"One of the positive injunctions of the Ten Commandments requires us to honor our parents so that we may merit a long life. Five other Commandments, I guess the more negative ones, tell us what *not to do*; among them is *not to be envious* of your neighbor's possessions.

"So how can *honor* be among the three factors that pave a man's path to death?

"The Mishnah must be referring to *honor gone bad*. Not respect of others, but rather, *ga'avah*, hubris, only requiring respect for oneself. This egocentric use of a Commandment is punishable by death.

"While we see that cupidity and desire are necessary for existence, negative lust and desire are destructive to the very fabric of our society, breaking the bonds between husband and wife and the whole community makeup."

Here, I add that the Mishnah in *Sotah* begins with "When a man is jealous of his wife." The story of the *sotah*, the suspected wife, and her subsequent drinking of the "bitter waters," is indeed the basis of *shalom bayit* (domestic harmony) and demonstrates the importance Hashem places on honor and trust versus the "poison" jealousy can imbue in a marriage. He permits His Holy Name to be destroyed in the search for truth and *shalom bayit*.

"Not bad," smiles Chaim, "for a woman," referring to my Mishnaic reference. "So here is positive envy, positive lust and positive honor."

"Chaim," I ask, "how do you manage to be so *mefargen*?" – a Hebraized Yiddish word, meaning unselfish understanding of and benevolence towards others.

"It's not easy at all. I have difficult days and nights, but I realize that jealousy of others will not bring me what they have, it will only poison my soul and the possibility of having relationships with those I care for.

"I'll give you an example. Recently on a Shabbat when my married sister and brother were visiting, my brother-in-law picked up my brother's daughter. This may sound complicated, but he isn't a blood relation, he's my sister's husband

and the baby was my brother's child. Anyway, his own son became very jealous. He wanted his father's love, exclusively. He was crying, 'Abba, pick me up.'

"One of the other guests quoted this very sentence in *Pirkei Avot* and explained it wisely: 'When we are babies we are jealous, when we are adolescents we have *ta'avah*/desire, when we get old we want honor and in the end we are removed from the world'."

As you can see, though Chaim K. may not get around freely and seems "stuck" in many ways, his mind knows no boundaries. His views of life are kinder and more *mefargen* than most. He is always processing information and has insights into life from which we can all learn.

As we end our session, Chaim says: "Honor and dignity, I lost them the moment the car hit me and left me paralyzed totally, a quadriplegic; desire and cupidity, I haven't ruled them out yet." Winking at me, he ends with: "Before I 'leave' [*sic* this world], I still hope to achieve those goals."

Giving a "Loan" from the Emotional Bank

W<small>HEN HE WAS</small> wheeled into my office for our weekly appointment, I noticed a change. He seemed to be bursting with something that I couldn't place. No sooner had his aide left the room, Chaim K. started speaking.

"You can't believe the number of '*einei aigel*' [literally, calf eyes, but in the vernacular, looks of amazement] I received this week! I have started to visit the Critical Care Units in hospitals with my sister. She propels me and gives out bags of candies and cookies, from a box that is on my wheelchair tray. We present these to anxious people sitting outside these critical care units. They see me, and their eyes pop out and some say: 'Here you are, so handicapped, and yet you are concerned about us; how can we complain about our state!'"

Chaim K. digresses and speaks of actor Christopher Reeve. Until his death, one of the most talked-about people with SCI (Spinal Cord Injury) was Reeve, best known for his reoccurring role in the Superman movies. Thrown from a horse in 1996, Reeve suffered an incomplete C1-C2 injury – his spinal cord was damaged between the first and second cervical vertebrae, just at the base of his skull. Reeve's sheer determination was inspiring to most. He worked to raise awareness (and money) for spinal cord research. "I have the same injury as Christopher Reeve. He came to Israel to publicize the cause, and I even have a picture of him and me together."

I tell Chaim how excited I am for him for his "rounds" in the hospital. He continues to tell me about another "pusher," as I call his aides. "Nachum [not his real name] has become stronger in his observance. He told me that being with me and my family and visiting the yeshiva with me, has made him rethink and strengthen his observance of *mitzvot* and belief in God."

Chaim K. has also received quite a few letters of support by email giving him the validation that he has something to offer – even in his quadriplegic state.

This change is significant because it illustrates a point I try to make to patients and their parents. One can't give a loan if one has no "money" in the *Bank HaNafshi* (emotional bank). Chaim K. has difficult days and nights thinking about life in general, and his future, in specific. It is so hard seeing his classmates and siblings moving ahead in life, or just plain *moving* on their own.

"When I see the world going by, I think of myself as 'a goldfish in a bowl,' staring at the world, imprisoned in a fixed space, without even the privacy to cry. I don't even have the ability to hide myself under the covers and be alone; I have to ask someone to do that for me."

I nod in agreement, and add that the goldfish can cry "privately" as he is in water which camouflages his tears. Chaim smiles and winks at me, as if to say: "That's a good point." Then he continues: "I do feel good though when we go to the hospital and hand out the bags. Even in this wheelchair with the respirator 'breathing,' people say they get strength from me."

I am reminded of the book, *The Giving Tree* by Shel Silverstein. "Once there was a tree . . . and she loved a little boy." Every day the boy would come to the tree to eat her apples, swing from her branches, or slide down her trunk . . . and the tree was happy. But as the boy grew older he began to want more from the tree, and the tree gave and gave and gave.

First, the tree is a place for the boy to play and munch on apples, later its branches serve as a source of lumber to build a house, and later still, its trunk provides the wood for a boat. By the time the boy has become an old man, he has used so much of what the tree has to give, that all that remains is a stump. Yet, all that the old man needs at this point, is a place to sit and rest – a function the solitary stump can still provide. The story ends with a sad: "and the tree was happy" (from the Online Editors of Barnes & Noble). I never liked this story, even though millions of readers love it.

We are told that a person who gives *tzedakah* (charity) should give only a percentage (10 percent) of his money. Moreover, someone who gives more than that amount (over 20 percent) is considered a *rasha* (evil person), but what about the recipient of acts of kindness? In one of the Haftaras (biblical chapter read weekly), Elisha asks the woman who prepared a special room for him when he made his annual sojourn in that part of the country, what he could do for her – as a sign of his gratitude.

In the Torah reading preceding the Ten Plagues, Rashi notes that Moses did not execute the first three plagues, because of his relationship with the Nile, the Ye'or, in which his mother placed him in a basket, and thus the river saved him.

"The Giving Tree" story always afforded me an opportunity to teach, to whomever I was reading the story, how Hashem wants us to give *tzedakah*, but that, equally as important how central *hakarat hatov* (acknowledgment of munificence) is to the process. In this story, the boy *took* throughout his life and the tree never taught him responsibilities or boundaries of taking. In the end, the boy, now an old man, came to *take* again. The tree was finally nothing but a stump, so the old man sat down on it. The book ends with: "The tree was happy," but one who looks at the picture of the old man, can see that he wasn't happy. He is alone, in his taking. He has reduced goodness and charity from the world, by taking from a tree and never planting anything in return.

In Chaim K.'s daily schedule, he is very dependent on others, but in his actions and words, he gives so much. The fact that his aide/pusher has been suffused with newly acquired *emunah* (faith), speaks volumes. I can attest that, in retelling this experience, I saw how "the goldfish" was pleased.

Is It Better to Have Loved and Lost than to Never Have Loved at All?

I hold it true, whate'er befall; I feel it,
when I sorrow most;
Tis better to have loved and lost,
Than never to have loved, at all.

(From Alfred Lord Tennyson's poem "In Memoriam: 27")

CHAIM K.'S MOOD is mercurial and I sense another change in the wind.

"What other cases like mine do you have?" This is a loaded question that many patients/clients ask. Behind the obvious, lie the age-old questions children ask their parents: "Am I the one you love the most?" "I am special, right?" "There is no one who you feel this way about?" "Our relationship is unique."

And then there is: "Am I the worst case you have seen?" "Am I the least serious case of my disease you have ever seen?"

All of these questions, stated or implied, are minefields for both therapists and parents.

We all try to convey that each of these statements is true and can co-exist for everyone at the same time, even when there is a patient who has just left the office and another who will be coming at the close of this session.

But I had the feeling that Chaim was asking another question. This afternoon he is pensive. "What purpose could God have for me? What sin could I have committed that was so horrible, that being jailed to this chair, not being able to breathe on my own and watching the world and everyone in it go on with their lives is my sentence? Even murderers get a specific amount of time in jail, not the life sentence I have. The guy who hit me had his driver's license revoked for three months. Boy, that must have been awful for him," he says cynically.

I don't begin to venture a facile (or even difficult) response. Chaim K. has been to more *Mekubalim* and *Rabbanim* (saintly men) than I. He knows the *pesukim* (verses) that give him succor and relief better than I.

I decided to take this discussion somewhere else. "Tell me, on your way here today, what did you see from your van or near your house, even before you boarded your 'magic carpet'?"

Chaim becomes thoughtfully quiet. Though he frequently has to take time between talking while his ventilator breathes for him and kicks in, this time he sounds a little choked-up and says, "I still remember the wind going through my hair when I was whizzing by on my bike."

I am actively listening. A few moments go by. In a whisper, he says: "I don't remember how it felt anymore when my feet touched the ground."

"How terribly, terribly sad," I say. "There is nothing I can say to change this but –"

His eyes smile a bit and he looks at me with the glint that bespeaks for him: "You're right; there is nothing you can say."

All the while I wonder what I will say now. "Yours is a tragic example of the famous question: 'Is it better to have loved and lost, than to never have loved at all'?"

"Why would one want to fall in love if you couldn't stay in love and if the person wouldn't love you?"

"Ah," I say sagely. "There is a phenomenon in psychological literature, known as an addiction to love. It refers to a compulsion where one is addicted to falling in love, but once that stage is achieved, and the couple moves on to a commitment stage, the person breaks off the relationship. Another variation of this is when they understand that they have set themselves up for a form of abuse. Falling in love with people who abuse them, they may come to understand (through a lot of therapy) that there is more to being in a relationship with someone who loves you, than only falling in love. At any rate in both cases, it is indeed better to have loved and lost."

A quick Internet search of Barnes & Noble reveals just a few of the following titles:

- *Is It Love or Is It Addiction?* Brenda Schaeffer
- *Facing Love Addiction: Giving Yourself the Power to Change the Way You Love,* Pia Mellody, J. Keith Miller, Andrea Wells Miller
- *How to Break Your Addiction to a Person,* Howard M. Halpern

As usual, though smiling, he stares at me as if I speak Martian and not our "Hebrish" (Hebrew and English mishmash). He says the Hebrew equivalent of: "It figures that you would not answer like anyone else. You psychologists are always talking of love and not life!"

"Sure, there are feelings and sensations that you have lost, but *B'Ezrat Hashem*, Love is not one of them. Though people sense it in their hearts and even in their stomachs, Love is in the brain. And your brain is in just dandy condition!"

"Sure I'll find love," he says unbelievingly.

"Yes," I say. "Just like in the songs you listen to, and if you found love and lost it once, I know you'll find it again, because you know how to be receptive to it."

I am curious though, about what we have in our literature: the Torah and/or Mishnah, Gemara and Midrash, that discusses the question of which is better, "to have never experienced love or to have lost?" We finished our meeting with homework on this topic for both of us.

Soon after, I attend a wedding where I meet Dr. Eliezer Be'eri, the rehabilitation physician from Alyn Orthopedic Hospital who had first referred Chaim K. to me for therapy. He is wonderfully committed to his patients, and visits Chaim weekly. Chaim shows Dr. Be'eri our articles upon publication. I mentioned the homework – finding a Jewish source for this specific question.

"That's easy," the physician says. "Check Tractate *Berachot* 28a."

To paraphrase the Gemara: R. Eliezer ben Azariah was asked to come to the famous Rabbinic Academy that had ousted R. Gamliel. He said he would seek the counsel of his family, and asked his wife, who noted that they may overthrow him as they had R. Gamliel. Whereupon, R. Eliezer quoted a proverb: "Let a man use a cup of honor [one used for state occasions, a delicate filigree one] for one day, even if it be broken the next" (*Berachot* 28a, Soncino Edition Translation). The allegory's meaning is that it is important to experience something wonderful just once, even if it may be destroyed thereafter. Clearly, a Talmudic answer to our question.

Once again, I am awed by the *zechut* I have living here, for I know that only in Jerusalem, can one solve philosophical questions overlooking the strobe-lit Old City Walls while hearing klezmer music from the wedding, mixing with rock music from the Sultan's Pool amphitheater. The fact that the source of the solution was a chance meeting with Chaim's Torah/Gemara-knowledgeable doctor, at a wedding, was surely not lost on me, nor will the confluence of events be lost on Chaim K.

May all of God's children find *refua shleima* – complete recovery, and their *basherte* – designated love.

The Gift that Was Too Expensive

We outsiders, civilians in the army of WH or Wanna-Helpers, don't understand the price of our help. One example is the gift that was too expensive.

What could be a greater compliment to a fledgling writer, than to be offered a reward for his writing? One of the articles that I co-wrote with Chaim K. – "I Understand You . . . ," caught the eye of Zelda Harris of the Metuna Organization for Road Safety (in Israel). She was in charge of the annual Metuna Conference, which took place at a Dead Sea resort.

After Zelda read the article, Chaim K. and I were invited to the conference. They offered Chaim K. a gift, he could stay overnight at the hotel to divide up the over two hour drive so it would not be too taxing for him. He was asked to be part of a panel and discuss what he wrote and his experiences over the years since his life changed drastically after he was hit by a car.

He was thrilled. This was the first real, in terms of financial recognition of his writing. A FREE two days and a night at a five star hotel! Then reality struck. He requires two people to move him from his chair to bed, and someone with him 24/7. His father was going to come as the second person; he wanted to give his mother the opportunity of getting a respite and coming too. But where would the other person/aide sleep? Even when that problem seemed to be surmountable, the cost of paying the aide for the sixty-hour shift became impossible. And so, the gift was too expensive, and they didn't go.

We in the army of WH or Wanna-Helpers don't understand the overwhelming obstacles that even gifts present. We also don't appreciate the consequent price paid for the exercise – that of disappointment, frustration, sadness, and more than anything else, dashing the hope of "being almost normal just this once."

Not to be dashed, and using the positive letters of feedback for the articles that Chaim K. and I penned, I wrote a proposal to *The Jewish Press*. It was accepted. Chaim K. would be paid for the articles. That payment would be the first time he had a paying "job" since that night when he was hit by the car on his way home from baking *matzot* at a factory.

At an appointment about six weeks later, we are talking about life. Chaim K. has learned since his injury not to trust or share his feelings. It is generally too painful for him, surprisingly not because he doesn't wish, or can't access them, but rather the effect these feelings have on those around him. He sees their pain. Though much of his physical body does not feel anything – he intensely feels the discomfort, hurt, and agony of those who love him and whom he loves. So he screens, or as he says "censors" what he says.

Weekly, in the safe place of my office, our conversations are a challenge to both of us. To Chaim K., censoring is habitual at this point, and with a glint in his eye he challenges me to read the "chapters" between the lines, or not even lines, but syllables of his utterances. Sometimes, he says: "No, Dr. Judi, you didn't get it." I glow with pride when he sheepishly smiles, and says: "*Bull*" (in Hebrew that means "right on the mark" as in bull's eye). After the Expensive Gift experience, he barely spoke at all. Finally when he did, he told me about a song that was playing in his head. Robbie Williams, "Angels." Not knowing it, I went online with him in the room, and looked it up. Here is some of it:

> *So when I'm lying in my bed*
> *Thoughts running through my head*
> *And I feel the love is dead*
> *I'm loving angels instead.*
>
> (From "Angels," lyrics by Robbie Williams)

I read the lyrics to him, and tried to relate to the message, and reframe it in a way to verbalize that hope and love are to be found in this world, though there is no doubt that he has gotten a large dose of disappointment and sadness now. The Metuna Organization recognized that even in his pain and sorrow, he could express feelings to outsiders that others were not capable of doing. The fact that they invited him to speak to real people, not angels, meant that they saw in him the ability to contribute his thoughts, the act of offering the gift proved that.

At our next meeting, he told me about another song "that was in my head" – "Feel," also by Robbie Williams.

> Feel
> *I just wanna feel*
> *Real love fill the home that I live in*
> *I got too much love*
> *Running thru my veins*
> *To go to waste*
> *I just wanna feel*
> *Real love and the love ever after*
> *There's a hole in my soul*

You can see it in my face
It's a real big place.

(From "Feel," lyrics by Robbie Williams)

I related to the hope of normal relations, his capacity to feel so much more than many people who had neural sensations in their limbs and bodies. The fact that he is now thinking in terms of here and now options, and not talking to Angels was optimistic. That was an improvement since our last meeting.

When I read him this article which we wrote, the Censor smiled.

Dumb Things that People Say

W ORDS ARE VERY POWERFUL indeed. So much so that "mute" – unable to speak (Merriam-Webster Online Dictionary) is in the vernacular, "dumb." In Judaism, we may hear terms such *as lashon haRah* and *nivul peh* used to describe certain words in a context.

With the expert help of Nefesh Israel's "CEO" Elana Walhaus, I began the Nefesh Israel ListServ, which has expanded to be both Nefesh International and Nefesh Israel and as such reaches around the world. Many topics are raised on this Internet forum between *frum* professionals in the field of mental health.

In a discussion related to the topics of *lashon haRah* and *nivul peh*, Rabbi Dr. Ephraim Becker noted that "the 'official' definition of *nivul peh* is any usage which could have been said in a more refined manner (e.g., referring to that which could readily be called *Lo Tahor* as *Tameh*). Anything less than the most refined way of speaking, can be defined as *davar meguneh*, and not directly as *nivul peh*. . . . The test is that *nivul* is much more far-reaching than the use of popularly acknowledged foul language. As such, the degree of violation would seem to be relative to the language skills of the speaker."

He went on to explain that: "*Lashon haRah* refers to words which damage another's reputation when the besmirching utterance is true. *Motzi shem ra* is the term applied when the utterance is untrue. *Rechilus* is the term that applies to speech that causes friction between two other Jews (creating ill-will between them)."

These concepts are specific ways of bringing home the idea that speech needs to be controlled. But how many of us are aware that we may be hurting another with our "compliments" or just day-to-day language.

Chaim sits in my office in a wheelchair. We talk about stupid things people say, especially to him. He is kinder than I am; he says they don't mean to hurt by saying the things they do, "but I still get hurt."

It's hard for Chaim to specifically recall instances, but he has a number of songs he knows that he wouldn't sing to people in specific situations.

"*Kum v'hithalech ba'aretz*" (rise and walk around the country) is one such song and isn't for people who can't walk.

Chaim believes that no one would intentionally hurt another person, especially one who they see as handicapped in some way, but often when we speak we don't always pay attention to the meaning of what we are saying. A person in a wheelchair is supersensitive to the expression: "Rise and Shine."

Ruth is blind. She tells me that people tend to shout at her when they notice her white walking stick. "They figure I'm blind, and that means I'm 'handicapped'; they feel that they have to make some type of adjustment. Then they raise their voice to tell me that the traffic light is green! Once, someone called out to me and said: 'Ruth, do you know you're outside?' 'No,' I felt like saying, 'I thought I was in the bathtub!'

"Dumber yet, are those who say: 'See you later' and then uncomfortably say: 'Oops, I'm so sorry.' Don't they think I know I'm blind!?"

There are sensitivities and sensibilities that are not always obvious. A mother who has dark hair but whose children are blond (as is her husband) once painfully related that in the supermarket someone approached her and said: "You are really good with those children, how much do you charge?" A red-haired child told me that she was often asked: "Are you adopted?" because none of her other siblings (nor parents) were "gingy."

A compliment to a mother of a couple of children such as: "Each is prettier than the last," can cut through the heart of the eldest of the family.

A child, whose father was killed in a terror act, once told me that many people have asked him: "How do you feel?" "What was I supposed to say to that!?" he weepingly asked.

When I made a (weak) attempt at humor, and mentioned to Chaim that in the Mishnah discussing the High Priest's preparations for Yom Kippur, his wife is referred to as *"Beito,"* his house. Wasn't his wife insulted when her being overweight was so blatantly noted?

"No," said Chaim. "Rav Yehuda HaNasi didn't mean to insult her, but rather to make a point. Without a woman, the *Kohen HaGadol*'s house was just walls. And even though he worked in the most glorious of places, his home would be just walls without his wife." I am quiet, and sit in awe of Chaim, again reminded how the kindness and benevolence of those we help puts us all to shame.

The Higher the Expectation,
the Bigger the Fall

CHAIM K. COMES into the office and immediately begins to speak, as if our last meeting had never ended.

"A few years ago, someone told my mother about a doctor who maybe could help me improve my condition. I was waiting for an appointment with all my heart. Maybe he could help me *just improve* my situation a little. After months of waiting, we drove to Tel Aviv and I met the doctor and he checked my whole file.

"Then he called another neurologist and another doctor and then a few more. They all consulted with each other and looked at me again and again. Finally the moment I had been praying for, they were going to tell me something life-changing. I visualized my heart doing flips in my chest; my pacemaker was firing like crazy. This famous doctor, whom I had waited months to see, came into the room, and this is what he said: 'The possibility that something will help your situation or change it, is less than zero percent. The possibility that someone will win the lottery is greater than someone in your situation improving.'

"When I heard this it hit me like a sledgehammer, I was depressed for months. Later, when I started thinking about it, I tried to understand why I was so disappointed. This wasn't the first time I had heard this same news from doctors. I have been in this SCI condition for a few years already, why am I so surprised by it?

"I posited (good word, Dr. G., huh?) the reason being that I had *expected* something else. I expected a miracle worker. I was waiting, dreaming maybe, there is something, some kind of surgery, anything, that will change my situation. Because I had built my expectation so high, the crash was so painful.

"The story taught me a great lesson. Take everything in proportion, even your expectations of something have to be measured with their relationship to reality.

"Let's not confuse expectation and ambition. For example, a man who just started working in a big company does not (and shouldn't) expect to become the CEO within a year. He needs to retain the ambition to achieve his goal; he needs to adjust his expectation to reality. With hard work it may take him over twenty years or even more to achieve his ultimate goal.

"After this happened, and after I took to heart what I had learned, I now try to take everything in proportion and have 'under-expectations' rather than heightened expectations. I learned this the hard way.

"So I want to pass this on to you," says Chaim K. "If your expectations aren't high, then the disappointment is less steep. I'm still disappointed but not to the same extent as *that* time.

"Expectation can be a great tool in life. For example, when a person is set up on a blind date, he develops certain hopes, anticipations, and expectations that will come to fruition when he does meet that girl. He is more anxious and excited to meet her; at the same time he shouldn't expect that she will be *the* one."

Smiling, Chaim says: "He shouldn't buy a ring or take out a mortgage on a house, for example, yet!

"Now, Dr. G.," he winks and smiles, "I did my part on this article, you add the psychological and other stuff." I agree and disagree at the same time. "I didn't expect anything else," he says. His arched eyebrow seems to say: "bring it on."

In their article, "Discounting delayed and probabilistic rewards: Processes and Traits," Myerson, et al. describe disappointment, and an inability to prepare for it.[1] Disappointment has also been hypothesized as the source of occasional immune system compromise in optimists. While optimists generally are thought to exhibit better health, they may alternatively exhibit less immunity when under prolonged or uncontrollable stress, a phenomenon which researchers have attributed to the "disappointment effect." Further amplifying on the disappointment effect, Suzanne C. Segerstrom's (1990s) research suggested that rather than being unable to deal with disappointment, optimists are more likely to actively tackle their problems and may experience some immune system compromise as a result of this "work."

Ian Craib in his book *The Importance of Disappointment* (1994) drew on the works of Melanie Klein and Sigmund Freud in advancing the theory that disappointment-avoidant cultures – particularly the Therapy Culture – provides false expectations of perfection in life and prevents people from achieving a healthy self-identity.

Oddly enough I came in contact with this culture when I bought the little kids' game "Candy Land" for my grandchildren. The original game was a sort of Snakes and Ladders where the players moved forward on a board and

---

1. J. Myerson, L. Green, D. D. Holt, J. S. Hanson, S. J. Estle: "Discounting Delayed and Probabilistic Rewards: Processes and Traits," *Journal of Economic Psychology* (2003:24).

sometimes went *up* a ladder beating a co-player, or sometimes landed on a snake and slid *down* and landed below a co-player. The new version doesn't "allow" for any disappointment and is basically no fun to play. It doesn't teach the skills of competition, anticipation and success tempered by disappointment any more.

In a 2004 article, *Psychology Today* recommended handling disappointment through concrete steps including accepting that setbacks are normal, setting realistic goals, planning subsequent moves, thinking about positive role models, seeking support and tackling tasks by stages rather than focusing on the big picture.

Margaret Marshall of Seattle Pacific University and Jonathon Brown of the University of Washington, Seattle, found that students who expected to do badly, actually felt worse when they did mess up, than those who predicted they would do well but similarly botched their test. This suggests that gloomy expectations could actually exacerbate the wretchedness felt when a person fails. The old advice of "preparing for the worst" does not seem like a successful strategy.[2]

In Parshat Korach (Numbers 16:1–18:32), we have an opportunity to read about raw emotions and the consequences of ambition and disappointment. Korach was Moses's and Aaron's first cousin. Moses received *malchus* (kingship); Aaron received the *kehuna* (priesthood), and Korach who was the next in chronological line was sure he would receive the *nesi'ut* (presidency). Hashem had other considerations and awarded this position to the youngest cousin Elitzaphan.

Instead of trying to understand what might be the intrinsic requirements of the position, Korach lashes out at Moses's decision. The resulting divisive revolt caused death and destruction and teaches a strong lesson in how to deal with personal disappointment. Instead of trying to learn about the roles and respect Hashem's understanding of the requirements of the position of president, Korach sowed anger, jealousy and blame. He lost an opportunity for introspection, self-feedback and learning from disappointment.

Our ambitions and our expectations are gifts from the Almighty. To help us to achieve, grow and constantly seek to improve our situations we must learn to use frustration and disappointment as stepping stones to reach a sense of *shelaimut* – wholeness and peace.

---

2. J. M. Grohol, Psy.D. http://psychcentral.com/blog/archives/2006/02/04/is-it-best-to-expect-the-worst-psychologists-test-long-held-theory-of-emotional-cushioning/.

Chaim B'Seret –
Living in a Movie

Almost immediately on entering my office, Chaim K. begins with the title and says: "I have thought about this title, and I think the best way to describe my day-to-day life is to say it is 'life in a movie.' This is an expression of people whose lives are lived out in a surreal dreamlike fashion.

I think to myself, *wow*, this is going to be an appointment to remember! His opening remarks can be immediately understood as a double entendre of his nom de plume, "Chaim," and his life. As a CSI person on a respirator, his life hangs on a thin cord (*seret*=string/ribbon). He continues: "I feel that I am living in a way that one might think is *in* a movie script. No one writes this script of life, only God. Sometimes I feel it is a comedy; sometimes a horror movie; sometimes a tragedy; sometimes a drama; most of the time it is a *very* boring movie. Nothing anyone would pay an entry price to watch." Touched, and a bit surprised, feeling a bit surreal myself before the onset of a new year, a new year of work together, I murmur: "You feel your life is boring." "Definitely boring. I live in a bubble; my own bubble."

I allow the moment, like another empty bubble signifying non-conversation in a cartoon and add: "What are the benefits?"

He looks at me a bit surprised by that unexpected remark. "My life has no surprises and that's a good thing. Everyone else doesn't know what will happen day-to-day; I can tell you where I will be every second and every day. Therefore my life is calmer than that of others. Surely some things may happen which are unexpected – I could get sick, a flu, an infection, but this won't really interrupt the routine of my life; it might kill me," he smiles. "That won't be boring. "The main negative side is that every person needs something to wake up for. What's mainly missing for me is some level of responsibility, besides just staying alive. For me, that is the main missing element."

He goes on after some thought, "It is a serious problem. Lately, every day is the same thing; I don't really have anything to wake up for. This saddens me, and disappoints me. Of late, instead of staying in bed, in my room and not getting out at all, I try to find all sorts of things to do, but at the moment something very important is missing for me – motivation with a capital *M*.

"The *M* word is something you need in order to work or study or love. "I've been thinking." (I smile and say that thinking is always a sign that there is a problem in the horizon.)

"You've got it; it's not only me who lives in a movie. I look at the Singles Scene, and I think that they are living in an unreal world. They are afraid to change the script of their life to something unknown.

"A friend of mine told me that although he has a girlfriend, whom he loves, he's not sure if it is worth it to marry her. I asked him why. 'What if it doesn't work out?' he says. 'What if, after three years, we have problems and we'll have to divorce?' "So I told him." (Chaim winks at me as if to say, "See, now I am the expert!")

"I said to him, 'First of all, if you love her and you are going to marry her, you probably will have a very nice life; everyone has problems, but you'll be together and able to work out those problems together as a couple.'

"The Rebbe of Gur said finding a person's mate is as hard as crossing the Red Sea. What does this mean? A person who marries has to jump in the water. Nothing in life is 100 percent sure. You have to jump in and you have to swim. Nachshon ben Aminadav kept walking into the Red Sea, having faith as the water rose and rose, to his very nostrils, when all of a sudden his faith was rewarded and the waters parted and Bnei Yisrael followed him to miraculous safety.

"So too the singles; they have to have faith that they won't drown, they'll have a good life, children and stuff. Other people say they just haven't found the 'right person.' They might say to themselves, 'Why should I compromise when I waited so long already?' I ask them, 'What have you done so far in order to find a wife? Have you done enough in going to *shadchanim* (marriage brokers), Internet sites, *Shabbatonim* (weekends) and just the old way of asking family and friends to fix you up'?"

The unsaid words in Chaim's bubble are still hanging about the room; it is heavy with hope, expectations tinged with deep, deep sadness, fear against fear of unrequited love, rejection, loneliness.

He continues: "I see your look and I hear myself sounding so judgmental and un-empathetic, maybe even unkind, but there is something called Singles with a capital *S*. I think someone who is waiting and waiting for the perfect person, the perfect opportunity, and doesn't marry in order to have children, is selfish. It is a waste. From my point of view they are lazy; they're upset that they'll have to wake up at night (with crying babies); divide their salary."

"Wait a minute!" I say. "I think you are being a bit insensitive to people who have tried. They go to *shadchanim* and have gone out on first and even second dates many, many, many times; they have also been disappointed again and again with those recommended to them; they live in such constant pain of rejection, and more than that – not fitting in. Wherever they go, the communities they are in are couple and/or family focused. Every place they go, every wedding, Bar Mitzvah, *brit*, *zeved ha'bat* (celebration for baby girls) and every Shabbat, is a dagger in their hearts, where so much blood has dripped out that it seems dry to the onlooker. This dry, tearless, cry is more painful and more constant than most of those who mete out their opinions or, should I say judgments, can even imagine. Another oft-avoided result of do-gooders is the recipient of others' advice or ideas for a *shidduch*, may be the feeling that the choice presented them was hardly appropriate. Going through this process often makes volunteering to go out, to put one's whole self, one's very being, making one's right to life a virtual foray into a *makom sakana* – a place of horrible danger, which the rabbis tell us to avoid.

"Also, do you realize that singles are 'singled out' – by marrieds and now, you too, for that matter – as people who should be blamed for their single state? How dare you be so insensitive to blame the victim? Do you realize that people take time out of solving their own problems to analyze singles, generally behind their backs, and figure out what the psychological problems may be?! They always know the answer, too! They *pasken* on mother issues, or father issues, as they presume to explain singlehood and myriad other 'pathologies'." With an exaggerated theatrical pouted-lip, Chaim says: "Hey, you're making me out to be a bad person and cold-hearted supercilious jerk."

Smiling, I say, "If the shoe fits okay, you're not cold-hearted." We both laugh at all the other qualities I didn't bother denying. "Okay, I'll come down a peg, but now that you mention it, let's just say I'm just presenting another vantage point. I am not blaming someone who has a physical or emotional problem. I am referring to people who are selfish. If I could move my finger, I am pointing it, at them. They don't want to get married because they are comfortable in their very single, easy life, without responsibilities," he retorts.

Hold the phone right there! I'm rethinking "cold-hearted." "How do you feel when someone explains 'you to you,' tells you how you feel and what you need to be doing to solve your problems; how lazy you are because you aren't married, or whatever they get into their pathetic heads!"

"Calm down, Dr. G, this can't be good for your blood pressure," he winks. "We're just having a discussion."

He goes on: "From people who are close to me, I take their criticism as constructive even if it hurts, and even if I don't agree. But I know that if after I get to Heaven and they ask me 'why you didn't do *p'ru u'revu* (be fruitful and multiply) and bring another generation to this world,' I will say that I did everything in my power to try to achieve that very important mitzvah."

I look at him askew.

"You have to believe me that by the time I get to Heaven I will have tried everything in my power to do this – to get married and have children. I want to re-emphasize that what may sound like criticism is not really so."

"Are you criticizing yourself?"

"Always!" "What is on your To Do list? You are twenty-one, almost twenty-two, and it says *'ben shemona esrei l'chuppah'* (eighteen for marriage)?" I ask.

"Why did my parents get married and have eleven children? They slaved to feed us, worried and still worry about us, our education our life and our getting married and raising families. Why did they do it?

"They did it in order to establish another generation of *ovdei Hashem*, who will be mitzvah-observant and will honor *Shem Shamayim*. And also there is *nachat* and *simcha*. When I see my nieces and nephews, my parents' grandchildren, it brings joy to them; the way I see it, there is no greater joy.

"It's obvious from my choice of a topic, that this is something I think a lot about. In my condition which is, let's say, medical, I think my chances are slight, but not impossible for achieving this type of mitzvah," and then in a whisper, he adds, "this level of joy." "What do you have to do to make it a bit more possible?" I inquire. "Pray to Hashem to direct me in the right way, to help me and send me a wife. I truly believe that this is a possibility.

"I am trying to not live in my bubble, to get out of the *chaim b'seret*, life in a movie, and use the opportunities that are out there. Just know that I will go anywhere for any *shidduch* date with someone, who knowing my situation, would even consider going out with me."

And then, as he moves his wheelchair towards the door and adds: "My ad would say: SFYM in WC&R interested in SFYW for serious purposes only with marriage as main goal." I add: "Bright, sensitive, and funny even though he often thinks too much and criticizes mostly himself."

The Miracle of God Given Breath

CHAIM K. ROLLS into my office with a determined look on his face and a twinkle in his eye. I am filled with relief that his dark days seem to be coming to an end. Over the past six years (starting four years after his accident), we have achieved a level of comfort with each other. Awe, mutual respect, friendship, frustration and excitement have often joined hands during the almost weekly sessions. We have learned to understand each other in a way that sometime resembles an old married couple.

I see the old twinkle in Chaim's eye replacing the dull and sad resignation of previous months. He begins talking immediately; he is in a different mode, he feels he has something to contribute to others, not just take, a word he uses to connote his extreme dependence.

He begins: "One morning, I awoke to find myself in the hospital with tubes coming out of me from every possible, and even some impossible places. I didn't understand what had happened to me.

"I tried to get up, but I couldn't. I tried to sit, but I couldn't. I tried to speak and I couldn't. I went into a panic. They told me that I had been in a *very* serious car accident and was injured in my C2, which is the second cervical vertebra.

"They told me I was paralyzed; my whole body was paralyzed; I would never be able to move or breathe on my own again.

"The first time I was disconnected from the external breathing machine I was very frightened. Suddenly, I felt as though I was being choked. I couldn't breathe! I was so afraid. Instantaneously, one of the disconnected machines started to beep – almost screaming – but I couldn't raise a peep from my voice. I had the realization that I had no air to scream, but worse than that, to even breathe.

"I didn't understand what had happened to me; it seemed like forever until 'they' galloped in and hooked me back on to the respirator. From that time to now, almost ten years, I have a tube from my trachea to the ventilator, 24/7.

"It is hard to live with the knowledge that your life is totally dependent on a machine which can mess up at any second. A number of times already over the course of ten years the machine has gone *kaflooey* – I can't breathe, and the same choking sense envelops me. The only difference between the first time and now is that I am not as panicked, because I know what is happening and that help will soon arrive.

"One of the downsides of being hooked up to a respirator is that the machine requires electricity at all times. When I am home the machine is plugged into the wall. When I go out of the house, I have a battery on my electrified wheelchair which keeps the respirator fully juiced all the time. The battery lasts just a few hours a day, so that I have to plan for every eventuality, all the time.

"A few months ago, my pulmonologist explained that Israel is just about to import a new machine that will change my life. In the States it isn't at all that new, but here I would only be able to receive it if I qualified for a grant and fit the profile of one who could succeed with this type of technology.

"The device known as a Diaphragm Pacer and it is very much like a heart pacemaker. It sends an electric pulse to the nerve that causes the diaphragm to raise and lower itself, thereby allowing the lungs to rhythmically fill and empty of air.

"This will allow me to breathe without the respirator. I can't imagine what it will be like not hearing the constant noise of this infernal machine – day in and day out, night in and night out.

"*Baruch Hashem*, I completed the surgery to implant the device in my body just three weeks ago. After the surgery one has to wait over a month before they activate the device giving the body a chance to heal from the surgery and the imposition of this new machine into it. Next week my Doc is going to turn it on, and my diaphragm and I will begin 'training' for the big day. Day one is just a few minutes of me breathing on 'my own.' Every day we will increase the amount of time the Diaphragm Pacer works and I breathe without the respirator.

"I can hardly imagine that in about two months I will be – *tra-ra-tra-rom* – breathing on my own.

"I lie in my bed and try to imagine when my diaphragm, my body, will move on its own. For ten years, I have forgotten how my body feels when it is breathing.

"Every day I thank God that He created the minds of the inventors of this and other medical miracles. I keep praying and hoping that one day they will find a cure for the situation I and other spinal injured people are in.

"You probably do not pay attention to the rhythmic pulsing of your diaphragm, your chest rising and lowering at an even pace.

"You probably don't pay attention to your first morning prayers especially the following:

> *Elokai neshamah shenatata be tehora he. Ata nafachta be.* My God, the soul with which Thou hast endowed me is pure. Thou hast created it. Thou

hast formed it. Thou hast breathed it into me. Thou dost preserve it within me, and Thou wilt hereafter reclaim it and restore it to me in the life to come. So long as there is soul within me, I avow before thee, Lord my God and God of my fathers, that Thou are the Sovereign of all creation, the Ruler of all living, the Lord of all souls. Lord who does restore the soul to the dead, blessed art Thou.

"Next time you inhale a deep breath, stop a moment to savor it and think about the wonderful gift Hashem gave you. For me this is not a given, it is a Miracle."

Pure Belief

CHAIM K. HAS BEEN going through a difficult time. It is impossible to imagine oneself confined to a chair 24/7 for a week, let alone ten years! Over the years that we have known each other, I have been privy to Chaim K.'s indomitable spirit and the highs and lows of his mood.

Without going into the specifics, what can only be seen as Hashem's intervention, caused a situation where Chaim K. was presented with a choice, maybe the first choice in his life since the car that hit him destroyed his carefree adolescence. Chaim K. *chose* to see the opportunity presented to him in its entire awesome proportions. He chose life. His belief in Hashem's miraculous ways were revitalized, re-energized; his battery was recharged. He entered my office and began speaking immediately.

"For ten years already, I ask God for an answer to my question of 'Why me? Why *davka* me?' There has to be order in Hashem's world, there has to be an explanation for chaos – this mess I am in. This is the tenth year of me being a quadriplegic on a respirator. I can't move or feel anything but my face. The one thing I do have is time, time to think – so, so, so much time.

"I realized such a question couldn't be answered. I'll explain my thinking to you through a parable:

"Let's say a person steps on an ant. The friends of the ant, not unlike me, my friends and my family, ask why did this person step on our beloved son, brother and friend and squash him. He was a good ant; he was hard working and a member of our society. Why him?

"The person, who stepped on the ant, can try to explain to the ant's friends why he did that. 'People don't like ants in their houses; they aren't aesthetic or clean; they carry disease and make me look like a bad housekeeper.'

"You can try to explain for fifty years straight – until you are blue in the face – why he killed their friend, but the ant will never understand. Because the 'squasher' is a human and the ant is just a lowly ant. Ants will never understand human forms of communication and language.

"So too, we are ants before Hashem. Hashem can try to explain for fifty years straight, why *davka* this is happening to me, for example. But we can never truly understand.

"Our intelligence can never comprehend this.

"So where does that leave me, a lowly human in my questioning for reasons? After ten years of questioning, I have arrived at a somewhat bittersweet acceptance of the answer. Belief!

"We have to believe that Hashem makes no mistakes and wants what is best for us; even if it seems so unrealistic that *this* thing is good for me. How can this be good for me? I am paralyzed; I'm always in a wheelchair; I can't breathe on my own; my heart even needs help to beat on time (a pacemaker).

"How can this situation be understood as Hashem doing what is best for me?

"Believe me, I can't say this is an easy life, a life that one can easily be grateful for having, but as a believing Jew, I trust in Hashem. His decision is that there is no other way for me to *be*, to exist, in this world. Hashem asks of us to believe in something we will never understand. That's it.

"I want to sharpen this point with the following story:

> One day students of the Baal Shem Tov came to him and asked why are those who do evil rewarded and those who are holy and honest punished in this world.
>
> The Baal Shem Tov told them to go to a river at the edge of the town and hide on the side of the way and observe what is happening at noon.
>
> The students went and waited by the stream. They saw a man coming on horseback. When he reached the riverbank he sat under a tree in the shade to rest and drink a bit of the fresh water.
>
> After a while he got up and jumped on his horse to continue on his way. When he mounted the horse unbeknownst to him a package of money fell from his pocket to the ground. The man continued on his way crossing the river and going to the next town.
>
> A few minutes later a stranger walking on the side of the river reached this spot. He found the package of money on the ground. He picked it up, looked inside and joyfully continued on his way.
>
> Moments later, another person went by and sat under the same tree to rest. Meanwhile, the horseman noticed that the money was missing. He panicked and raced back to the spot that he had been at under the tree. From afar he saw a man sitting under the tree. He approached him and yelled: "Where is my money, give me back my money." The hapless man under the tree had no idea why this rider was screaming at him, because he had neither found nor taken any money. The man told the rider, that he had no idea what he was talking about.
>
> But the rider didn't believe him. He started to seriously beat him up. When he saw he wasn't getting anywhere, he re-mounted his horse and went on.

In a bit, the wounded limping hapless victim of this unexplainable abuse went on his way.

The Baal Shem Tov's students returned from this tableau they had just observed. They went to the Rebbe and said: "What is this injustice that we just saw? How could this happen?"

The Baal Shem Tov responded by telling them a story:

"In a previous incarnation (*gilgul*), the horseman was a business partner of the man who had found the money. The rider owed his partner money, but he didn't want to pay. They went to a *din Torah*, a Rabbinic Court, and the rider knew that he would lose the case so he bribed the *dayan* (judge) to rule in his favor.

"What you saw was a resolution of an injustice. The rider was the person who owed the money to his partner, the one who found the money was the partner to whom the money was owed, and the third man, who was beaten to a pulp, and who seemed to just be an innocent bystander, was the *dayan* who took the bribe."

Such was the fashion in which the Baal Shem Tov demonstrated to his students how their limited view of the events led them to assume that Hashem metes out injustice, the evil are rewarded and the honest are punished.

"And now to me. I have spent all these years wondering what happened in my previous *gilgul*, what I am here to correct. I can only *believe* with all my soul that I am a part of Hashem's just world."

On Siblings, Jealousy
and the Normal One

"When I was healthy and my brothers were young and bothered me," said an exasperated and frustrated Chaim K., as we began another session, "I'd shout at them or even hit them. Now, even my younger siblings don't listen to me. I have to yell at them for at least ten minutes to get them out of my room, if they are annoying me.

"My younger brother thinks that it's funny to hit me. He's fifteen years old and I yelled at him more than once or twice. You can't hit me, you have to respect me as your older brother, and you can't hit me and think it's a joke."

Dr. G.: Where does he hit you?

Chaim K.: He slaps me on my face. I told him that I don't think it's funny.

Dr. G.: Does he think it's a way of connecting with you and treating you like you're okay?

Chaim K.: No, he knows I'm angry at him for doing it and that I don't think it's funny.

Dr. G.: How would you act?

Chaim K.: I would act towards him appropriately. If he was my older brother I would respect him, not bother him. I would help him in any way I can.

If I could walk, I'd break every bone in his body, and send him to the emergency room; now, the situation is different.

He's the only one who hits me; the others bother me, annoy me. They come and they kiss me; they know I don't like to be kissed. They wet their mouths first and then kiss me; they do it on purpose to annoy me. They spread their spit all over my face when they kiss me. I know they love me a lot, but it still makes me sad and angry. I yell at them, but it doesn't help so much.

Dr. G.: Do you think that maybe they are jealous? (He is now looking at me as if astounded by what I said.)

Chaim K.: Of what?! Can't you see I am a quadriplegic, I can't move anything but my face, of what would they be jealous?!

(I sit quietly and wait a few minutes.)

CHAIM K.: My mother spoils me, I can understand it; she wants to make me happy, to put me into a good mood. It's hard for her to see me like this.

(I sit quietly.)

Why do you think? Because she can't do anything that can help me! It is the feeling of helplessness for a mother to feel that is so hard for her, for a mother to see her son suffer like this and not be able to do something to help him. Because of this she spoils me.

And maybe that does make them jealous.

DR. G.: You are nineteen years old, what can you do to change this? Are there any adults that treat you with disrespect? Maybe you should live with people your age.

CHAIM K.: I love to be at home.

DR. G.: Tell me about that, being at home.

CHAIM K.: It's different being at home, with family, everything has its benefits and its negative sides.

(He has an uncontrolled spasm, and his hand and arm fall off the tray of his wheelchair, I ask him if I can touch his hand to raise it and put it on the tray, he acquiesces.)

CHAIM K.: When this happened the first time (during our first visit), I wouldn't have asked you to help me and give you permission to lift it up.

When I was in Alyn (Children's Orthopedic Hospital), I only drank water once a day. I didn't want to ask anyone to get me anything, even water, I was embarrassed to ask anybody to help me.

Our time is finished and I think that we might discuss Joseph and his brothers from the Torah portion.

SIBLING RIVALRY

Sibling rivalry is a normal part of family life. All children become jealous of the love and attention that siblings receive from parents and other adults. When a new baby is brought home, older children may, as part of normal development, feel betrayed by their parents and become angry, directing their anger first toward the parents and later toward the intruder who is usurping their position. How many of us (we Sephardic wives "out there") would easily acquiesce to our husband bringing home his second wife? (Even though Sephardim did not accept the *takana* of Rabbainu Gershon against the biblically-permitted state of bigamy, they may marry more than one wife in countries where this is permitted.)

Just imagine your husband saying: "Hashem saw how much I love you so he blessed me with another one just like you; you'll grow to love her; you'll be best friends" – or other such statements, that we expect an older sibling to accept with equanimity.

We have to look no further to read about this type of conflict than the in the Bible: Abel and Cain, Abraham and Nahor, Isaac and Ishmael, Jacob and Esau, and Jacob's preferential treatment of Joseph over his other sons are only a few examples. Physical as opposed to verbal fights usually peak before the age of five. All these biblical cases had violent sequelae.

ANOTHER TYPE OF SIBLING RIVALRY: THE NORMAL ONE

There exists another type of sibling rivalry which is hardly ever addressed, either by most parents or by professionals (or educators and rabbis). In her excellent book, *The Normal One: Life with a Difficult or Damaged Sibling,* psychotherapist Jeanne Safer interviewed sixty adults who grew up with a disabled brother or sister, and they themselves may have been labeled "the normal one." She used her own personal experience as a catalyst.

The book examines the pathology of this experience in a systematic and nosological manner. She noted that "the normal ones" exhibited very clear, similar and definable behaviors in their childhood and later in life: premature maturity, emotional and intellectual perfectionism and deep guilt about their own health. She analyzes Shakespeare's *The Tempest,* and the character, Caliban, using some psychological theory, but it's the memoir and her candid style that makes the book unique. (You don't have to know Shakespeare's works or any psychology to understand the syndrome.)

She examines the double-edged reality of normal ones: how they both compensate for their siblings' abnormality and feel guilty for their own health and success. With both wisdom and empathy, Safer describes what she calls the "Caliban Syndrome," a set of personality traits and characteristics of higher-functioning siblings: premature maturity, compulsion to achieve, survivor guilt, and fear of contagion.

When Chaim K. and I meet, we discuss "our articles," we edit them, and he gives the "final okay" as to what we send in. Even though the articles are very personal, Chaim K. feels that if it helps one person or changes their way of thinking/behavior for the better, it is worth the effort.

We may not say everything that is on our minds. Both of us, though, experience a lot of incidental learning, and I guess that is what life is all about.

FOR FURTHER READING:

M. Wallace, M.S.W., *Birth Order Blues: How Parents Can Help Their Children Meet the Challenges of Birth Order* (NY: H. Holt, 1999).

J. Safer, Ph.D., *The Normal One: Life with a Difficult or Damaged Sibling* (N.Y.: Free Press 2002).

Love with Respect

"In the nine years since the car hit me, the options available to me for work, narrowed dramatically. You see the only part of my anatomy that I can manipulate is my face.

"This being the case, there are very few vocations for which I can apply. One of the fields with the most potential for me, though, is to work with the computer. There is a special mouse I can use, and over time I have perfected my skill level.

"You see, since the accident I have had a lot of free time and spend a lot of it on the computer. So, I have learned a great deal. However, until now I haven't had any opportunity to use all this knowledge rolling around in my mind.

"My sister works for a charity called Shalva. This is a very unique institution that works with very handicapped children. My sister is a Hydrotherapist which means that she does therapy with her clients in water. One day she introduced me to the director of the organization and he asked me what I do.

"I mentioned my interest in computers and he said that this was a true *min haShamayim* (Heaven sent) moment because they were looking for a webmaster. He offered me the job and I accepted. I have started working there and am really enjoying it. Most of the work I can do from home, they send me memos or notes over the Internet, and once a week I go into my office in their building in Har Nof.

"The work I do includes putting up pictures on the website and trouble-shooting when there are problems – in essence things I love to do. And best of all, I can work at times that work well for me.

"When I arrive at the building, my sister comes to visit me in my office. I am very goal-oriented, so when I arrive I go straight to my office and do my work. When it's time for me to go home – I leave.

"As I have said before, I am quite closed in my own bubble. I don't mingle and socialize. In the Amuta Shalva there are many young women doing their National Service, Sherut Leumi in lieu of serving in the army. This week my sister told me that some of these volunteers came to her quite insulted, saying that they were surprised she is so nice, as her older brother (me) is such a snob.

Even though he doesn't speak to anyone, he must think he is too good for them, and all he has managed to do is hurt everyone's feelings when they have approached him just to say hello.

"But let me tell you, my readers, the real reason for my reticence in opening up lines of communication with these Sherut Leumi young women.

"The story began six years ago – when I should have been attending high school, but because of my situation was at home. The Ministry of Education assigned a *bat sherut* whose job it was to study and do homework with me twice a week. I was 17 years old and she was 18. After a while we really connected – not just as student and volunteer, but with a stronger bond – at least on my part. I had fallen in love with her. During the whole year that she came to work with me, I never told her how I felt. When the year was over, she continued on with her life and went to study in university. I began to miss her. One day I spoke to her and asked that she come and visit me, just like that. I told her how I felt, that I felt I was really in love with her. It was so hard for me to tell her these intimate feelings. I was so vulnerable and wasn't sure how she would respond.

"Her response was one of shock and panic. She said that the feelings I had towards her were not love, but rather gratefulness for the work she had done with me. 'What do you want me to say,' she asked. 'You know what your situation is, and that there can never be something real between us,' she continued.

"I was very hurt by her response. But I don't judge her, because I don't know how I would have behaved if the tables were turned.

"In the ensuing six years, I maintained a connection with her; we met occasionally and spoke on the phone. The reason I kept up contact with her was that it was just too hard to completely disconnect from her. During those six years I prayed, fantasized and dreamt for a miracle – to be cured and be able to just walk up to her. That miracle hasn't happened yet. A few months ago, I was in a bookstore with my father and I saw her as she came in. There was a big change in her – her hair was covered. She had gotten married. The site hit me like lightening, and I felt as though an ice-pick had gone thru my heart. My heart was shattered into a million pieces and bleeding through and through.

"During the six years, the pain had been great, but there were also glimmers of light. From the day I saw her in the bookstore, I haven't spoken with her, the contact which I thought would be impossible to break was gone; the glimmers of light that hope had allowed to seep through, dimmed to darkness.

"I put myself into a shell, not allowing feelings, clearly such as these, to enter or leave the protective coating of my bubble. It is like a moth who loves the heat and light of the fire, but as he flies closer and closer he gets singed, not warmed. He can't resist the light or the heat and he moves yet closer and closer until he gets totally burned and dies. But I am not a moth. Once I got close to the fire, the feeling was warm and the light was bright and nice. But the second I got burned, I learned my lesson and now I stay away from the fire – notwithstanding the glorious feelings the light and heat bring with it.

"I have a job I love; I enjoy going to work once a week. I don't want to get burned and I don't want to hurt anyone the way I was hurt. I hope one day to be strong enough to take down the shield I put up and maybe meet another nice girl, and hope for a different ending. I have learned though, from King Solomon who wrote in *Shir Hashirim*, the Song of Songs: 'Many waters cannot quench love, nor will rivers overflow it; If a man were to give all the riches of his house for love, It would be utterly despised'.

"In my case, that means that though the fire of love stills burns deeply in my heart I will not open myself and take a chance on being derided or despised by throwing all my riches, the totality of my 'house,' after love. I pray and I know it will come to me, one day on its own."

IN MEMORIAM

We Lost Our General
on the Battlefield

Tuesday, September 9, 2003, 6:00 p.m.

I AM WRITING THIS to give you a *temunat matzav*, a picture of "the situation" during the terror bombing onslaught targeting Israeli civilians in buses and restaurants throughout the country, specifically in Jerusalem.

The *matzav* in Israel vis-a-vis them and us.

Life here is never either/or. We cannot dress-up, or down and melt into surroundings to have a few hours off of being Israeli – Jewish or Arab – for that matter. When I'm on a plane, just before the flight attendants ask "are you *the* kosher," I have a feeling that I am anonymous and "just like everyone else," for example, the person sitting in the seat next to me.

No matter what ethnicity or color we are, in Israel, we are never anonymous, as my scheduled appointments show on a typical day: someone who lost a spouse on the August bus bombing; a little girl (no relation) who was near that bus; someone whose trauma was being in the "one before" bus. Among the sundry other problems: a person who discovered her brain tumor returned; two PDD kids; a 3-year old Arab girl who was in a car accident and I am the court-appointed neuropsychologist; a learning-disabled adolescent whose parents are more disabled than he in so many more important ways; and a little boy who has school issues – the one his parents and teachers didn't mention is that he is scared stiff that the guard, who "just sits" in the school yard, will not be able to keep him safe.

6:45 p.m.

I hear the news that there was a *pigu'a* close to Asaf HaRofeh Hospital near Tel Aviv. More dead, more wounded. Jerusalem and the rest of Israel is on emergency alert for more terrorist activity – heightened alert, if possible – we are already required to keep our beepers on through the night.

11:30 p.m.

After hearing a loud boom, and then the ambulances, I went off to the hospital. Instead of the usual noisy excitement and dread of the ER and MCI (Mass Casualty Incident) personnel, I was met with a quiet pall. Almost immediately I was told by the chief psychiatrist that the head of the ER was at the café (the scene of the terrorist bombing) having a "quiet" moment with his daughter the night before her wedding.

Hours later, he, Dr. David Appelbaum, 50, and Nava, his 20-year old daughter, the bride-to-be, were not to be found in any hospital. The family, the groom-to-be and his family, friends of all the family and each of the seven children, overseas guests arriving for the wedding who went to the hospital instead of their hotels, all rallied around the family until 3:30 a.m. when the final identification of Nava was made at Abu Kabir, the country's pathological institute.

Dr. Appelbaum had just returned from a lightening visit to New York University Hospitals where he presented innovative ER responses to trauma. He started his work at the Magen David Adom (the Israeli Red Star of David) and then founded an independent emergency clinic (in which he felt he bypassed the bureaucratic mire). At his death, he ran both that clinic and Shaare Zedek Medical Center's ER. He was a doctor's doctor, *the* expert in triage and instant trauma attention. He treated thousands of people of all nationalities, colors and stripes. How many people that he might have treated, Arab and Jew alike, will suffer because of that anonymous bomb.

Wednesday, September 10, 2003, 10:30 a.m.
They are being buried now. She was eloquently eulogized by her father-in-law-to-be as an "Eternal Bride." Daughter and father joined together forever in death and not off to a new start, a new life at the wedding.

This was not the only family to lose a loved one at the hospital last night, but to the ER staff and the Shaare Zedek Family, the loss was palpable. We lost our general on the battlefield, and we are left to manage alone and anonymously.

Continuing the Legacy
of Chezi Goldberg
and Roberta Bernstein

CHEZI GOLDBERG, HY"D, May God Avenge His Blood, the columnist who wrote the weekly "Chezi's Corner" for *The Jewish Press*, was a member of Nefesh Israel, and was on its conference committee for the second, third and fourth annual Nefesh Israel Conferences.

During our preparations for the Eighth Annual Conference in 2008, the image of Chezi making his last presentation, less than two weeks before he was killed by a suicide terrorist in 2004, was one of the catalysts that mobilized us as we chose programs for the conference.

Chezi Goldberg's work with youth and teens and the articles he wrote dealt with issues still under discussion. Among the topics that is always in the forefront of our work here, and especially so when we think about Chezi and other victims of terrorism, both the living and dead, is how to work with children and youth following such catastrophic events.

Unfortunately, as the army has made the country safer – "vehicular terrorism" – the carnage on the roads, claims more victims daily. During Sukkot 2007, Chuck Chaim (Charles) Bernstein, 54, his wife Roberta, 49, and their 18-year old daughter, Batsheva, were killed (their 11-year old son, Moshe, was gravely injured), leaving their eldest child, Orly, aged 19 and in the army, the only member of this family "whole."

Roberta, z"l – a seasoned social worker and a tireless voice for children and families who were terrorist victims – worked with me on many occasions. She and her wonderful husband and daughter will be sorely missed by everyone she touched.

I am frequently asked what we do here to help children cope with the seemingly endless round of funerals for their young friends or family members. I'm not sure if it is primarily an Israeli situation, but, unfortunately with the death of so many young men, elder and younger brothers, fathers in the armed services, and the continuing increase of terrorism by both external and internal sources (road accidents), we, the world-weary, have put together previous methods that seem to help youngsters and teens.

Below are some examples of situations and strategies:

THE MEMORY BOOK

There is a feverish urgency in the searching for pictures. All the friends are looking in their homes for pictures and mementos from the last tiyul – school trip. Shira is drawing a picture; Motti who is great at writing poems is working hard, tears streaming down his face. Everyone will write something that will capture the essence of one who will never get old. All this work is goal-directed, which is to make a memory book for their classmate that will be something the mourners will have during and after the shiva.

The Memory Book is a very important way of showing the parents of a child or adolescent who died how the many people outside the family were touched by him/her. There may be thirty classmates, friends from youth groups such as Bnei Akiva that are only "Shabbat Friends," who knew the child in ways the parents and other family members did not. Each page adds a dimension to the life cut down with such finality. The Memory Book gives those close to the deceased an opportunity to say things to their friend that they may not have said in words during her/his life. It is their last gift.

MULTIPLE DEAD, THE FUNERAL, SHIVA IN DIFFERENT ROOMS, SHIVA IN HOSPITAL

Funerals are always sad, but this one was heart wrenching. Five open graves. So many members of this one family killed on such a bright summer day. Two of the children who were together with what was a big family, were seriously wounded. They were at the cemetery too, on hospital gurneys, faces white with bandages and tubes of transfusion lines coming out of their arms.

At the funeral: What do you say to the living? What is there to say except "take care of yourself," "hope the pain is not too bad," "we are still here for you," "we'll never forget you," and yes, you cry for the dead.

WHAT ABOUT THE SHIVA WHEN MORE THAN ONE PERSON WAS KILLED OR DIED?

They were once a family – father, mother, sisters and brothers. Now three people did not return from the outing to town. The apartment has four rooms and a kitchen. In every room one or a few of the family members are sitting shivah. The son, daughters and mother all have their own friends. The grandparents, aunts and uncles are also sitting Shiva. Going into the house causes an overwhelming feeling of the heart being squeezed. Will I remember the stories

I want to tell them? Will I be able to stand the pain in my throat and heart? Will the words come out?

Take your lead from those already in the rooms. Frequently someone there, a friend, will include you into the "circle" and fill you in as to what they were talking about. You can smile, make a joke, or tell a story, or you can just sit there and cry. Even if you are not actively included in the exchange of memories, just sit there, and even if you say nothing, your presence sends an important message: "I am here for you, you can count on me."

AWARENESS OF LIFE AND DEATH

Little hand in the bigger hand of his brother, Yossi walks the same route every morning and afternoon to his *gan* (kindergarten). On a sunny morning they pass one of the buildings on the way and see a white notice edged in black taped onto the front gate of the building. "Who was *niftar*?" asks 3-year old Yossi. They look at the *moda'at aivel* (the death announcement) and see the words: *b'seivah tovah* (at a ripe old age). Yossi's older brother says: "It was someone who was old and waiting for Hashem to take him to Gan Eden."

Here in Israel, more than in other parts of the Jewish world, death is a way of life. Our "awareness" of death comes to us early in childhood, and it is a familiar concept to young children being walked to *gan*.

The car with the blaring loud speakers rushes around the religious neighborhoods, it is on a mission, its loud message cuts through the quiet night, or the bustle of the day. "The funeral for Ploni ben Ploni (so-and-so) is going to take place in an hour or two."

It is a mitzvah to bury someone before nightfall on the day of death. The mitzvah is also to bury someone as soon as possible, so in Jerusalem, burials take place at night.

In Israel, and specifically in Jerusalem, the *meit* or deceased is buried, wrapped in a *tallit* and not in a coffin.

Devori saw the *tallit* being carried on a stretcher. At first she wondered why four people were carrying a *tallit* in that fashion? Then she understood; the *tallit* held within it, the body of her grandmother. How little and small it looked. It couldn't be a person wrapped in "that!" This could not be my grandmother, she said to herself; Savta was so big, and she filled my life with her stories and her recipes. And then another thought took the place of the first one. When Hashem takes the neshamah, the person we knew is no longer a "resident" in the body. Devori felt comforted by that thought.

LOSS OF A BODY PART

Yermi fought in a tough battle in the Golan. What he remembers most is the light, fire and sounds of the battle. The biblical description of The Merkavah came to mind seconds before he felt something, and then looked down toward his right hand. A "silly" thought came to mind. He had always worn his watch on his right wrist so that he wouldn't have to take it off, and possibly lose it, when he put on his *tefillin* in the morning. Now it was gone, as was his whole arm. His *chavruta* from yeshiva was with him in the tank. He put his hand in the "hole" left on Yermi's body and held on to the veins and arteries as tightly as he could, until they were transferred to a field hospital.

When I visited Yermi as he was convalescing, he told me that the Army Rav (Chaplain) had come to visit him earlier in the day, and brought him something. With his one hand Yermi unwrapped the "gift." It was his watch. Yermi was relieved, because it meant that his hand was found and buried, as is the mitzvah regarding body parts separated from someone before death.

Research by thanatologists – scientists who study death – has shown that there is a minimization of reported phantom limb pain in those who know what happened to their body part. We, as Jews, for 5000 years, have had this *chochmah*, built into our way of life.

May the times of the Mashiach be near and with it, *techiyat hameitim*, the rebirth of souls in the Holy Land. Until that time, may organizations such as Nefesh, and its credo of synthesis and networking of Torah-true mental health professions continue to be a strong source of hope and help to those it serves.

FOR FURTHER READING:

The following book has other ideas suggested for an American audience: N. C. Goldberg, M. Liebermann, *Saying Goodbye: A Handbook for Teens Dealing with Loss and Mourning*.

An Open Letter to
You . . . Woman!

I CAN'T BELIEVE IT! I can't believe you are gone from this world. I can't believe it is Erev Shabbat and Erev Sukkot, and I am debating which earrings and shoes to wear as I wait for my lift to the Eretz HaChaim cemetery in Beit Shemesh, Israel, where the sun never sets.

I recall our first meeting at a Nefesh conference as though it was yesterday. Both of us were escaping, as unobtrusively as possible, from a less than enlightening, invited speaker. We looked at each other and said almost in unison, "Why don't they use our 'own' people?" We smiled at the coincidence. Your energy propelled you; I just held on to your pushchair as we went to another lecture.

At another point, people were coming over to you and either breathing heavily or saying: "How *are* you?" After I was introduced, you asked me the same question. I looked perplexed and you told me you know how difficult this last year must have been in Israel. You were wondering how I was holding up, working in the ER at Shaare Zedek Medical Center, what with the terrorists and all.

How does she know so much about me, when I didn't even know her name, I wondered. I answered: "I'll tell you, if you'd tell me why you were getting all those 'How *are* you's'." The Big C, the Big MS and assorted other letters of the alphabet followed. I nodded that I had gone through some alphabet letters as well, but by comparison, I was just balmy/bomb-y. You gave your wonderful laugh, and said: "Woman, we have to be friends!" It wasn't an invitation; it was a command, as well as a prophecy.

Over years of Nefesh conferences and telephone conversations, we were indeed friends in mind and spirit.

At another Nefesh conference, I took a break and high-tailed it to a nearby wholesale shoe store. I returned, with not too much time to spare, to sit on a panel on T/trauma – big *T* and little *t*, as it is called in "EMDRese." I wasn't sure who else was sitting on the panel with me and was thrilled – it was you. "Where were you, Woman?" you asked. I showed you my very new, green shoes and after that, whenever we spoke you asked: "What are you wearing, Woman?"

I counted myself very fortunate to be among your panel of outside "eyes and ears." This panel crisscrossed the U.S., Europe and Israel. For the many years that you were home- or hospital-bound, you did better information gathering than the CIA and Israel's Mossad combined! I would call you to find out what was doing in my hometown and everywhere else, for that matter.

I wasn't interested in gossip or slander, but rather involved in the burning issues in the overlapping venues of Torah-true Judaism and mental health.

How I will miss our transatlantic conversations which always began with: "Woman, what are you thinking?" And hearing you laugh as we enjoyed yet another foray of mental gymnastics enhanced by your sagacious input, which allowed our minds to soar.

So as I chose my large dangling earrings and donned my purple Crocs, I did so because I knew you'd be asking: "Woman, what are you wearing?" soon to be followed by: "Woman, what are you thinking?"

I'm thinking of you, Rivka, watching over your beloved family, and the rest of us – richer and wiser for knowing you.

Woman, May your memory be blessed.

— Judi

In memory of Dr. Rivka Ausubel Danzig, z"l

Twenty Extra Years

WHILE READING THE AUTOBIOGRAPHY of the late David Servan-Schreiber, *Anticancer: A New Way of Life*, along with his summation of experiments and treatment for cancer, I was reminded of the very last prayer after the *Neilah* – the closing service on Yom Kippur (in the custom of Spanish and Portuguese Jews):

> Go, eat thy bread with joy, and drink thy wine with a happy heart, for God has now accepted thy works. (*Book of Prayer Yom Kippur*, Dr. David de Sola Pool)

Dr. Servan-Schreiber, M.D., Ph.D. writes about his own cancer experience. How when he was thirty-one years old and just beginning his career as an experimental neuropsychiatrist, a patient didn't show up for an MRI. Rather than waste valuable machine time, he and his colleagues decided to use themselves as guinea pigs. When it was his turn in the machine, they were silent. He asked what the problem was. Gingerly, they told him they thought they had found a tumor in his brain.

His new life began after that. Was he to be no longer the examining physician and researcher, but rather a cancer patient with a six-month to a year prognosis to live? As he wasn't prepared to accept that, he began reading and researching.

Surprisingly after the choices of surgery, chemotherapy and radiation there was nothing else in the oncological medical bag of tricks. He went through the interventions and had a few months hiatus until the cancer returned. The doctors had warned him this was a serious probability. Again he went the accepted medical route of surgery, chemo and radiation.

After he was declared NED (No Evidence of Disease) the second time, he asked: What can I do to help myself? "Just go home and enjoy your life as best you can, when it recurs we will do more interventions," he was told.

Yes, but he wondered if there was something "alternative" he could do in the meantime? Nothing, he was advised, just go home and enjoy your life. This is a standard conversation that takes place between doctor and patient.

It is important to note the Dr. Servan-Schreiber himself, in one of his last interviews, highly recommends sticking to the conventional oncological/medical treatments, but during the time conventional treatments are in a break or have been exhausted, he suggests other interventions, mainly those relating to the intertwined relationship between the mind/body and diet.

He began to use his prodigious scientific and medical skills to examine multi-continental research in the area of cancer interventions. He developed a methodology which essentially involves mind/body continuum as well as diet. His clear and readily available book has helped, supported and cajoled many cancer patients into prolonging their life spans. His book, *Anticancer: A New Way of Life*, is also available in Hebrew and other languages.

In July 2011, after a twenty-year battle with cancer, David Servan-Schreiber passed away. In the twenty extra years he was given, he expanded his horizons, as well as the lives of hundreds of thousands of patients and those in charge of their care. His life's work was to bring an anticancer life to everyone. His book is preventative as well as reparative and recuperative.

David Servan-Schreiber's seventeen rules below are gleaned from his website:

FOOD RULES

1. Go retro: Your main course should be 80 percent vegetables, 20 percent animal protein – like it was in the old days. Opt for the opposite of the burger topped with a token leaf of iceberg lettuce and an anemic tomato slice. Meat should be used sparingly for taste, as when it used to be scarce, and should not be the focus of the meal.

2. Mix and match your vegetables: Vary the vegetables you eat from one meal to the next, or mix them together – broccoli is an effective anticancer food, and is even more effective when combined with tomato sauce, onions or garlic. Get in the habit of adding onions, garlic or leeks to all your dishes as you cook.

3. Go organic: Choose organic foods whenever possible, but remember it's always better to eat broccoli that's been exposed to pesticide than to not eat broccoli at all (the same applies to any other anticancer vegetable).

4. Spice it up: Add turmeric (with black pepper) when cooking (delicious in salad dressings!). This yellow spice is the most powerful natural anti-inflammatory agent. Remember to add Mediterranean herbs to your food: thyme, oregano, basil, rosemary, marjoram, mint, etc. They don't just add flavor, they can also help reduce the growth of cancer cells.

5. Skip the potato: Potatoes raise blood sugar, which can feed inflammation and cancer growth. They also contain high levels of pesticide residue (to the point that most potato farmers don't eat their own grown potatoes).

6. Go fish: Eat fish two or three times a week – sardines, mackerel, and anchovies have less mercury and PCBs than bigger fish like tuna.

7. Remember not all eggs are created equal: Choose only omega-3 eggs, or don't eat the yolks. Hens are now fed mostly corn and soybeans, and their eggs contain twenty times more pro-inflammatory omega-6 fatty acids than cell-growth regulating omega-3s.

8. Change your oil: Use only olive and canola oil in cooking and salad dressings. Go through your kitchen cabinets and throw out your soybean, corn and sunflower oils. (And no, you can't give them to your neighbors or your relatives . . . They're much too rich in omega-6 fatty acids!)

9. Say "Brown is beautiful": Eat your grains whole and mixed (wheat with oats, barley, spelt, flax, etc.) and favor organic whole grains when possible since pesticides tend to accumulate on whole grains. Avoid refined, white flour (used in bagels, muffins, sandwich bread, buns, etc.) whenever possible and eat white pasta only al dente.

10. Keep sweets down to fruits: Cut down on sugar by avoiding sweetened sodas and fruit juices, and skipping dessert or replacing it with fruit (especially stone fruits and berries) after most meals. Read the labels carefully, and steer clear of products that list any type of sugar (including brown sugar, corn syrup, etc.) in the first three ingredients. If you have an incorrigible sweet tooth, try a few squares of dark chocolate containing more than 70% cocoa.

11. Go green: Instead of coffee or black tea, drink three cups of green tea per day. Use decaffeinated green tea if it gets you too wired. Regular consumption of green tea has been linked to a significant reduction in the risk for developing cancer.

12. Make room for exceptions. What matters is what you do on a daily basis, not the occasional treat.

NON-FOOD RULES

1. Get physical: Make time to exercise, be it walking, dancing or running. Aim for 30 minutes of physical activity at least 5 days a week. This can be as easy as just walking part of the way to the office or the grocery store. Choose an activity you enjoy; if you're having fun, you're more likely to stick with it.

2. Let the sun shine in: Try to get at least 20 minutes of daily sun exposure (torso, arms and legs) without sunscreen, preferably at noon in the summer (but take care to avoid sunburns!). This will boost your body's natural production of Vitamin D. As an alternative: discuss the option of taking a Vitamin D3 supplement with your doctor.

3. Banish bad chemicals: Avoid exposure to common household contaminants. You should air out your dry-cleaning for two hours before storing or

wearing it; use organic cleaning products (or wear gloves); don't heat liquids or food in hard plastics; avoid cosmetics with parabens and phthalates; don't use chemical pesticides in your house or garden; replace your scratched Teflon pans; filter your tap water (or used bottled water) if you live in a contaminated area; don't keep your cell phone close to you when it is turned on.

4. Reach out (and touch someone!): Reach out to at least two friends for support (logistical and emotional) during times of stress, even if it's through the Internet. But if they're within arms' reach, go ahead and hug them, often!

5. Remember to breathe: Learn a basic breathing relaxation technique to let out some steam whenever you start to feel stressed.

6. Get involved: Find out how you can best give something back to your local community, then give it.

7. Cultivate happiness like a garden: Make sure you do one thing you love for yourself on most days (it doesn't have to take long!).

Sure, most of you will say: I have no self discipline; how will this work where everything else has failed.

To you, dear readers, I ask a simple question. Sometimes non-kosher food looks good, but do you drool over it? We all know serious smokers who were unable not to smoke almost every waking hour, only to be completely abstemious on Shabbat and holidays. Because Hashem's injunctions are stronger than even the fear (or knowledge) of certain early and painful death.

You don't have to make everyone in your family crazy with this diet; it isn't so hard to follow. But be aware that major health centers advise following the Mediterranean Diet to promote health.

My prayer for the Jewish People is to be in touch with our primary roots, those of our forefathers and mothers, Avraham and Sara, Yitzchak and Rivka, and Yaacov and Rachel and Leah. Isn't our core from the Mediterranean Basin?

SPEECHES FOR AWARDS

The Maimonides Award

May 1998

FIRSTLY, I WOULD LIKE to bring a fresh report from what will be called "Charlie's Floor" – of the Woman and Infant Center – in memory of my dad, Charles Henry Bendheim, z"l, who in his lifetime, and with my mother Els's support, worked tirelessly for Shaare Zedek. The tiles are a restful Pinkish Terra Cotta, the wood lintels are oak. It looks airy, spacious, unfinished, but great! With your continued support Charlie's Floor will soon be ready for business and my wish to you is that many of your children, grandchildren and great-grandchildren, will be born there. *Bli ayin hara,* many of my grandchildren have been born at Shaare Zedek, and I look forward to the beautiful and exciting new developments.

I also want to add how honored I feel to be chosen as the recipient of the Maimonides Award, not only for my work at Shaare Zedek, but also as an opportunity to share a life lesson with you. What unites us as the Shaare Zedek family, is that we each could, in Candide's words, have "tended our own garden" – or taken care of our own lives. Instead, we have been fortunate to have had the choice and opportunity to use the vector, energy of those feelings for others. I have the pleasure to be sandwiched between Ilse Falk who might have used her successes in life for her family and herself, but indeed chose to erect in the ashes of the Shoah – and I'm referring to the Israel Center, in Jerusalem, a place where thousands of kids have found a physical and spiritual home away from home. And Julie Stern Joseph – whose father Stanley, z"l, I grew up with, and whose mother Marsha, z"l, was as a newlywed, among the founders of Yeshiva University's Junior League. Julie Stern Joseph might have used her personal, intellectual and academic abilities to further only herself, but rather than doing that, she has chosen to be the harbinger of a new and exciting mode of spiritual and religious interaction within the Orthodox community.

I personally feel blessed that God has given me the gift of waking up each morning and running to work for a ten-hour day. My work as a neuropsychologist involves what I call "a search for the healthy part of the child." Most, if not all of the children I see have been referred as a result of some form of disability that affects their brain/behavior relationship. That is the definition of the field of neuropsychology: the study of the brain behavior relationship in order to diagnose, analyze and develop rehabilitation means for circumventing the area of the brain affected, and the behaviors compromised. In so doing, we endeavor to help the child maximize her or his potential. These might be the disabilities that one can see – physical malformations, or those that are not obvious to the eye. They may be brought about by injuries sustained at birth, genetically transmitted, head trauma as a result of car accidents, brain malformations, cancer, or serious learning disabilities with no known cause. In any event, these realities prevent the child from being who she or he otherwise might have been.

What most of you don't know is that I was, and to some extent am, that child. I was born with a physical malformation that became life threatening. My parents – I was the first of my seven siblings – were in their young twenties at the time, and they were told to leave me in the hospital and I would be dead in three days. I was blessed with parents who would not accept no for an answer, they took me home and fought for my life. That fighting spirit I now try to convey to my patients and their parents. With a great deal of support from my children, and especially my husband, I pursued my studies throughout my marriage and the raising of our children. We married when I graduated high school. My BA took eleven years and studying over three continents to complete. My Masters took "only" four years and two coasts. I finally earned my doctorate in 1990 – by then I was a grandmother. Today is a closing of many circles for me. Indeed, I am thanking God and many individuals through my work at Shaare Zedek Medical Center.

My parents accessed doctors and hospitals that indeed did save my life. In 1996, when I had cancer, doctors and hospitals again came to the rescue. My first coming-out party at age three was at Aunt Erica and Uncle Luddy Jesselson's wedding – I was the flower girl. And I am so happy to see her here today. My wedding was at the Essex House and some of the people in this audience were present. And finally the Maimonides Award, with which you are so graciously presenting to me, joins me with my husband's heritage, as both Maimonides and my husband, Rabbi Dr. Harris Guedalia, are of Spanish/Sephardic origin. I am also especially grateful to see my my mother-in-law, Selma Guedalia and father-in-law, Judah Guedalia, as well as my Aunts Guetchen Herlands-Engelberg and Erna Steindecker, all of whom made a special effort to be here today.

Before I close I would like to particularly thank Eva Zweibel, *z"l*, her daughter Dorothy Zenilman, and the Tobin Family Foundation, for their contribution to the Pediatric Neuropsychology Clinic. They have allowed the Clinic to grow. Today we receive referrals from all over the country. In closing I would like to especially thank my dear friend Lee Weinbach, my co-recipients, and you, the women who have made, and are continuing to make – Shaare Zedek Medical Center in Jerusalem – truly the hospital with a Heart, Soul and Brain.

Thank you.

The Mercaz Harmony Award

February 12, 2001

Firstly, i want to thank Joan and her committee for choosing me as an honoree for the Harmony Award. When Joan called and left a message, I was sure I was going to say yes. Yes – I would see whomsoever it was she was sending, and yes, I would find a few hours in a chocker-block schedule to make that appointment happen, in the nearest future. I was speechless – not a common occurrence for me – when she told me why she had phoned.

My first response was: Why me? I'm not accustomed to public stuff of this sort, and there are so many more worthy people out there. After some persuasion, I said: Let me think about it and I'll call back. I called my sister Karen, and told her about it. She said: "How many people want to honor you anyway? Quick, call Joan right back before she calls all the other people who really should get the award."

After tonight, a German saying comes to mind:

> *Man wird so alt wie eine Kuh(e);*
> *Und immer lernt man noch dazu:*

Loosely translated it means that even though I may be as old as a cow, I can still learn something. Well, I have learnt to enjoy this.

When I was thinking about what to say tonight, two people, widely different, came to mind. Not in order of importance – don't laugh – Abraham Lincoln, and my grandfather Ivan Salomon, *z"l*. Today, February 12, is the date of Abraham Lincoln's birthday, so he was an obvious association; my Opa Ivan might be a bigger stretch. Most of you know that Abraham Lincoln was the president of the United States, but many of you might not have known that he suffered from Marfan's Syndrome, an hereditary disorder of the connective tissue that affects many organ systems, including the skeleton, lungs, eyes, heart and blood vessels. His great height is a common symptom of Marfan's Syndrome, as is pain, discomfort and shortsightedness, which were all a part of his life.

My Opa Ivan, who died at age 92 in 1972, contracted meningitis in 1899, at the age of 19. He fortunately survived the dread disease, but suffered headaches day in and day out, for the rest of his life. I once asked him what it was like to

379

have a headache all the time, and he said something that has been a guiding principle to me in my life and work. He said: "You learn to think 'over' the pain."

Abraham Lincoln looked very different from those around him, suffered daily, but he thought "over" the pain. It was maybe this pain and these differences that shaped him and made him sensitive beyond his time to the differences of others, and toil for the equality of all, in society. He made a difference to the world.

My Opa Ivan, headaches and all, saw the nazi threat, and with his family and the friends that would listen to him, left "peaceful" Holland for Canada. His strident belief in his judgment, notwithstanding others who scoffed at his vision of the dangers ahead, allowed me to be born – he allowed me to be a part of this world.

Abraham Lincoln and my Opa Ivan taught me the value and importance in "seeing and thinking 'over' the pain." The parents of the children I see at the hospital have taught me these same lessons. Yes, there is pain in not being the same as those around you, but yes, you do make a difference to the world when you "think" and "live" above the pain.

I personally feel blessed that God has given me the gift of waking up each morning and running to work for a ten-hour day.

My work as a neuropsychologist at Shaare Zedek Medical Center, involves what I call "a search for the healthy part of the child."

Most, if not all of the children I see have been referred as a result of some form of disability that affects their brain/behavior relationship. That is the definition of neuropsychology: the study of the brain/behavior relationship in order to diagnose, analyze and develop rehabilitation means for circumventing the area of the brain affected, and the behaviors compromised. In so doing, we endeavor to help the child maximize her or his potential.

These might be the disabilities that one can see: physical malformations, or those that are not obvious to the eye. They may be genetically transmitted or brought about by injuries sustained at birth, head trauma as a result of car accidents, brain malformations, or developmental lags; or they may be serious learning disabilities with no known cause. In any event, these realties prevent the child from being who she or he might otherwise have been. In my work, I try to communicate to the child and the family that, yes, you have a disability but no, you are not the sum total of your disabilities. You are whole.

It is with this attitude and philosophy that in 1986 I found a kindred spirit. That partner was and is Mercaz Harmony as exemplified by its founder Joan Sheransky. From its inception, Mercaz Harmony has stood alone in being a child-centered institution. Certainly it goes all out to help parents and school, but if there ever is a question of who goes first, in regard to feelings or sensibilities, then the children always come first. I too, am proud to align myself with this oftentimes less than popular approach. I know that I can call Joan and use my *protexia* to push for a child to be accepted into an already closed class. The advent of the outreach program has permitted this "class" to be almost anywhere. The children have only benefited. Mercaz Harmony's credo that every child has a right to be included and integrated harmoniously into society, resonates in me, and fuels my work.

Before I close, I would like to thank all those who worked so tirelessly on making this evening a very special one for me, especially Vanessa Broch and Michael Goldstein.

I am grateful, that my mother, Els Bendheim, is present to share in this evening, my siblings for their ongoing support.

I thank my children, for being the wonderful people that they have become, and apologize that they who sometimes have to wait their turn because "I am in the middle."

Most importantly my husband, for his patience and fortitude, and also for his role as a model of *tzedakah* and Community Service.

I would like to especially thank the children and their parents for being unique, teaching and challenging me in so many ways, and allowing me to have a very, very small part in Hashem's plan to make their world harmonious.

Thank you all.

The Esther Solomon
Memorial Award

December 2011

Before i begin I would like to say *"She'hechiyanu ve'kimanu ve'higianu la'zman ha'zeh."*

I am truly honored to be a recipient of the award in memory of Esther Solomon, *z"l*.[1]

Coming from Israel to the Nefesh Conferences, I would always come the night before to get my "land legs," so to speak. Frequently, that meant helping out with last minute gluing and stuffing on the floor with my swimming *chavruta*, Esther Solomon.

The women's swim was at 7 a.m. and Esther and I would be there with another few stalwarts. After doing our laps, we would chat. Esther always had great ideas for *shidduchim* and made quite a few. I was less fortunate, having made just one *shidduch*, but I benefited from the ones that she made. Esther made a single condition for a *shidduch* – a trip to Israel. And we would have coffee or lunch on my home turf celebrating each of her successes. May we all be *zocheh* to follow in her footsteps and be at Hashem's service and be *mezaveg zevugim*, join souls.

I received the call telling me of the award just minutes after another fateful call, that one informing me that my latest CT had come back with not such good news, the cancer that was discovered a year ago and excised *and* chemo-ed, was back full force and had succeeded in making a new tumor.

My first reaction was I don't want to get the award of the best Nebbish Story of the Conference. I was assured that the committee had me on the short list for three years already, well before I was ill, and that now I was the natural shoo-in.

Once hearing that, which happened to be the day after the Nobel Prize was announced and retracted because the recipient had croaked three days previously; I said "No Backsies." I was again assured that that would be the case. Parenthetically, the Nobel Awards committee did reinstate the late Professor Ralph Steinman's Nobel Prize in Physiology and Medicine. And now for the

---

1. The Esther Solomon Memorial Award for Outstanding Contributions to Mental Health in the Torah Community is awarded at the Nefesh International Conference. It is in memory of Esther Solomon, the wife of Dr. Nosson Solomon, President of Nefesh International.

difficult part: the previous honorees were, as you all know, Rabbi Dr. Abraham Twerski, Rav Dovid Cohen, Rabbi Dr. David Pelcovitz and Reb Ronnie Greenwald. I recalled the song from Sesame Street: "One of these things is not like the others," ME! If I was to accept the reward, I had a lot of responsibility to future FEMALE recipients.

(1) One, they don't all have to have a Chronic Terminal Illness;

(2) Two, they don't have to wear Black Suits and white accessories, and three . . .

(3) To quote Rick Perry, the Republican hopeful, I forget what Number Three is . . .

What should I wear, and of similar importance, what would I say?!? Just being here today took a tremendous toll, not just on me but also on my family and my beloved husband, Rabbi Dr. Harris Guedalia. Hashem aligned the stars and moons and even as I write this I am not quite sure how and if my attendance will work out.

This time, I diagnosed the cancer recurrence on Rosh Hashanah, and finagled a CT scan immediately following the holiday which confirmed a tumor a day later. There were many *sevarot* (opinions) what would be the best way to treat it. Most doctors said surgery was out of the question, rather shrink it with chemo and then surgically remove it; or the trickier more risky way, do surgery first and then do the chemo to ensure that the little buggers will not return any time soon.

Most of the doctors in Israel and the States to whom we spoke were not in favor of doing the surgery first. But how could I let this unwanted "guest" live in me for months before evicting it? I wanted it O-U-T, and OUT as soon as possible, before it could grow a millimeter larger. The surgeon who operated on me fifteen months before in New York, when the wretched disease was first identified (by me), said he could do the surgery and felt that doing it immediately was the way to go. I had it O-U-T in New York, the day after Sukkot. Both times I had no symptoms and my blood tests were just dandy. My main complaint was stubborn constipation, even as the bowel system seemed to work alright independently.

Since the surgeries, last year's and now this one, the *beracha* I say with the most *kavana* (intention) is "*Asher Yazar*." The more I looked into the meaning of this blessing, the more I felt that it is an all-encompassing special prayer that was so much deeper than its mere literal translation, a blessing with a message that we, as Torah-True Mental Health Professionals, need to integrate into our personal and professional lives.

When Theodore Reik spoke of Listening with the Third Ear, he described how psychoanalysts intuitively use their own unconscious minds to detect, decode and decipher the unconscious wishes and fantasies of their patients.

When talking to my son David about the *gadlus*, the greatness of the *Asher Yazar beracha* for its psychological insight, I noted that I visualize Hashem sitting on-high, permitting and allowing our soma and stoma to receive and express so much more than the peristaltic flotsam of basic day-to-day life. The sharpened awareness of "what's going on" is the essence of true communication with ourselves, with others, and of course with our Creator. My son David mentioned that I should look up the Queen of Sheba's riddles to King Solomon in Louis Ginzberg's *The Legends of the Jews*. He was right.

Here is riddle number 7:

> The Queen of Sheba poses this riddle: "There is an enclosure with ten doors, when one is open, nine are shut; when nine are open, one is shut."
>
> King Solomon responded: "That enclosure is the womb; the ten doors are the ten orifices of man – his eyes, ears, nostrils, mouth, the apertures for the discharge of the excreta and urine; the navel is open and the other orifices are closed, but when it issues from the womb, (i.e., the child is born), the navel is closed and the other 'doors' are opened."

This might be a weird association, but I felt it was Right-On the mark as a segue for my speech this afternoon. When Leah Abramowitz and I attended our first International Nefesh Conference, we both felt that with Nefesh International as our mother ship, our placenta as it were, connecting and nurturing us, we could attempt birthing Nefesh Israel. Rabbi Dr. Mordechai Glick and his wife Nina, the then Presidential pair, and all the Board members were very positive that our endeavor was possible, and so began the nascence of Nefesh Israel. Today, the proof of the pudding is in the eating, with an attendance of around three hundred Torah-True Mental Health Professionals a day at our two-day conferences, and scores at our year-round lecture series, Nefesh Israel is more than off the ground, it's flying!

Thank you, again, Awards Committee and Nefeshers for bestowing on me the Esther Solomon Award and as such recognizing Nefesh International's role in the birthing and nurturing of Nefesh Israel. The ListServ was "developed and set afloat" in Israel under the combined stewardship of Elana Walhaus and myself and later spun off into two: Nefesh International ListServ, under Rabbi Dr. Mordechai Glick's and now supplemented with Dr. Abe Worenklein's able leadership, and the Nefesh Israel ListServ. Both are entities which have joined our world of Torah-True Mental Health Professionals intergalactically as we would never have imagined possible.

To sum up,

Blessed art Thou, Lord our God, Ruler of the universe. In wisdom Thou hast formed man, creating within him channels innumerable. In Thy sublimity Thou knowest that were they rent (torn) or obstructed we could not subsist even for a short while. Blessed art Thou, Lord who workest the miracle of healing for all flesh. (Dr. David de Sola Pool's translation of "*Asher Yatzar*")

I will loosely translate it for us today, and the present and future Torah-True Mental Health Professionals:

Blessed is Hashem whose wisdom abounds, and created within us many channels for getting in and releasing "stuff" that we and others, our patients, for example, carry about. Channels of Spiritual, Secular and Humanistic communication. Most importantly You have taught us the importance of releasing and clearing these channels so that we will be available to exist as healthy individuals doing and working for ourselves, our families and Klal Yisrael.

That is my prayer to us all, keep the lines of communication open, learn from one another, and enjoy Life and Work – in that order.

Thank you.

PEER REVIEWED ARTICLES

Birkhat Ha'Gomel:
Community Response to
Acute Stress Disorder

Judith B. Guedalia, Ph.D.

T HE AIM OF THIS PAPER is to propose the introduction of a communal ritual as a post-trauma early intervention technique. There are specific community oriented methods for dealing with trauma survivors; we believe that, in particular, the Jewish ritual of *Birkhat Ha'Gomel* (the blessing recited when saved from danger) is helpful for reducing chronic effects of trauma. Similar post-trauma traditions are seen in other ethnic groups, such as the Navajo; those will be briefly discussed as well. It is important to note that therapies that are currently employed as the result of years of research have many similarities to those rituals that have existed for thousands of years. When providing early intervention for a trauma survivor, it is important to be aware of culturally appropriate treatments as well as the most commonly used professional methods. A combination of these techniques may be effective to alleviate acute stress disorder and prevent chronic post-traumatic stress in the general public.

INTRODUCTION

Biblical-rabbinic and modern psychological definitions of trauma overlap, both viewing a traumatic event as an experience in which an individual is faced with the possibility of death or serious injury. Specifically, the DSM-IV® (*Diagnostic and Statistical Manual of Mental Disorders*) defines a traumatic event as an event that is experienced or witnessed which involves an actual or threatened death or serious injury or a threat to the physical integrity of self or others.[1]

The Talmud sages qualify trauma as a situation of being faced with danger to

* "Birkhat Ha'Gomel: Community Response to Acute Stress Disorder" by Judith S. Bendheim Guedalia was originally published by *B'OR HA'TORAH Journal of Science, Life and Art in the Light of the Torah* (2008) vol. 18. www.jct.ac.il/site/borhatorah

1. American Psychiatric Association, *DSM-IV: Diagnostic and Statistical Manual of Mental Disorders*, 4th ed. text revision (Jaypee, 2000).

one's life.[2] The Talmud, completed in 200 BCE, enumerates four situations after which an individual is required to say *Birkhat Ha'Gomel* (the blessing recited when saved from danger): crossing a desert; traveling by sea; recovering from illness; being released from prison.

Interestingly, the major criterion for performing this post-trauma ritual is identical to the major criterion for PTSD – a person's perception that his or her life was in danger. According to many rabbinic authorities, this blessing is recited whenever one's life was in danger, even if the circumstances do not exactly match the four situations defined by the Talmud.

CLINICAL TREATMENT

Survivors of traumatic incidents (including illnesses) suffer from many psychological effects. Although some people enjoy an initial phase of excitement and hope as the result of having been saved from death, many other survivors begin to engage in risky behavior, such as non-compliance with medical treatment.[3] R. S. Blacher[4] finds the development of depression and guilt in postoperative patients who seemed to feel that they were getting "too good a share" in life in comparison with others who did not fare as well through a disease or surgery. Holocaust survivors, paradigmatic examples of trauma survivors, have been found to suffer from depression, anxiety, survivor guilt, and social withdrawal.[5] Other survivor symptoms include fear, insecurity, anxiety, and uncertainty.[6]

Studying the guilt that results from trauma, Lewis[7] believes that guilt is a major outcome for most people who have experienced a severe life stress. Berger[8] writes that guilt is one of the four major therapy themes of Holocaust survivors. People suffering from survivor guilt display a prominent self-perception of unworthiness and indifference; they are preoccupied with those who died. They

---

2. Talmud *Brakhot* 54b.

3. S. N. Broun, "Understanding 'Post-AIDS Survivor Syndrome': A Record of Personal Experiences," *AIDS Patient Care and STDS*, vol. 12, no. 6, (1998), pp. 481–488; M. Vamos, "The Survivor Guilt and Chronic Illness," *The Australian and New Zealand Journal of Psychiatry*, vol. 31, no. 4 (1997), pp. 592–596.

4. R. S. Blacher, "Paradoxical Depression after Heart Surgery: A Form of Survivor Syndrome," *Psychoanalytic Quarterly*, vol. 47, no. 2 (1978), pp. 267–283; R. S. Blacher, "It Isn't Fair: Postoperative Depression and Other Manifestations of Survivor Guilt," *General Hospital Psychiatry*, vol. 22, no. 1 (2000) pp. 43–48.

5. A. Kruse and E. Schmitt, "*Erinnerungen an Traumatische Erlebnisse in der Zeit des Nationalsozialismus bei (Ehemaligen) Judischen Emigranten und Lagerhaftlingen,*" *Gerontol. Geriatr.*, vol. 3, no. 2 (1998), pp. 138–150.

6. National Center for PTSD (2005).

7. H. Lewis, *Shame and Guilt in Neurosis* (New York: International Universities Press, 1980).

8. D. Berger-Reiss, "Generations after the Holocaust: Multigenerational Transmission of Trauma," in *The Handbook of Infant, Child, and Adolescent Psychotherapy*, ed. B. S. Mark and J. A. Incorvaia, vol. 2: *New Dimensions in Integrative Treatment* (Northvale, NJ: Jason Aronson, 1997), pp. 209–219.

often appear dysthymic, feeling undeserving of life and believing that others died so they could live.[9]

Immediately and within the first month post-trauma, some survivors develop acute stress disorder (ASD), a psychiatric diagnosis which was introduced into the DSM as recently as 1994. The current diagnostic criteria for ASD are similar to the criteria for PTSD. ASD criteria, though, encompasses a greater emphasis on dissociative symptoms, and its diagnosis can be given only within the first month after a traumatic event. Statistics of prevalence vary; studies of survivors of motor vehicle accidents have found rates of ASD ranging from 13 percent[10] to 21 percent.[11] A rate of 19 percent was found in survivors of violent assault.[12] A recent study of victims of robbery and assault found that 25 percent met criteria for ASD,[13] while a study of victims of a mass shooting found that 33 percent met the criteria.[14]

An ASD diagnosis permits early identification of trauma survivors who are at risk for developing chronic post-traumatic stress disorder. To prevent the onset of chronic PTSD, there are many early intervention options.

Recently traumatologists in Israel have presented a Position Paper to hospitals and medical centers recommending that treatment for ASD begin in the hospital and up to three days following a traumatic event. They posit that treatment of ASD has been shown to reduce the number of people who will suffer later from PTSD (personal communication, June 2008, Bituah Leumi/National Insurance of Israel).

Arieh Shalev, MD, Chair of the Department of Psychiatry and founding director of the Center for Traumatic Stress at Hadassah University Hospital in Jerusalem stated at a recent American College of Neuropsychopharmacology (ACNP) annual meeting:

> We found that cognitive therapy and cognitive behavioral therapy
> worked well on these patients, whose symptoms and duration of

---

9. R. E. Opp and A. Y. Samson, "Taxonomy of Guilt for Combat Veterans," *Professional Psychology: Research and Practice*, vol. 20, no. 3 (1989), pp. 159–165.

10. A. G. Harvey and R. A. Bryant, "The Relationship between Acute Stress Disorder and Post-traumatic Stress Disorder: A Prospective Evaluation of Motor Vehicle Accident Survivors," *Journal of Consulting and Clinical Psychology*, vol. 66 (1998), pp. 507–512.

11. V. Holeva, N. Tarrier, and A. Wells, "Prevalence and Predictors of Acute Stress Disorder and PTSD following Road Traffic Accidents: Thought Control Strategies and Social Support," *Behavior Therapy*, vol. 32 (2001), pp. 65–83.

12. C. R. Brewin, B. Andrews, S. Rose, and M. Kirk, "Acute Stress Disorder and Post-traumatic Stress Disorder in Victims of Violent Crime," *American Journal of Psychiatry*, vol. 156 (1999), pp. 360–366.

13. A. Elklit, "Acute Stress Disorder in Victims of Robbery and Victims of Assault," *Journal of Interpersonal Violence*, vol. 17 (2002), pp. 872–887.

14. C. Classen, C. Koopman, R. Hales, and D. Spiegel, "Acute Stress Disorder as a Predictor of Post-traumatic Stress Symptoms," *American Journal of Psychiatry*, vol. 155 (1998), pp. 620–624.

PTSD were compared at the end of three months of intervention. At that time, their symptoms were significantly less severe than in patients who were treated with medication, placebo, or no treatment at all.[15]

Shalev added that although antidepressants did not work during this early post-trauma period, it is important to continue exploration of pharmacological interventions for early treatment of PTSD. Shalev says that other research[16] suggests that both pharmacotherapy and cognitive behavioral therapy can be partially effective for PTSD when given three months or more after a traumatic event. He adds that it is important for PTSD survivors to know recovery is still possible even if treatment is not received immediately. Nevertheless, Shalev adds that his results indicate that it is best for survivors to be treated as early as possible.

One medical method, *abreaction*, is the discharge of repressed emotion by way of talking about a disturbing experience. This is often done while under hypnosis, allowing the patient to discuss the traumatic event and discharge the emotions that cannot be released during the normal state of consciousness. Hypnotic techniques have been reported to be effective for symptoms often

---

15. Arieh Shalev, "Psychotherapy Useful in Treating Post-Traumatic Stress Disorder in Early Stages," *Science Daily* (9 Dec 2007). When treated within a month, survivors of a psychologically traumatic event improved significantly with psychotherapy, according to a new study presented at the American College of Neuropsychopharmacology annual meeting.

See also: "Cognitive Therapy Can Reduce Post-Traumatic Stress in Survivors of Terrorist Attacks," *British Medical Journal* (13 May 2007) *Science Daily*. Retrieved 7 Jul 2008 from http:www.sciencedaily.com/releases/2007/05/070510194055.htm.

A. Bleich, M. Kotler, Ilan Kutz, and A. Shalev, *A Position Paper of the (Israeli) National Council for Mental Health: Guidelines for the Assessment of and Professional Intervention with Terror Victims in the Hospital and in the Community* (Jerusalem, Israel: 2002). EMDR is one of only three methods recommended for treatment of terror victims.

Ilan Kutz, "Mental Health Interventions in a General Hospital following Terrorist Attacks," The Israeli Experience (2005), pp. 425–437. Dr. Kutz directs the psychiatric services of Meir General Hospital in Kfar Saba.

American Psychiatric Association, *Practice Guideline for the Treatment of Patients with Acute Stress Disorder and Post-traumatic Stress Disorder* (Arlington, VA: American Psychiatric Association, 2004). SSRIs, CBT, and EMDR are recommended as first-line treatments of trauma.

E.B. Foa, T.M. Keane, and M.J. Friedman, *Effective Treatments for PTSD: Practical Guidelines of the International Society for Traumatic Stress* (New York: Guildford Press, 2000). EMDR was listed as an effective treatment for PTSD with further research needed for an "A" rating. Such research has now been completed and the proposed revised "Practice Guidelines" (posted 2007) have given EMDR an "A" rating for chronic adult PTSD.

16. "Cognitive Therapy Can Reduce Post-Traumatic Stress in Survivors of Terrorist Attacks," *British Medical Journal* (13 May 2007) *Science Daily*.

associated with PTSD such as pain,[17] anxiety,[18] and repetitive nightmares.[19] Most of the studies which report that hypnosis was useful in treating post-trauma disturbances lack methodological rigor, however, and therefore strong conclusions about the efficacy of hypnosis to treat PTSD cannot be drawn.[20]

Another therapeutic method of coping is psychoeducation technique,[21] recommended for the prevention and treatment of PTSD and its related symptoms, including guilt.[22] This technique consists of education regarding the symptoms and treatments available for PTSD and any other disorders presented by the patient. Blancher's 1978 study on depression after heart surgery shows one example of the effectiveness of this method.[23] Once the depressed patients in the study were informed of the phenomenon of survivor guilt, almost all of them recovered quickly.

Psychological debriefing (PD) has been advocated for routine use following traumatic events. Its purpose is to review the impressions and reactions of survivors shortly after a traumatic incident, avoiding psychiatric labeling and emphasizing normalization. Recent studies show, however, that while PD is generally well received by clients, there is little evidence that early PD prevents later PTSD. Additionally, some studies of individual PD have raised the possibility that the intense reexposure involved in the PD can retraumatize some individuals without allowing adequate time for habituation, resulting in negative outcomes.[24]

Eye Movement Sensitization and Reprocessing (EMDR) is a post-trauma technique that has the patient imagining the trauma while making back-and-forth eye movement, or alternating his or her attention to both sides of the body (bilateral 'use' of motor cortex).[25] Different variations of this therapy have been

17. E. Daly and J. Wulff, "Treatment of a Post-Traumatic Headache," *Br J Med Psychol*, vol. 60 (1987) (Pt 1):85–8. D. Jiranek, "Use of Hypnosis in Pain Management in Post-Traumatic Stress Disorder," *Australian J Clinical and Experimental Hypnosis*, vol. 21, no. 1 (1993), pp. 75–84.

18. Etzel Carena, "Hypnosis in the Treatment of Trauma: A Promising, but not Fully Supported, Efficacious Intervention," *International Journal of Clinical and Experimental Hypnosis*, vol. 48, no. 2 (Apr 2000), pp. 225–238.

19. Burr Eichelman, "Hypnotic Change in Combat Dreams of Two Veterans with Post-traumatic Stress Disorder," *Am J Psychiatry*, vol. 143, no. 1 (Jan 1985), pp. 112–114. S.J. Kingsbury, "Brief Hypnotic Treatment of Repetitive Nightmares," *Am J Clin Hypn*, vol. 35, no. 3 (Jan 1993), pp. 161–169.

20. B.O. Rothbaum, et al., "Virtual Reality Exposure Therapy for Vietnam Veterans with Post-traumatic Stress Disorder," *J Clin Psychiatry*, vol. 62, no. 8 (Aug 2001), pp. 617–622.

21. E. B. Foa, J. R. T. Davidson, and A. Frances, "The Expert Consensus Guideline Series: Treatment of PTSD," *Journal of Clinical Psychology*, vol. 60 (1999), Suppl. 16.

22. L. E. O'Connor, J.W. Berry, J. Weiss, D. Schweitzer, and M. Sevier, "Survivor Guilt, Submissive Behavior, and Evolutionary Theory: The Down-Side of Winning in Social Comparison," *British Journal of Medical Psychology*, vol. 73, no.4, pp. 519–530.

23. See note 4.

24. B. Raphael, L. Meldrum, and A. C. McFarlane, "Does Debriefing after Psychological Trauma Work?" *British Medical Journal*, vol. 310 (1995), pp. 1479–1480.

25. F. Shapiro, *Eye Movement Desensitization and Reprocessing: Basic Principles, Protocols, and*

found to be extremely effective with victims of terror in emergency rooms.[26] EMDR has been shown to be more effective than psychodynamic, relaxation, or supportive therapies.[27] Research comparing EMDR to cognitive-behavioral treatment (CBT), however, shows significantly better results with CBT at the three-month follow-up. CBT results also show greater sustainability.[28]

There are many other treatments utilized for early trauma intervention. Currently, EMDR during the acute aftermath of a traumatic incident has shown itself to be most effective in preventing subsequent PTSD.[29] Bryant and others[30] have conducted the only studies that specifically assessed and treated ASD. They have shown that a brief cognitive behavioral treatment may not only lessen the severity of ASD, but it may also prevent the subsequent development of PTSD. In a 1999 study, Bryant and colleagues randomly assigned individuals with ASD to five individual, ninety minute sessions of either a cognitive behavioral treatment or a supportive counseling control condition. The

---

Procedures (New York: Guildford Press, 2001).

F. Shapiro, ed., *EMDR as an Integrative Psychotherapy Approach: Experts of Diverse Orientations Explore the Paradigm Prism* (Washington, DC: American Psychological Association, 2002).

F. Shapiro and M. S. Forrest, *EMDR: The Breakthrough Therapy for Overcoming Anxiety, Stress and Trauma* (New York: Basic Books, 2004).

F. Shapiro, *Handbook of EMDR and Family Therapy Processes* (Wiley, 2007).

26. J. Guedalia and F. Yoeli, Presentation at the EMDR European Conference on EMDR under Fire: EMDR in the ER, Université des Saints-Pères, Paris (Jun 2007).

27. M. M. Scheck, J. A. Schaffer, and C. Gillette, "Brief Psychological Intervention with Traumatized Young Women: The Efficacy of Eye Movement Desensitization and Reprocessing," *Journal of Traumatic Stress*, vol. 11 (1998), pp. 25–44. J. G. Carlson, C. M. Chemtob, K. Rusnak, N. L. Hedlund, M. Y. and Muraoka, "Eye Movement Desensitization and Reprocessing (EMDR) Treatment for Combat-Related Post-Traumatic Stress Disorder," *Journal of Traumatic Stress*, vol. 11 (1998), pp. 3–24.

28. G. J. Devilly and S. H. Spence, "The Relative Efficacy and Treatment Distress of EMDR and a Cognitive Behavioral Trauma Treatment Protocol in the Amelioration of Post-Traumatic Stress Disorder," *Journal of Anxiety Disorders* (2000).

29. Y. Gidron, R. Gal, S. A. Freedman, I. Twiser, A. Lauden, Y. Snir, et al. "Translating Research Findings to PTSD Prevention: Results of a Randomized Controlled Pilot Study" *Journal of Traumatic Stress*, vol. 14, no. 4 (2001), pp. 773–780.

R. A. Bryant, A. G. Harvey, C. T. Dang, T. Sackville, and C. Basten, "Treatment of Acute Stress Disorder: A Comparison of Cognitive-Behavioral Therapy and Supportive Counseling," *Journal of Consulting and Clinical Psychology*, vol. 66, no. 5 (Oct 1998), pp. 862–866.

E. Echeburua, P. deCorral, B. Sarasua, and I. Zubizarreta, "Treatment of Acute Posttraumatic Stress Disorder in Rape Victims: An Experimental Study," *Journal of Anxiety Disorders*, vol. 10, (1996), pp. 185–199.

CIGNA Health Care Coverage Position; subject: Eye Movement Desensitization and Reprocessing (EMDR); coverage position number 0374; revised date 15 Jun 2008. A June 2008 CIGNA Health Care Position Paper recommended supporting the use of EMDR for ASD, noting that "while questions remain regarding some aspects of EMDR, such as the theoretical basis and the role of eye movements, the literature appears to indicate that EMDR is as effective as other established treatments for PTSD and ASD, and in the practicing behavioral health community EMDR is an accepted treatment for PTSD and ASD.

30. Bryant et al., 1998. R. A. Bryant, T. Sackville, S. T. Dang, M. Moulds, and R. Guthrie, "Treating Acute Stress Disorder," *American Journal of Psychiatry*, vol. 155 (1999), pp. 620–624.

assignment was done approximately ten days after an individual experienced a non-sexual assault, motor vehicle accident, or work accident. They found that fewer CBT subjects met criteria for PTSD post-therapy six months later. They have also studied different CBT techniques (prolonged exposure plus anxiety management, and prolonged exposure alone) and compared them to supportive counseling intervention. The results indicated that both CBT groups showed significantly greater reductions in PTSD symptom severity compared to the supportive counseling group. Research comparing EMDR to cognitive-behavioral treatment (CBT), however, shows significantly better results with CBT at the three-month follow-up. CBT results also show greater sustainability.

THANKSGIVING FOR SALVATION

In addition to the aforementioned early intervention techniques, we would like to propose another coping method seen in multiple cultural groups. In Jewish culture, this method can be traced back to biblical times, when – after escaping life-threatening situations – individuals would bring a thanksgiving offering to the Tabernacle and later to the Temple to express thanks to God. The thanksgiving sacrifice consisted of a huge amount of food that was to be eaten in a short amount of time. The time limitation compelled the bearer of the sacrifice to share it with a large group of people. In addition to taking the individual out of social isolation, the thanksgiving process probably induced the survivor to talk about the traumatic event many times over and as such brought about a therapeutic catharsis.

After the Temple was destroyed, the rabbis instituted *Birkhat Ha'Gomel*, a short prayer of thanks, to replace the thanksgiving sacrifice. The blessing, which must be recited aloud in a group of at least ten, states:

> Blessed are You, God our Lord, King of the universe, Who bestows goodness [even] to the guilty, Who has bestowed upon me all that is good.

All those present respond: Amen.

> May God Who has bestowed upon you all that is good, bestow upon you all that is good, forever.

Another version of the communal response is:

> God, blessed and exalted above all blessings and praise, has bestowed on you His goodly favor, love, and grace. May He in His love ever guard you henceforth and grant you all that is good.[31]

---

31. *Shulhan Arukh, Orah Hayyim*, chap. 219.

Survivors often make arbitrary inferences (conclusions without any solid evidence) that since they were lucky this time, they have "used up" all of their merit. The phraseology of both the blessing and its reply may serve to guard the survivor against such maladaptive cognitions. The words imply that God may save us even if we are unworthy and that God can continue to save us repeatedly (more than "just" once).

The public recitation of this blessing creates an opportunity for the survivor to discuss his or her experiences with those present.[32] It is crucial to note, however, that he or she is not required to do so. This fits smoothly with Foa's guidelines for trauma response, which emphasize that the therapist should listen actively and supportively but not probe for details or emotional responses.[33]

Reciting *Birkhat Ha'Gomel* may also help the survivor recover by removing excessive guilt caused by personalizing the blame for the event to begin with. At first glance, it might appear that the more commonly used form of the blessing psychologically "harms" the survivors by labeling them as guilty rather than reassuring them of their innocence. However, we have discussed above the importance of facing and experiencing one's own guilt in order to be freed from it. Once it is acknowledged, guilt can be worked through in the hope of eliminating it completely. Recognizing a higher authority – in this case, God – as responsible for the event may remove feelings of blame from the survivor, bringing him or her one step closer to recovery. This is similar to the popular twelve-step recovery method, in which an individual feels free to heal after turning responsibility over to a higher power.[34]

A similar custom is seen among members of the Navajo Nation (Native Americans), who conduct a "Sing" to heal tribe members who have returned from combat. Sings are attended by the community at large, who come in support of the traumatized individual. The Sings reflect on the individual's experience, focusing on the fact that he or she is being reintegrated into society and will soon return to a normal state. Topper[35] remarks that the Sings restore the ego function and integrate the warriors back into the social setting from which they had been separated. Sandner[36] analyzes the process further. He finds four major reasons for the efficacy of the Sing: 1. herbal remedies are often presented that have psychopharmacological effects; 2. the intricate psychological structure

32. S. Scheidlinger, "The Minyan as a Psychological Support System," *Psychoanalytic Review*, vol. 84, no. 4 (1997), pp. 541–552.

33. M. Shacham and M. Lahad, "Stress Reactions and Coping Resources Mobilized by Children under Shelling and Evacuation," *Australasian Journal of Disaster and Trauma Studies* (2004).

34. Alcoholics Anonymous, "Chapter I: Bill's Story" (New York: Alcoholics Anonymous World Service, Jun 2001) 1–16.

35. M. D. Topper, "The Traditional Navajo Medicine Man: Therapist, Counselor, and Community Leader," *Journal of Psychoanalytic Anthropology*, vol. 10 (1987), pp. 217–249.

36. D. Sandner, *Navaho Symbols of Healing* (New York: Harcourt Brace Jovanovich, 1979).

of the chants repeatedly encourages the survivor's expectations of healing; 3. the survivor is socially supported by the entire community; 4. the words of the chant guide the survivor to find culturally appropriate answers to difficult cosmological problems, such as the management of evil. Studies by Manson and colleagues[37] show that Native American war veterans who do not experience this type of ritualized trauma treatment have significantly higher rates of PTSD.

The Lakota Times reported on February 22, 2006 that

> Navajo and Hopi veterans of northern Arizona will now receive the counseling services and traditional ceremonies they may need to help them re-adjust to civilian life after the traumatic stress of combat or military service. . . . the Northern Arizona Veterans Administration Health Care System officially launched its expansion of services for the Navajo and Hopi nations with a dedication at the Chinle Community Center.[38]

Likewise, a comparable phenomenon was found among the Betsimisaraka Tribe of east Madagascar, where an influx of communal ritual activity, mainly cattle sacrifices, were used to heal the community after a rebellion that took place in 1947. According to the Betsimisaraka tradition, if people forget their ancestors, the ancestors will punish their descendants until they reconnect with them. Therefore, cattle sacrifices – a ritual directed towards the ancestors and offered after war or illness – were seen as a purifying ritual in which the community becomes cleansed from any evil they may have done. The performance of the sacrifice, along with a ritual speech containing explanatory and responsive elements, helps to remove feelings of guilt or blame accompanying the traumatic event. Cole's research in the Betsimisaraka community led her to conclude that rituals have the ability to aid the reconstruction and processing of painful memories. Archival documents, including the Betsimisaraka testimony, suggest that Betsimisaraka were active participants in the 1947 rebellion. However, afterward, sacrificial speeches stated that "We didn't mean to hurt each other; it was all the government's fault," thus greatly reducing their own guilt.[39]

---

37. J. Beals, S. M. Manson, J. H. Shore, et al., "The Prevalence of Posttraumatic Stress Disorder among American Indian Vietnam Veterans: Disparities and Context," *Journal of Trauma Stress*, vol. 15 (2002), pp. 89–97. Jay H. Shore, S. M. Manson, and M. Spero, "Telepsychiatric Care of American Indian Veterans with Post-Traumatic Stress Disorder," *Telemedicine Journal and e-Health*, vol. 10 (2004), S-64.

38. See also: Michelle Roberts, "Medicine Man Uses Ancient Arts to Help Care for Veterans," Associated Press (2005), http://www.usatoday.com/news/nation/2005-12-10-medicine-man_x.htm.

39. Jennifer Cole, "Painful Memories: Ritual and Transformation of Community Trauma," Culture, Medicine, and Psychiatry, vol. 28, no. 1 (Mar 2004), pp. 87–105.

COMPARISON OF THE JEWISH AND NAVAJO APPROACHES TO PROXIMITY IMMEDIACY EXPECTATIONS

Both the Jewish and Navajo cultures place significant value on the necessity of a supportive community ritual. There is an understanding that once a traumatic event occurs, the survivor is not expected to continue as if nothing has happened. Instead, there is a ritualized way of coping that is very similar to the popular PIE[40] early intervention for soldiers in battle conditions. PIE connotes Proximity Immediacy Expectations.

Proximity

The principle of proximity – to ensure attachment to the Army unit – is met by promoting attachment to a social support group. It is important to note that in both Navajo and Jewish rituals, there is a quorum present when the ritual is performed.

Immediacy

Immediacy is met by rules regarding the recitation of prayers. *Birkhat Ha'Gomel* is preferably recited within three days, or, if not, within thirty days, although it can be said for a significant time after that if necessary.[41] It is interesting to note that PTSD is only diagnosed if the qualifying symptoms for the disorder last for over thirty days. If they last for a shorter time, the diagnosis is ASD. Considering that the timing of the diagnosis coincides with the period in which *Birkhat Ha'Gomel* is recited, it is possible that the blessing might help prevent the shift to the more severe and lasting PTSD. Among the Navajo, the ritual is performed as soon as possible, because they believe that the entire community is connected. Therefore, if one individual is "out of balance," all are affected.

Expectations

A clear message that the individual will return to full functioning is given in the text of the blessings and chants themselves, the support of the community, and the existence of the ritual aimed at normalizing events. We have seen many

---

40. E. Jones, A. Thomas, and S. Ironside, *Shell Shock: An Outcome Study of a First World War 'PIE' Unit: Psychological Medicine* (Cambridge University Press, 2006) doi: 10.1017/S0033291706009329.

Zahava Solomon, "Battlefield Functioning and Chronic PTSD: Associations and Perceived Efficacy and Causal Attribution," *Personality and Individual Differences*, vol. 34, no. 3 (Feb. 2003), pp. 463–476.

41. According to *Shulhan Arukh, Orah Hayyim*, chap. 219:3 and chap. 219:6, *Birkhat Ha'Gomel* is preferably recited within three days. According to *Mishnah Brurah, Orah Hayyim* 219:8, *Tsits Eliezer*, part 19, chap, 53, and *Yehaveh Da'at*, part 3, chap. 14, people who cannot find a *minyan* (quorum of ten men) may wait up until thirty days until they have a minyan to say it.

instances in which the recitation of *Birkhat Ha'Gomel* normalizes the experience for survivors, probably preventing chronic PTSD.

CONCLUSION

While no formal tests have been conducted, anecdotal evidence repeatedly proves that a community response is beneficial for post-trauma for the reasons stated above. We highly recommend that individuals perform a ceremony within a group of friends and family as soon as possible after a traumatic event. As we have discussed the aspects of the *Birkhat Ha'Gomel* prayer in particular, it is possible that a survivor can also benefit from recitation of a personally meaningful prayer or text.

This information is particularly relevant to us as Israeli mental health professionals. Since the start of the Al-Aksa Intifada in Israel, we have had extensive contact in hospital emergency rooms with victims of traumatic events. According to a recent study of emergency room patients in Jerusalem, the ratio of physically injured to emotionally affected individuals following critical incidents is 1:12.[42] Reactions such as those described above are almost commonplace in Israel. While a communal ritual is helpful to all patients, it is especially helpful to recommend *Birkhat Ha'Gomel* to Jewish patients as a therapeutic early intervention.

ACKNOWLEDGMENTS

I wish to thank E. Acobis, D. Appel, and G. Mintz for their indefatigable efforts during their tenure as research interns at the Neuropsychology Unit of the Shaare Zedek Medical Center. I also wish to express my gratitude to my husband, Rabbi Dr. Harris Guedalia, for a lifetime of teaching and learning, this article being just a small example of this blessing.

---

42. See note 33.

Ben Sorer U'Moreh:
Using a Biblical Metaphor in
Diagnosis and Therapy

Judith B. Guedalia, Ph.D., and Leah Haber, Ph.D.

ABSTRACT

THE BIBLE'S ACCOUNT of the *Ben Sorer u'Moreh* (recalcitrant, or literally, "stubborn and rebellious" son) (Deuteronomy 21:18–21) is one of its most puzzling and, seemingly, psychologically incomprehensible. However, upon closer investigation, it may be interpreted as a passage that reflects the Torah's understanding of individual psychopathology, dysfunctional behaviors of the couple as individuals and as a parental unit, and the impact of these factors on family dynamics.

We propose to discuss how this passage acts to guide and give a role to the larger community (through the Beit Din, the Jewish court system) in taking responsibility for children in unhealthy, abusive family environments. In this paper, we hope to use a specific case and demonstrate how a formulation of the *Ben Sorer u'Moreh* aided the therapist in both comprehending the family dynamics and proposing therapeutic change.

The *Ben Sorer u'Moreh* is identified as the recalcitrant son (defiant child) who does not listen to his parents, one who steals money presumably for food.[1] He eats not to satiate his physiological hunger, but rather in a gluttonous manner.[2,3] Specifically, he drinks wine without diluting it,[4] as was the custom at that time to make the thick brew palatable. He eats a grotesque amount of meat in a thoughtless manner.[5] He acts out of control to his parents' wishes in this fashion and in regard to "hanging out with a bad crowd."[6]

---

* "Ben Sorer U'Moreh: Using a Biblical Metaphor in Diagnosis and Therapy" by Judith B. Guedalia and Leah Haber was originally published in *ASSIA: Journal of Medical Ethics*, vol. 5:1, August 2005, pp. 49–55.

1. Maimonides, Laws of Mamrim, 7:7.
2. Ibid., 7:1.
3. חוץ מרשות אביו.
4. *Sanhedrin* 70a – יין חי.
5. Ibid., 72a – תרטימר.
6. Ibid., 72a – תרטימר.

The procedure that must be followed, according to Jewish oral tradition, is that both parents[7] must approach the elders of the city[8,9] and use identical words in order to describe the behavior of their son. Although the text of the Bible seems to state that the BSM receives the death penalty, the Sages explain that if he runs away until such time (three months)[10] that secondary sexual development occurs, he is free, as he no longer fits the legal definition of a BSM. We propose that he is actually held under observation by the courts until he reaches puberty, at which point, he is no longer his parents' responsibility, and may go free.[11]

Our hypothesis is that this passage presents a mechanism to remove this child from an untenable and abusive family situation.[12] We view the BSM as a child who is desperate for attention and affection, who turns to food for nurturance. It is well documented that eating disorders are highly correlated with childhood experiences of physical abuse,[13,14] and we see the "symptoms" that the Bible reports as indicative of family pathology.

Jewish oral tradition links the description of the BSM with one of the passages which immediately precedes it (Deuteronomy 21:10–14), which deals with the laws of the *Yifat Toar* (literally "woman of beauty"), a woman who is taken captive in war by an Israelite man, and ultimately he chooses to marry after going through a process of masking her physical beauty and enabling her to mourn her lost family. In other words, this man chooses a wife who is isolated: alone, debased, forcibly removed from her society, her family, her support system, and all else that is familiar to her. According to the Talmud, the product of this union is destined to be a BSM. A picture emerges of a marriage between a controlling, abusive man, and a vulnerable, dependent woman. She is emotionally abused, neglected and desperate for attention; he is forced to resort to desperate measures in his attempts to obtain emotional nurturance.

An example of the pathological family dynamic which the Jewish oral tradition elaborates on is that in order to be considered a case of BSM, both husband and wife[15] must use the identical language when describing their son to the

---

7. אומרין להן – בננו זה סורר ומורה. Maimonides, Laws of Mamrim, 7:7.

8. בית דין של שלשה Ibid., 7:7.

9. If there are no elders in his city, he must be brought to a city with elders.

10. *Sanhedrin* 69a; Maimonides ז-ו. כל ימיו של בין סורר ומורה איני אל

11. If he runs away and there is a change in his "status" – secondary sexual development; he is free, *Sanhedrin* 71b.

12. תשובות הרדב"ז חלק א,סימן רסג where it is discussed that the Beit Din should remove a child from a "toxic" family situation and place the child with another family. The main author would like to thank Harav Naftali Bar Ilan for sharing this source.

13. See note 27.

14. K. J. Zerbe, M.D., *The Body Betrayed: A Deeper Understanding of Women, Eating Disorders, and Treatment*, (Gurze Books, 1995).

15. Had one or another parent refused to testify against their son he would not be considered BSM.

court.[16,17] The wife allows herself to be used to simply parrot her husband's words instead of speaking in her own voice. Against her motherly instincts to do whatever has to be done to save her child's life, this woman is prepared to say "He is a recalcitrant child and the only recourse is death." This, in direct contrast to the classic story of King Solomon, who was approached by two women who both claimed that a baby belonged to them, and that the child of the other woman had passed away. In his wisdom, Solomon suggested that the baby be cut in half, so that each mother could have half.[18] He knew that a "real" mother would love her child so much that she would rather give him up than let him die. And indeed, that is exactly how he identified the true mother – while the other woman agreed to Solomon's "compromise," the real mother insisted that the child be left alive, even if he was in someone else's care. One can only wonder, what has happened to the mother of the BSM that forces her to suppress her motherly instincts and allows herself to, in effect, sacrifice her child?

In the specific case we intend to use, a very similar family dynamic was present, in which a child referred to by his parents as a BSM exhibited remarkably similar symptoms to those presented by the Bible. Predictably, the relationship of the parents also matched that of the "conqueror" and the "vanquished" *Yifat Toar* in many ways as well.

We conclude that this formulation of the biblical passage can serve to sensitize Jewish society to its social responsibility to provide for the welfare of "families in crisis," and to alert its leadership to its social responsibility to intercede as a sort of "Child Protective Services" in certain cases.[19,20] This mandate is not just limited to such extreme cases as the one outlined in Deuteronomy 21. We propose that using the BSM as a metaphor will sensitize both the religious community and at risk families in understanding and interpreting acting-out behavior in children. In using the biblical model in this fashion, we hope to focus on the mental health concerns of individual families as communal issues that must be addressed and remedied.

We see this case as an example of how ethnographic understanding of patients will benefit the therapist in his/her work, specifically in the Orthodox Jewish community (and certainly in the larger therapeutic community as well). Fluency with the cultural milieu of one's patients allows the therapist to hear and be heard with a sort of "third ear,"[21] namely a sensitivity to the subtext that is unique to each ethnic group.

---

16. מדרש תנאים בדברים כא' פסוק יט'.

17. ילקוט שמעוני פרשת כי תצא – רמז ככקכ'ט – שוה בקול.

18. I Kings 3:16–27.

19. Prof. Abraham Abraham, M.D. שו"ת רדב"ז חלק א סימן רסג

20. *Torah She'Beal Peh*, ed., Yitzhak Rephael; vol 12, p. 156, (Mossad Harav Kook, 1970).

21. Theodor Reik, *Listening With the Third Ear: The Inner Experience of a Psychoanalyst*, (Farrar Straus Giroux, 1983).

When working with a client (either an individual or a family), the metaphors that they use in their speech are an extremely powerful tool which can help the therapist understand conscious and unconscious dynamics operating in the family.[22] These metaphors are often cultural, and it is important for the therapist to be attuned to the meanings which resonate for the person speaking even if they do not hold the same significance for the therapist and/or someone with a different canvas of cultural symbols. Listening to the patient in this way opens up doors to understanding the patient on a fundamental level, and may also suggest directions for treatment.

This phenomenon was encountered when interviewing the family of a fourteen-year old boy who had been referred for psychological evaluation. His parents reported out of control and aggressive behaviors on his part and expressed their frustration and anger at not being able to control him. Words which they used to describe his behavior were "loud, needy, clingy, uncommunicative verbose, lacking appropriate affect, aggressive, sadistic, spoiled, and grasping." They went so far as to compare him to the *"Ben Sorer U'Moreh,"* the "incorrigible son" described in the Bible.

As both parents and the identified patient elaborated on the dynamics within themselves and within the family, a picture became clear, one that was remarkably similar to the genesis of the *"Ben Sorer U'Moreh"* as it is seen to evolve in biblical and rabbinic sources. Sensing the importance of the metaphor, the therapist began researching the rabbinic sources to understand the "family's language."

Our first introduction to the concept of the *"Ben Sorer U'Moreh"* is in Devarim 21:18–21:

> If a man has a stubborn and rebellious son, who will not obey the voice of his father, or the voice of his mother, and that, when they have chastened him, will not hearken to them: then shall his father and his mother lay hold of him, and bring him out to the elders of the city, and to the gate of his place; and they shall say to the elders of the city, This our son is stubborn and rebellious, he will not obey our voice; he is a glutton and a drunkard. And all the men of his city shall stone him with stones that he die: so shalt thou put evil away from among you, and all Yisra'el shall hear and fear.

Even with a very basic text based reading of this passage, it is clear that the Torah is determined to construct a society in which each family must not exist as a discrete unit in which it alone is responsible for its own problems. When a family experiences trouble, such as an uncontrollable child, they approach the

---

22. R. Bandler, J. Grinder, *Frogs into Princes: Neuro Linguistic Programming,* 1979.

Beit Din (BD), a communal body. It is the BD which has the authority to deal with this very difficult issue. However, there seem to be some difficulties with this passage as well. Does not the death penalty seem to be a rather harsh punishment for a defiant child? What is the significance of the peculiar phraseology that the parents use when describing their son?

The Talmud elaborates on this passage in the Eighth Chapter of *Sanhedrin* (titled *"Ben Sorer U'Moreh"*), and succeeds in minimizing the possibility that such a phenomenon will ever come to pass. A minor cannot become a BSM, it is only possible for someone to achieve this status in between the appearance of primary sexual characteristics and secondary ones – a very narrow window of time. Only a son can become a BSM, not a daughter. The Talmud and Mishneh Torah remark that the BSM must continue his habits, such as eating raw meat and drinking unadulterated alcohol and they reason that a female would not do these acts for a protracted amount of time, which is a necessary element of the identification of a BSM.

Very specific amounts and types of food and/or drink must be ingested, as well as the type of people with whom the food is eaten (are they people of ill-repute?)[23] and the reason for the feasting (if it is to honor the new moon, he does not qualify), and the source of the money used to buy this food and drink (if it's *maser sheni* funds in Jerusalem, he is OK). To "qualify" as a BSM, the Mishnah and Gemara go on to specify that the money used to purchase the food must have been stolen from the parents of the youth in question, and the food must have been eaten in property not belonging to his father, as well as in front of his father in a gluttonous fashion and the food considered "uneatable" under normal circumstances: wine that is unadulterated and meat that is undercooked if not even raw.

In addition, both parents must agree that their son is indeed a BSM. They must be similar in appearance and height, speak in an "identical voice" and say the same words. To become a BSM, the youth must continue his wayward behavior after he was warned by his parents in front of a court of three judges, and flogged by this court. The chances of both parents being the same height, weight and have the same timbre of voice is well nigh impossible. As is the "requirement" that they will use the "same words" to describe their son. Then, he must be judged again by a court of twenty three judges which includes the original three. However, if his secondary sexual maturational characteristics appeared before he was judged this second time, he is exempt from punishment as a BSM. Chazal also puzzle over the fact that any mother would willingly turn her son over to be stoned. Didn't we learn from King Solomon's famous "decision" that no normal mother would let her child be killed; she would sooner

---

23. See note 6.

give him up. Moreover, if he is "taken to the *zekainim* of the city[24] (there is a *sugiah* about if there are no *zekainim* in his city – he is taken to another city),[25] we posit that this period of three months is for "observation." During that time he will certainly develop secondary sexual characteristics.[26] There never was a *Ben Sorer U'Moreh*,[27] nor will there ever be one in the future. And why then was the law of *Ben Sorer U'Moreh* written in the Torah? God says: Expound the passage and you will receive reward for doing so (*Sanhedrin* 71a). In other words, use this case as a prototype.

These sometimes painfully specific and detailed halachic wranglings accomplish a dual purpose for Chazal. First, they for all intents and purposes negate the possibility that the event of a BSM will ever come to pass. How could one person possibly fulfill all these criteria? Secondly, they manage to create an abstract psychological portrait of a child and a family who are desperately in need of the community's intervention, both of whom are screaming out for help in action as well as in behavior.

By using the metaphor of the *"Ben Sorer U'Moreh,"* Moshe's[28] parents were drawing a parallel between their domestic situation and that of the one cryptically described above. On the surface, they no doubt were referring to the frustration and helplessness that they experienced in dealing with Moshe, as well as their sense that there was nothing that they could do to change the situation, and their desire to hand him over to someone else, no matter what the consequences. However, a sensitive listener would also be attuned to the subtext of what they were saying. Moshe's parents were unconsciously touching on the toxic undercurrents in their own family relationships which led to their disgusted and despairing feeling God dynamics which are also present in the family of the *Ben Sorer U'Moreh*.

They came to my office (JBG), on the face of it, no different than the hundreds of other parents that have made appointments to see me over the years regarding their children. What made this family different was how they "introduced" their son. They said he is a *"Ben Sorer U'Moreh."* I tried to discover if they were using this term as a metaphor. They said that he stole food, acted in a disrespectful and surely he fit the total description of a *Ben Sorer U'Moreh*. Coming from an Orthodox family, who knew the biblical "punishment" concerning the intransigent son, death, their identification of him as such was jarring.

What type of food did he "steal" and from whom, I asked. Well, for example,

---

24. Deut. 21:19,20.

25. Talmud *Makkot* 10b. Interestingly this issue of having a city with "elders" is discussed also regarding the *egla arufa*, the heifer whose neck was broken in the case of an untraced murderer. Possibly the juxtapositioning of these two cases might be a seen as another example of the "perception" of the BSM as an "untraced murder" – a child whose very soul was at risk of annihilation.

26. See note 10.

27. *Sanhedrin*, chap. 11.

28. An assumed name.

said the mother, I buy my seven children Bamba for Shabbat. Okay, I thought so? Well, I give each child five Bamba for Shabbat, and he has taken more than that at times. More than Five Bags of Bamba, I ask. No, more than the five pieces of Bamba that he is given at the beginning of Shabbat.

This mother was speaking about giving each of her seven children, five pieces of Bamba for the entire Shabbat, as a treat. She also added that his son stirs the food in the pot, when he knows only his father and mother are permitted to do this. I'm not sure I understand, I say, the food is cooking on the stove and . . . That's right, she says, my husband's rule is that only he or I can stir food in the pots, you know how some people taste the food in the pot, we only – he and I – are allowed to do this. Questions kept popping into my mind: It might have been better not to give them any "treat" than to create a situation such as they did. What kind of "nurturing" environment exists in this family? What was the family history, of each parent? If this son was the oldest, was he "acting out" to help his other siblings too? What was going on with the other children in this family?

As a firm believer in looking at the "symptoms" as a "window" to the problem, as when a child presents with a problem of "selective mutism" ("the persistent failure to speak in specific social situations, [e.g., school, with playmates] where speaking is expected, despite speaking in other situations."),[29] I consider "selective mutism" a pathnomonic sign. This "sign" directs my "diagnostic search" for a developmental disability in the area of language. This is not always the case, but in my experience[30] it has been found to be a reliable indicator. In this case I felt that the use of the BSM description of their son was a "pathnomonic sign," a clue, to the answer to these questions.

As clinicians, we are constantly on the lookout for an entrée into the internal world of our clients. Exploration of the individual's conflicts and dynamics is an important way to enter into this world. However, there is also a social/cultural context that also expresses itself during the session. Being attuned to this context and using it as a tool in therapy is an extremely effective way of understanding the individual and working with him or her in therapy. This paper will focus on the utility of being sensitive to this cultural context as it appears in the *metaphors* used by the client.

A metaphor is an image, idea, or story captured in a word or phrase, and yet much more evocative than simply a piece of vocabulary. It expresses a very specific and meaningful belief system inherent to a specific culture.

By understanding the metaphors used by our clients, we are able to enter

---

29. *DSM-IV - Diagnostic and Statistical Manual of Mental Disorders*, American Psychiatric Association, 1994.

30. The main author is the Director of the Neuropsychology Unit at Shaare Zedek Medical Center, Jerusalem and a senior supervising specialist in the areas of Medical, Rehabilitation and Developmental Psychology.

a sphere of consciousness which is more primitive, yet at the same time more powerful than the conscious and the rational. We can tap into a very fundamental belief system, communicated through metaphors as a "meta-language" and use this language to then communicate more effectively, and at a more "visceral" and genuine level with our clients.

The efficacy of addressing the potency of a particular culture's specific images and "meta-language" has been acknowledged by the greater psychological community. We know, for example, that Ethiopian *shamans* are able to cure mental illness in traditional Ethiopians where other forms of more current treatment have failed. Other examples of this in various cultures are the phenomena of the "Dybbuk" in Eastern European Jewish lore, and the idea of the "Exorcist" in some forms of Christianity which has some manifestations in our contemporary culture. (In fact, some of these terms appear in the appendix of the DSM!)[31] All these methods can be successful because of the ability to "meta-communicate," not through mere words but through larger beliefs and assumptions about the nature of reality that a particular culture holds true. It seems clear that for meaningful psychological change to take place, it is best that communication occur between "practitioner" and client at the deepest, most fundamental level possible. This level is not a conscious, rational one, but rather the most primal way that we have of expressing ourselves, through communal images that we have taken in before we even knew how to express ourselves verbally.

What does it mean practically, to use metaphors in contemporary psychotherapy? How is the therapist to use this idea as a therapeutic device or tool? Of prime importance is the ability to listen for metaphors in the client's presentation. Once a therapist has an idea of what this metaphor may mean, she is able to use it in therapy as a way, not only of coming to an increased understanding of the patient, but as an extremely effective way of communicating with him or her and determining which intervention will be most constructive.[32]

The use of metaphor as a therapeutic tool assumes that no client is "incomprehensible"; the skilled therapist will be able to, through careful listening, learn how to speak to each client, no matter how "disturbed," in his or her own language (the language of the *client*).[33]

Using both professional *and* religious literature, we were able to detect and use a metaphor which the mother of a client used in the initial consultation. In describing her sixteen-year old son, she said, "He is a *Ben Sorer U'Moreh*." We used the metaphor of the biblical Wayward Son in formulating the case and determining treatment.

---

31. *DSM-IV - Diagnostic and Statistical Manual of Mental Disorders*, American Psychiatric Association, 1994.

32. J. Hayley, M. H. Erickson, *Conversations with Milton H. Erickson, Volume I: Changing Individuals*, (Norton Professional Books).

33. Ibid.

Looking at the metaphor of the BSM, the gluttonous eating, the alcoholic intake of wine that was unadulterated with water and therefore considered "undrinkable," we get a picture of the BSM who is giving us the signs of the pathology that he is living with at home. The requirement that he do this behavior not just at home, in front of his parents, but also "outside" is an all important factor in demonstrating how the Gemara understood the behavior as a "call for help." He is eating food publicly in a clear fashion that his eating is not nutritious. As if to say: "Look at my symptoms, I am not getting nurtured properly in my environment. I am 'raising the volume' to demonstrate the problem in my family." (See the description of the anorexic in Psychosomatic Families by Salvador Minuchin).[34]

In discussing the family and etiology of the possible family dynamics and history of the parents' original "getting together and courtship," Rashi brings forth (because of the proximity of both *sugiot*) the hypothesis that the father was the soldier who on the battlefield could not "control" his sexual/aggressive urges, and "took/raped" the "*Yifat Toar*" – the beautiful woman of the vanquished "tribe" – as a spoil of war, as it were. The Gemara/Halacha "connect" on the biblical reference, discusses that if he cannot control his urges and may "have her once."[35] If he still wants to marry her, she must undergo a month of mourning – separated from her kin forever, "letting herself go" – by letting her hair and nails grow long, becoming ugly.[36] If he still wants to marry her under those circumstances he may. These then, according to Rashi, are the parents of the BSM. When the BSM parents go to the BD *separately* and "speak in the same voice",[37] and be identical in size, etc., what are we seeing? We propose that this woman is acting as an abused wife/mother and/or suffering from co-dependency similar to the Stockholm Syndrome/Effect, whereby the captive strongly identifies, and feels protected by the aggressor.[38]

This woman, the mother of the BSM, seems not to have a shred of her own personality, so much so that she even sounds and looks like her husband. The man who vanquished her, separated her from her family and cultural ties, her emotional support system and denied in her the normal vestiges of "*Ezer Kenegdo*"[39] that we learn are created with Adam and Eve in the Garden of Eden. When Abraham, our forefather, asked God how he could send away his second

---

34. S. Minuchin, B. L. Rosman, L. Baker, *Psychosomatic Families: Anorexia Nervosa in Context*, (Harvard, 1978).

35. Deut. 21:11–13.

36. Ibid.

37. See note 7.

38. The Stockholm Syndrome is the case in which a hostage begins to identify with their captors and at times then joins them. This was noted in Stockholm after a bank robbery when hostages were held in a bank vault. It has also been discussed in the legal case of Patty Hearst, a young woman kidnapped, taken captive, repeatedly abused and raped, and then photographed robbing a bank with her captors.

39. Gen. 2:19.

son, God said "Everything Sarah your wife says, listen to,"[40] she had seen that the son of his Egyptian handmaiden was a bad role model for their son and the future of Am Yisrael. Clearly not a case of the wife echoing exactly what the husband requires of her, clearly not the case here.

So great is her separation from normal maternal feelings supplanted by this man who having terrorized her, denied any aspect of an individualized ego. The father, a man who could not control his basest aggressive/sexual urges married a woman he vanquished and then made her devoid of all that is attractive physically and spiritually.[41] How could she nurture his child when she didn't exist as a separate entity in this family's dynamic? One might see the BSM's behavior pointing up the pathology of his nuclear family. (He had no maternal grandparents to go to for help, as his mother was cut off from all his familial ties.)[42] The stealing of "money" from the father, "the currency" of sustenance, points to the lack thereof from the father. The gluttonous eating in public is not for sustenance, but just to be *full* (we posit: to be nurtured by his parents?).[43] This behavior which was enacted publicly may be seen as to point to the lack of maternal nurturing; bring this family to the "wise-men" of the community.[44] Might he be saying "I am approaching manhood and don't have my most basic needs of nurturing met. Help me and help my mother/parents who are unable to help either of us."

To see a similar relationship between father and son, man and wife, in "more modern" times (19th century), one is directed to the unique study by Morton Schatzman. He describes schizophrenia and family psychopathology in the famous Schreber family.[45] The father of the family was a famous pedagogue and physician Daniel Gottlieb Moritz Schreber (1808–1861). His sons were Daniel Gustav, who went mad and committed suicide,[46] and Daniel Paul Schreber (1842–1911), an eminent German judge, who went mad at forty-two, recovered and eight and a half years later went mad again.[47] The father practiced his "philosophy" on his own children, forcing them to sleep in halters tied to the bed, wear head restrainers to keep from fidgeting their heads, and other similar contraptions. He proposed to "battle the weaknesses" of his era by making children obedient and subject to adults. The title of the book describing the surviving son's schizophrenic "visions," most of which were parallel to "torture" in the guise of child rearing, is called *Soul Murder: Persecution in the*

40. Ibid., 18:15.

41. Deut. 21:10–14.

42. Ibid., 21:13.

43. See note 21.

44. See note 22.

45. M. Schatzman, *Soul Murder: Persecution in the Family*, (Random, 1973). The main author (JSBG) would like to thank Prof. Moshe Halevy Spiro, for his recommendation of this book.

46. Is not suicide the murder of self?

47. One might note the fact that both his sons carried his name (where normally just the first son would do so) as an example of his extreme narcissism.

Family. Where was the children's mother, Anna? you might ask. As Schatzman writes: "We can infer from Dr. Schreber's own writings what sort of role his wife played (interestingly her name never appears in the entire book!):

> When the man can support his opinions by reason of demonstrable truth, no wife with common sense and good will want to oppose his decisive voice. If one wants a planned upbringing based on principles to flourish, the father above anyone else must hold the reins of up-bringing in his hands. (p. 17)

Schreber, the father, was wont to consider himself a god in his home. This is brought home in an excerpt from a letter by his daughter, Anna Schreber after he died. In the letter she writes:

> ... how God was present in their childhood world at all times, not merely in their daily prayers, but in all their feeling, thinking, and doings. All this was finished with the sudden death of our beloved father.

In relating the process the BSM undergoes might not we posit that the Beit Din hear the BSM's plea. The requirement that there be "Elders" in the city, seems to create a situation where both the parents and the child are under "supervision?" Might this not be a sign that the BD recognizes that this home is a poisonous environment and mandates, during this final stage of a child's emotional and spiritual development, to take the child away from the parents?[48] This "process," obviated by inadequate and odious parenting, would most assuredly create a sick individual, uncaring and unable to understand and appreciate the life of another – a murderer,[49] whose own soul was murdered by his family.

Here then, we see the glory of the Torah and our Hachamim (Elders), having identified the problem they are presenting us with a solution. There is community responsibility for inadequacies of individuals.[50] In this case, the Elders provide a means of saving the soul and life of a child of a troubled environment.[51]

The authors wish to thank Prof. Moshe Halevy Spero for his contributions and suggestions.

---

48. Prof. Abraham Abraham, M.D. שו"ת רדב"ז חלק א סימן רסג
49. Rashi, Deut. 21:18 על סופו.
50. See note 25.
51. In the case at hand and using the lesson of the BSM, I recommended that the child be sent to his grandparents (elders?) for the period of three months during which time he would be under the supervision of the guidance counselor gauging his school work and behavior. It is interesting to note that during this period no "acting out" was observed.

Accidental Death: A New Look at an Ancient Model

Judith B. Guedalia, Yocheved Debow & David Debow

I N THIS PAPER we present an integrative model for helping perpetrators of accidental killing accept the consequences of their actions and their
"new" selves. We use the model described in the Bible of the "city of refuge,"
a place defined as a sanctuary to protect the "accidental killer." Based on an
understanding of the psychic trauma experienced by accidental killers, we
classify their response to the specific event as a form of Post-Traumatic Stress
Disorder (PTSD). We then present a model for rehabilitation that could be used
to facilitate the rehabilitation of accidental killers and facilitate their re-entry
into society.

> In our nature, however, there is a provision, alike marvelous and
> merciful, that the sufferer should never know the intensity of what
> he endures by its present torture, but chiefly by the pang that rankles
> after it.
>
> Nathaniel Hawthorne, *The Scarlet Letter* (1906)

PROPOSAL

For the accidental killer – a person who inadvertently caused the death of
another human being – the aftermath of the fatal accident is overwhelmingly
painful. Accidental death occurs frequently; traffic and military accidents often
claim fatalities. Such death becomes a double-edged tragedy, for both the bereaved family and the accidental perpetrator, whose experience often sentences
him/her to a lifetime of turmoil. The Bible discusses the concept of a "City of
Refuge" (Hebrew: *Ir Miklat*), a sanctuary to protect the accidental killer, who
was to move to one of these forty-eight cities and live there for an indeterminate
period of time (Exodus 21:12–14; Numbers 35:9–29; Deuteronomy 4:42; 19:1–13).
We suggest that an analysis of the guidelines and directives clearly stated in

* "Accidental Death: A New Look at an Ancient Model" by Dr. Judith Guedalia, Yocheved
Debow and David Debow was originally published in *Bekhol Derakhekha Daehu*, 14 (March 2004),
pp. 25–37, © copyright Bar-Ilan University, Ramat Gan, Israel.

the Bible and Rabbinical commentaries may not only provide insight into the psychological trauma experienced by an accidental killer but also help provide ideas for a contemporary rehabilitation model. We have selected concepts from studies of Post-Traumatic Stress Disorder (PTSD) and have also used the diagnostic framework of the *Diagnostic and Statistical Manual of Mental Disorders, Fourth Edition* (DSM-IV). Moreover, we examine the *Ir Miklat* (IM) from a psychological perspective. It is our contention that the IM concept can serve as a model for understanding the effects of accidental death on the accidental killer (or, in the words of the Bible, "*Rotzeah Beshegaga*," hereafter RB), his/her family and the surrounding society.

PURPOSE

Accidental death is a frightening prospect, as it may occur to anyone. Most people would like to believe in the orderliness of events in this world, yet accidental deaths occur under many different circumstances. Recently, the secrecy surrounding incidents of accidental killing in the Israeli Defense Forces has been lifted. Live ammunition is used regularly in training exercises, and the dangers of accidental killing in the army are felt more acutely than in everyday life. Nevertheless, newspapers are filled with reports of fatal traffic accidents, which are the major locus of accidental killing. From 1982 to 1992 in Israel alone there were 4879 people killed in traffic accidents.[1] An extensive search for empirical data, including a computer search of the psychological literature since 1987, revealed only twenty-four papers mentioning accidental killing. Of these, not one dealt directly with the impact of accidental killing on the person who caused it. It thus emerges that despite the large number of people facing this tragedy and the ensuing distress, attempts at helping the perpetrators of accidental killing face their own future are insufficient. In searching for a model, we examined the IM concept presented in the Bible.

Ir Miklat

The *Ir Miklat* (IM), or City of Refuge, is a biblical concept described in several biblical texts (Exodus 21:12–14; Numbers 35:9–29; Deuteronomy 4:42; 19:1–13) as a city to which an accidental killer could flee to escape the vengeance of the victim's family. The plan as described in the Bible calls for six such cities to be set up, specifically dedicated to being Cities of Refuge (Numbers 35:6). Another forty-two cities, which were set aside for the Levites to live in, were also available to be used as Cities of Refuge[2] for Israelites who had committed

---

1. Ministry of Transportation: Road Safety Authority (1993). *Road Safety in Israel: Facts and Figures.*

2. Maimonides, M. *The Codex of Jewish Law.* Sabbatical and Jubilee Laws 13:1.

an accidental killing. Immediately after the accident, before a court had decided whether the death indeed conformed with the legal definition of "accidental killing," the perpetrator would flee to an IM and would be protected within the clearly marked boundaries of this "sanctuary." S/he would thus no longer be vulnerable to "blood avengers," family members of the deceased who would not be tried for murder if they took the life of the accidental killer outside an IM (Numbers 35:27). Rabbinical sources and biblical commentators, who continually re-evaluate and re-interpret the biblical sources, have endeavored to find a precise legal definition of accidental killing. It is distinguished from criminal negligence on the one hand and total circumstantial involvement on the other. In this paper we are discussing the "inadvertent" homicide – homicide in which there is a slight degree of negligence. Once a person was adjudicated an accidental killer, s/he was permitted to live in the IM and continue his/her normal existence there. The exact time of release was arbitrary, as it depended on the death of one of the three High Priests who functioned at any given time. Only then was the accidental killer permitted to leave the IM and return to his/her previous home (Exodus 35:25). It is this concept of *Ir Miklat* that we wish to explore.

The Accidental Killer – "Rotzeach Bishgaga"
In any fatal accident, the focus is usually on the deceased and his/her relatives. However, there is often someone who feels responsible for having caused the death, however unintentionally.[3] There are many and varied types of situations in both army and civilian life which can lead to accidental killing. A search of papers published in psychological journals since 1987 reveals almost no literature dealing with the problem of the accidental killer. One book, *Fatal Moments*,[4] is based on interviews conducted from 1980 to 1990 with nearly 200 people who responded to their call to explore this phenomenon. The study presents the following model of the experience of the accidental killer, claiming that, despite some individual variation, most accidental killers experience a similar pattern of responses. Generally, psychological shock comes first. During this brief period of numbness, the mind hides from the full realization that one has caused the death of another human being. This is followed by preoccupation with the accident. In the struggle to make sense of the event, many accidental killers replay it over and over in their minds. Anger often engulfs the accidental killer, directed at every aspect and player in the accident, including the victim. Guilt is nearly universal, causing accidental killers to torture themselves for unfounded reasons as well as for error and oversight. Depression, also common, may occur

---

3. Gilliam, G. and Chesser, B.R. (1991). *Fatal Moments: The Tragedy of the Accidental Killer.* Lexington Books.
4. Ibid.

in various forms. Their internal turmoil may cause them to withdraw from family and friends and keep them from normal social interaction. They usually experience some form of social tension, often resulting from the failure of their friends and associates to respond or act supportively, due to their unfamiliarity with the situation. Family stress occurs as well. At some point, virtually all accidental killers begin the process of healing. Nevertheless, the aftermath of the event extends throughout their lives.[5] Thus most accidental killers themselves become victims of the event. All the symptoms experienced by accidental killers are included in the definition of Post-Traumatic Stress Disorder. DSM-IV[6] lists several diagnostic criteria for PTSD:

A. The person has been exposed to a traumatic event in which both of the following were present:
  (1) The person experienced, witnessed or was confronted with an event or events that involved actual or threatened death or serious injury, or a threat to the physical integrity of self or others;
  (2) The person's response involved intense fear, helplessness, or horror.
B. The traumatic event is persistently re-experienced in one (or more) of the following ways:
  (1) Recurrent and intrusive distressing recollections of the event, including images, thoughts or perceptions.
  (2) Recurrent distressing dreams of the event.
  (3) Acting or feeling as if the traumatic event were recurring (including a sense of reliving the experience, illusions, hallucinations, and dissociative flashback episodes.
  (4) Intense psychological distress at exposure to internal or external cues that symbolize or resemble an aspect of the traumatic event.
C. Persistent avoidance of stimuli associated with the trauma and numbing of general responsiveness, as indicated by three or more of the following:
  (1) Efforts to avoid thoughts, feelings, or conversations associated with the trauma;
  (2) Efforts to avoid activities, places, or people that arouse recollections of the trauma;
  (3) Inability to recall an important aspect of the trauma;
  (4) Markedly diminished interest or participation in significant activities;
  (5) Feeling of detachment or estrangement from others;
  (6) Restricted range of affect;

---

5. Ibid.
6. American Psychiatric Association (1994). *DSM-IV: Diagnostic and Statistical Manual of Mental Disorders, Fourth Edition*. Washington, DC: American Psychiatric Association, 427–428.

(7) Sense of a foreshortened future (for example, does not expect to have a career, marriage, children, or a normal life span).

D. Persistent symptoms of increased arousal.

E. Duration of the disturbance is more than one month.

F. The disturbance causes clinically significant distress or impairment in social, occupational, or other important areas of functioning.

There are so many stimuli that can engender an emotional reaction that it is hard to avoid the cues that evoke the memory of the trauma.[7] A study of police officers who had witnessed or taken part in shooting incidents found that many suffered from a reaction that took the form of severe PTSD symptoms.[8] It would indeed seem that these people have experienced a psychologically distressing event and that their reactions often fit the DSM-IV criteria of PTSD listed above.

Although recent research indicates that all these symptoms are usually experienced at the same time, it is still interesting to note the similarities with the classic model of the stages of mourning described in Kubler-Ross's seminal work.[9]

There is a difference only in the final stage: "aftermath" in accidental killing and "acceptance of death" in the Kubler-Ross model. We propose that what may make it difficult for RBs to experience "acceptance" in any way may be that they actually remain in the state of mourning. They are mourning not only for the victim who actually died but also for themselves, who are still alive, but no longer in their former state of innocence – the person they were before the fatal moment. At some point RBs apparently realize that they can never be this old self again; the moment of accidental killing has irrevocably changed them and in a certain way perhaps "deadened" an innocent and unburdened self. Thus they may actually be mourning for the person they can no longer be. Shalev[10] offers a psychodynamic formulation of PTSD as "incomplete processing of traumatic experiences similar to pathological mourning." Although he considers this definition insufficient to encompass the full nature of PTSD, it could certainly serve as a partial explanation of the psychic processes occurring in the PTSD patient, particularly the RB.

Accidental killers are frequently acquitted in court for the crime of manslaughter. Legal exoneration, however, cannot reverse the accident and return

---

7. Keane et al.,1985, quoted in Solomon, Z., Bleich, A., Shoham, S., Nardi C., & Kotler M. (1992). The "Koach" Project for treatment of combat-related PTSD: Rationale, aims, and methodology. *Journal of Traumatic Stress*, 5, 175–193.

8. Heath, Gersons, B. P. R. (1989). Patterns of PTSD among police officers following shooting incidents: A two-dimensional model and treatment implications. *Journal of Traumatic Stress*, 2, 247–257.

9. Kubler-Ross E. (1969). *On Death and Dying*. New York: Macmillan.

10. Shalev, A. Y. (1993). Post-traumatic Stress Disorder: A Biopsychological Perspective. *Israel Journal of Psychiatry and Related Science*, 30 (2), 102–109.

the dead person to life, nor can it render the RB a person who has not killed anyone, albeit accidentally. Often, an RB's reaction after being acquitted is to say that the person is still dead, and "it was still my finger on the trigger."[11] Although the law has judged them to be not guilty, their own acute awareness of loss prevents them from accepting that judgment. The RB is no longer the same person s/he was before the event and must spend time mourning the loss of his/her former, "untainted" self. The importance of allowing accidental killers to experience these feelings of guilt has recently been recognized. Terr[12] in her book on psychic trauma in childhood, emphasizes the importance of guilt as an adaptive mechanism. It allows trauma victims to feel that they had a certain amount of control, even in a situation in which their control was actually minimal. The event can then be faced and worked through. Where there is no working through of the guilt, shame frequently becomes the predominant emotion. It is usually compounded by feelings of helplessness, which make it more difficult for victims to forgive themselves and move on to redefinition and acceptance of the self.[13]

Ir Miklat – An Understanding Based on the Biblical Text and Commentaries

The biblical injunction ordering RBs to proceed to an IM contains highly specific directives: All homicides, whether inadvertent or not, fled to an IM and were then brought back to their own town for trial. An RB had to immediately leave the environment in which s/he was living and go to the nearest City of Refuge. Inherent in the command is the immediacy and specificity of the directive. It is imperative to gather oneself together and proceed actively. At every intersection there were signs pointing to the nearest IM, so that it was always accessible.

The IM was inhabited by members of the Tribe of Levi and accidental killers. Traditionally, the Levites had no land of their own, thereby freeing them from agricultural responsibilities. Instead, they were the teachers and the social workers, the caretakers of the nation. Their life was dedicated to the soul and spirit of the people, and it would seem that part of their responsibility was to live in the Cities of Refuge, perhaps as the "support staff" for those RBs who needed moral support during healing.[14] It is explained that the city must be neither too large nor too small.[15] This ensured a sense of community, while guaranteeing the RB privacy as well. Another important structural feature was that RBs were never to be a majority of the population.[16] This stricture kept the

---

11. *The Jerusalem Post* (October 1993).

12. Terr, L. (1990). *Too Scared to Cry*. New York: Basic Books.

13. Janoff-Bulman, R. (1992). *Shattered Assumptions: Towards a New Psychology of Trauma*. New York: The Free Press.

14. Hirsch, S. R. (1860). *A Commentary to the Bible*.

15. Maimonides, M. *The Codex of Jewish Law*, Homicide 8:8.

16. Ibid., 7:6.

population healthy and prevented the group malaise that might otherwise be self-perpetuating. The number of people suffering from trauma was never so large that the support mechanism could not function efficiently. The city always had a group of empathic people who were not caught up in working the land, but were free to be helpful and supportive as necessary.

Once an RB was sentenced to spend time in an IM, he would not go there alone; he was encouraged to move there with his family and a "Rabbi" or mentor. (Here we must use the masculine form, as apparently the rule that the RB's family and mentor must accompany him to the IM applied only to males. The husbands of female RBs were enjoined to continue supporting them, but they were not required to accompany them to the IM. Thus women in this position were given some support, but not as much as men; it is the model as proposed for males that we suggest for emulation.) The RB was to be separated from his previous life, but only partially. Perhaps "relocation" would be a more appropriate term. Clearly, the resettlement of the teacher and family would be difficult, yet it was essential for maintaining the RB's existence. The importance of taking along parts of one's former life to the IM was understood. Perhaps another purpose was to make sure the RB would not be able to cloak himself in secrecy. On his arrival in an IM he was announced as an RB.[17] This publicity was not a public branding of shame, but rather meant for the purpose of integration. While the RB was not required to part from his immediate family, the act of relocation clearly separated him from the rest of society. This might have helped prevent the RB from sensing social tension in those around him.

Finally, the "release time" for a RB from the IM was always dependent on an arbitrary event – the death of the High Priest. The random nature of the accident is reflected in the release, which is similarly out of the RB's control.

HOW THE IR MIKLAT MODEL ADDRESSES THE SYMPTOMS OF PTSD

Current models for the explanation and treatment of PTSD are generally found to be unsatisfactory.[18] The complexity of PTSD symptoms seems to call for a multi-dimensional approach. Although this is generally agreed on in theory, much of the literature based on clinical work relies on one-dimensional approaches, and so there is a great deal of dissatisfaction with treatment results.[19] There is still widespread debate about the various treatment options for PTSD, but what seems clear is that an effective treatment model must be multi-dimensional. The

---

17. J. *Minchat Chinuch*: A Commentary on the Commandments of the Bible.

18. Shalev, A. Y. (1993). Post-traumatic Stress Disorder: A Biopsychological Perspective. *Israel Journal of Psychiatry and Related Science*, 30 (2), 102–109.

19. Ibid.

literature on PTSD generally states that avoiding situations similar to the one that caused the trauma or attempting to deny the event gives rise to the most severe PTSD symptoms.[20] However, attempting to force the trauma victim to place himself in this type of situation may further exacerbate the symptoms. What is healing is an attempt to treat the psychological reactions to the trauma with a cognitive approach as soon as possible and encourage the trauma victim to face the situation.[21] Seligman in his study of "learned helplessness," described how his experimental subjects learned to be passive when they came to believe that they were unable to control their environment.[22] Once an event such as an accidental death has occurred, the initial feelings of shock, numbness and preoccupation give rise to a need to escape. This need is satisfied by the injunction to flee to the IM. In a situation of total disorientation and turmoil, fleeing to the IM gave accidental killers a way of mobilizing their energy in defense of the ego, thus helping them avoid the internal dialogue of self-defeating talk in which such people may become mired.[23]

It forced them into action, which can give one a certain sense of control. This commandment also helped reorient the RB; s/he realized that s/he was not the only accidental killer in the world; the signposts put him/her into a new category with others, so that s/he could redefine him/herself and not feel so alone. The IM thus addresses the unavoidable change in self-concept following trauma, a notion that is often a basis for modern-day dynamic psychotherapies for PTSD. Thus, although RBs were running "away" from the scene of the trauma, they were also running "towards" a place that would redefine them specifically through this trauma, and force them to face the consequences of their acts, albeit within a therapeutic and supportive setting. This combination of running away from the scene of the crime, while running towards a place where help could obtained, creates an apparently paradoxical combination of avoidance and activity. Activity seems important for giving one a feeling of control over one's body, something RBs may feel they have lost by doing something which seems to have been uncontrolled.[24] In her book describing her work with the Chowchilla children, Terr shows that those who were able to actively do something to try and save themselves from the disaster emerged less traumatized, apparently because they had been active in protecting themselves. She notes in particular that one child, who was explicitly told not to help because he was "too weak

20. Solomon, S. D., Gerrity, E.T., Muff, A.M. (1992). Efficacy of treatments for Post-traumatic stress disorder: An empirical review. *Journal of the American Medical Association*, 268, 633–638.

21. Terr, L. (1990). *Too Scared to Cry*. New York: Basic Books.

22. Seligman, M. E. P. (1975). *Learned Helplessness*. San Francisco: Freeman.

23. Solomon, Z., Bleich, A., Shoham, S., Nardi C., & Kotler M. (1992). The "Koach" Project for treatment of combat-related PTSD: Rationale, aims, and methodology. *Journal of Traumatic Stress*, 5, 175–193.

24. Terr, L. (1990). *Too Scared to Cry*. New York: Basic Books.

and too fat," spent years trying to prepare himself for the next time he could be a "hero" until he died at the age of fifteen in an accident.[25]

Although this is only a single case, it nevertheless supports the contention that being active provides a certain sense of control that facilitates recovery. Activity can also help alleviate the psychological numbing defined as a common symptom of PTSD in DSM-IV (1994). Flooding therapies can exacerbate symptoms by evoking emotions associated with the trauma. However, seemingly unrelated activities can work as occupational therapy to provide inputs that give rise to unassociated feelings. Thus allowing the person to have safe emotional experiences that do not have to be suppressed through numbing.

An added function of the signposts placed all over the country, directing people to the IM, might be to desensitize the population in general to the idea of accidental killer and thus facilitate their acceptance within the community. They became a part of people's awareness and thus may have served to minimize the accidental killer's sense of being a "pariah." In describing the City of Refuge, the Midrash, a homiletic commentary on the Bible, calls it "a healing for you."[26] This seems to imply an understanding that accidental killers indeed need a place to escape to for the purpose of introspection, far from the normal routine of life, which should help them confront the enormity of the events. The Bible displays sensitivity to the RB's traumatic experience, realizing that under such circumstances people cannot be expected to return to their usual lifestyle without taking time out to work through the trauma. Moreover, being accompanied to the IM by one's mentor and family changed the nature of the exile. Perhaps its purpose was to demonstrate that one's lifestyle should not be altered. There is clear evidence of the importance of family support in facilitating the recovery of trauma victims despite the fact that they cannot always provide all the support a trauma victim needs.[27,28] Another purpose may have been to prevent a reaction that is fairly common in PTSD – the feeling that the future is foreshortened that there is nothing more to live for, that one's life is basically over.[29] Thus the RB was not allowed to be cut off from his immediate supportive environment, even though he was forced to move away from a society which might well have difficulty taking him back. Since the RB might be unable to face the flooding that often accompanies repeated return to the scene of the trauma,[30] he was protected from it at the same time that he was encouraged to face himself and his new identity. In addition, it was recognized that cloaking

---

25. Ibid.
26. Midrash Devarim Rabbah.
27. Herman, J. L. (1992). *Trauma and Recovery*. New York: Basic Books.
28. Terr, L. (1990). *Too Scared to Cry*. New York: Basic Books.
29. Herman, J. L. (1992). *Trauma and Recovery*. New York: Basic Books.
30. Solomon, S. D., Gerrity, E. T., Muff, A. M. (1992). Efficacy of treatments for Post-traumatic stress disorder: An empirical review. *Journal of the American Medical Association*, 268, 633–638.

oneself in secrecy would only foster an unhealthy reaction to the trauma. It was for this reason that the RB's arrival at the IM was announced in advance. The environment did not permit avoidance. This addressed a major symptom of PTSD. As mentioned previously, RBs generally experiences guilt feelings despite legal acquittal. By bringing them to an environment in which they would be with others in a similar situation, the IM directive eased their bewilderment and provided a sense of comfort and fraternity. Family or friends who never had this sort of experience may be unwilling to listen to repeated descriptions of the horrors of the event.[31] Sharing experiences with others in similar circumstances can help the RBs in many ways. It encourages them to confront the fact that they do indeed have a new identity, similar to that of others in the new environment. This confrontation, which may occur in the face of denial, often serves to relieve some of their anxiety by demonstrating that there are other people in the same predicament. This, in turn, may help alleviate guilt feelings. Living in a place with others who may be more advanced in the healing process, can encourage them to face the future. Although separated from their previous way of life and aware that guilt feelings cannot be ignored, the RBs are not alone in their experience and reactions to it. Clearly, sharing these feelings with others and being exposed to others in various stages of recovery from their trauma can facilitate rehabilitation. There are various reports in the literature about the use of group and milieu therapy for the treatment of PTSD, particularly with Vietnam veterans.[32,33] The first of these reports describes a week-long program for a group of Vietnam veterans at Camp David, an area surrounded by mountains and isolated from nearby towns. The treatment program included traditional treatment methods for PTSD, as well as Native American healing techniques. An evaluation immediately after the program, and a three-month follow-up, indicated a significant reduction of symptomatology for nearly every measure of psychopathology.[34]

Another helpful factor is that the IM was primarily inhabited by Levites – an important sector of the community, mentors of the population. Thus the RBs' knowledge that they were not being sent to spend their "sentence" with a socially undesirable community, but were worthy of the company of the Levites, may also have served to help them re-acquire a favorable sense of identity. It is interesting to note that the Levite community also served a primary role in preparing the sacrifices for the Temple. They were known to be people characterized by great precision.[35] It might also have been important for accidental

---

31. Ibid.
32. Wilson (1989).
33. Johnson, D. R., Feldman, S. C., Southwick, S. M., and Charney, D. S. (1994). The Concept of the Second Generation Program in the Treatment of Post-Traumatic Stress Disorder Among Vietnam Veterans. *Journal of Traumatic Stress*, 7,(2).
34. Ibid.
35. Grodner, M. (1970). Intention and Homicide in the Talmud. Unpublished doctoral thesis,

killers to be exposed to this trait as part of their battle against the randomness of the event that had so dramatically changed them.

Finally, there is the arbitrary release time. This awareness of non-control is essential in mitigating the RBs' sense of personal responsibility for themselves and the community, and in facilitating rehabilitation and a return to the larger society.

DISCUSSION

Modern society appears to respond to killing dichotomously – either it is accidental and therefore not punishable, or it is intentional and therefore punishable. Ancient Jewish society added a middle possibility – even if the killing may be accidental, so that the killer is innocent of a crime, s/he is nonetheless responsible for a death, and must therefore be punished. The biblical injunction ordering RBs to proceed to an IM has traditionally been understood as serving as a punishment for the RB and a necessary step in facilitating *Kapparah* for causing, even accidentally, the death of another human.

Today, accidental killers are aware that they have caused someone's death, yet there is no formal reaction from society. The implicit message is that the RBs are not at fault and may therefore disassociate themselves from the tragedy. This situation makes the natural process of mourning and subsequent rehabilitation into society more difficult. It leaves the RBs without the means to integrate this traumatic event into a new personal identity, and thus leads to behaviors that are defined as PTSD symptoms. The palpable result is heightened PTSD. A powerful symptom of PTSD, which exacerbates the RB's suffering, is avoidance.[36] Healing is a long, slow process that comes with introspection and facing the reality of what has happened.[37] The concept of IM provides many lessons. Society needs to separate from the RB, and that the RB needs to be distanced from the physical cues of the environment in which the accidental killing occurred. This relocation permits the RBs to mourn for their old, *unconfounded* self, and construct a new, acceptable personal identity. Being in a supportive and accepting societal environment in which RBs are recognized as such – in this new and as yet *unintegrated* identity – could facilitate their rehabilitation. As the modern outlook appears to recognize formally only one dimension of the situation – guilty as opposed to innocent of a crime – there is no place for the paradoxical psychological needs of the accidental killer. Establishing a middle ground – innocent and yet responsible – accepts the reality that this person's

University of Washington, Seattle.

36. Solomon, Z., Bleich, A., Shoham, S., Nardi, C., & Kotler, M. (1992). The "Koach" Project for treatment of combat-related PTSD: Rationale, aims, and methodology. *Journal of Traumatic Stress, 5*, 175–193.

37. Herman, J.L. (1992). *Trauma and Recovery*. New York: Basic Books.

two losses (of the person who was killed as well as his/her own previous "innocent" self) must be accounted for. This allows RBs to redefine themselves in a way that is congruent with his/her psychological state.

CONCLUSION

The treatment of PTSD remains a challenge for the health profession. The complexity of the disorder underscores the difficulty in establishing a clear treatment of choice, or perhaps a constellation of treatments of choice, for patients suffering from PTSD. Moreover the paucity of literature on the subject of accidental killers reflects the lack of attention given them as a group. Perhaps it is easier for those in the helping professions to comfort and work with "pure victims" rather than "victim-perpetrators." They are, however, undoubtedly people who have undergone a traumatic event, and as such deserve our attention.

In this paper we have attempted to present the biblical model of the *Ir Miklat* as an all-encompassing approach to the treatment of the specific trauma of accidental killers.

Nevertheless, the model as it existed in ancient times clearly cannot be transferred as a whole to modern-day society. It must be kept in mind that an important element in the efficacy of the IM model, which would be difficult to replicate nowadays, is the idea of ritual integral to the procedure. The clearly set out rules and processes were an accepted form enabling RBs to expiate their sense of guilt. At present, when these practices are not accepted by the larger society, there is no prescribed way for RBs to act. However, the model of a separate community can certainly be operationalized today in the form of group homes or special facilities. The experimental model for treatment of Vietnam veterans at Camp David was very similar to the IM model. There are other models for rehabilitation of drug abusers – for example, the Gateway Drug Rehabilitation Clinic in Pittsburgh – which could perhaps serve as a model for creating a rehabilitative environment for RBs. There may even be existing facilities which could be redefined in line with the IM model. The Israel Defense Force presently has a facility that seems to have a similar aim. It could certainly serve as a basis from which to launch a more encompassing model that would take into consideration the various symptoms experienced in PTSD.

Although the Levite Tribe no longer serves the functions it had in ancient times, the psychologists and social workers of today could serve similar functions, at least as a therapeutic staff, if not as a community in which RBs could live. The fact that biblical practice foreshadows many of the same techniques currently used in modern-day psychotherapies for the treatment of PTSD seems to invite using the wisdom of long ago for those who still suffer today as accidental killers.

The "Unorthodox" Therapy of an Ultra-Orthodox Adolescent

Judith B. Guedalia, Ph.D. and Leah Haber, Ph.D.

Editor's note [ASSIA]: In addition to the rabbis consulted by the authors, ASSIA-Jewish Medical Ethics has approached a number of leading halakhic authorities, seeking their opinions on the course of treatment outlined in this case study. These authorities were kind enough to provide us with their written responses, including halakhic sources, justifying the therapy. They emphasized that this is not a generally applicable ruling; each case must be individually dealt with by a competent halakhic authority.

Acting out can be an expression of a conduct disorder. When a person experiences conflict, his or her frustrations are often played out through inappropriate behavior, of which there are many subcategories. In the following case report, we will discuss an instance of conduct disorder and the effective cognitive therapy as best exemplified by Colin A. Ross's model. It must be noted that not only the therapy model used but also the referral itself can be described as "unorthodox" given the cultural realities of this case, as will be seen.

THE PATIENT

The patient, whom we will call Yisrael, was a sixteen-year old boy from a close-knit Hasidic sect that, like many Haredi groups, sets strict parameters on its members' lifestyles. These communities are not open to the attitudes or developments of secular society and attempt to shield their members from its influences. Nonconformist behavior is frowned upon and eliminated, especially violations of Orthodox Jewish law (halakha).[1]

Yisrael had already been expelled from one yeshiva entirely and from the

---

* "The 'Unorthodox' Therapy of an Ultra-Orthodox Adolescent" by Dr. Judith B. Guedalia and Dr. Leah Haber was originally published in *ASSIA: Journal of Medical Ethics*, vol. 4:1, February 2001, pp. 35–40.
    1. Bilu, Yoram, and Witztum, Eliezer. "Working with Ultra-Orthodox Patients: Guidelines for a Culturally Sensitive Therapy." *Culture, Medicine and Psychiatry* 17 (1993): 197–233.

dormitory of another because of repeated incidents in which other boys sexually stimulated him, brought him to ejaculate, and he did the same to them. Yisrael stressed that finding willing partners was not difficult and he never forced anyone to participate.

Understanding the Jewish position on masturbation is essential to fully grasping the severity of Yisrael's conduct disorder. According to *Kitsur Shulhan Arukh*, a popular work on Jewish law, "spilling seed" is among the most severe prohibitions in the Torah, similar to that of adultery. Loss of any potential for creating life is comparable to killing, and therefore one who engages in it is ostracized. Many restrictions are placed upon the Jewish male so that he should not come to perform this sin: he is not allowed to think about women in a sexual way, he is not allowed to watch animals copulating, certain foods are prohibited at night, and he may only sleep on his side, not on his back or stomach.[2] For a boy who cannot – or does not want to – control his urges, repeated masturbation can cause tremendous feelings of guilt.

Over the course of therapy, it became clear that Yisrael was acting out certain conflicts. Shortly before the problem began, his young, married cousin died. He was profoundly affected by this and it raised serious questions in his mind about death and the injustice of a young man dying, leaving a widow and orphans. To make matters worse, the Rebbe or *Admor* ("our master, our teacher, our rabbi"), the revered leader of his community, had assured the family that the cousin would live. Not long afterward, the Rebbe died as well. Yisrael's religious beliefs, which were tied into a magical faith in the powers of the Rebbe, were deeply shaken.

In Hasidic communities, mythic qualities are ascribed to the Rebbe. He is seen as the intermediary between his followers and God. Everything he comes into contact with takes on mystical significance – for example, it is considered a great merit to be present at the Friday-night gathering called the *tisch* and to receive a piece of bread that the Rebbe has touched (*sherayim*). The Rebbe is the source of advice, often about the most minute matters. His words are cherished and his instructions are obeyed to the letter. One can understand, therefore, why the Rebbe's death had such a devastating effect on Yisrael, especially considering his particular circumstances.

Yisrael's antisocial behavior can be understood as a cry for help, for a way to reconcile the conflict that was shaking the very foundations of his faith, his lifelines: his connection to religion and his community. From the halakhic perspective, masturbation is intimately connected to the interplay between life and death, the potential for life and its destruction. "Spilling seed" might have been

---

2. Gantzfried, Rabbi Shlomo, *Kitsur Shulhan Arukh* 151.

his way of challenging or defying God: "Will you kill me just as you killed my cousin?"

Masturbation can also be seen as part of normal development. In Yisrael's community, however, this normalcy is repressed and seen as an inability or lack of desire to control the sexual urge.

It must be noted that Hasidic boys are, for the most part, separated from women (other than their immediate family members) starting at the age of three. Their contact with women, therefore, is limited. After Bar Mitzvah (thirteen years of age), their daily routine involves sitting and studying for most of the day. No time is allotted for exercise or any other sort of physical release, which is seen as glorifying the body and therefore forbidden. Even non-Hasidic teenagers have trouble maintaining a healthy, balanced attitude toward their bodies and growing sexuality. In the Hasidic context, Yisrael's behavior was much more aberrant, widening the circle of damage.

Yisrael's parents were interviewed by the therapist and his father in particular presented as a disorganized person who had difficulty setting limits. He appeared disheveled and clearly did not know how to relate to the therapist in a professional manner – for example, at the end of the first session he asked Yisrael in the office whether he felt the therapist had done a good job. The lack of standards and limits in the boy's household undoubtedly contributed to his inability to control his urges in an appropriate way.

There may be another reason why Yisrael's conduct disorder took on such a pronounced sexual tone. It seems that the patient grew up in a household where sexual tension was rife and actions with a sexual overtone may have been a way of expressing frustration and/or asserting control. The salience of this particular symptom of his crisis, therefore, was hardly surprising.

Yisrael's conduct disorder was not simply a repressed sexual urge gone awry or the result of growing up in a home with inappropriate parameters for behavior. As stated, it was a cry for help from a confused and torn individual. Only an extremely severe and pressing conflict would cause him to endanger his position in his community – as he said to the therapist early on, "If I don't have *hasidut*, I don't have life." Yisrael knew perfectly well that his behavior would result in ostracization from his community – as previously mentioned, he had already been expelled from one yeshiva entirely and from the dormitory of the yeshiva he was then attending.

COURSE OF TREATMENT

Yisrael was treated over a ten-month period, first in one-hour biweekly sessions, then in weekly sessions. Therapy was based on a model formulated by Colin

A. Ross for dissociative identity disorder.[3] This therapy follows the cognitive model and is based on collaboration between patient and therapist. In this particular therapy, the therapeutic relationship was emphasized. Yisrael was made to feel valued as a person by the therapist and, as a result, he began to value himself independently. The atmosphere was a comfortable one in which he and the therapist built a relationship based on mutual respect, even friendship.

Ross states that gentleness, flexibility, humor, and the therapist's ability to listen should characterize the therapy. The therapy style is problem-oriented and a historical, focusing on the problem at hand and its solution as opposed to probing into the past.

The relationship aspect of Ross's model was particularly important. Yisrael had entered the therapy believing that he was worthless and the relationship with the therapist demonstrated that he was not. Someone in a position of importance – a doctor in a hospital, no less! – found him worth befriending. That his parents, who were not well-off, had found the money to pay for the therapy sessions seemed to reinforce his growing sense of self-worth. Despite the asocial quality of his problem and the embarrassment he was causing his family, he was not being written off. In addition, his yeshiva allowed him to continue attending (although he was stigmatized by not being allowed to board).

Ross's first step is to address the faulty learning model. Yisrael's dysfunctional behavior was attributed to maladapted learning. An important part of his therapy, therefore, was to acquire more functional learning methods. At the beginning of the therapy, it was immediately clear that Yisrael was ignorant of – and curious about – human anatomy in general and sexual matters in particular. This was due to his extremely parochial upbringing, which censored all information about such matters, deeming them immodest.

To correct his ignorance, the therapist showed Yisrael a children's book about the different parts of the human body and their functions.[4] For the first time, he was able to be open about these taboo topics.

He was able to converse openly with a woman, something which simply was not possible in his community, and this boosted his confidence as a young man. The ignorance and unclean atmosphere that had, for him, characterized sexual issues were replaced with awareness and a sense of control. The sanitized atmosphere of the hospital and his white-coated therapist helped him regard sexuality in a different, more positive way. He began to feel better about himself as a man and developed an understanding of the feelings and urges he had been unable to discuss with anyone else.

Another form of relearning occurred when Yisrael became more aware of his

---

3. Ross's model can be found in Blackburn, Marie, and Davidson, Kate. *Cognitive Therapy for Depression and Anxiety*, 51–53.

4. Gina Ingoglia, *Look Inside Your Body* (n.p.: Grosset and Dunlop, 1989).

emotions and moods. The "How Am I Feeling Today?" poster, which shows different faces displaying various emotions and states of mind, was a particularly helpful tool.[5] Yisrael would, on his own initiative, search the poster for a face that matched his mood. He realized that the "guilty" face was one he used when he was insulting someone else. It was in the safe environment of the therapist's office that he felt secure enough to admit this. He also realized that through his own actions he was degrading himself and creating his intense guilt feelings.

Yisrael's new environment, during therapy, was unlike any he had ever experienced and may have been an important factor facilitating his learning. It was easier to reconstruct his idea of reality after his reality had, indeed, changed. Yisrael had been in therapy before. His therapist – a religious, bearded male – reminded him of the world from which he came. He had terminated the therapy because he "did not feel that it was helping." Now he was seeing a female therapist who, though religious and able to understand his background, was part of the larger world and thus able to help him see a broader reality.

THERAPEUTIC HOMEWORK

Homework is an integral part of Ross's therapeutic process. The idea is to give the patient a more active role in the therapy, thereby cementing and developing what is accomplished during the therapy sessions. In this case, the therapist took something over which Yisrael felt he had no control – masturbation – and attempted to give him a certain amount of control. Paradoxically, his assignment was to masturbate. Five times per day, three days per week, he had to masturbate, immersing himself in the ritual bath (*mikveh*) each day that he masturbated (the *mikveh* is prescribed by Hasidic custom for anyone who ejaculates sperm). His actions – which, until now, he could not control – were raised to a voluntary and controllable level. The nexus of control was thus shifted from Yisrael to the therapist and then back to Yisrael again. The realization that he was in control of his actions increased his self-respect; he no longer saw himself at the mercy of mysterious, uncontrollable urges.

Yisrael was given a second "homework assignment." He would occasionally travel by bus to visit relatives in an ultra-Orthodox enclave about an hour away. Because of security considerations in Israel, the passenger seated in the front seat of the bus must be physically able to help the bus driver in case of a terrorist attack (much like the airplane passenger seated by the emergency exit). Yisrael's assignment was to sit in the front seat every time he went to visit his relatives, putting himself in a position of responsibility, thus reinforcing his

---

5. Therapeutic Interventions. "How Am I Feeling Today?" (poster).

growing self-confidence. It served a second purpose: it kept him from the back of the bus, where troublemakers tend to sit.

As stated above, collaboration between therapist and patient is a prominent characteristic of Ross's therapy model.[6] In this case, the therapist contributed her medical, psychological, and worldly knowledge, and Yisrael contributed by sharing parts of his world that the therapist had no access to – the Rebbe's *tisch*, for example.

Ross's therapy is active and directive. While the therapist must create a warm atmosphere, he or she must also be focused and fairly strict about the treatment. This particular therapy's structure was consistently maintained. Each session opened the same way. Yisrael would report how often he had masturbated, how he felt about it, and whether he felt he was developing more control. The discussion would take its own course from there, but even if only briefly, each session began the same way.

Ross's model uses the method of Socratic questioning, which leads the patient to independently identify his own feelings rather than passively be diagnosed by the therapist. Since this method of questioning is used in the Talmud, it was familiar to Yisrael and he was able to internalize it to help identify his problems even though the therapy process itself was completely foreign to him. A bridge was built between the two worlds, and his ability to relate the two helped in the progression of the therapy.

Socratic questioning succeeded in taking Yisrael on a cognitive journey starting in his own community and reaching the new and different world of the therapist's office. He was ultimately able to return to his own community with a deeper understanding of himself. He came to realize what was truly important to him: his community and the sense of belonging it engendered.

Openness is another characteristic of Ross's therapy model. It was imperative that Yisrael and the therapist be open with each other. During the first appointment, when Yisrael told the therapist that he engaged in homosexual acts, she was very clear with him about the unacceptability of his conduct. She told him that he was abusing himself as well as others, stressing that just as he would not allow someone to reach into his pocket and steal his money, so was this a form of being taken advantage of, of self-abuse, and she would not tolerate it. He mentioned frequenting a public park where male and female prostitutes gather and where unprotected sex takes place. Again, the therapist made it very clear that she would terminate the therapy if he continued going to this park. "I don't want to work with a dead person," she stated, because of his risk of contracting AIDS through unprotected sex.

---

6. See Heilman, Samuel, and Witztum, Eliezer. "Patients, Chaperons and Healers: Enlarging the Therapeutic Encounter." *Social Science and Medicine* 39, no. 1 (1994), 133–43.

The therapist came to symbolize openness because she acted as a window to the outside world. For someone who was not even allowed to read the secular press (the Hasidic community generally reads its own, censored newspapers), this was an eye-opening experience. It was at this time, the summer of 1997, that the *Sojourner* vehicle, *Rover*, was exploring planet Mars. Yisrael was interested in *Rover*'s progress and the therapist kept him updated on its journey, a journey that became a symbol for Yisrael's own. Just as *Rover* had to navigate rocks and hard places to gain knowledge and understanding, so did Yisrael have to endure the difficulties of therapy to gain a deeper understanding of himself.

Ross outlines five session targets, goals to be achieved over the course of therapy: defining the problem, identifying associated negative thoughts, answering negative thoughts, evaluating the effect of the answer on belief in original thought and on emotion, and establishing how the answer could be pursued in action.

Once his conduct disorder and acting out were identified, Yisrael and the therapist began identifying his associated negative thoughts, or mindset. In addition to the religious conflicts previously described, Yisrael's problem with masturbation created feelings of alienation from and anger toward his community. He felt trapped because he had no outlet for his sexual urges. Engaging in a practice forbidden by Jewish law – which he equated with murder – created intense feelings of guilt, frustration, and worthlessness.

The therapeutic relationship was effective in battling these negative thoughts. Through it, Yisrael began to feel valued as a person. He formed a friendship with the therapist as they laughed together, talked together, and built a relationship of mutual respect and fondness, and this relationship played a large role in disproving his belief that he was worthless and "bad." He began to realize that while his behavior was unacceptable, he had the power to control it and to set boundaries. This was further reinforced by the homework assignments discussed earlier. Additionally, continuing to attend yeshiva and to board there once a week allowed him to test and verify his new perceptions in the "real" world.

For someone from a community where innovations are frowned upon and suspected, where openness about feelings and opinions is not the norm, the therapeutic experience had the potential to be frighteningly unsettling. Yisrael's *rosh yeshiva*, therefore, appointed a teacher from the community to discuss his problems with him and to explain why it was unacceptable from the community's perspective. The parallel processing was effective in keeping him rooted in his own world while journeying to new and unknown, yet often enlightening and liberating frontiers.

DISCUSSION

From the perspective of cognitive therapy, the therapy was effective because of its success in changing the way Yisrael thought. Faulty thought processes were identified, analyzed, and replaced.

Certain beliefs had irrevocably changed. Even before he entered therapy, the bases of his religious belief had been shaken by the deaths of his cousin and the Rebbe. To help reconcile this, the therapist introduced the concept of death and new beginnings. She had recently lost her father at almost the same time that her grandchild was born. Her experience acted as a metaphor for his. Through the new insight and more sophisticated understanding he had gained, he was able to resolve his own issues through the experiences of the therapist. As Bowen suggests, it is not only the therapeutic alliance that can be therapeutic, but the therapist him or herself.

It is significant that Yisrael shared a Talmudic insight (*devar Torah*) that the Rebbe had delivered before his passing. It showed that he was able to reaccept him as a pious and wise man.

Another aspect of his new mindset was a greater respect for women. His therapist was an Orthodox woman who was also a professional, respected by his father and by the leaders of his community. He had confided in her and worked through his problems with her. She had been able to understand him and even to discuss Torah, a topic seen by his community as beyond the abilities of a woman.

Just as the *Rover* metaphor was so significant, so too were others used during the therapy. Metaphor is effective in therapy because it functions as meta-communication; its meanings are absorbed on a number of different levels.

A significant symbolic exchange occurred when Yisrael brought sunflower seeds to eat during the session. Sunflower seeds are a popular ethnic snack in Israel. Their flesh is tasty, but the shell is large and messy to remove. When Yisrael asked the therapist whether she would mind if he ate them during the session, she said that she felt that they had their place, but that they mostly create more mess than food. They may look big, but there is little nourishing value in them. While it may be acceptable to eat them, it is important to put the mess in its place. Implicit in her response was that she was prepared to accept his faults, but that he had to learn to identify them and deal with them directly – in other words, to put them in their place.

Another symbolic event occurred on Purim, when children dress up in costumes and deliver packages of food to friends and neighbors. Yisrael dressed up as a monster for the therapist. Hiding and revealing at the same time, he used the customs of the holiday to test his own identity. Was he a monster, as he appeared on the outside, or a "good guy," as he was on the inside?

Through the therapy, particularly through metaphors such as these, healthier and more positive metaphors replaced Yisrael's negative thoughts. Many of his former ideas about the world had been shattered, but he replaced them with new, healthier ones.

What was there in the relationship between patient and therapist that allowed changes in such basic, ingrained patterns of thought to take place? A psychodynamic perspective on the therapy will help explain why the cognitive changes occurred.

Transference and countertransference played pivotal roles in the therapeutic relationship. Boys in his community live in dormitories from the age of thirteen until they are married. Even beforehand, as mentioned, once they reach the age of three and begin to attend *heder*, they are separated from their mothers and sisters for most of the day. This highlights the uniqueness of Yisrael's interaction with the female therapist, and the transferential experience that simultaneously occurred on many levels.

The therapeutic relationship became the relationship with his mother that Yisrael never had. Separated as he was from her, and from any other loving, nurturing female figure, he had no one to turn to when experiencing sexual or existential confusion. The therapist was an accessible female who cared about him (as demonstrated by her firm refusal to allow him to engage in any behavior that would endanger his life), who valued him as a person, and who wanted to help him work through his issues. Through the relationship with the therapist, he resolved the relationship with the mother he had never, for all intents and purposes, had.

Although in reality he never would have been able to have such an open relationship with his mother, the transferential relationship with the therapist gave Yisrael the opportunity to attach to his "mother" and then separate from her when he had gained the self-confidence and maturity (from the relationship itself) to do so. Yisrael's cognitive and emotional perspectives underwent a change once he had resolved an early deficiency in his psychological development.

Countertransference occurred on the part of the therapist. Since Yisrael was in need of a mother, the therapist adapted to play that role. She created an atmosphere in which he felt comfortable disclosing himself, making himself vulnerable but also open to help. She showed respect and trust for him and he ultimately reciprocated. This partnership is what allowed for resolution of Yisrael's issues and his return to a predominantly male world.

The therapy sessions were to end at the conclusion of the yeshiva academic year, roughly corresponding to the month of July. As July approached, the sessions took on a different tone. Yisrael began bringing stories of the late Rebbe's acts of piety and also related lessons he had learned in his Talmud studies. At the therapist's request, the yeshiva increased the number of times he was allowed board, from once a week to twice. This was a tangible effect of his newfound faith in himself and proof of the yeshiva's faith in him. These events seemed to signify a rapprochement with his community, with himself.

Is reentry into the environment that fostered the problem considered a success? We maintain that it certainly is. When assisting individuals from different cultural backgrounds, avoiding imposing one's own values is imperative. The therapist must, whenever possible, assume the patient's perspective and help him achieve his goal without transplanting him into the therapist's world, which may be foreign to him. This particular patient wanted, more than anything else, to return to his community as a functioning member. This desire was reflected in his "contractual statement" at his first meeting with the therapist: "If I don't have *hasidut*, I don't have life." Yet, although he was able to return as a functioning, contributing member of the Hasidic community, his journey into a broader and more accepting world had rendered him different.